FUNDAMENTALS
OF
COMPUTATIONAL PHOTOGRAMMETRY

About the Author

SANJIB K. GHOSH worked as a Surveyor in the Survey of India for 11 years, and as a faculty at the Ohio State University for 20 years and Laval University for 12 years. Also, he served the United Nations as a Consultant on World Cartography. His professional experience in research and development involved, among others: Air Photo Mapping of India - E. Pakistan Boundary; Ice flow movement studies in Antarctica; Calibration of the Lunar Orbiter IV (for Moon mapping by NASA); Calibration of the world's largest radio telescope (at Arecibo, Puerto Rico); Mapping blood cells (Electron-micrographic); Calibration of Electron Microscopes; 3-D Mapping of human brain (Stereo-radiographic); and Self-calibration used in unconventional photogrammetric systems.

He also served as Visiting Professor at various institutes and universities in Brazil, Canada, India, Japan, Korea, Malaysia, Morocco, Nigeria and Thailand. He has authored around 200 scientific publications, three books as sole author and four books as a contributing author. Inventor of a New Method of Determining Latitude and Azimuth, Dr. Ghosh holds a patent on the use of 'Floating Line' in Stereo-radiographic surgery of epileptic human brains.

FUNDAMENTALS OF COMPUTATIONAL PHOTOGRAMMETRY

SANJIB K. GHOSH
Professor (emeritus)
The Ohio State and Laval Universities

CONCEPT PUBLISHING COMPANY, NEW DELHI-110059

Cataloging in Publication Data—DK
Courtesy: D.K. Agencies (P) Ltd. <docinfo@dkagencies.com>

Ghosh, Sanjib K., 1925-
Fundamentals of computational photogrammetry / Sanjib K. Ghosh.
p. cm.
Includes bibliographical references.
Includes index.
ISBN 818069187X

1. Photogrammetry—Mathematics. 2.Photogrammetry—Data processing. I. Title.

DDC 526.9 21

ISBN : 81-8069-187-X (HB)

First Published 2005

Published and Printed by
Ashok Kumar Mittal
Concept Publishing Company
A/15-16, Commercial Block, Mohan Garden
New Delhi-110059 (INDIA)

Phone : 25351460, 25351794
Fax : 091-11-25357103
Email : publishing@conceptpub.com

... Man is not travelling from error to truth, but from truth to truth, from lower to higher truth . . .

—Swami Vivekananda, 1893,
Chicago Lectures

PREFACE

The science of photogrammetry has been rather dynamic in recent years. Certain new data-reduction techniques and numerous analytical instruments have been introduced in the world. Computational photogrammetry is being applied in numerous fields other than the conventional field of mapping (topographic, cadastral or engineering), like architectural and biomedical fields. Photogrammetry is recognized for having the inherent capability of non-contact and rapid spatial measurements. The fact, however, remains that the technique would not be accepted in all such applications in all countries unless it is cost-effective to provide enough economical and technical advantages over other existing measuring techniques suitable to their needs. Automobile construction, metal working, mining engineering, shipbuilding, traffic engineering and machine construction are certain industrial fields where adequate success has already been achieved.

The main purpose of this book is to establish aspects of computational (or call it analytical) photogrammetric concepts and procedures, the backbone of which consists of various "Mathematical Models". In scientific usage, the word 'model' is often applied to physical or conceptual systems that are meant to represent the involved chain of events in a phenomenon under study. A variety of languages is used in conceptual models. A system can be expressed in ordinary English, in terms of specialized scientific jargons, or through the abstract symbolic languages from the domain of Mathematics. Systems of the last type, called 'Mathematical Models', have been used in physical sciences for centuries. There is, however, no mystery about the way in which the insight into the underlying chain of events is achieved. Mathematical models have no scientific values until and unless they have been adequately validated with factual data through experience or research.

Mathematical models are often 'crippled' by lack of informational backgrounds, and the task of making the connection to reality is difficult. In this respect, the involved ones, both the scientist and the mathematician, strive for 'generality'. The mathematician is concerned with generality in the form of the statement, and the scientist with generality in its content. The former objective – the generality of language, and the latter – one of fact, can be incompatible in some cases. Such differences in the goals of mathematics and sciences may lead to differences in strategies of model-making. Traditionally, this task of model making has been carried out by mathematically minded individuals, often yielding headway in unproductive directions.

The strategy for a productive direction is simple. Firstly, one seemingly correct mathematical model is set up. Secondly, implications of the model are explored. Thirdly, outcomes due to the model are compared with reported results. If the theory fits the facts, it provides scientific validation. Whatever its mathematical virtues may be, the model has no specific value unless it has been validated. Scientific validation is an open-ended process. When a tested mathematical model shows success in repeated performances, it becomes established for all practical uses. Otherwise, depending on its degree of failure, it stands to be changed, modified or simply rejected.

There is no mathematical-scientific approach that can guarantee completely successful results in the complex circumstances of major problems. The user of ideas presented in this book must be aware of this reality of practical life. In the context of action, it is not easy to move from the abstract ideal of mathematical generality to the discrete goals of science-engineering generality, where it is the content and not the form of the mathematical statement that matters. The reader, therefore, often may benefit in modifying a mathematical model such that the form is adaptable to the circumstances without really changing its basic contents. Numerous suggestions in this direction are included in the text.

Modern computational photogrammetry seems to be overwhelmed with the techniques of Adjustment Computations. A rigorous solution, even by using the method of Least Squares, would not always justify the trouble expended. This is because the data, observed or calculated, do not depend merely on errors of observation but also have their origin in the inequalities of the terrain, atmospheric conditions, measuring instrument, camerá, etc. as well as the inadequacy of the mathematical model(s) used for the purpose of processing, assessing and analyzing the data.

This book must be taken in these perspectives.

Intended for students and practitioners in photogrammetry and remote-sensing, this book presupposes a good background in physics and mathematics as generally required in undergraduate level college curricula. The author has made concerted efforts to present a self-contained book. Detailed derivations are given wherever feasible. Related relevant publications are cited in the text by the authors' names and years of publication. Bibilographies of such cited works as well as others deemed useful for further studies have been given at the end of each chapter. Although each and every symbol or notation has been explained when first introduced in the text, a list of symbols and a list of abbreviations and acronyms are separately added in order to assist the reader.

Observational and photographic/sensing techniques which are necessary in any practical job are deliberately omitted as being out-of-place in this, theory oriented, presentation. With similar justification, discussions on the basic tools, viz., the camera or the sensing device, have been omitted also. The reader would benefit in this respect by examining other available publications, such as the Manuals of Photogrammetry and Remote Sensing. Although some computer programs would have enhanced the value of this book to the uninitiated reader, they were not included in view of the bulk and the associated cost for such a proposition. Nevertheless, a self-calibration program (on photographic imaging systems) developed under the author's guidance is added as Appendix C. This program would prove to be unique. It is flexible enough to be used in conventional (aerial or satellite imaging) as well as unconventional (like X-ray or Electron Micrography) systems, as has already been used successfully in numerous projects in several countries.

The book is presented in nine chapters and three appendices. The decimal numbering system has been used for sections, figures, tables and equations according to chapters. Chapters are arranged in an order found most convenient by the author from his many years of teaching. Each chapter is self-contained in order that any teacher using this book as a class room text should find no difficulty in following any different order of the subject matter. Moreover, considerable blending of details has made for presenting a logical and meaningful flow of the text.

Special appreciation is expressed for the generous and constructive contributing comments received from numerous colleagues around the world, the outstanding ones being from Dr. Olubodun Ayeni, Dr. Arthur Brandenberger, Dr. (Late) Duane Brown, Mr. Gouribhusan Das and Dr. Taichi Oshima. All of their comments have been considered. The author also thanks the instrument manufacturers and individuals who provided many of the illustrations or diagrams or ideas, which have been assimilated in the text. All these have been appropriately acknowledged in the text. The group directly involved in publishing and marketing the book, i.e., all of the Concept Publishing Company deserve special appreciation for their excellent cooperation.

Perhaps some points in this book could have been more elaborated, some more derivations could have been added or some examples from actual cases could have been presented. This is a task for the future. Time and *economics* of publication could not permit these in some cases, while in others it was felt that the general flow of the text would have been disturbed. It is hoped that the book would serve its purpose and would encourage all readers further to develop the computational photogrammetric procedures far beyond the current scopes as presented here.

Columbus, Ohio, USA
September 2002

SANJIB K. GHOSH

CONTENTS

LIST OF FIGURES

LIST OF TABLES

LIST OF SYMBOLS

Symbol	Description
A	Coefficient matrix of observations (composed of partial derivatives of observations in condition equations, Chap 4)
a	Semi-major axis of an ellipsoid (Chap 3); Transformation coefficient; Format size of square photographs; Expansion coefficient of air due to temperature (Chap 5)
$\underline{a}_1, \underline{a}_2$	Shifts due to decentering distortion (Chap 5)
B	Coefficient matrix of parameters (composed of partial derivatives of parameters in condition equations, Chap 4, 8, 9)
$\dot{B}$	Coefficient matrix of estimated orientation parameters (Chap 8, 9)
$\ddot{B}$	Coefficient matrix of estimated ground coordinates (Chap 8, 9)
B	Atmospheric pressure (Chap 5)
Bx, By, Bz	X, Y and Z components, respectively, of base in model or ground
b	Semi-minor axis of an ellipsoid (Chap 3); Transformation coefficient; Photographic base
$\underline{b}$	Blur of image
$\vec{b}$	Vector representing base in a model
bx, by, bz	X, Y and Z components, respectively, of base at photo-scale
C_f	Differential film shrinkage
C_x, C_y	X and Y components, respectively, of the projection distance in view of scale-affinity
c	Camera constant
$\dot{C}$, $\ddot{C}$	Estimated unknowns for orientation parameters and ground coordinates, respectively; Contributions to Normal equations
D	Object distance from camera perspective center
$\vec{D}$	Parallax vector (total parallax)
D_i	Certain constants (Chap 3)
d	Prefix indicating differentials; Scalar multiplier to parallax $\vec{D}$ (Chap 4); Target diameter (Chap 7)

d¢ Measuring mark diameter

d_i Certain constants (Chap 3)

dr Radial distortion

dx, dy, dz Translational constants; Coordinates error

e, e¢ Ellipsoidal eccentricities, first and second, respectively

e Error (specifics identified with appropriate subscripts)

F, F_O Function and Function evaluated with approximate values, respectively

f Function; Camera focal length

H Elevation in ground or in model above datum

h Flying height; Elevation above geodetic ellipsoid

h_o Elevation of Origin in Local Space Coordinate-system

I Identity matrix

i Subscript indicating sequential numbering in a series; Angle of incidence (reflection or refraction)

J_i Profile function coefficients in decentering lens distortion

j Subscript indicating sequential numbering in a series

K Constant, a factor in atmospheric refraction

K_{im} Image motion constant

k Scale factor; Scalar multiplier (Chap 4); Distortion coefficients (Chap 5)

k¢ Atmospheric refraction coefficient

L Observation (Chap 8)

M Rotational matrix (elements identified with appropriate subscripts); Coefficient matrix of Normal equations

M Row matrices corresponding to the general rotation matrix; Radius of curvature of geodetic meridian

M_B Photo scale

M_K, $M_{K'}$ Map scales, of publication and compilation, respectively

M_M Model Scale

$\boldsymbol{M}_\Omega$, $\boldsymbol{M}_\phi$, $\boldsymbol{M}_K$ Rotation matrices representing W, f and K rotations, respectively

m Elements of rotation matrix (identified with appropriate subscripts); Standard errors/ deviations; Subscript indicating influence of IMC)

N Normal equations matrix

N	Radius of curvature of geodetic prime vertical; Coefficients of Normal equations; Augmented rotation matrix (Chap 5); Submatrices of Normal equations (identified with appropriate subscripts)
n	Number of observations; Atmospheric refractive index
O	Exterior orientation parameters
P	Weight matrix associated with observations (Chap 7, 8, 9)
P	Lens distortion coefficients (Chap 5); Point on ground or model
p	Subscript, indicating panoramic effect; Point on photograph
px, py	X-and Y-parallaxes, respectively
Q	Weight coefficient matrix (Chap 4)
q	Bandwidth in recursive partitioning (Chap 8)
R	Radius of Earth-sphere (Chap 3, 5); Radius of Critical circle (Chap 4)
$\vec{R}$	Vector defining location of a ground point with regard to perspective center (identified with appropriate subscripts)
$\vec{R}_O$	Unit vector in object space
R_M	Mean radius of Earth-sphere (Chap 3)
r	Radial distance of an image point; Border width in recursive partitioning (Chap 8)
$\vec{r}$	Vector defining location of an image point with regard to perspective center (identified with appropriate subscripts)
$\vec{r}_O$	Unit vector in camera space
S	Distance on ground of a point from Nadir point; A parameter (Chap 9)
S_i	Polylateration quantities
s	Distance on photograph of a point from Nadir point
T	Thickness of film or plate; Resection coefficients (identified with appropriate subscripts, Chap 6)
t	Temperature; Time; Third partition in recursive partitioning (Chap 8); A parameter (Chap 9)
t_e	Exposure time (Chap 5)
U	Constant vector associated with Normal equations (Chap 4)
u	A parameter (Chap 9)

V	Vector of residuals (of photo coordinates, Chap 4, 8, 9)
V	Column vector composed of residuals to observations; Ground speed of aircraft (Chap 5); Fundamental ellipsoidal quantity (Chap 3)
V, v	Error, deviation or alteration (identified with appropriate subscripts)
v_F, v_I	Speed of movement of film and image, respectively (Chap 5)
W	Weight matrix associated with observations (Chap 4)
W	Fundamental ellipsoidal quantity
$\mathbf{X}$	Solution vector associated with Normal equations (Chap 3); Coordinates . vector
X	Columns vector of alterations (corrections) to values of parameters (Chap 4)
X, Y, Z	Ground or Model Coordinates, in three dimensions
$\overline{\mathbf{X}}$	Vector of coordinates before transformation (Chap 3)
$\overline{X}, \overline{Y}, \overline{Z}$	Three, dimensional coordinates before transformation; Universal Space Rectangular coordinates (Chap 3)
X_o, Y_o, Z_o	Coordinates of an origin (a perspective center in particular)
$\overline{X}_o, \overline{Y}_o, \overline{Z}_o$	Coordinates of the Origin of a Local System
$\overline{\mathbf{X}}_o$	Vector of three shifts (Chap 3)
x, y, z	Photo coordinates (three dimensional, z being a constant)
x_o, y_o	Photo coordinates of Principal point
$\dot{x}, \dot{y}$	Image velocities in X and Y directions, respectively (Chap 5)
x¢, y¢	Réseau point coordinates from calibration (Chap 5)
x', y' / x_1, y_1	Photo coordinates on the left-side photograph
x'', y'' / x_2, y_2	Photo coordinates on the right-side photograph
α, β, γ	Angles for Direction Cosines, with X, Y and Z axes, respectively (Chap 4)
α	Camera field angle; Angle at a station (Chap 7); Local slope of terrain (Chap 7); Angle of deviation due to refraction (Chap 5)
β	View angle (of incidence of ray, Chap 5)
α, β	Tangential off-sets at Multilaterative comparator (Chap 2)

γ	Angle of intersection; Parallactic angle
Δ	As a prefix, diminutive error/deviation to a parameter; Certain values used in Space Resection (Chap 6); Column vector composed of corrections to parameters (Chap 4)
δ	As a prefix, diminutive correction to a parameter; Correlation coefficient (Chap 8)
$\dot{\delta}, \ddot{\delta}$	Correction to estimated orientation parameters and ground coordinates, respectively, (Chap 8, 9)
$\in$	Function with estimated values of unknowns (Chap 8); Discrepancy vector (Chap. 9)
$\dot{\in}, \ddot{\in}$	Vector of discrepancies for orientation parameters and ground coordinates, respectively (Chap 8, 9)
θ	Angle of convergence; Direction angle in Plane-polar system;
$\dot{\theta}, \ddot{\theta}, \dddot{\theta}$	Scan-rate, Scan-acceleration and Scan-jerk, respectively
λ	Geodetic longitude
θ	Azimuth (Chap 7)
λ, μ, ν	Certain constants used in transformation (Chap 3)
ρ	Atmospheric density (Chap 5)
Σ	Variance-covariance matrix; Summation (Chap 4)
$\dot{\Sigma}, \ddot{\Sigma}$	S for orientation parameters and ground coordinates, respectively
σ	Standard error/derivation (identified with appropriate subscripts); Elements of a covariance matrix (Chap 9)
ψ	Angle of deviation of ray in atmospheric refraction (Chap 5)
ϕ	Geodetic latitude
ϕ_o	Direction angle of maximum tangential lens distortion (Chap 5)
Ω, ϕ, K	Model rotation angles around *X*, *Y* and *Z* axes, respectively
ω, ϕ, κ	Photo rotation angles around *X*, *Y* and *Z* axes, respectively
$\omega_o, \phi_o, \kappa_o$	Rotational angles referred to calibrated positions
$\dot{\omega}, \dot{\phi}, \dot{\kappa}$	Angular velocities in w, f and k, respectively
∇	Angles at perspective center (identified with appropriate subscripts; Chap 4, 6)
ℓ	Distance between fiducial marks (Chap 5); Dimensional indication of matrices (Chap 9)

LIST OF ABBREVIATIONS AND ACRONYMS

ACIC	Aeronautical Chart and Information Center (in the DMA)
ACSM	American Congress on Surveying and Mapping
AMS	Army Map Service (currently in the DMA)
ANOVA	Analysis of Variance (from Statistics)
APPS	Analytical Photogrammetric Positioning System
ARDC	Air-force Rome Development Center (of the USA)
ARME	Automated Réseau Measuring Equipment
ASCE	American Society of Civil Engineers
ASP	American Society of Photogrammetry (currently ASPRS)
ASPRS	American Society for Photogrammetry and Remote Sensing
ATL	Army Topographical Laboratories (also known as ETL)
BL	Bildmessung und Luftwildwesen (journal of the German Society of Photogrammetry)
BRATS	Bundle Refinement Aerial Triangulation Solution (of J. F. Kenefick)
BRL	Ballistic Research Laboratories (of the USA)
BSOR	Block Successive Over-Relaxation
CADMAP	Computer Aided Drafting, Mapping and Photogrammetry
CGS	Centimeter-Gram-Second
C&GS	Coast and Geodetic Survey (currently NOS, NOAA)
CI	Contour Interval
CRT	Cathode Ray Tube
DBA	Duane Brown Associates
DMA	Defense Mapping Agency (of the USA)
DOD	Department of Defense (of the USA)
DTM	Digital Terrain model
EDM	Electromagnetic Distance Measuring
ETL	Engineering Topographical Laboratories (US Army)
FORTBLOCK	Fortran Block Triangulation (program at The Ohio State University)
FPS	Foot-Pound-Second
GIS	Geographic Information System
GPS	Global Positioning System

ICAO	International Civil Aviation Organization
IEVP	Instantaneous Equivalent Vertical Photograph
IMC	Image Motion Compensation
ISP	International Society for Photogrammetry (currently ISPRS)
ISPRS	International Society for Photogrammetry and Remote Sensing
ITC	International Training Centre (currently The International Institute for Aerial Surveying and Earth Sciences, The Netherlands)
KDMS	Kork Digital Mapping System
LFC	Large Format Camera (of NASA, USA)
MKS	Metre-Kilogram-Second
MSS	Multispectral Scanner Subsystem
MUSAT	Multiple Station Analytical Triangulation
NASA	National Aeronautics and Space Administration (of the USA)
NAVSTAR	Navigation Satellite Timing and Ranging
NBS	National Bureau of Standards (of the USA)
NGS	National Geodetic Survey (branch of NOAA, USA)
NOAA	National Oceanic and Atmospheric Administration (of the USA)
NOS	National Oceanic Survey (branch of NOAA, USA)
NRC	National Research Council (of Canada)
OEEPE	Organisation Européene d'Etudes Photogrammétriques Expérimentales (European Organization for Experimental Photogrammetric Research)
OS	Ordnance Survey (of the UK)
PE	Photogrammetric Engineering (currently PERS)
PERS	Photogrammetric Engineering and Remote Sensing (journal of ASPRS)
PR	Photogrammetric Record (journal of the British Photogrammetric Society)
RABATS	Rapid Analytical Block Triangulation System (of J. F. K. Inc.)
RBV	Return Beam Vidicon
RMS	Root Mean Square
SAPGO	Simultaneous Adjustment of Photogrammetric and Geodetic Observations
SI	Système Internationale (International System of units)
SMAC	Simultaneous Multiframe Analytical Calibration
SPOT	Système Pour l'Observation de la Terre (French Satellite imaging system)
UNO	United Nations Organization
USAF	United States Air Force
USCGS	United States Coast and Geodetic Survey (currently NOS, NOAA)
USGS	United States Geological Survey
UTM	Universal Transverse Mercator (Projection)

1

INTRODUCTION

Photogrammetry (GK. Photos = light; GK. Gramma = writing; GK. Metron = measure) is defined by the American Society for Photogrammetry and Remote Sensing (ASPRS) as, "The art, science and technology of obtaining reliable information about physical objects and the environment through processes of recording, measuring and interpreting photographic images and patterns of electromagnetic radiant energy and other phenomena" (ASPRS Manuals, 1980, 1998).

1.1 BASIC PRINCIPLES

1.1.1 Photogrammetric

Included within the above definition are two distinct aspects of photogrammetry: (1) *Quantitative* (or metric), which involves precision measurements to obtain information related to size and shape of object or derived information such as change (e.g, velocity, volume change, etc.), statistical- (e.g., area distribution, time variation, etc.), or associated- (e.g., stress, force, etc.) parameters; and (2) *Qualitative* (or interpretative), which deals with recognition and interpretation of objects. Digital, graphic or visual representation of such information is almost always implied.

Qualitative photogrammetry does not fall within the scope of this book. The interested reader would benefit from the Manual of Remote Sensing (3rd Ed., ASPRS 1998) or other books in that subject area. Within the scope of Quantitative aspects, *Computational* (also universally known as *Analytical*) *Photogrammetry* deals with the solution of problems by mathematical computations, using measurements made on the photograph or image as input data. Suitable mathematical models are used to represent relations between points in the object space, their corresponding images and errors in the system. Principles of perspective projective geometry are inherent in this. In the conventional use, the image on a photographic film is a projection of the object being photographed, where the projection is "central". The perspective center of the camera lens is the projection center.

During recent developments of the analytical (computational) procedures (see History, the following section), the interest of numerous photogrammetrists has been to somewhat duplicate the performance of analog instruments for standard mapping problems. For such applications, analytical approaches have demonstrated efficiency (in terms of accuracy, time and cost), such as are comparable to the instrumental approaches without any great improvement, however.

The analytical photogrammetrists have tried to justify their efforts on the basis that they should be able to obtain more accurate results in less time than in the instrumental approaches. The application over which much discussion and efforts have been made with not so much results is that of aero-triangulation. This is due to both the strength and weakness of the procedure under the state of the art. Its weakness lies in the fact that it frightens away a great majority of the practitioners and involves considerable cost; and causes the reluctance to make use of it. Its strength lies in the freedom it permits in the data reduction with a computer. The real strength of analytical photogrammetry, however, lies beyond this and justifies its continuous application and growth.

The principal justification lies in the recent applications on the tracking of ballistic missiles, satellites, etc. and others which are completely outside the capabilities of the instruments of only optical-mechanical scopes. The second justification lies in those applications where the concept of a simple central perspective projection is no longer adequate. Examples of these are strip and panoramic photography systems, electron micrography systems, etc. Also included are the applications in the which the accuracy is required in eliminating mensural errors due to lens distortion, atmospheric refraction, deformations of emulsions, comparator errors, etc., which are difficult or impossible to incorporate in optical-mechanical devices but are easily accomplished through mathematical models with a computer. The third justification lies in the inclusion auxiliary information data and numerical adjustment procedures in a fully satisfactory manner. Such information may be obtained from various sources like electronic positioning, inertial navigation systems, etc. Often, such information may not be directly and rigidly enforced but may be entered as adequately weighted parameters to reinforce rather than override the geometric strength of the normal photogrammetric procedures.

The basic material used in all these are photographs, negatives or diapositives of various types. The basic inputs are the photo-coordinates in a *x,y* (rectangular two-dimensional) system. The outputs may be of various types, like *X,Y, Z* ground coordinates, orientation elements, derived information on specific relations and conditions, etc.

The working system (Fig. 1.1) involves, broadly speaking, the following: object (terrain or other), sensor (camera or other), environment (media items like atmosphere), data acquisition tool (instrument or comparator), data processing mechanisms (computer, accessories and the mathematical models), and the human worker. Each, with its working limitations, contributes towards errors of various nature. The comprehensive knowledge of such limitations and error contributions is essential for an efficient job.

The provision of control in the classical topographical sense my not be necessary or even usable in some non-topographic applications. Furthermore, computer utilization may not be needed in many cases of data processing. Yet, one of the major trends in the development of photogrammetry during the past two decades has been the increasing use of electronic computers for data processing and analyses. The computer utilization can be viewed in the following:

Data Acquisition

1. Digitizing existing charts obtained from analogical or graphical photogrammetric techniques;

2. Measurements of photo-coordinates at a comparator or stereoplotter;
3. Digitizing spatial coordinates from a stereo-model (3-D) at a stereoplotter.

Information (output in Fig. 1.1.) required in various applications

1. Mensuration parameters like area, volume, curvature, gradient, shape and perimeter;
2. Change parameters like velocity, acceleration, volume change and change with regard to time or to parameters other than time;
3. Statistical parameters like area or volume distribution, time variation and probabilistic inferences;
4. Associated parameters like stress and force.

The software potentials throughout these are enormous. Generally speaking, an efficient and appropriate file handling and computer programming system is essential in most of the applications.

Analytical photogrammetry is, however, rapidly becoming more and more complex. Increased complexity does not necessarily mean increased worth. By being more complex, it may become less used because of the concern of the potential user. In this respect, it will be pertinent to emphasize that such situations call for the wisest possible treatment of the photogrammetric resources and the involved technologies with sensible innovations at all stages.

1.1.2 Mensural

Mensuration [L. mensura = a measure] is defined in Webster's New Twentieth Century dictionary as: (i) The act, process or art of measuring or taking the dimension of anything, or (ii) Branch of mathematics that treats of methods for finding length of lines, area of surfaces and volumes of solids. In this treatise we would emphasize, nay insist that our subject matter goes beyond the bounds of mathematics into all branches of science and engineering.

The mensural systems are characterized by saying that it is the study of figures or bodies that are unchanged when the figures (or bodies) themselves are subjected to rigid motions or changes, viz., translations, rotations and changes of size (scale or volume) or of shape (form).

The term "mensuration" also refers to dimensional measurements made to obtain *direct* information on the object being measured, or *derived* information (for example, changing parameters such as velocity; statistical parameters such as area distribution and standard deviation; or other associated parameters such as stress and force). This discussion will be limited to the "direct" part, the "derived" being considered beyond the scope of this book.

Many authors use the two words "measurement" and "observation" interchangeably. However, a subtle difference exists between them. Measurement is the assignment of numbers to objects to represent the relations existing among them with respect to particular properties (Eisenhart, 1969). In the mensural sense, one does not measure an object but rather its dimensional properties—i.e., *quantities* like length or volume. Observation refers to the operational process and its outcome, both, especially with respect to the associated "adjustment" procedure. In the context of both terms, nevertheless, the following fundamental considerations are essential:

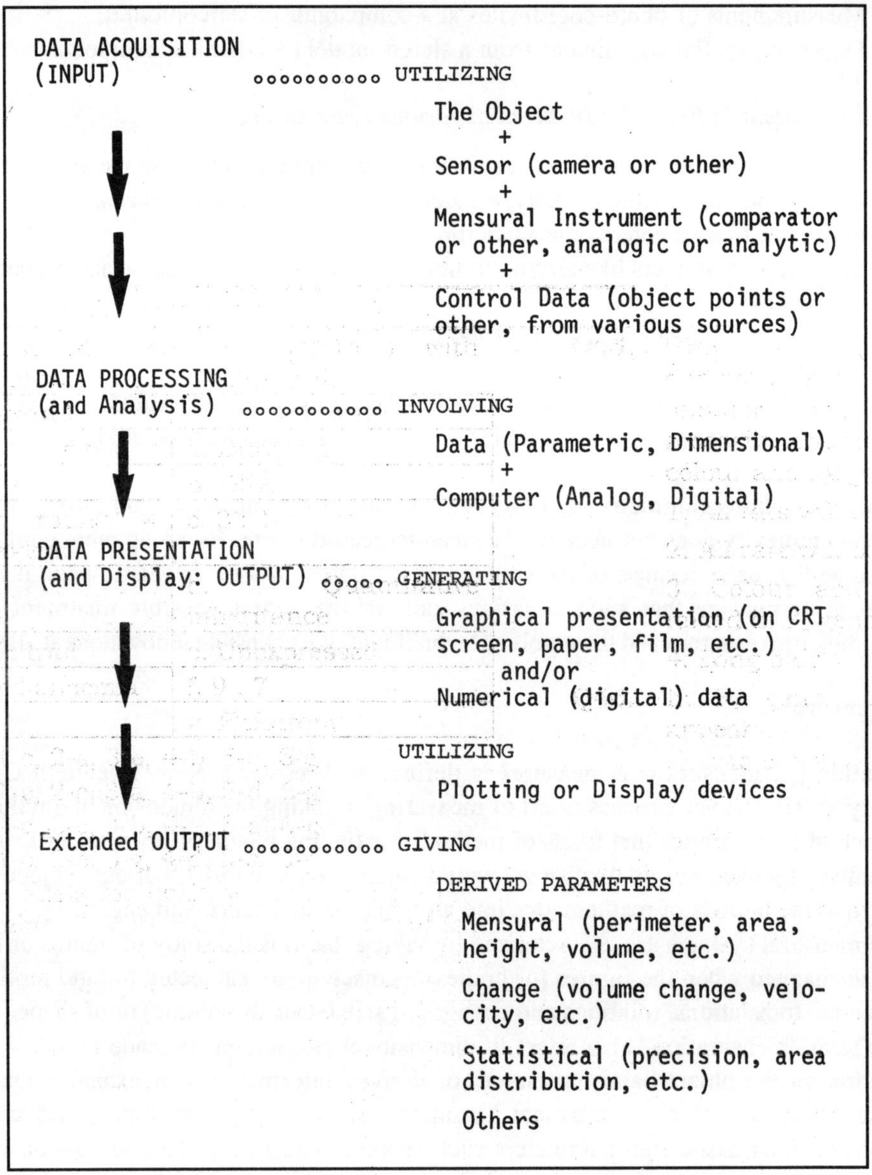

Fig. 1.1: General working system in analytical photogrammetry

1. Measurements are made with simple or complex *instruments* or with the aid of physical phenomena or *entities* (wavelength as for a meter, or a grain of wheat). Associated with this is the operator (human observer) with his individual characteristics.
2. Measurements must be referred, directly or indirectly, to the corresponding *standards* with which comparisons are to be made. Associated with this are the corresponding dimensions and their units.

3. The numerical data obtained in the *observation* process represent the measurements. The data imply the circumstances and conditions under which the observations are made.
4. The mensuration process involves a physical operation. However, often several more operations are implicated, such as preparation (prior calibration, setting up, etc.), pointing and comparing.
5. Measurements are usually the means to other ends (even within the measuring instrument). For example, angles and distances are measured to obtain locations and coordinates, giving derived data, arrived at directly or indirectly.
6. Such derived data are based on *theoretical concepts*, which may be expressed by "mathematical models" based on physical laws. The possibility remains, however, that such concepts and certain associated assumptions are not fully established or understood.

A physical situation can be expressed through the abstract symbolic language of mathematics. Symbolic expressions, known as *mathematical models,* are meant to represent the involved chain of events in a phenomenon under study. Although such conceptual systems can be expressed in ordinary wordage of a language or in terms of specialized scientific jargons, the use of mathematical models has been conveniently made in science and engineering for centuries.

The mathematical models, however, have no scientific value until and unless they have been adequately validated against factual data through experience or research. Scientific/ validation is an open-ended process. The "model" becomes established when it has been tested successfully for repeated applications. Otherwise, depending on its degree of failure, it stands to be modified or even rejected. Mathematical models in practical applications should describe the situations as exactly as possible. They also should be simple enough to provide solutions without undue complications. These two requirements are not always compatible. Thus, one may compromise by way of generalizing the "model" to obtain useful results, knowing that the results may not be exact. One usually looks for computer compatible forms of such "models". In the generality for applications in science-engineering, it is the content and not the form of the mathematical statement that matters. Therefore, often one may benefit from modifying a model so that the form is adaptable to the circumstances without really changing its basic contents.

Mathematical models are composed of two parts: (1) the *functional* model, which describes the deterministic properties of the considered physical event. For precise mensural work, usually a static (time-independent) situation is assumed. Dynamic mensural problems are beyond the scope of this book. (2) The *stochastic* model, which describes and defines the nondeterministic or probabilistic (stochastic) properties of the involved variables. These models are subject to statistical evaluations, which can offer ways of estimating the quality of the operation.

Our discussion covers basically the functional model with adequate consideration of associated stochastic states. For ideas on stochastic models and corresponding principles of "adjustment" theories, the reader is referred to numerous books in that area (e.g., Hirvonen, 1971; Mikhail, 1976).

1.2 HISTORICAL DEVELOPMENTS

1.2.1 Fundamentals and Precursors

Development of mathematics as a discipline of logic did not exist before about 1000 B.C. The Greek philosopher Aristotle (~350 B.C.) referred to the process of optical *projection* of images. Leonardo da Vinci explored the disciplines of optics, geometry and mechanics. In 1492, he demonstrated the principles of optical perspectivity (MacLeish 1977), which provides the foundation of photogrammetry even today. Albrecht Dürer (1471-1528) in 1525 constructed samples of mechanical devices to make true *perspective* drawings of nature and studio scenes even for producing *stereoscopic* drawings (ASPRS 1980). The German astronomer Johannes Kepler in 1600 gave a precise definition of stereoscopy. Aughtread of England in 1574 developed the first *slide rule* and soon thereafter John Napier (1550-1617) published *tables of logarithms* and Blaise Pascal (1623-1662) established the concept of *metrology* and gave the world a *desk calculator*. Isaac Newton (1642-1727) and Gottfried von Leibnitz (1646-1716) firmly established the concepts of differential and integral *calculus*. Concepts of *inverse central perspective* and *space resection* of cojugate images were first discussed by J. Henry Lambert (1728-1777) in his book "Freie Perspective" in 1759.

Fig. 1.2: Albrecht Dürer (1471-1528)

Wheatstone of England presented in 1838 the *stereoscope,* one most important tool used in photogrammetry. The practice of photogrammetry could be started only after Arago and Niepce announced a "Heliographic Process", based on which Louis J.M. Daguerre (1789-1851) presented to the French Academy of Arts and Sciences in 1837 the *photographs* which he called "daguerrotypes". The coining of the term "photogrammetry" in 1855 by Kersten with its introduction by Meydenbauer in 1867 to international literature, the first German textbook on photogrammetry by Koppe (1889) and Aimé Laussedat's classic work on French photogrammetry (1898) are some of the milestones of analytical photogrammetry recorded in history (ASPRS 1980).

Fig. 1.3: E. Abbé (1840-1905)

Fig. 1.4: C. Pulfrich (1858-1927)

Hauck (1883) established the relationship between *projective geometry* and photogrammetry. This should be considered to be the most fundamental geometric concept and the basis of most classic analytical photogrammetric developments.

Ernst Abbé, the cofounder of the German Zeiss Works in 1871 started intense studies and tests for *optical elements* on the basis of rigorous *mathematical analyses*. F. Stolze discovered the principle of the *floating mark* in 1892 while Carl Pulfrich also of the Zeiss group developed a practicable method of measuring and deriving *spatial dimensions* from stereo-photographic images with floating marks. He presented in 1901 the Zeiss-Pulfrich *stereocomparator* by supplementing Eduard von Orel's (1877-1941) first prototype stereoautograph at the 73rd Conference of Natural Scientists and Physicians held at Hamburg. Separately, a similar stereocomparator was invented in 1901 by Henry G. Fouprcade (1865-1948) of South Africa. He presented this at the Philosophical Society of Cape Town.

Sebastian Finsterwalder (1862-1951) in a series of publications during 1899 to 1937 established a very strong foundation for analytical photogrammetry. In these he brought about the geometric relations which govern *resection* and *intersection* as well as *relative* and *absolute orientations*. He predicted the future possibility of *nadir point triangulation* and the application of photogrammetry to astro-geodetic measurements. He also formulated the basic laws of *error propagation* in long strip triangulations. He was probably the first person to use *vector terminology* in photogrammetry literature (Finsterwalder, 1932).

Eduard Dolezal (1862-1955) of Vienna, Austria provided great international driving spirit as he became the founding President of the *International Society* for Photogrammetry in 1909. He also created the *International Archives* of photogrammetry.

1.2.2 Pre-World War II Developments

Although organized civil aviation in the early 1900s and the dirigible airships (like Zeppelins and Parsivals) and balloons opened up new explorations, there was a serious setback by the outbreak of World War I in 1914. However, the period between the two World Wars and extended through World War II (1918 to 1945) witnessed tremendous developments in establishing sound mathematical bases and computational tools to provide the necessary foundation for analytical photogrammetry.

During this period developments in analytical photogrammetry were rather infrequent and mainly limited to countries and individual organizations with certain international interlocking involvements and implications. The following would give the highlights of basic developments during this period. One would notice some developmental efforts started during this period extended into the postwar years, as well as certain disappointing events to slow down possible progress.

Reinhard Hugershoff (1882-1941), a professor at the Technical University of Dresden, Germany introduced in 1921 the Autocartograph, the first universal photogrammetric plotter and later at the Second ISP Congress in 1926, the Aerokartograph, a lighter instrument of the universal type which incorporated capabilities of control extension and phototriangulation. Here is an interesting story, which the author learned from Prof. Schermerhorn during his stay at ITC, the Netherlands, indicating one of many undesirable hurdles in the progress of analytical procedures. In 1920 the Dutch government contracted the German Luftbild GmbH (supported by Zeiss) for mapping several islands and a stretch of the Netherlands coast line. Hugershoff applied the pyramid method by using oblique photographs (Hugershoff 1919) and Luftbild applied a method developed by Fischer (1921). The ground control being inadequate, both the results were very unsatisfactory giving scale errors of upto 10 per cent and azimuth errors upto 7 degrees. These obviously created furore in Europe against any further practical application of analytical triangulation in mapping for almost twenty years..

Otto von Gruber (1884-1942), a professor and scientific collaborator of Carl Pulfrich became famous for his landmark publication “Single and Double Point Resection in Space” (1924). His lectures in the Vacation Courses on Photogrammetry at Jena, first published in 1930 (with English reprints published in 1942) provided pioneering *theoretical concepts* (von Gruber 1942) on differential formulas of projective relations between planes. It was von Gruber who observed in strip triangulation the influence of errors in ϕ on scale and on height. Based on experiments at his initiative, two important facts were emphasized, viz., the usefulness of auxiliary data and instruments in order to avoid propagation of systematic errors in strip triangulation and the practical advantage of using wide-angle cameras.

Heinrich Wild (1877-1951) presented in 1926 at the Second International Congress at Berlin his modified plotter prototype known as Police Autograph. Subsequently he founded a factory in Switzerland (Wild Heerbrugg Ltd.) where hundreds of well-known and widely used opto-mechanical *autographs, comparators* and (now) *analytical plotters* have been developed and manufactured.

The Kern Co. (now in the Leica group) of Aarau, Switzerland joined the photogrammetric industry in 1930 and continued its contribution up to this date. Umberto Nistri (1895-1962) of Rome, Italy and Ermeneguildo Santoni (1896-1970) of Florence, Italy also contributed essentially in designing and manufacturing instruments of various kinds as also in developing numerous corresponding mathematical concepts. Nistri patented in 1919 a method of spatial aerotriangulation. This method, however, was practically applied for the first time to the use of the Multiplex equipment around 1932-33. Georges Poivilliers (1892-1967) of France, Edgar H. Thompson (1910-1976) of the UK are credited with numerous analytical contributions and with designing instruments and stereo-comparators. Thompson's finest contributions were in analytical (matrix algebra) developments, réseau techniques and aerotriangulation by the method of independent models. Thompson edited the British journal "The Photogrammetric Record" for 14 years. Martin Hotine (1898-1968) of the UK War Office, although primarily a geodetist, published two landmark articles on photogrammetry concepts, "Stereoscopic Examination of Air Photographs" (1927) and "Calibration of Surveying Cameras" (1929).

Willem Schermerhorn (1894-1977) of the Netherlands who became a professor at Delft in 1926, began systematic tests of aerotriangulation in 1932 and applied these ideas to uncharted lands in the East Indies. In close cooperation with Otto von Gruber he contributed much to the understanding of error sources and *error propagations* in phototriangulation. He was also the initiator of the ISP journal "*Photogrammetria*". A post World War II Prime Minister of the Netherlands, he was also the founder (in 1950) of the International Training Center (ITC) for Aerial Survey at Delft (now located at Enschede).

His life was dedicated to the promotion of photogrammetry.

V.P. Nenonen and Y. Vaisälä of Finland developed in 1936 a method of aerotriangulation aided by horizon photographic records and statoscope readings. This initiated the concept of using *auxiliary data* for phototriangulation.

Bertil Hallert (1910-1971) a professor of the Swedish Royal Technical Institute at Stockholm contributed much in developing *numerical relative orientation* procedures and establishing the concepts of *calibration* and *standards* for testing cameras, comparators and stereoinstruments. The term "standard error of unit weight" was first used by him.

Starting in the early 1930s through the 1950s, some theoretical and conceptual analytical developments were made at the Federal Institute of Technology, Zurich by Professor Max Zeller and his associates, some of whom continued their contributions well into the 1970s. Arthur J. Brandenberger and W.K. Bachmann, two outstanding ones of the group made numerous contributions in various orientation concepts. Hugo Kasper, also of Zurich, Switzerland contributed considerably to the general concepts during the 1940s and later.

Earl Church (1890-1956) published a series of 19 articles on *computational photogrammetry* in the 1930s after the first American Institute of Photogrammetry was established in 1929 under his direction at Syracuse University. The first six articles were bound in a book (Church 1934). Church started a trend in which numerous scientists made significant contributions in the USA for solving problems of space resection, orientation, intersection, etc. One of the approaches developed by Church, on the determination of the camera station (perspective center) coordinates by utilizing an *approximate position* and an *iterative approach*, has in effect remained virtually unchanged to this day. He, however, separated the solution for the orientation angles from the camera station coordinates. He also tackled another problem which he called "Determination of scale data" i.e. to compute the dimensions of objects from the photographs without reference to their absolute positions in space. He also turned his attention to the calculations of rectifier settings. He later formalized his procedures by codifying his derivations in the direction cosine notations (Church 1948). The approaches of Church were, however, explicit i.e., with no consideration of redundant observations or data. Also. he never applied any error analysis to his solutions.

1.2.3 Post-World War II Developments

World War II had a major effect on developments in all countries. Nonetheless, within each European country postwar efforts were somewhat continuation of previous developments. Destruction of manufacturing and service facilities on the European continent had brought the industry to a virtual standstill. However, during the postwar period the centers of evolution were greatly extended to the North American continent where a tremendous relatively high need in mapping and associated control network existed with untapped scientific and industrial resources and capital to support the growth. Real advancements were made with regard to analytical methods only after World War II, although it is recorded (ISP Archives, 1948 and 1952 Congresses) that numerous "experts" would define photogrammetry as the "art of avoiding calculations". Many of them felt that analog plotting machines had achieved sufficient accuracy with regard to detail plotting and contouring. They considered that the only area where further developments were required was aerotriangulation, in which supplementary computational work was always necessary. In this regard, governmental and commercial interests with academic collaboration were successful in establishing steady growths in various aspects in numerous countries. Although these were peace-time efforts, international competitions, national priorities (in planning and developments) and the challenge of outer space provided the stimuli while technological advancements continued to provide the necessary support.

Furthermore, at the beginning of this period, the basic principles of statistics were no novelty to the photogrammetrist. The theory of errors and the method of least squares had served him well. However, at this stage more and more people started to realize that the modern statistical principles would show how to improve the reliability of various minor operations, analogic or analytic. They even started to realize as to how to plan a job to obtain the maximum amount of information from the number of observations which one can afford to make (due to economic and time considerations) and how to determine the reliability of inference from them.

The units to measure distances remained an unresolved entity to the photogrammetrists. Centuries ago, a foot was defined as the length of 36 barley grains strung end to end and the yard was the distance from the tip of King Edgar's nose to the end of his outstretched hand. Since then we have come a long way. However a confusion did exist internationally, particularly between the two major systems: CGS (Centimeter-Gram-Second) and FPS (Foot-Pound-Second). The CGS system with two variations devised by European scientists in the 1800s was unified in the early 20th century into the MKS (Metre-Kilogram-Second) system. Then in 1954, at the X General Conference of Weights and Measures held at Sèvres, France the Ampere (A) being chosen as the fourth base unit, this system was referred to as the MKSA system. Finally in 1960 at the XI General Conference of Weights and Measures, the system of units proposed in 1954 was officially entitled "Systeme International d'unités" with its abbreviation being SI. This being a coherent system, it is now used by over 80 per cent of the people of the world. Although ISPRS encourages this system, its full official implementation encounters difficulties.

As with the units (meter, foot, etc.), there existed a confusing multitude of systems of coordinates. After numerous deliberations finally an International System of Coordinates was accepted in 1956 (ISP Archives, 1956 and 1960 Congresses). Its universal implementation, however, remains yet to be fulfilled.

In view of computational-analytical approaches, the photogrammetrist started to understand in the early 1950s the necessity and importance of items like "random sampling", "test of hypotheses" or "degrees of freedom" at even minor stages of operations involving also such effects as film shrinkage, lens distortion or temperature variation. Questions related to consideration of, for example, "weight" and "correlation", "observation equations", "condition equations" or "observations" against "quasi-observations" started to be raised in the computational approaches.

Ideas on specific technical developments with regard to uses of Single Images, Stereo Images, Multiple Images and their adjustments in Strips or Blocks will be discussed in the appropriate chapters in the book.

The major thrust in analytical photogrammetry has been made in the USA, Canada and in Europe. Everett Merritt published the first book on Analytical Photogrammetry in 1958. The first analytical system to become operational in an organization of the USA was in the C. & G.S. (now, NOAA). Numerous other public and private organizations have since been involved in these approaches.

In the meantime, sincere efforts have been made in developing analytical procedures in various applications in many countries. The credit of doing outstanding work during the last few decades goes to numerous scientists like K. Rinner of Austria; G. Konecny and F. Ackermann, both of Germany; U. Bartorelli and G. Inghilleri, both of Italy; K. Ryokichi and T. Oshima, both of Japan; A. N. Lobanov of the U. S. S. R.; and many others; omission of whose names here is due to lack of space and limitations of the author (thus, not intentional).

Analytical photogrammetry is now on the way of a great expansion in its applications. This is indicated by the recent developments of several comparators. Another landmark has been the Analytical Plotter, which utilizes a computer on-line to perform functions too numerous to list here (see chap. 2). The last two decades have witnessed a tremendous growth for analytical approaches. The technology continues to change, with the digital computer playing a key role. All-digital systems are in their initial stages of development. On-line analytical photogrammetry is indeed favoured for various tasks.

The efforts of the International Society for Photogrammetry and Remote Sensing (ISPRS), through seven service area related commissions with considerable support from around eighty national agencies and societies, particularly the American Society of Photogrammetry and Remote Sensing (ASPRS), have been greatly instrumental in helping develop the analytical approaches of photogrammetry to its present state. International cooperation is essential for progressive developments which will benefit all human beings.

1.3 APPLICATION EXPANSION

The success of conventional (frame camera photo related) photogrammetry has prompted its extension into various unconventional imaging systems for mensural applications in numerous fields. Modem computer technology contributes innovative adaptations even though the approaches are not always rigorous. Uses of systems like Radiology, Return Beam Vidicon

(RBV) and Electron Micrography (EM) can be made by purely digital or analog-digital procedures provided sufficient knowledge is acquired and applied to correct for image distortions (caused by factors internal and external to the sensing or imaging mechanisms). Brief ideas on representative systems are presented here in three broad groups:

1.3.1 Macro-range

A. *Strip Camera Photography*: First developped and used in 1932 (ASP Manual, 1983), it was further developped in the 1960s and has been used in low-altitude, high-speed reconnaissance and highway planning jobs. The camera records a continuous strip of ground as the aircraft flies over it. With a fixed lens and open shutter, the film in camera is advanced (during exposure) in the direction of flight at the rate of image motion due to the aircraft flight. Both collinearity and coplanarity condition (stereoviewing provided by two strips) equations, modified, have been used (Case, 1967 and Derenyi, 1973).

B. *Panoramic Photography*: Developped in the 1950s, it has been used in mapping.

Of the scanning type, it 'sweeps' the ground from side to side across the direction of flight. Continuous ground coverage is obtained by properly spaced exposures timed to give sufficient overlap between frames. Various movements contained in the imaging system tend to create distortions and image smear. Corrective procedures, mechanical and computational are necessary. The projective equations, modified, have been used with success at analytical plotters for earth and lunar mapping (Gill, 1964; Kratky, 1983 and Peterson, 1973).

C. *Lunar Orbiters* (Satellite imaging systems developped for mapping Lunar surface, auspices of NASA, USA): The first three (of five) were for the Lunar equatorial areas and the last two for the remaining areas. These used frame cameras with onboard (Earth-based remote controlled) dry processing of negatives. The pictures were scanned and transmitted through space via TV monitoring systems and plotted pixel (Picture Element)-by-pixel at a computer facility. The photographs were, therefore, computer generated. In view of the inherent distortions, with reseau control, modified projective equations were used with success (Morgan, 1971).

D. *Earth Satellite Imaging Systems*: Developped during the 1970s and later, there are several systems used worldwide. Landsat and Spacelab (USA), SPOT (France), Radarsat (Canada, USA and UK) as also MKF-6 and KFA-1000 (USSR), to name a few, have excellent cartographic potentials (Ghosh, 1992). These were primarily developped for Remote Sensing. However, with certain necessary modifications of the projective equations and proper corrections being applied, these provide good results.

1.3.2 Close-range

A. *X-ray (Radiography) Photogrammetry*: This is an area of worldwide application.

The system contains a central (perspective) projection although the focus is not a point but a small surface area and it differs from one tube to another. Distortions depend on (a) Film deformation; (b) Double emulsion effect; (c) Refraction; and (d) Focal region effect. Analytical plotters are effectively used in this area. Carl Zeiss (Germany) marketed a special plotter (StR Instrument System) for plotting from X-ray stereopairs.

B. *Holography and Speckle Metrology*: The technique is based on electromagnetic wave fronts scattered from an object and recorded on a 'hologram'. The 3-D data are extracted from double exposure holographic interferometry. The light must be coherent and monochromatic. Measurements of motions and deformations ranging from 1 mm to 1.5 mm with a potential accuracy ofupto 0.3 nm have been reported. The advantage of unlimited depth of focus and the ability to look around an object makes it well suited to the study of small objects.

C. *Moiré Contourgraphy*: It has been mainly used in biostereometrics to measure human body forms, volumes and deformations. Image resolution of 25 lines/mm and accuracies ofupto 0.1 mm have been reported. The potential exists here for real-time computer processing analyses of moire images.

D. *Raster Photogrammetry*: It involves the projection of a grid of known dimensions on the object. It permits obtaining 3-D information from a single image with simple and relatively inexpensive instruments. The technique is adaptable to automated digitizing and real-time data processing. Accuracy of the order of 4 mm has been reported with the use of a metric (calibrated) camera and this technique. Its application potential exists in robotics and in computer vision.

E. *Tomography*: Tomodensitometry obtained through X-ray scanning at 360 degrees around an object is extensively used in medical applications around the world. It gives a sectional view of the object (e.g., a human limb). By integrating data through several such tomographs, one can obtain 3-D information (detectable features, both internal and external) of the object. On-the-job calibration and 3-D data generation with an accuracy of better than 0.3 mm has been reported.

1.3.3 Micro-range

A. *Electron Micrography (EM)*: Both Transmission Electron Micrography (TEM) and Scanning Electron Micrography (SEM) systems have been found to contain distortion patterns (of Scale affinity. Radial, Spiral and Tangential types), for which mathematical models have been developped (Adiguzel, 1984 and Nagaraja, 1974). The near parallel projective imageries are compatible with analytical plotters. Magnifications of upto 500,000x in TEM and upto 200,000x in SEM with limiting resolutions of 0.3 nm in TEM and 3.0 nm in SEM have been reported. Their applications include surface topography (SEM) and studies with tissue and cell biology (TEM).

B. *Ocular Fundus Photogrammetry*: By using stereofundus cameras (with 35 x 35 mm format images) in opthalmological studies, volume and shape determinations with success have been reported. Image resolution of 120 lines/mm and accuracy of upto 7 urn are easily obtained. Digital data and graphical plots are obtainable at analytical plotters (reported by Dr. T. Takamoto, Tufts-NEMCH, Boston, Mass. at the ISPRS Congress, Kyoto, 1988).

BIBLIOGRAPHY

Adiguzel, M.; *Problems Related to Three Dimentional Mapping with Electron Micrographs* (Ph.D. Thesis, Laval Univ., Quebec: 1984).

American Society for Photogrammetry and Remote Sensing; *Manual of Remote Sensing* (3rd Ed.), ASPRS, Falls Church, Virginia; 1998.

American Society of Photogrammetry; *Manual of Photogrammetry* (4th Ed.), ASPRS, Falls Church, Virginia; 1980.

Arthur, D.W.G.; *A Stereocomparator Technique for Aerial Triangulation,* Ordnance Survey Professional Paper, New Series No. 20, London; 1955.

Case, James B.; The Analytical Reduction of Panoramic and Strip Photography, *Photogrammetria* 22, No.4; 1967.

Church, Earl; *The Geometry of the Aerial Photograph*, Syracuse University, N.Y.; 1934.

Church, Earl; *Theory of Photogrammetry*, Bull. No. 19, Syracuse University, N. Y.; 1948.

Derenyi, Eugene E.; Orientation of Continuous Strip Imagery, *PE* 39, No. 12; 1973.

Doyle, Frederick J.; The Historical Development of Analytical Photogrammetry, *PERS* 30. No. 2; 1964.

Eisenhart, Churchill; *Precision Measurement and Calibration* (NBS Special Publication 300, Vol. 1: 1969).

Finsterwalder, Sebastian (1932): Die Hauptaufgabe der Photogrammetrie. (Sitzungsberichte der Bayrischen Akademie der Wissenschaften, München).

Fischer, T. (1921): Uber die Berechnung des Räumlichen Rückwärtseinschnitts bei Aufnahmen aus Luftfahrzeugen (G. Fischer, Jena).

Fourcade, H. G. (1903): On a stereoscopic method of photographic Surveying (Transactions of South African Philosophical Society, 14).

Ghosh, S.K. and M. Boulianne; Adaptation and Utilization of a Conventional System of Radiography (X-Ray) for Precision Measurements; *Proceedings ofASPRS Annual Convention:,* 1984.

Ghosh, S.K.; *Quantitative Aspects of Remote Sensing* (Historical Dimensions of Agriculture, Vol.1; Ed. Noor Mohammad; Concept Pub. Co., 1992).

Gill, Charlene; Relative Orientation of Segmented Panoramic Grid Models on the AP-II,P£30,No.6;1964.

Hauck, Guido (1883): Konstruction einer Dritten Perspektive einer Objektes aus zwei Gegebenen Perspektiven.

Hirvonen, R. A.; *Adjustment by Least Squares* (F. Unger Publishing Co., N. Y. : 1971).

Hugershoff, R. (1930): Photogrammetrie und Luftbildwesen (Springer, Wien).

Lambert, J. H.; *Freie Perspektive,* Zurich; 1759.

Laussedat, Aime; Recherches sur les instruments, les méthodes et le dessin topographiques, Gauthier-Villars, Paris; Vol. I, 1898; Vol. II, 1901-03.

MacLeish, H. (1977): Leonardo da Vinci, A Man of All Ages; National Geographic, 153/3, pp. 296-319.

Merritt, Everett; *Analytical Photogrammetry*, Pitman, N. Y.; 1958.

Morgan, Peter; *An Investigation into Some Problems of Lunar Orbiter Photography System* (Ph.D. Dissertation, The Ohio State Univ., Columbus, Ohio: 1971).

Nagaraja, Hebbur; *Application Studies of Scanning Electron Microscope Photographs for Micro-measurements and 3-D Mapping* (Ph.D. Dissertation, The Ohio State Univ., Columbus, Ohio: 1974).

Peterson, C.G.; Compilation of Lunar Pan Photos, *PE* 39, No.l; 1973.

Thompson E.H. (1959): A Rational Algebraic Formulation of the Problem of Relative Orientation (PR 3/14).

Von Gruber, Otto; *Photogrammetry, Collected Lectures and Essays,* American Photographic, Boston, 1942.

2

INSTRUMENTATION

Instruments used in computations photogrammetry can be classified in the following functional groups :

1. Instruments for *data acquisition* (comprising comparators, point marking and transferring devices);
2. Instruments for *data processing* (comprising image space plotters, analytical plotters and hybrid or converted plotters); and
3. Instruments for *data display and presentation* (comprising plotting tables, software systems and orthophotoprinters).

One would note, however, considerable interactions amongst such components in view of diverse activities, conventional (in aerial and terrestrial mapping) and unconventional (technologies or application related). All the same photogrammetric data-acquisition is primarily to obtain the input data (coordinates x,y) of photographic image points. There are two approaches in this, viz., monocular and stereoscopic measurements. With regard to the data-processing, the approach is mathematical, with the help of a computer. This can be done either *off-line* (where the devices in the computer systems are not in direct communication with the data-acquisition outfit), or *on-line* (where the operations of terminals, files and other auxiliary equipment are in direct communication with the data-acquisition outfit in order to eliminate or minimise the need for human intervention at any stage between initial input and computer output). Apart from the comparators, analytical plotters or the hybrid (basic analog stereo) plotters, one may consider the Radial Triangulators, discussed later in Section 2.5. They are much less in use now-a-days, However, before discussing the specific instruments, it would be pertinent to know the basic components therein.

2.1 BASIC COMPONENTS

The basic components of an instrument are: (i) the viewing system, (ii) the measuring system; and (iii) the readout and recording system.

2.1.1 Viewing Systems

The role of a viewing system is to bring the measuring (or, floating) mark into coincidence with the image (photo) and to present the combination to the eyes of the observer at an appropriate magnification. There are various kinds used in the instruments, as follows:

(a) *Single eyepiece.* This, the simplest viewing system uses one objective (for focussing the illuminated photograph) and one eyepiece to examine the combined image. There are several elaborations and variations of such systems, e.g., with zooming eyepieces, interchangeable eyepieces of different magnifications, and prisms added to incline the eyepiece for comfortable viewing.

(b) *Binocular eyepiece.* In single-image instruments, both eyes see the same image, making such an instrument very comfortable to the observer. In a double image instrument, however, each eye sees one image such that a 'fused' stereo-image is viewed only after appropriate settings are made.

(c) *Projection viewing.* In some instruments, both the measuring mark as well as the photo image are projected on a screen where the observer's viewing can be made without the aid of additional optical elements.

(d) *Photo-electric setting.* Such systems, of recent development, can be attached to the instruments. This is to assure that the reticle is exactly centered on a symmetrical image. For example, a beam-splitter is used in the Mann Comparator so that visual observations on a viewing screen at 22x magnification may be coupled with photoelectric settings. Such systems are excellent for symmetrical images like marked points or star images. Some viewing systems (e.g., the Autometric-Gilliland instrument) have image detecting devices which automatically locates the center of the image. The detector determines the center of gravity of image-density within the area being scanned. These are, therefore, ideal for symmetrical images.

2.1.2 Measuring Systems

The function of a measuring system is to obtain the relevant data on the photograph. The various available devices are listed below.

(a) Leadscrews

The most common measuring device is the leadscrew or spindle (in combination with a nut). A large drum attached to the end of the screw, graduated in decimal divisions would give the distances (and coordinates, accordingly) to the smallest unit possible in such a system. For example, if the pitch of the screw is 1mm (which is very common) and the graduations on the drum are 1000 divisions, this would give each division to represent 1 μm translation. A supplementary revolution counter or scale would give the full revolutions (corresponding to pitches of the screw), while the partial revolutions can be read with an index on the graduated drum.

Some comparators have the viewing microscopes moving over fixed photographs while others have fixed viewing systems with the possibility of translating the photographs. The movements can be made faster with added motor drives.

Some comparators (e.g., Mann, Type 841) have single leadscrews with which only one coordinate can be read at a time. After all points are read in one coordinate (say, x), the plate is rotated through 90° and the other coordinate (y) for all the points are read next. This requires double pointing, and consequently, more time and some complications in data refinement result. Accordingly, double leadscrew comparators are generally preferred. The plate carriers in these are usually rotatable for making the photograph fiducial lines approximately parallel to the measuring axes.

The leadscrew comparators can have errors in the observed coordinates caused by lack of straightness and orthogonality of the screws, variations in the pitch of the screws, instrumental back-lash and effects of temperature variations.

(b) Scales and Micrometers

The movements of the plate under the viewing system are referenced to scales (glass or metal) parallel to the measuring axes. When a point is observed, the measuring mark may fall between two full divisions of such a scale. A micrometer or vernier measures the translation necessary to bring the index to the closest full division. The sum of the full divisions of the scale and the micrometer reading will then give the complete coordinate value. Such a system, in general, uses the *Abbé Comparator Principle.*

Note: Abbé Comparator Principle, first presented in Ernst Abbè, *Gesammelte Abhandlungen,* vol. 2 (Zeiss Jena, 1906), p.207, states: The object to be measured and the measuring standard or agent must be in contact or lie in the same plane. To quote Abbé, "The design be based on the following requirements: (i) To exclusively base the measurement in all cases on a longitudinal graduation with which the distance to be measured is directly compared; (ii) To always design the measuring apparatus in such a way that the distance to be measured will be the rectilineal extension of the graduation used as a scale."

It has the following advantages: (i) Mechanical errors in straightness or orthogonality of axes have only secondary effects on the measurements. (ii) If the scales and diapositives (and negatives) are both made of glass, their temperature variations are nearly identical. This reduces the need for temperature control in the laboratory. (iii) The micrometer (or, vernier) needs to be only of the length of the increment between two scale divisions. This makes the instrument very convenient in manufacturing and in precision measurements.

The spiral micrometer (like one used by Zeiss, Jena) is one of the simplest devices of this kind, which permits easy reading to 0.1 μm.

(c) Grid (réseau) Plate and Micrometers

The basis of measurement is a glass grid plate with a series of points which is superimposed on the photograph to be measured. The grid can be precalibrated. The increment from the nearest grid point (or, line) to the image point is measured with micrometers. Such grid plates usually represented by crosses (e.g., in Zeiss PSK stereocomparator) or black dots (e.g., in Canadian NRC monocomparator).

Minor variations in this systems are in the movements of the grid plate or of the optics. A typical example is the Zeiss PSK stereocomparator where the grid plates are translated in the

x-direction (along with the superimposed photographs) while the viewing optics are translated in the y-direction. The leadscrews for x and y translations need to be precise enough to count the full divisions (in cm) on the grid plate. When the image to be measured has been brought into coincidence with the reticle, an optical switch brings the reticle and the micrometer plate simultaneously into focus. Rotations of the x and y handwheels translate this micrometer plate to measure the increments to the nearest grid lines.

The greatest advantage of this system is that once calibrated, the grid is not subject to variations from wear. Its temperature expansion coefficient is the same as that of the photo (diapositive or negative) and all accuracy requirements are met by the glass grid.

(d) Ferranti Fringes

In this system a length of an optical diffraction grating having a precisely known number of lines per unit length (e.g., 2160 lines per mm) is used. A grating as long as the axis to be measured is attached to the movable carriage and a short piece is placed over the photocells which do the counting. With two sections of such a grating superimposed with the line structure at a slight angle to each other, a moiré fringe pattern with an approximately sinusoidal distribution of density is produced at right angles to the grating lines.

When one grating moves along the other, the fringe pattern moves across the grating at the rate of one fringe cycle per grating pitch. A set of Ferranti silicon photocells are used, either directly for coarse gratings or by means of a special lens and slit assembly for finer gratings (e.g., 40 lines to a mm). A high speed bidirectional electronic counter is essential for successful applications of moiré fringe measurements.

Such a measuring system is entirely free from friction and wear. Minor sources of errors like dust or scratches have no appreciable effect on the measurements. The signal on each photocell is derived from a strip of grating (about 1 cm × 0.25 cm). Metric gratings with structures of upto 250 lines per mm corresponding to the least count of 1 μm are readily available.

(e) Interferometer Measurement

Such a system is based upon the interference phenomenon produced by superimposing beams of monochromatic light. This has been used in ballistic photogrammetry where occasional operational problems have been reported (Chitayat, 1960).

(f) DIG Linear Measurements

This is a non-incremental system capable of determining absolute positions over an unlimited range (developed by Bausch & Lomb, Inc. and General Measurement Research, Inc.) with a least count of 1 μm. The essential elements in this are: a precise glass scale, a reading head and a display panel. It has several interesting features including the possibility of measuring along up to three axes. It has not, however, been used in conventional applications of photogrammetry.

(g) Computer-controlled Measurements

In a developed system (Roos, 1975), the Automated Réseau Measuring Equipment (ARME), it is possible to accurately center on réseaus, stars and marked points on photographs with homogeneous or heterogeneous background. It is a precise computer-controlled comparator with a TV camera, an operator console, a point locator and a computer system with card, magnetic tape and hard copy output possibilities. The most interesting feature of this equipment is the automatic centering program, in which the largest number of bits that can be stored is 255 or, 65,025.

2.1.3 Readout Systems

The function of a readout system is to permanently record all the measured coordinates. The various available systems are given below:

(a) *Manual, optical-mechanical.* This is the simplest approach, which involves an optical readout by the operator and manual recording by the operator from verniers, micrometers, drums or scales of the instrument. Such manual recordings can be time consuming and are liable to human faults and errors.
(b) *Hard-copy printout.* The output from such a system (e.g., with shaft encoders) can be fed to various kinds of typewriters. Some units also permit typing desired comments, associated with particular points in addition to recording point numbers (for identification) and their coordinates.
(c) *Automated, complete systems* permit point identification, recording of coordinates on punched cards/tapes or compact discs in formats as are directly usable by a digital computer or an automatic plotter. Such an automated recording system, adapted to any photogrammetric instrument, has several advantages. Firstly, the system eliminates human blunders and mistakes. Secondly, this increases the speed of observational work. Thirdly, it presents the data in computer compatible forms. Additional refinements in the form of photographic recording of each image point (which identification) is possible in some instruments.

2.2 COMPARATORS

2.2.1 Standard Monocomparators

Monocomparators make measurements (*x, y* coordinates) of points on one photo at a time. In such an approach, the point images to be measured have to be recorded on the photo as natural features on the object or, marked, artificially, by a point marking (or, transferring) device in appropriate locations, i.e., these points must be unmistakably identifiable on the photo.

There can be three categories of points: (a) Signalized points, marked on ground (object) before photographing, e.g., paneled control points; (b) Detail points, as are readily identifiable on the photograph, e.g., a street intersection on a photograph taken from air; and (c) Marked (artificial) points, which are directly marked or transferred (by a point marking/transferring instrument) in proper locations.

A representative example is the PK-1 Monocomparator (see Fig. 2.1) introduced in 1976 by Carl Zeiss, Oberkochen, West Germany. In this, a photo-holder carries the photograph on its upper side and the index grating on the under side moves along a plane surface. There is a

Fig. 2.1: PK-1 Monocomparator

guide ensuring parallel motions of the photo-holder. Test points are set by first shifting the photo-holder by free hand and tilting a plate (provided for this purpose) to obtain a precise shifting motion. One glass scale is mounted on a U-beam which at the same time serves to guide the carriage with the scanning head. An image of the photograph is formed in a nearby intermediate image plane in which the measuring marks are located. It offers the operator a choice of using one of three types of luminous floating marks or a black floating mark. Binocular viewing is possible with 5×, 12×, 20×, or 30× magnification. The two dimensional linear measuring system of this monocomparator is illustrated in Fig. 2.2. This uses a photoelectric linear measuring system. The index grating is contained on the photo-holder. This grating, in

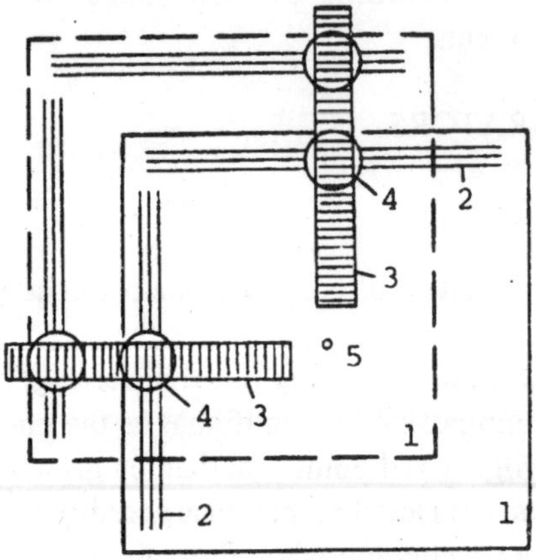

1 Photo-holder plate
2 Index qrating
3 Scale
4 Scanning head
5 Measuring mark

Note: Broken line indicates centre position and solid line indicates off-center position.

Fig. 2.2: Two-dimensional linear measuring system with index-grating and fixed scales of Zeiss PK-1 comparator

conjunction with the scale-grating, produces Moiré fringes, which are required for counting. The length of scale lines is equivalent to the test length in the opposite coordinate. The design combines the principles of linear pulse measurements with that of guide-error compensation.

Another example is the Mann comparator type 422-F (see Fig. 2.3), in which three motions are incorporated. Two translatory motions permit the photo-holder (or, stage plate) to be transported along two mutually perpendicular directions (*x* and *y*). The other motion allows

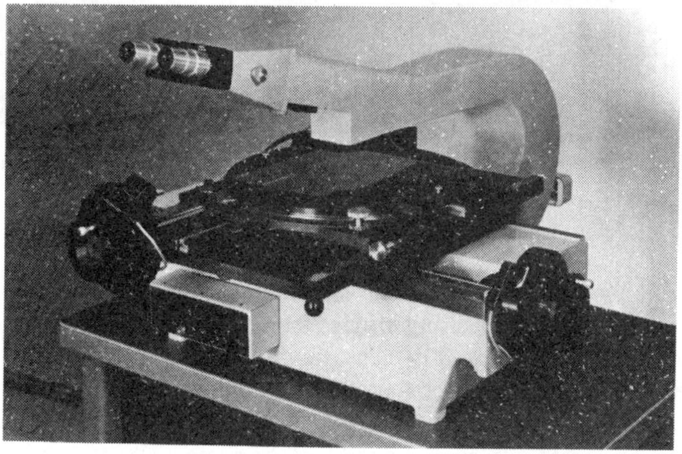

Fig. 2.3: Mann Monocomparator Type–F

the stage plate to be rotated. There are slow motions screws for fine adjustments usually provided for each motion. Another popular monocomparator is the Space Optic comparator. In order to measure the coordinates of a point, the photograph is placed on the photo carrier, which is rotated and adjusted so that one of the fiducial axes of the photo becomes parallel to one of the instrument axes. The movement of rotation is then locked and readings of the *x, y* coordinates of all points along with all of the fiducial marks are made with regard to the translatory motions only. The fiducial center coordinates are obtained by averaging the observed values of the fiducial marks. The coordinates of the fiducial center are then subtracted from the coordinate readings of all the points to obtain the initial (i.e., unrefined) photo coordinates.

In practice, more than one set of readings should be taken on each point to eliminate the possibility of blunders and improving on the precision of observation. It is better if such repeat observations are taken with care by eliminating the possibilities of errors due to instrumental backlash, personal/(observer) bias, etc. The actual number of repeat observations may be influenced by time and cost considerations.

2.2.2 Multilaterative Monocomparator

During recent years, the general availability of digital computers has made feasible an altogether new approach in designing (by DBA, Inc.) this large format (245 × 245 mm) plate measuring comparator (with Least Count 1 μm.). The instrument is (see Fig. 2.4) a single-image, portable (weight, 10 kg.) comparator, available both with and without automatic digital readout. It

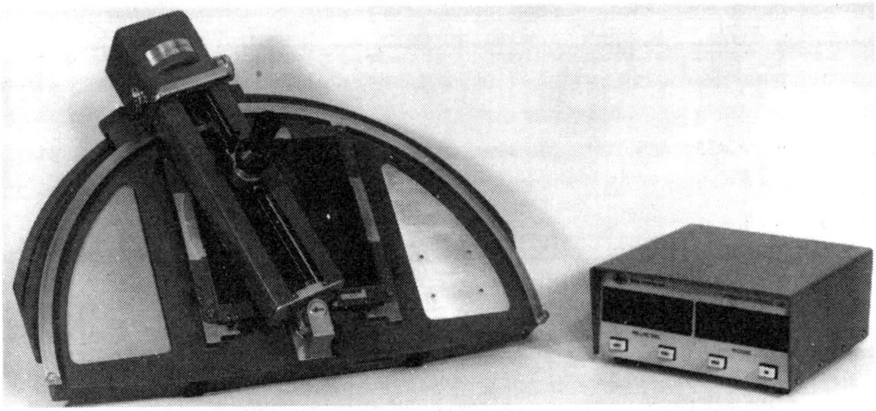

Fig. 2.4: Multilaterative monocomparator by DBA system

operates on the principles of trilateration. The essential measuring element is a glass scale arm with precision graduation. The measuring arm is free to rotate about a pivot at its base. Length measurements are made by rotating this measuring arm about the pivot and simultaneously moving the eyepiece (microscope) such that the point to be measured comes within a circular reticle. The glass scale along with a micrometer reads the distance. Four distances between the pivot and the particular point (with rotations of 90° of the photo on the stage plate) are measured. The *x, y* coordinates of the fiducial marks and all image points are obtained by computation in an arbitrary *x, y* system.

Figure 2.5 (after Brown, 1969) illustrates the theoretical basis of this comparator. Four measurements (distances), r_{1j}, r_{2j}, r_{3j} and r_{4j} of a point are made. The actual measurements,

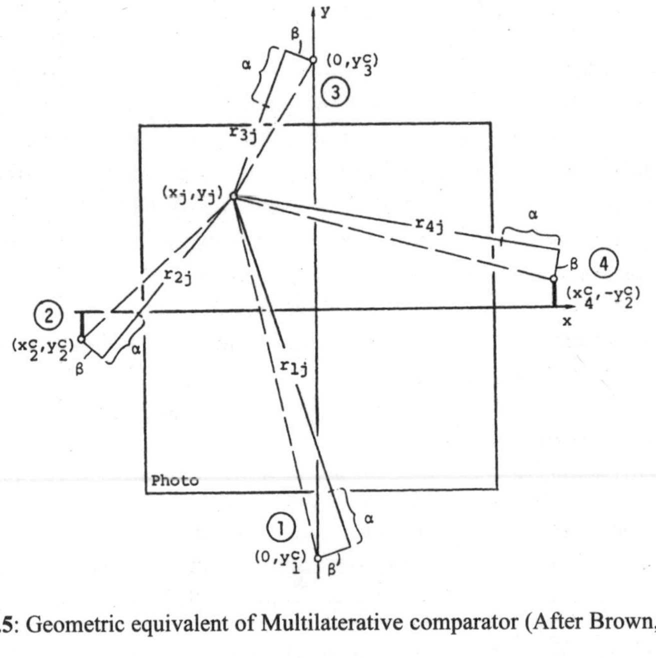

Fig. 2.5: Geometric equivalent of Multilaterative comparator (After Brown, 1969)

r_{1j}, are from the zero mark of the scale to the point, rather than from the pivot. To convert the measurements to radial distances from pivots, one must consider the tangential offsets (α and β).

If x_i^c, y_i^c are the coordinates of the pivot corresponding to the i th position (i = 1, 2, 3, 4) of the photograph, one can write the following set of observation equation where x_j, y_j are the desired photo coordinates:

$$\left.\begin{aligned}(r_{1j}+\alpha)^2 &= (x_j - x_1^c)^2 + (y_j - y_1^c)^2\\(r_{2j}+\alpha)^2 &= (x_j - x_2^c)^2 + (y_j - y_2^c)^2\\(r_{3j}+\alpha)^2 &= (x_j - x_3^c)^2 + (y_j - y_3^c)^2\\(r_{4j}+\alpha)^2 &= (x_j - x_4^c)^2 + (y_j - y_4^c)^2\end{aligned}\right\} \tag{2.1}$$

If the ten parameters of the comparator (i.e., α, β and four sets of x_i^c, y_i^c) were exactly known, the process of coordinate determination would be reduced to a four-station, two-dimensional, straightforward Least Squares trilateral solution.

In practice, however, the comparator, parameters are not known with sufficient accuracy. Therefore, a self-calibrating solution to recover those parameters (while simultaneously executing the trilateration) is desirable. This can be done by enforcing certain simplifying conditions such that the eight unknown pivots coordinates are reduced to five. These are: $x_1^c = x_3^c = 0$ and $y_4^c = -y_2^c$ (see Fig. 2.5). This choice has also the merit of placing the origin of the photo coordinates near the fiducial center.

By virtue of this arrangement, only seven independent parameters of the comparator (viz., α, β, $y_1^c, y_3^c, x_2^c, x_4^c$ and y_2^c) need be recovered. This means, if n number of points are measured on the plate, the number of unknowns is $2n + 7$. For each point one writes four equations of the type of Eq. 2.1. Accordingly, if $n \geq 4$, there will be more observation (or, condition) equations than unknowns. A Least Squares adjustment solution leading to $2n+7$ by $2n+7$ system of *Normal equations* can then be performed. The size of the normal equations would increase linearly with the number of measured points. However, they possess a patterned coefficient matrix that can be exploited to collapse the system to one of order 7×7, which would involve only the comparator parameters. Hence, their solution presents no difficulty.

The manufacturer (DBA System, Inc.) has developed a FORTRAN program, fully documented, for the data processing in order to obtain adjusted photo coordinates (i.e. x_j, y_j) of all measured points. This is available to the customer.

2.2.3 Stereocomparators

A stereocomparator is used for measuring simultaneously the coordinates of corresponding points on a stereo pair of photographs, particularly when such readings are made without resorting to some form of point transfer. Usually, the measuring, viewing and readout systems are of the same type as those employed in the monocomparators. Alternately, each stage of a stereocomparator can be used as a monocomparator.

It is advantageous for the computational photogrammetric techniques to have completely separate measuring systems for the two photographs of a stereo pair. It is, however, necessary to translate both stage plates simultaneously under the viewing optics in order to continuously scan the stereo pair (without losing the stereo impression). In the classical construction of a stereocomparator (see Fig. 2.6), two stages are utilized: (i) the *x*-carriage (upper-stage) with its own measuring system, carries the photographs. The right side photograph can be moved in

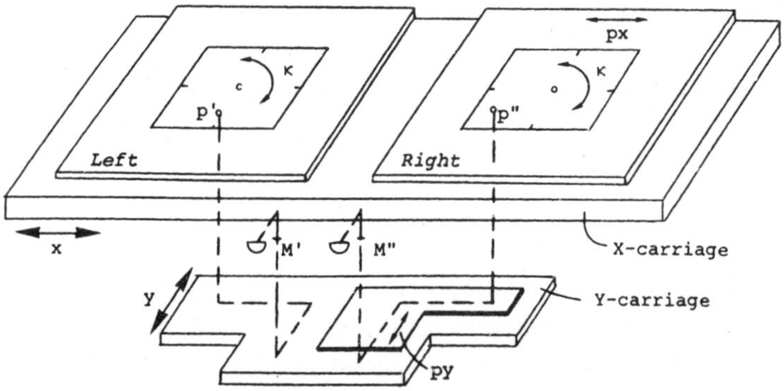

Fig. 2.6: Schematic of a stereocomparator, 1818 of Zeiss Jena
(M' and M" are the measuring marks; optical paths are shown in broken line

x relative to the left photo. It records the coordinate (x_1) of a point on the left photo and the differential *x* movement (*px*) corresponding to the right photo; and (ii) the *y* carriage (lower stage) containing the rest of the necessary measuring devices, can be translated by the amounts necessary to remove and record the y_1 coordinate for the point on the left photo and the differential y movement (*py*) corresponding to the right photo. The values *px* and py are the *x* and *y* parallaxes, respectively. Thus, the observed values are: x_1, y_1, *px* and *py*. Coordinates, x_2, y_2 for the right photo are:

$$x_2 = x_1 + px \text{ and } y_2 = y_1 + py$$

Brief characteristic features of some of the numerous stereocomparators are discussed below:

Zeiss-Jena Stecometer

In this instrument (see Fig. 2.7), the common *x* motion is given to the lower stage and common *y* motion is given to the optics (microscope). The *px* motion is given to the right photographs on one upper stage and the *py* motion to the left photograph on a second upper stage. It can use photographs up to 23 × 23 cm size. The photographs are illuminated through a condenser from above and are observed from below with a magnification, 6×, 12× of 18×. It is possible to choose one of six luminous measuring marks, each differing in size and shape. Three different colours of measuring marks can be selected also. One can optically transform *px* into *py* with built-in Dove prisms.

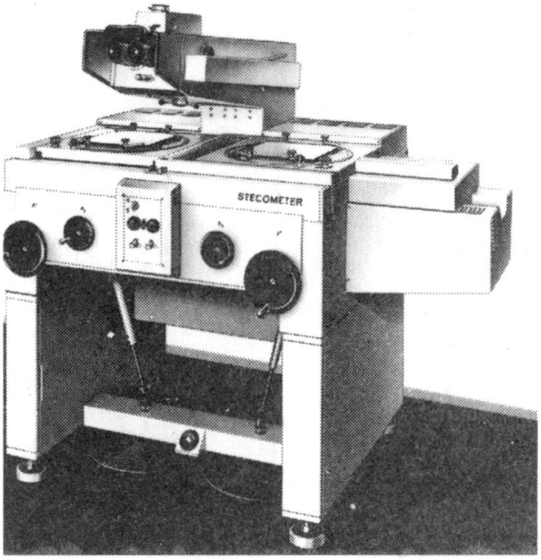

Fig. 2.7: Stecometer of Zeiss Jena

Hilger-Watts Recording Stereocomparator

In this instrument, the measuring system is based on the use of a 1 cm grid, which is defined by fine crosses. It can be printed on the negative at the time of exposure or a grid plate can be placed on the negative in the stereocomparator.

The grid permits the elimination of the influence of film distortion and permits simple corrections for distortions due to lens and the errors of the grid marks as known from calibration. Scanning in the x direction is by moving the stage plates and in the y direction by moving the optics. The instrument is provided with a device for plate rotations up to ±22.5 degrees. Magnification is possible between 6x and 12x. A single control can give a differential magnification up to ±1.2 times between the left and right photographs. The built-in Dove prisms permit rotations of the images as may be necessary for convenient stereoscopic viewing. Additional coupled Dove prisms can be used to rotate images jointly through 90° for transforming *px* into *py*.

In view of the grid (réseau), an observation method developed by J.G.F. Lawrence (Ordnance Survey, UK publications, 1949) is used in this stereocomparator. In this, the réseau crosses serve the following purposes: (a) Control the distortion of the negative and print material, (b) provide a convenient source of 'minor control' as may be necessary in photo-triangulation, and (c) define a coordinate system on the photograph. The binocular observing system has floating (measuring) mark graticule half crosses in the left and right sides, which are fused stereoscopically to form a cross with arms parallel and at right angles to the eye-base (Fig. 2.8).

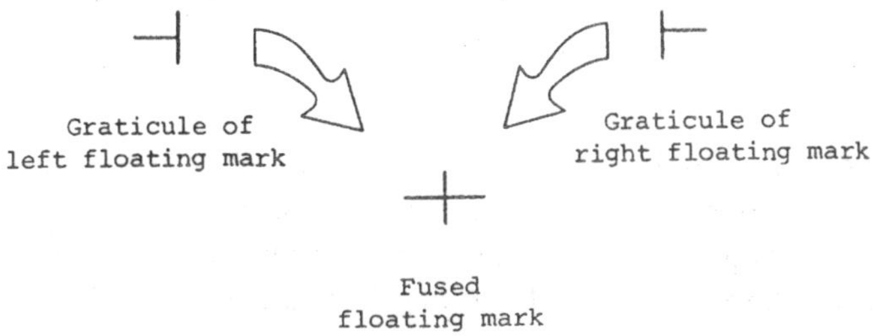

Fig. 2.8: Floating marks in Higher-Watts stereocomparator

The operation can be visualized through Fig. 2.9. Photograph No. 1 is aligned so that its lines of réseau crosses are parallel to the instrument axes. Photograph No. 2 is adjusted to give

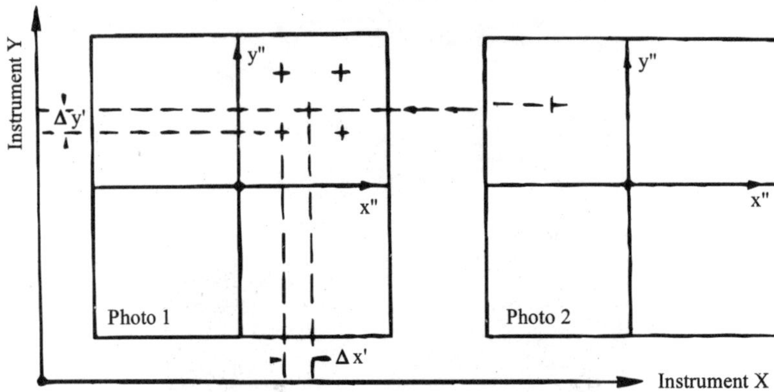

Fig. 2.9: Lawrence method of observation

comfortable setereo vision over the area around the point to be observed. The stereoscopic pointing is completed with the finer adjustments so that the two halves of the floating mark appear as a single cross resting on the ground model, bisecting the observed point. the *x,y* readings for the aligned photo No. 1 are recorded. The half mark associated with photo No. 1 is then brought over the réseau cross nearest to the observed point and the readings for photo No. 1 are again recorded. The differences of the second readings from the first ones give $\Delta x'$ and $\Delta y'$, the *x*- and steps from the réseau cross to be observed point, with respect to photo No.1. These are then added to the calibrated réseau coordinates of the cross to obtain those of the point. For points on the ground (trigonometric stations, pass points, etc.), the procedure has to be repeated by aligning photo No. 2 with its line of réseau crosses parallel to the instrumental axes, adjusting photo No. 1 to give comfortable stereo vision over the area around the same observed point. Thus, one obtains, New $\Delta x''$ and $\Delta x''$ values, i.e., new *x*- and *y*-steps from the réseau cross to the observed point with respect to photo No. 2. These are then added to the calibrated réseau coordinates of the cross to obtain those of the point.

In this system, *minor controls* are generally réseau crosses. If so, these have to be coordinated on the photo on which they are not marked. The coordinates on the photo on which they are recorded are already known from the calibration data for the réseau. Thus, left-hand points, have to be observed on the right-hand photo and the right-hand points, likewise, on the left-hand photo.

Zeiss PSK-2 Stereocomparator

This instrument (see Fig. 2.10) is worthy of notice because of its design and portability. Plates with measuring réseau grids are used. Photographs are placed with emulsion surface directly in contact with these grid plates, one on either side of the instrument. Prisms permit inversion of images and change of viewing sequence as may be necessary in bridging (left side photo to

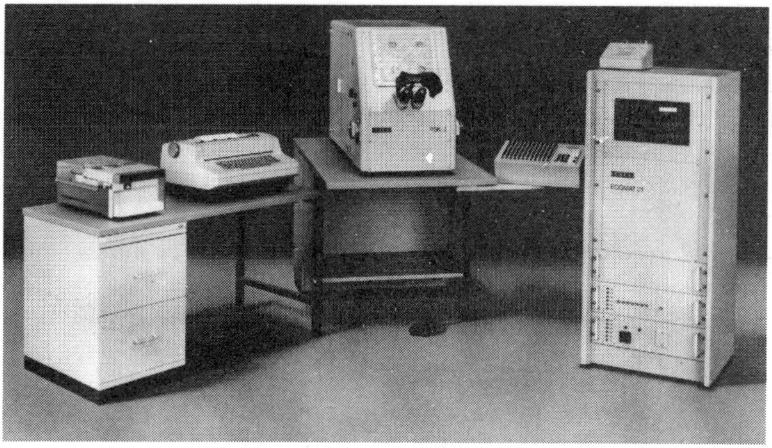

Fig. 2.10: Stereocomparator PSK-2 with Ecomat 21 by Zeiss

be viewed by right eye and vice versa). Built-in *amici* (or, roof-angle) prisms can optically adjust any rotation required for stereo viewing.

During the observation procedure, the photo holders are moved in the *x*-direction while the optical element containing the measuring mark moves in the *y*-direction. After the measuring mark is stereoscopically focused on the point to be measured, the photo coordinates of this point are read by means of a measuring grid and a *mm* reticle (*G* and *R*, respectively, in Fig. 2.11)

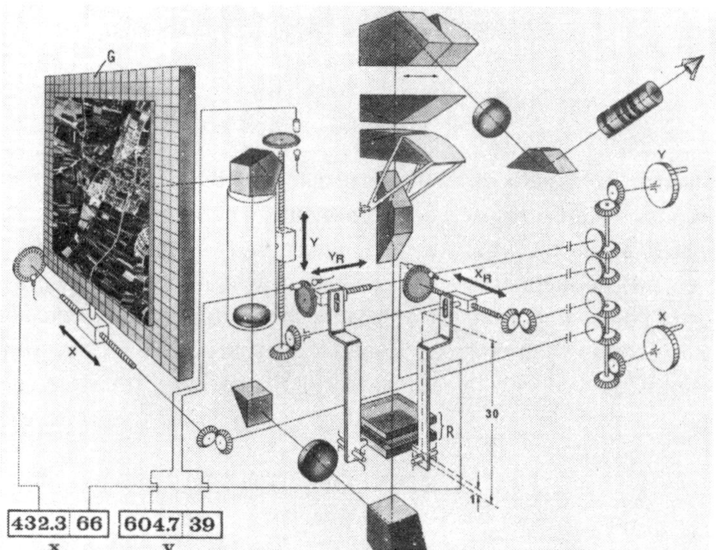

Fig. 2.11: Functional diagram of stereocomparator PSK-2
(*Courtesy*: Carl Zeiss, Oberkochen, Germany)

placed in the fieled of view of the eyepieces. The coarse readings of the x and y coordinates are obtained with reference to the réseau and the fine readings by coincidence between the reticle and the réseau.

The six digit coordinate and parallax values, x_1, y_1, px and py are read (with the least count of 1 μm) at the illuminated instrument counters or computer cards are directly punched at the connectable card punching outfit. A recording unit, e.g., Ecomat 21, can be obtained from the manufacturer.

Our discussion on comparators would not be complete if we do not mention one uniquely designed instrument, Kern CPM 1 (Fig. 2.12), developed in the 1970s. This instrument serves as a point marking and transferring device as well as mono comparator and a stereo-digitizer.

Fig. 2.12: Kern CPM 1
(*Courtesy*: Kern & Co. Ltd, Switzerland)

Attempts were made as early as the 1960s to automate the stereocomparator, as exemplified in the OMI-Bendix TA3/PA. However, such instruments equipped with correlators, never arrived at sufficient accuracy. Finally these functions have been incorporated in the analytical plotters (Section 2.4), in the more recent versions of which the instrument is able to find the originally selected point solely from previously measured or program located positions, thereby reducing the necessity to even mark the points to be transferred and measured. Some highly promising experimental version of automated total (marking, transferring and measuring) systems did not, however, eventually materialize as they failed to be cost-effective.

2.3 STEREOPLOTTERS

In the absence of Comparator, if a precision stereoplotter is available, one can use that conveniently as a comparator. The operations are simple and straight forward. The procedures explained below are applicable in any precision stereoplotter like Leica (Wild) A10, (See Fig. 2.13). Zeiss C8, Thomson-Watts plotter or Galileo Santoni Stereosimplex.

Fig. 2.13: Autograph A10 by Wild

2.3.1 Monocular Measurements

Monocular comparator measurements can be made by using either the left or the right side camera (projector). All elements must be set to their zero position (i.e., $\omega = \phi = \kappa = bx = by = bz = 0$). The principal distance (camera constant) should be set to an arbitrary value ($\bar{s}$) in Fig. 2.14; e.g., 150.00 mm), regardless of the focal length of the taking camera. The carriage should be brought to a Z-column setting of a round multiple of the principal distance setting (e.g., $Z=2\bar{s}$ or $3\bar{s}$) such that the entire photograph can be observed within the instrument's limitations.

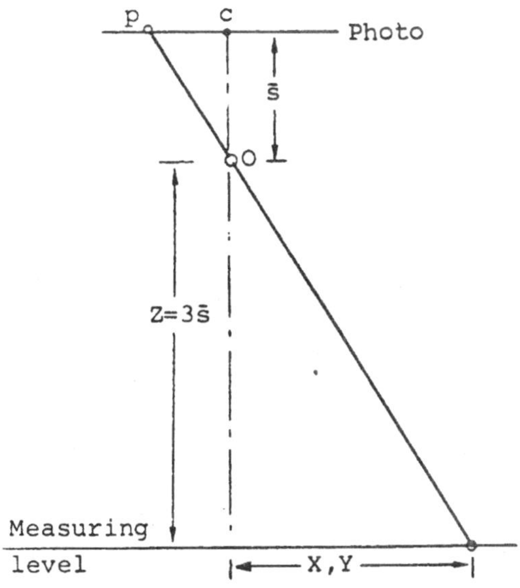

Fig. 2.14: Monocular measurement at a stereoplotter

The fiducial center of the photograph being *c*, the photo coordinates of a point (*p*) can be obtained from simple relations (considering *X*, *Y* as instrument coordinates in terms of the counters or scales connected to the carriages):

$$x = -\frac{\bar{s}}{Z}X \quad \text{and} \quad y = -\frac{\bar{s}}{Z}Y \tag{2.2}$$

where

$$X = X_{\text{observed}} - X_c$$

and

$$Y = Y_{\text{observed}} - Y_c$$

Note: X_c and Y_c are the instrument coordinates of the fiducial center of the photo, i.e., average of the observed *X, Y* coordinates of the fiducial marks.

2.3.2 Stereoscopic Measurements

A Stereoplotter can be used a stereo-comparator by using both the cameras (projectors) of the instruments with observations in stereo. The stereo overlap can be accomplished in either base-in or base-out mode. The base-in mode is illustrated in Fig. 2.15.

Note: *Base-in* and *Base-out* are permissible settings in some instrument systems. With alternate base-in and base-out settings, it is possible to perform instrumental strip triangulation with only two cameras in such instruments (Ghosh, 1975).

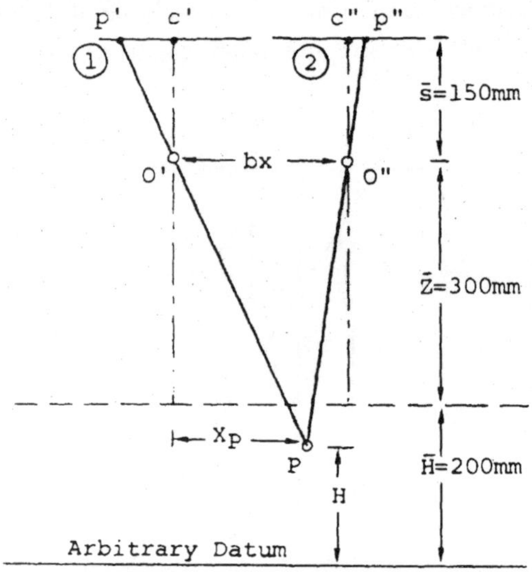

Fig. 2.15: Stereoscopic measurement at a stereoplotter

In a Base-in model (assuming an air-photo strip flown left to right, Photo No. 1 in the left camera of the instrument and Photo No. 2 in the right camera), all the elements excepting *bx* must be set to their zero positions, i.e., $\omega' = \omega'' = \phi' = \phi'' = k' = k'' = by' = by'' = bz' = bz'' = 0$.

The settings of *bx*, $\bar{s}$ and *Z* must be realistic round figures, in keeping with the intersection geometry of the stereo pair. For example, with *Standard* (i.e., Wide angle camera and 60 per cent forward overlap) photography, the possible settings are: $bx = 200.00$ mm, $\bar{s} = 150.00$ mm and $z = 300.00$ mm (see Fig. 2.15 drawn with these values in mind).

Other instrumental settings are: (i) Instrument gears and levers are set such that all readings, (*X, Y* and *H*) are in the same units (e.g., mm); (ii) The *H* counter must read positive values at all points in the stereo overlap. This can be done by initially setting the *H* index to read a large value (e.g., $\bar{H} = 200.00$ mm) at the instrument *Z* level (in Fig. 2.15, it is 300.00 mm).

The *X* and *Y* had wheels and the *Z* disc (or pedal) are to be used for scanning the stereo model and reaching the specific points. *Y*-Parallaxes are to be removed with the *by* element, whose readings are to be recorded along with the readings of the *X, Y* and *H* scales (or counters). The photo coordinates of a point in the left side photo are obtained by using the following expressions:

$$x' = -(X = X_{c'})\frac{\bar{s}}{(500.00 - H)}$$

$$y' = -(Y - Y_{c'})\frac{\bar{s}}{(500.00 - H)} \tag{2.3}$$

The photo coordinates of the same point in the right side photo are given by:

$$x'' = x' + px$$

$$y'' = y' + py \tag{2.4}$$

where $px = \bar{s}\frac{bx}{(500.00 - H)}$ and $py = \bar{s}\frac{by'' - by'}{(500.00 - H)}$ (2.5)

This procedure can be followed for both negatives and diapositives. Note that the number 500.00 appearing in the denominators of Eqs 2.3 and 2.5 is due to the sum of 300.00 (value in mm of the *Z* column setting) and 200.00 (value also in mm of the *H* index setting).

In a Base-out model, the data can be obtained in a similar manner, with Photo No.1 in the right side camera and Photo No. 2 in the left side camera and by using the *by'* element for parallax elimination. Many studies (Salmenpera, 1970) indicate that by using such stereoplotters one can obtain accuracies comparable with stereocomparators.

2.4 ANALYTICAL PLOTTERS

An analytical plotter consists of: (a) a Viewing Unit (precision stereocomparator with control) and (b) a Coordinatograph, interfaced with (c) an electronic Digital Computer (see Fig. 2.16). These instruments are capable of solving a wide variety of photogrammetric problems conventional and unconventional. The early models required a certain amount of manual operations. More recent ones, however, incorporate electronic image correlators and other components, which make them operate almost completely automatically. Their capabilities are limited by the dimensions of the photo-carriers in the comparator and the limitations of the computer. Many analogical solutions like Relative Orientation, Scaling, Absolute Orientation, Orthophoto printing, etc. are possible in such an instrument apart from it being used as a stereocomparator only.

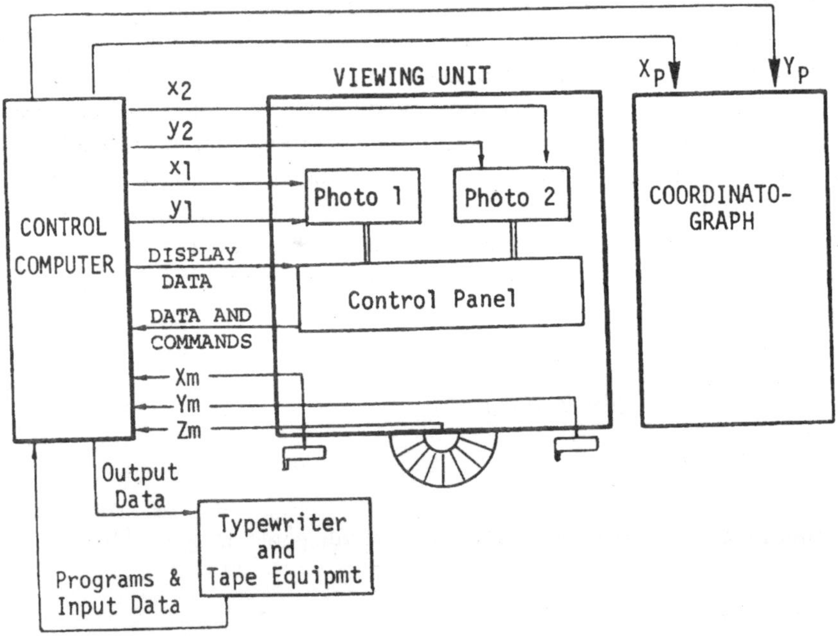

Fig. 2.16: System diagram for an analytical plotter

Several commercially available analytical plotters are shown in Figs. 2.17 through 2.19. Some of the numerous such plotters available on the market are: Aviolyt BC-1 of Wild, AP-C/

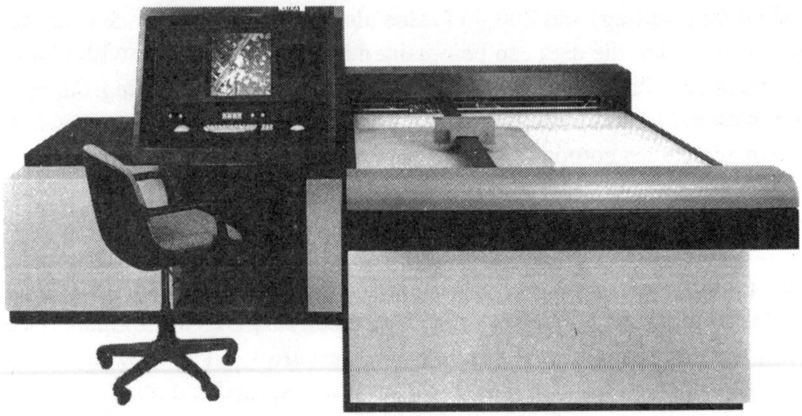

Fig. 2.17: Traster SST-77 by Matra
(*Courtesy*: Matra Optique, France)

4 of OMI Corporation, Planicomp C-100 of Carl Zeiss, US-2 of Helava Associates, Traster SST 77 of Matra Optique, DSR11 of Kern and Digital Streocartgraph if Galeo. Certain simpler versin with limited capabilities like Stereocord G2 of Carl Zeiss and APPS-IV of Autometric are also available. These indicate the worldwide trend towards on-line analytical solutions with computer capabilities.

The manufacturer, Carl Zeiss, claims that the HP 1000 minicomputer and additionall hardware and software components allow the C 100 Planicomp system to be expended into a photogrammetic plotting and computing center. Practical experience shows that this is a particularly valuable feature.

The PLANI-AS and PK-AS program systems support plotting with analog plotters and comparators. The measured data is identical in format, management and further processing capabilities with the data produced by the C 100.

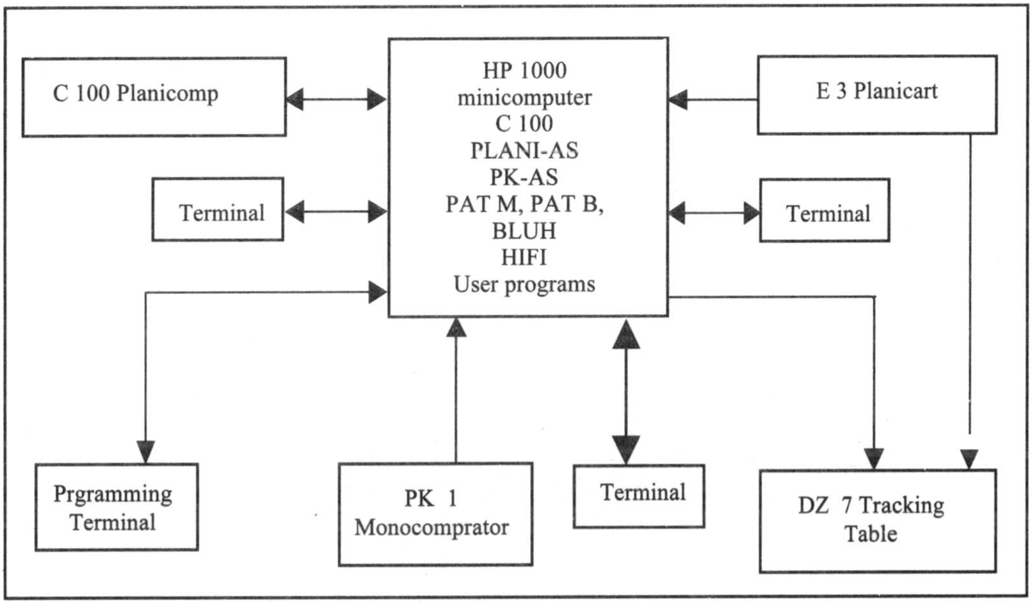

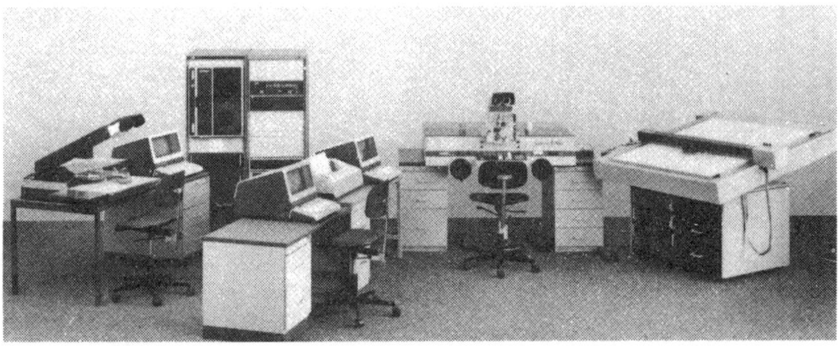

Fig. 2.18: Total working system and Planicomp C-100 by Zeiss

For further processing Carl Zeiss offers the PAT M, PAT B and BLUH programs for model or bundle block adjustment and the HIFI program system for digital height modles and the calculation of contour lines. The user can also write his own programs; they may be completely indepedent or can be bound into the C 100 software structure by means of Zeiss routines. Delivery, installatin and service of the overall system are the responsibility of Carl Zeiss.

Such an instrument operates by solving equations based on the observation data (points locations on photo), the stored data and the mathematical model relating the problem. Output from the comparator-computer combination activates servo motors to drive the coordinatograph plotting device (pencil or scriber), which presents the graphical, plotted information. Some of them can even provide computer support for analog plotters in parallel.

The new Alpha 2000 first-order analytical stereoplotter represents the latest advance in the closed-loop servo drives, an independent measuring system, close adherence to the comparator principle, open 32-bit distributed computer architecture, menu-based operator interface, and an on-line, high resolution interactive graphics and editing workstation — all the features expected of a first order analytical stereoplotter.

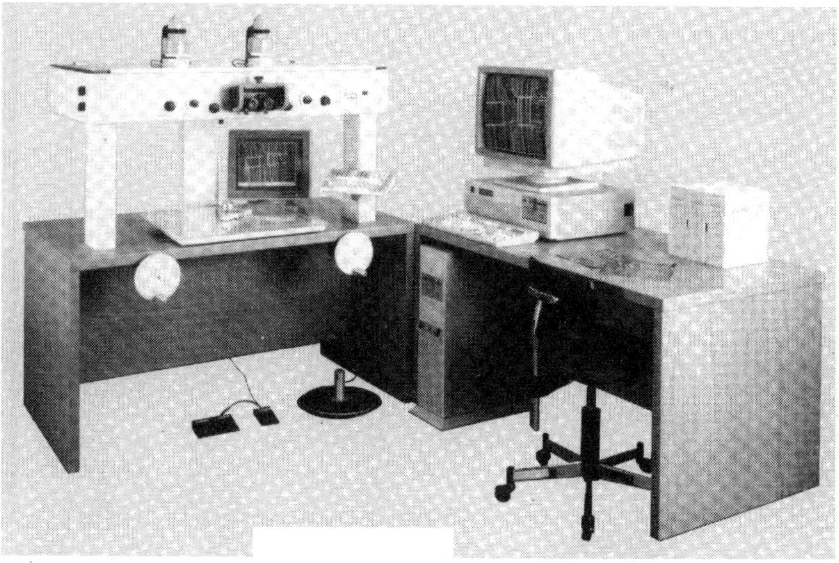

Fig. 2.19: Alpha 2000 System by I^2S

It should be recognized that there are always necessary communication (dialog) between the computer and other relevant components of the analytical plotter. This is essential for on-line solutions of various problems. The standard procedures involved in topographic mapping with a stereopair of aerial (or satellite) photographs are illustrated in Fig. 2.20

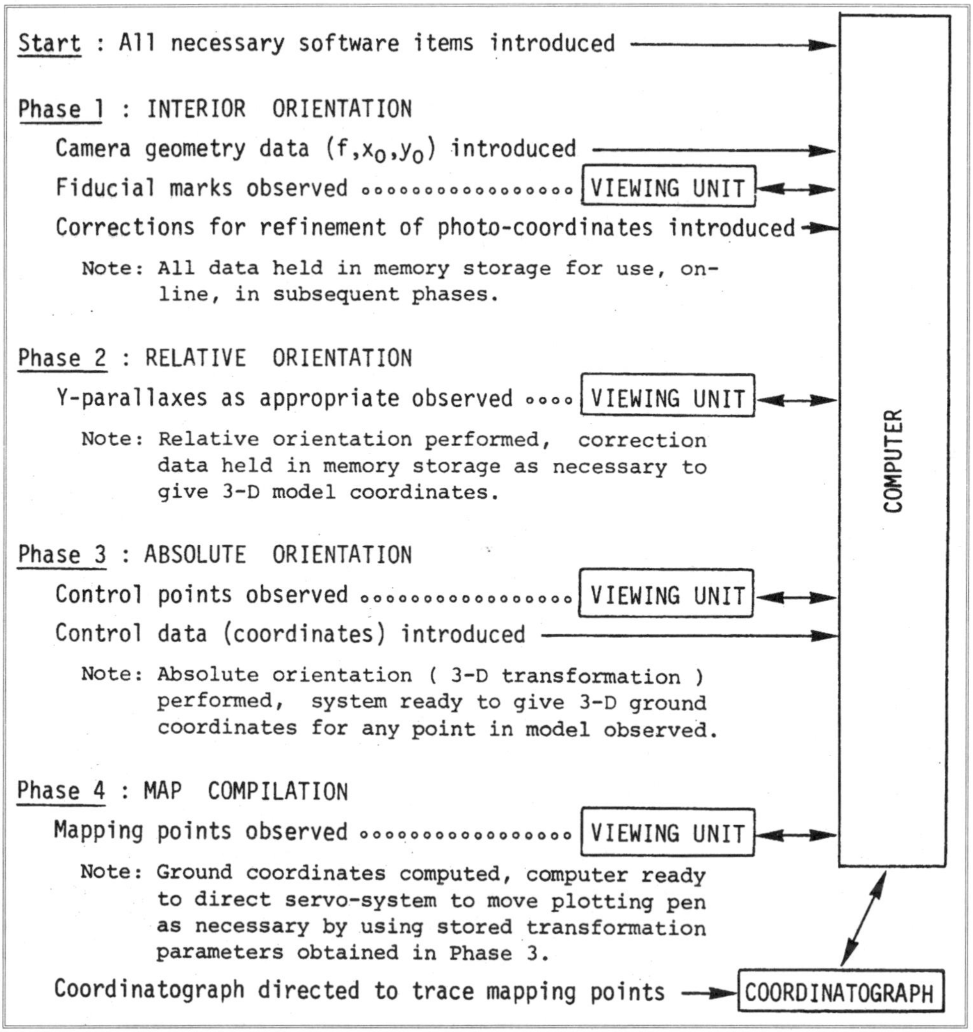

Fig. 2.20: Typical communication diagram for mapping of stereo-model at an analytical plotter

The adaptability of the analytical plotter to various systems and problems is its prime asset. For example, any portion of a photograph with the NASA Large Format Camera can be used inspite of the fact that the perspective center could be set off-center. The problems of orienting strip and panoramic photographs are solved easily and adequately at such a plotter. Likewise, radiographs or electron micrographs can be handled successfully. For their use with conventional (frame) photography, the operations follow a pattern similar to, yet more than, those at a conventional optical-mechanical stereoplotter. For example, the following steps would be pertinent with regard to panoramic photography: [*Note*: Standard Frame Photos do not need certain parameters, as mentioned.]

1. *Interior Orientation* of each photo. The inputs at this stage are,
   (a) Diapositives (or negatives) placed on the plate carriers of comparator,
   (b) Constants (for the computer);
   - F - Camera focal length corrected for uniform film shrinkage:
   - C_f - Differential film-shrinkage constant, which is used to calculate such correction as is applicable to one set of photo coordinates (say, y) compared to the other (say, x);
   - R - Radius of the Earth Sphere in the model scale;
   - $\overline{X}, \overline{Y}$ - The coordinates of the points in the model at which the Earth Sphere is assumed to be tangent to the X-Y plane of the model;
   - C_e, C_h - Correction constants which are determined by fitting correction equations to appropriate distortions due to lens and atmospheric distortions:
   - X_n, Y_n - Coordinates of the camera Nadir point in the model system;
   - K_{im} - The image motion constant which corrects for the Image Motion Compensation (IMC) of the camera;
   - K_{xr}, K_{yr} - These two apply to panoramic photography only, being the relative vehicle motion constants (relative to the Earth) during exposure.

   (c) Photo centers (x_o, y_o), established from the observed fiducial marks constitute the only observation data for Interior Orientation.
2. *Relative Orientation* of the stereo pair.
   (a) Y-parallaxes observed at five or more locations (in the stereo model);
   (b) The elements of relative orientation, generally 'Dependent'case (i.e., bx, by, ω, ϕ and χ) are computed and stored.
   Note: With appropriate software, the relative orientation can be performed by also applying the Collinearity or the Coplanarity condition.
3. *Absolute Orientation* of the stereo model.
   (a) Three control points (at least) are identified and used for absolute orientation (scaling and levelling). The elements of transformation between model coordinates and ground (survey) coordinates are computed and stored.
4. *Map Compilation* of necessary details and contour lines in the model.
   (a) δX and δY are computed from model coordinates and applied to the photo-carriages on a real-time basis.
   (b) Map coordinates are computed from model coordinates using the stored parameters of transformation from Step 3 above.
   (c) The compilation proceeds on a real-time basis. Alternately, model coordinates (X_m, Y_m, Z_m) or the corresponding map or ground coordinates (X_p, Y_p, Z_p) for discrete points can be recorded or displayed.

Simple versions of analytical plotters, some of them indigenous (for example, Ladouceur *et al.*, 1982), are becoming popular for applications where accuracy demand and scopes are limited. One recent example is the Stereocord G2 of Zeiss developed after the Analytical Photogrammetric Positioning System (APPS). The APPS, developed at the US Army Engineer Topographical Laboratories, is a modified Zeiss Stereotope, the analog mechanical computers having been replaced by an electronic desk calculator (Hewlett-Packard Model 9810). The measurement values are digitized with the aid of a commercial pulse generator in conjunction with a counter (e.g., DIREC-1 in Stereocord G2) and an interface system. All numerical data for each stereo pair (i.e., camera position, elevation, attitude, cameral calibration data, refraction corrections, etc.) are stored on a magnetic tape cassette together with the calculator program required for data reduction. The Stereotope part is used as a stereo viewer. A shaft-angle encoder, mounted on the Stereotope x-parallax micrometer, provides X measurements which can be used to determine the elevation of any point being viewed in stereo. All data reduction is performed automatically by the calculator and three-dimensional coordinates are displayed. When a plotter (e.g., Hewlett-Packard Model 9872A) is connected to the Stereocord G2, it becomes a complete analytical plotter (albeit, for limited applications).

Another simple analytical plotter is the APPS-IV of Autometric, Inc. This instrument has linear encoders on, x, y, Δx and (i.e., the two photo coordinates at a point and two parallaxes, Δx and Δy, at the same point) motions. These motions are driven by servo motors and are also displayed for manual uses. Other features include an electronic subsystem for internal data handling and facilities for communications with a computer.

2.4.1. Recent Developments

A wide range of development in analytical plotters took place since the 1984 ISPRS Congress at Rio-de-Jeneiro. PC (microcomputer) based low-cost technology has been behind several new instruments. These are typified in instruments like MPS instruments (by Adam Technology, Chamard 1987) and APY instruments (Yzerman 1987) or Wild BC-3 and BC-4, Kern DSR-15 [*Note*: Wild and Kern companies merged recently to form Leica] or OMI AP-5 (Klein 1987). Superb capabilities of analytical plotters have been enhanced in the 1990s through certain significant developments, the outstanding ones are the followings:

1. Integration of *graphic work stations* [e.g., Kern DEC PDP-11 based MAPS 300 system workable on line with either analog plotters like PG2 or analytical plotters like DSR-15 or Zeiss Planimap system workable with either Planicart (analog) or Planicomp (analytical)] to have an auxiliary monitor screen displaying the plotted manuscript map or chart. An excellent example of the versatility of such sytems would be seen in the following versions offered by Zeiss technology: (a) P3 Planicomp as a 3D Digitizer, with the basic module P3/PC for orientation and photogrammetric data acquisition, e.g., for CAD (Computer Aided Drafting) or GIS (Geographic Information System) systems, through conversion programs; (b) P3 Planicomp for digital mapping with the basic module and an AutoCAD and DAT/EM software optimizing for mapping projects; (c) P3 Planicomp for Intergraph compatible data acquisition with Micro-Station software; (d) P3 Planicomp with Kork Digital Mapping System (KDMS); and (e) P3 Planicomp as a photogrammetric data acquisition station for GIS pcARC/INFO, where the basic module and measuring functions enable on-line data acquisition directly in the pcARC/INFO environment. Below are some comments on the CADMAP and KDMS, since these two are currently the two most used programs with Analytical plotters:

(i) The CADMAP may be used to collect and edit graphic data but it may not be used to complete the final design on the job. This can be done with other available systems. The basic CADMAP graphic data structure contains upto 501 Layers (entities like roads, trees, streams or power-lines would use different layers), four Modes (Line, Splined Line, Symbol and Text) and four Graphic Pointers (two Line Font numbers, Symbol number and Text Pointer). There are several Mode Attributes (for miscellaneous parameters).

(ii) KDMS — a sophisticated computer workstation processes (inputs from most stereoplotters, tablet digitizers, Kork translators and mouse-based editing as also integrating graphic data. Each KDMS digitizer has a full colour video display. The output may be scribed or inked hardcopy with coordinated grids or KORKTRAN translators can be used to convert Kork map files to a variety of other digital mapping systems and for GIS applications.

2. *Superimposition and stereo-superimposition of graphics* [e.g., Wild S9-AP system or Zeiss Pl Planicomp system], whereby, for example, a monoscopic image of the plotted map can be compared with the 3-D image of a stereo-model.
3. *Image matching with correlators* [e.g., Kern Digital Orthophoto software system KDOSS or Gestalt Photomapper GPM], which conceptually followed the Bunker-Ramo UNAMACE system (Bertram 1965) developed by the US Army in the 1960s.
4. *Hybrid or Converted Plotters.* Conversion of several analog plotters into analytical has been successfully accomplished during the 1980s and later. Examples are provided in Quasco Analytical (QA) conversion of Kern PG2 and Wild B8, and E. Coyote's conversion of several Topocarts (Anacarts) by using computers (DEC PDP-11) and software provided by Helava Associates. Such low-cost PC based hybrid plotters are becoming popular world-wide.
5. *Data Display and Presentation Instruments*

   (a) *Plotting Tables.* During the last two decades, we have witnessed direct on-line or off-line plotting capabilities including data storage possibilities. Plotting is possible also with a wide range of tools, for example, tangential-control scribing devices, dual or quadruple plotting heads and software controlled plotting such as would provide automatic corrections based on prior calibration. Tiltable table surfaces and variable plotting speeds are now regular features at such plotting tables.

   (b) *Software Systems*. The world demands did help develop software systems for acquisition, processing, management and presentation (in graphical or digital forms) of data. Object-oriented and structured data management systems with graphic editing capabilities constitute newer generations of analytical plotters, like Zeiss PHOCUS or Wild-Leitz MS-DOS and UNIX. Associated computer work-stations are now commonplace. These are also generally usable with numerous peripheral hardware equipment, generally designed after customer requirements.
6. *Digital Photogrammetry*: In the 1990s, improvements in fast computers with available newer softwares, a knowledgeable customer base and image scanners capable of converting photos to digital images (with adequate resolution and stable geometry) have prompted the development of what is currently recognized as Digital Photogrammetry (Schenk 1999).

The analytical plotter still remains the optimum device. However, soft-copy plotters have been introduced, which present a purely digital approach to photogrammetry. Increasing interest in Geographical Positioning System/Satellites (GPS), Geographic Information System (GIS) and the use of image data in digital form have motivated several private firms to enter into digital photogrammetric workstations market. Such workstations are generally designed to perform not only the functions of analytical plotters but also other functions such as :

(a) Editing collected data or map.
(b) Implementing image processing functions (e.g., contrast enhancement and change detection).
(c) Integrating image and map data in raster and vector formats.
(d) Interfacing with GPS and GIS software for more complete information base.
(e) Generating on-line Digital Terrain Models (DTM) as also displaying data in perspective as well as in plan view.

Nonetheless, the current enthusiasm for digital photogrammetry workstations is tempered by cost and the need to handle large volumes of data efficiently as against the worldwide cost-effective use of analytical plotters.

2.5 RADIAL TRIANGULATORS

These were designed for computational radial triangulation, which may be performed now-a-days much better with other available instruments. The precision is extremely limited. Their use, accordingly, is much restricted. This brief description is presented here for the sake of completeness.

One oft-used example of such instruments is Wild RT1. In this instrument, the photographs remain fixed on the photo carriers during the measuring process while two rotatable glass scales, one on each photo of the stereo pair, are shifted. Each glass scale is provided with a series of measuring marks (engraved on the scale). To measure a point, the scale is rotated into the same polar direction of the point and the nearest measuring mark of the series on the glass scale is set on the point by a small shift and rotation of the scale. The values of the rotations of the two glass scales are read on two corresponding 'theodolite' horizontal circles (reading least count being 1^c, estimated to $\sim 0^c.1$). Similarly, the length of the radius vector (estimated to ~0.01 mm) for the points may be determined. These two measurement capabilities make it possible to use the instrument also as a stereocomparator for polar coordinates. Depending on the tilt, circumstances and job requirements, either the principal point, or the nadir point, or the isocentre (or any other reference point) of the photograph can be used as the radial center. Good stereo observation is possible by means of Dove prisms in the viewing system.

2.6 POINT MARKING AND TRANSFERRING DEVICES

With a view to avoiding possible ambiguity in the identification, selection and description of photo points obtained from natural details, it is often desirable to mark unmistakable points in the emulsion of the photograph. Depending on whether or not stereo- or mono-observations are desired, such points may or may not be transferred onto the adjacent photographs. In some areas (e.g., forest or desert) it may be impossible to locate natural points and the cost of providing presignalized points on ground may be prohibitive. Such artificial points are desirable in these cases. Several point marking and transferring devices are commercially available. Each device has, of course, its limitations in the type of point it can mark and the accuracy with which such points are marked and transferred. Brief descriptions of some of these are given below:

(a) MK Marking Device by Carl Zeiss (Fig. 2.21)

It has a rectangular metal frame within which is a glass plate with a spotting device (punctiform setting mark) and a marking device, both of which can be mutually adjusted so that the observed point appears in the center of the annular mark, engraved on the lower plane (in touch with the photograph). A stereoscopically selected point is marked in the emulsion of photo by a circle around the point of 1mm diameter. Artificial transfer points can be marked by a minute needle prick. A 10-power magnifying lens is provided to facilitate the observation of the point. Two such units are necessary for stereoscopic marking and transferring under a stereoscope.

Fig. 2.21: MK, Marking device
(*Courtesy:* Carl Zeiss, Germany)

(b) PM-1 Marketing Device by Carl Zeiss (Fig. 2.22)

It is much more sophisticated and precise than the MK cited above. It uses heated needles for marking the points. This creates annular bulges around the points and provides high contrast against bright or dark image details. It permits a viewing zoom magnification of between 6× and 26×. Point mark diameters vary from 40 μm to 200 μm for optimum matching to the floating mark size of the instrument to be used later for measurement. Photo carriers permit formats upto 42.5 cm × 48.0 cm. There is a choice of point- or ring-mark or both. Individual or common image rotations through 90° and 180° are permissible for point transfers between strips and for ortho-pseudo switching.

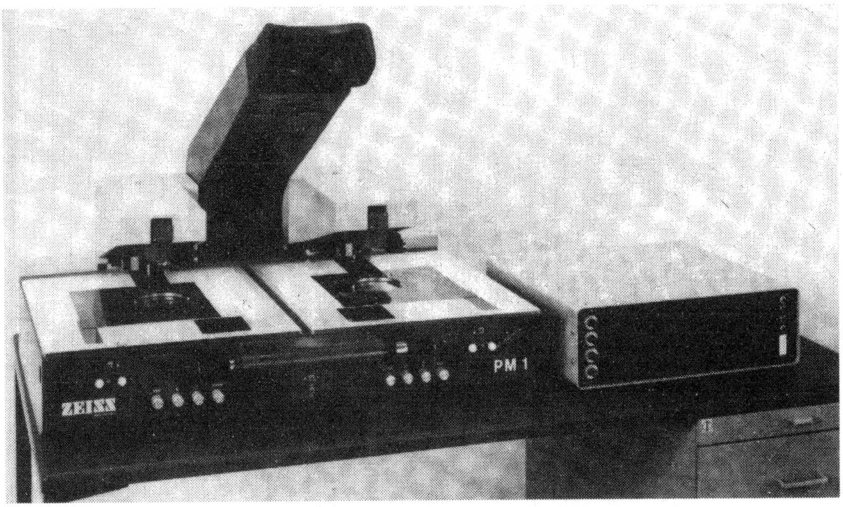

Fig. 2.22: PM-1 Marking Device
(*Courtesy:* Carl Zeiss, Germany)

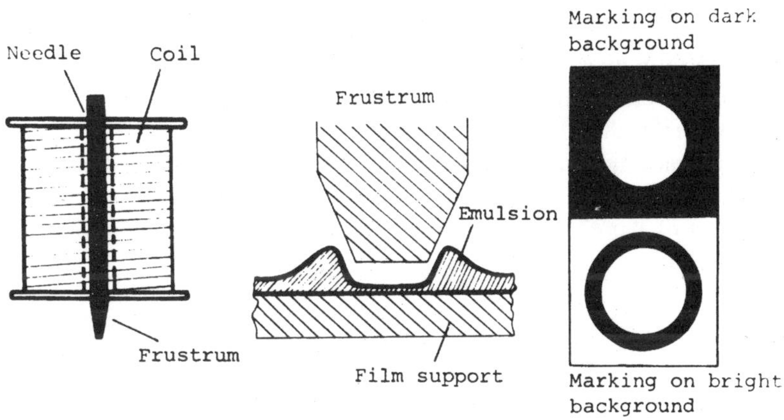

Fig. 2.23: Heat-marking principle in Zeiss PM-1
(*Courtesy:* Carl Zeiss, Germany)

(c) PUG-5 of Wild Heerbrugg (Fig. 2.24)

This instrument is meant for marking and transferring of points on glass or film by stereoscopically viewing the photographs and inscribing a circular mark in the emulsion. A metal box frame supports two glass plates, which act as picture carriers, with a range of 268 mm in x and y directions. Independent differential movements in both x and y directions are also provided.

Fig. 2.24: Wild PUG-5 (*Courtesy:* Leica, Switzerland)

Two ultrasonic marking heads, each consisting of a drive mechanism and a holder vibration mechanism are provided. When the marking lever is depressed, an electric vibration is transformed into a mechanical vibration to generate frictional heat. The mark is inscribed by the heated conical marking head as it penetrates the emulsion (see Fig. 2.25). PUG marks of 40, 60, 100 and 150 μm diameters are available. Zooming index marks of variable diameter are used for accurate setting under stereo viewing. Each optical system includes a zoom lens of range 1:5.5, whereby the magnification in each system can be varied continuously from 5.5× to 30×. The marking heads are motorized. The dependable speed and pressure ensure clean and sharp round marks. The viewing system is equipped with Dove prisms which permit necessary rotations of the observed pictures. The pictures are actually viewed form below through the carrier plates.

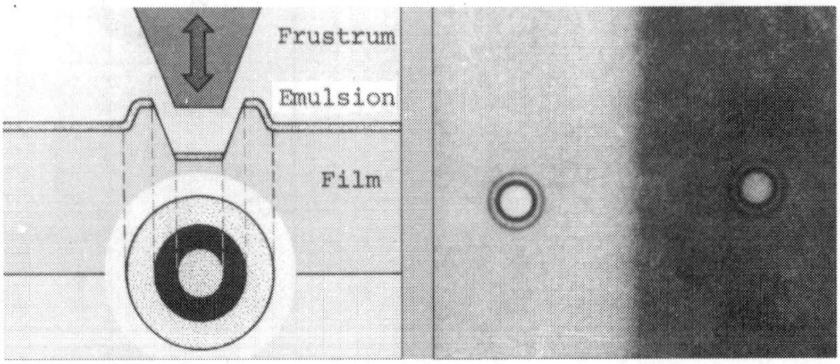

Fig. 2.25: Ultrasonic marking principle in Wild PUG 5
(*Courtesy:* Leica, Switzerland)

(d) Multiscale Marker by Bausch & Lomb

This was designed to handle photographs with large variations in scale and format. It can work with relative ease for scale ratios upto 1:16, can take film or glass plates upto a thickness of ½ inch and 9 × 18 inch format. The mark is made with a thermal marking die with a choice of six different types ranging from a 40 μm dot to 200 μm and 2000 μm circles. The die moulds a mark in the emulsion as it is lowered onto the emulsion and heated for a fraction of a second.

The optical system contains two identical trains, one for each eye, with continuous magnification ranging from 2.8 × to 48 × (in two steps), 360° image rotators and the binocular eyepiece having 5 × magnification. The instrument has two tables, one located above the other and each with a carriage which can travel in any direction at speeds from 0.5 mm to 25 mm (in coarse mode) or from 2 μm to 100 μm (in fine mode) per second. Each photo holder has a reference mark to position the photo, vacuum and acetate masks to hold it and three levelling screws to rectify the scanning and marking plane as may be necessary.

Interesting ideas on the working of such point marking and transferring devices, in themselves, and in combination with photogrammetric measuring instruments have been presented by Okang (1971, 1972). Okang's studies indicate that the performance of a point marking device depends primarily on three factors: (i) photo image quality; (ii) stereoscopic ability of observer and (iii) instrumental errors which includes also the incompatibility between the produced mark and the measuring mark of the measuring instrument. The statistical analyses of the results of computational relative orientation using the marked points give standard errors (at picture scale) of the relative orientation adjustment between 14 and 23 μm. Okang also observed that certain point marker and measuring instrument combinations work better than other such combinations. He suggested the method of Regression Analysis for calibration of point marking devices. Such a calibration would provide corrections to observed image coordinates for analytical-computational uses. Okang's studies also indicated that there is no significant difference between natural and artificial points so far as the final mensural accuracy is concerned at individual points. The transferred point may, however, be not always in the correct location.

2.7 CALIBRATION

Calibration is to be considered as (Eisenhart 1963) a refined form of measurement for the purpose of assigning numbers to specific properties, elements or parameters with statistically sound expressions for their systematic errors and precisions. Error prediction, intended to characterize the process, is obtained after the measurement procedure has achieved a state of statistical control in view of properly established specifications indicating allowable ranges or variations. The process seems simple enough, but there are some difficulties one must consider and try to eliminate:

1. The instrument's sensitivity to factors other than the desired input (in our case, the photograph and/or the control data);
2. The difficulty in obtaining the "standard" against which all measurements can be made or compared; and
3. The failure of the instrument to have the same output (say, photocoordinates) for repeated applications of a particular value of the input.

2.7.1 Difficulties to Consider

(a) *Sensitivity to Other Factors*

Unfortunately, an instrument may present an output due to factors of no interest. For example, a coordinate value may contain error input due to room temperature variation or power supply fluctuation. To avoid errors in calibration, it is necessary to control such unwanted inputs so that any change in output is due only to the corresponding change of the input being measured. Usually, this can be achieved by carefully controlling the environment in which the calibration is performed. In some cases it may be necessary to know the "static" characteristics of the instrument, i.e., when the unwanted factors (inputs) are varied singly and the primary input is maintained at a constant value. Therefore, it may be necessary to perform several such static calibrations, one for each possible factor. For the rest of our discussion, let us assume that we need to be concerned only with the principal input and that no unwanted factors are present. This concept requires that the calibration be conducted under circumstances which are reasonably representative of those "working conditions" in which the results would be applied.

(b) *Standards*

A standard is defined to be a quantity item that can be used as a reference in determining values of unknown quantities of the same item. Through the spirit of international cooperation and agreement, such a reference system has been established, known as the *International Prototype Standard.* From the International Prototype Standard are derived the *National Prototype Standards* as maintained by the various countries. In the USA the National Bureau of Standards (NBS) has been charged with maintaining the various standards. In order to protect the National Prototype Standard from deteriorations (e.g., due to wear and tear, oxidation, or other effects), it is not used routinely. A third level of standard, therefore, is derived from the National Prototype, known as the *National Reference Standard.* A fourth group, the *Working Standards* are next developed by comparison with the Reference Standards.

On the other hand, all these standards are carefully maintained and used under controlled and guarded conditions. They are not really intended to be used under the normal working conditions of the offices and laboratories. The standard normally used in such cases is the *Interlaboratory Standard.* This standard should have a calibration that can be traced to the appropriate standard at the National Bureau of Standards.

Since all the above mentioned derived standard are obtained by comparison, it is possible that the values will be somewhat in error. This error may be extremely small but one must remember that no measured quantity can be known exactly. Also, one should be aware that such standards are not known exactly, but should be (and generally are) guaranteed to be within some specific range (confidence limit or tolerance).

The use of such standards is imperative when 'absolute' values or data are required. However, for 'relative' information, An *Ad hoc Standard* (sometimes with assumed accuracy) may be used in practice. Yet, at other times, one may have to work with *Generated Standards* (e.g., generating a standard for the third dimension by using a two-dimensional standard grid. In such a case, however, the dependability of the generated standard would rest on various factors (including the application set-up). In all cases, nevertheless, it is desirable that one uses a reference standard of proven stability with the concept of 'repetition' being well established in the working system (see Eisenhart, 1969).

In this connection, it will be desirable to discuss the numerical values, *Units* (Wildi, 1991) — that are assigned to the various standards. We are familiar with the customary system of units that is used in our country. Similarly, other countries use their systems, each in a workable manner. In using them universally and internationally, there are two disadvantages: (i) The variety of units assigned to a particular quantity may require some conversion factors (e.g., to inches, feet or fathoms) and (ii) There are some differences among units known by the same name in various national systems. Such differences and inconsistencies should better be eliminated. In an effort to do just that, the *International System of Units* (SI) has been proposed. This system (a form of the 'metric' system is not yet completely developed but it is expected that it will be adopted by all the nations of the world.

(c) *Repeatability*

The enigma can be illustrated in the following problem of testing a scale of standard length (say, 100 mm). As we know that several trials are better than one, we repeat the measurement several times and obtain the following results:

Trial	Reading (Output)	Mean Value	Deviation from Mean	Standard Deviation
1.	101.3 mm	100.51 mm	0.8 mm	±0.77 mm
2.	99.3		–1.2	
3.	100.9		0.4	
4.	99.9		–0.6	
5.	101.1		0.6	
6.	100.6		0.1	

None of the readings is correct. The average of the readings (100.51 mm) is not the value of the input. The average result, inspite of a variety of individual indications, is useful. But the the question remains as to how one should deal with the individual readings. Supposing that it is possible to make only one reading, is there any way to indicate where this reading might be with respect to the mean? We must consider that for each possible input (scale value) there are infinite number of possible outputs and that the outputs are distributed in some fashion. The next question is, what is the nature of this distribution? Knowing full well that the instrument has its limitations, we can not expect the output to deviate from the true value of the input by an amount as large as infinity. We know that the chances of obtaining such extreme outputs are nil. Experience indicates that most of such outputs would be grouped near the mean value. A very strong assumption can now be made that the factors that cause the outputs to be in error are randomly active and are independent of one another. Now, the differences of the individual values from the mean would help us calculate the *Standard deviation* of the observations. The standard deviation is a measure of the way the outputs are scattered about the mean value. It is often adequate to simply report these two values, mean and standard deviation. But it may sometimes be more convenient to state the information in a different form such as to include the probability consideration at a certain per cent confidence limit. This is expressed by:

$$x = m \pm z \cdot \sigma \qquad (2.6)$$

where

- x is the expected output
- m is the mean value
- z is the degree of probability; it is obtainable from the probability table (see any book on Statistics) and
- σ is the standard deviation.

In the present case of example, m = 100.51 mm; σ = 0.77 mm and z = 1.65 at 90 per cent confidence limit. These give, x = 100.51 ± 1.27 (mm). This can be interpreted as follows: For an input of 100 mm, we can expect the output to be between 101.78 mm and 99.24 mm, at 90 per cent confidence.

It will be also helpful at this point to consider two terms: The first term is *Bias*. It is the difference between the input and the mean value of the output, i.e., Bias = Mean Value – Input. The second term, *Precision* indicates the scattering of the output values. It is defined as the measure of the ability of the instrument to give the same output for repeated applications of a given input. An instrument of high precision gives outputs which are very narrowly scattered. The standard deviation would indicate the precision. However, the outputs can be related to the input by *Accuracy* also in the entirety of the system. To specify Accuracy completely, we must specify both a range of values within which we expect the output to lie and the probability that this will occur. Therefore the following definitions are pertinent:

Precision : Degree of mutual agreement among individual measurements (made under prescribed like conditions).

Accuracy : Degree of agreement of individual measurements with an accepted reference value.

The concept of *System Calibration* in contrast to Components' calibrations can also be emphasized. This is, however, out of the scope of this book.

2.7.2 Calibration of a Comparator

Apart from the possibility of having accidental (random) errors, the following errors of systematic nature may occur in a precision comparator:

(a) Errors of the Instrument System
- — Scaling and periodic errors (of the x, y measuring systems involving scales, spindles, coordinate counters, etc.;
- — Affinity errors (being the scale difference between x and y directions);
- — Errors of rectilinearity (bending) of the guide rails;

— Lack of orthogonality between x and y axes (also known as 'rectangularity error').

(b) Backlash and tracking errors.

(c) Dynamic errors (e.g., microscope velocity does not drop to zero at points to be approached during the operation).

(d) Errors of automation in the system:

— Digital resolution (smallest incremental interval);

— Errors due to deviation of the direction. This is because the control system may not provide for the continuously variable scanning directions.

Each of the above mentioned errors can be mathematically modelled with respect to each comparator (even each carriage). However, in a systems approach, from the practical standpoint, the task can be performed by the transformation of the measured coordinates of a precalibrated array of points to the given (known) coordinates of the points in the array. The array of points would consist of a precision grid (réseau) plate. Considering all possible errors, the transformation equations (error model) of the form given below would be very appropriate (Kern publications, undated, on calibration):

$$
\begin{aligned}
x_c &= a_1 + a_2x + a_3y + a_4xy + a_5x^2 + a_6y^2 + a_7x^2y + a_8xy^2 + a_9x^3 + a_{10}y^3 \\
y_c &= b_1 + b_2x + b_3y + b_4xy + b_5x^2 + b_6y^2 + b_7x^2y + b_8xy^2 + b_9x^3 + b_{10}y^3
\end{aligned}
\tag{2.7}
$$

where

x_c, y_c are the known coordinates of measured points,

x, y are the instrument (observed) coordinates of measured points, and

$$\left.\begin{matrix} a_1, a_2 \ldots a_{10} \\ b_1, b_2 \ldots b_{10} \end{matrix}\right\}$$ are the coefficients of the error model (to be determined).

In this, each measured point generates one x equation and one y equation.. If more than ten points are measured, the system of equations is solvable by applying the method of Least Squares to yield the desired error model coefficients (or, calibration constants). In case points fewer than ten are used, the terms containing higher orders in x and y can be discarded (ignored) to obtain working solutions. Such a solution of limited scope may not portray the situation adequately, though. In such calibration jobs, it is recommended to use at least twenty five evenly distributed points.

Any such calibration procedure which accounts for nonlinear errors requires that an invariant coordinate system be adopted, i.e., the origin and the coordinate system as used at the time of calibration must be used for all subsequent work in which the calibration is to be utilized. Furthermore, the unit of instrument measurement must also be held invariant. Any such calibration should also be considered to be valid only for that area of the comparator surface (corresponding to the run of the screws or scales) over which the calibration is performed.

The parameters in Eq. 2.7 may be considered as uncorrelated. The right hand sides are identical and the 'normal' equations, would consist of a single coefficient matrix with two constant vectors (one for the x equation and one for the y equation). The inverse of the coefficient matrix multiplied by both constant vectors would yield the solution vectors for x and y. After the calibration constant are known, the equations may be evaluated for all checked points so as to determine the residuals (deviations) between the given (known) and the measured coordinates. The standard deviations for each axis (x or y) can next be computed from such residuals.

In some cases, it is possible that all ten terms in each of Eq. 2.7 are not really needed. It may actually be of interest to know as to which terms are superfluous. The polynomials are based on theoretically sound error propagation laws. Unfortunately, unless the handling process is controlled statistically, the nature of the required polynomial will vary for each application. On the other hand, in view of a fixed set of conditions, the performance of the instrument should result in a standard polynomial for each coordinate. These standard polynomials could be found empirically by using the analysis of variance (ANOVA) technique over a test grid plate. Any standard text book of Statistics may be referred to for the ANOVA technique. This way, many combinations of variables can be tested until the combination which gives the best reductions (in sum of squares of the residuals) is obtained. The final form of the best polynomials should then be used.

Alternately, for the practitioner's point of view, the equations can be solved several times, each time constraining certain terms to zero. Table 2.1 illustrates this suggested principle. Whether any of the higher order terms are necessary or not can be assessed by examining the residuals from each solution.

Table 2.1: Check of effective terms in calibration
(Note : e = term is effective)

Solution Number	*Terms*									
	Const	x	y	xy	x^2	y^2	x^2y	xy^2	x^3	$y3$
1	e	e	e	e	e	e	e	e	e	e
2	e	e	e	e	e	e	e	e		
3	e	e	e	e	e	e				
4	e	e	e	e						
5	e	e	e							
6	e									

Such a procedure of calibration would be applicable also to the analytical plotters. It is suggested that this be done separately for each photo carrier, such that the *model deformation* caused by the local deviations can be directly applicable to the generated three-dimensional coordinates, if necessary. See Ghosh (1972) for ideas on model-deformation.

Ideally, a complete calibration of a comparator should provide statistics to indicate the following:

1. Pointing precision (man-machine cooperation);
2. Quality (status) of instrument before calibration;
3. Quality (status) of instrument after removal of linear systematic errors;
4. Quality (status) of instrument after removal of non-linear systematic errors;
5. Quality of the given grid coordinates (against an accepted standard); and
6. An assessment of the time and cost involved in the calibration.

2.7.3 Calibration of a Project on Instrument

As in the case of a comparator, an improvement in the accuracy and efficiency of a stereoplotter (projection instrument) can be obtained by using redundant observation and a computer to handle the mathematical model describing the specific function for which the instrument is used. Calibration procedures for such instruments can be divided into three broad groups according to their functions:

1. These designed to determine the instrument parameters and zero-settings, viz.,
   (a) Elements of exterior orientation, $X_o, Y_o, Z_o, \omega_o, \phi_o, \kappa_o$, *bx by* and *bz*;
   (b) Elements of interior orientation, *f*, x_o and y_o.
2. Those designed to test the instrument and provide the information necessary for the operator/technician.
3. Those designed to speedily test the performance of the instrument in terms of one or more of the three coordinates (*X, Y* and *Z*).

Most frequently need information and their sample uses are listed in Table 2.2.

Table 2.2: Frequently needed parameters at a projection instrument

Parameters	*Notations*	*Sample Uses*
Principal distance	f	All uses of instrument
Principal point location	x_o, y_o	All uses of instrument
Perspective center	X_o, Y_o, Z_o	Photo-triangulation by Independent models method
Zero settings of rotation elements	$\omega_o, \phi_o, \kappa_o$	Terrestrial photogrammetry
Zero settings of base components (and their values)	*bx, by, bz* & *by', by"* *bz', bz"*	Instrument calibration Use of auxiliary data Instrument use as comparator
Elevation vlaues (in model)	Z	Compilation of contours
Planimetric model coordinates	X, Y	Compilation of planimetric details, use as comparator

Spatial resection of each camera (projector) of the instrument can be performed in order to obtain information on the aforementioned parameters. This can be done with a precision grid plate and having observations made at one Z = constant plane (in model space). The resection can be formulated in two ways (Dowman, 1973):

FORMULA I

$$\frac{X - X_o}{Z - Z_o} = \frac{a_{11}x + a_{12}y + a_{13}f}{a_{31}x + a_{32}y + a_{33}f}$$

$$\frac{Y - Y_o}{Z - Z_o} = \frac{a_{21}x + a_{22}y + a_{23}f}{a_{31}x + a_{32}y + a_{33}f} \qquad (2.8)$$

where

x, y are the photo coordinates (of grid intersections);
X, Y, Z are the model coordinates (observed at the instrument counters);
X_o, Y_o, Z_o are coordinates of the perspective center in model system; and
$a_{11}...a_{33}$ are nine elements of the rotation matrix.

The elements of the rotation matrix (explanations in Chap. 3) consist of sine and cosine functions of three independent unknowns (ω, ϕ and κ). There are, thus, six unknowns (X_o, Y_o, Z_o, $d\omega$, $d\phi$ and $d\kappa$), which can be determined from observations to at least there points in one Z=constant plane in the instrument. Equations 2.8, however, are not linear and the computations are more than what some desk calculators can handle. There is another disadvantage in using Eqs 2.8, that they make no allowance for errors in the interior orientation elements which may affect the results. On the other hand, because very small rotation angles are involved, one can express the space resection problem by yet other equations (see Ghosh, 1972 for the derivations of the equations):

FORMULA II

$$\left.\begin{aligned} dx &= -\frac{xy}{f}d\omega + f\left(1+\frac{x^2}{f^2}\right)d\phi - y\cdot d\kappa + dx_o - \frac{x}{f}df + \frac{f}{Z}dX_o + \frac{x}{Z}dZ_o \\ dy &= -f\left(1+\frac{y^2}{f^2}\right)d\omega + \frac{xy}{f}d\phi + x\cdot d\kappa + dy_o - \frac{y}{f}df + \frac{f}{Z}dY_o + \frac{y}{Z}dZ_o \end{aligned}\right\} \tag{2.9}$$

where

dx, dy are differences, at photo scale, between model coordinates and known grid coordinates;
$\left.\begin{matrix} d\omega, d\phi, d\kappa \\ dX_o, dY_o, dZ_o \end{matrix}\right\}$ are the six unknown parameters, corresponding to Eq. 2.8 and Table 2.2 (with observations made at one Z = constant plane);
dx_o, dy_o are the differences at the principal point; and
df is the error in the principal distance (corresponds to focal length).

In such a situation, f and Z being highly correlated to each other, if the observations are made on only one Z = constant plane, the solutions may not be conclusive in view of possible "critical geometry". However, if the observations are made in two Z = constant planes (rather than just one), the elements of interior orientation for each point (dx_o, dy_o and df) are also obtainable. In this connection, interesting ideas are given by Ghosh (1975).

In view of Eqs 2.9, a step by step procedure for this solution can be suggested such as can be performed at a desk or hand-held calculator:

Step 1: Set all elements to zero values (as previously obtained). These are good approximate values to start with.

Step 2: Rotate κ element to obtain κ_o setting. This being a tertiary rotation element, has no effect on any other element and thus, does not propagate any error.

Step 3: At this stage, if a programmable computer is available, a calibration can be undertaken by using Eqs 2.9, with respect to one camera (monocular grid observations) at a time. If not, one may continue as follows:

Step 1: The principal distance (*f*) and the perspective center coordinates (X_o, Y_o, Z_o) can be obtained by observing at least two points in two Z = constant planes (see the procedure described in Chap. 8, Ghosh, 1975).

Step 2: Set the measuring mark to X_o, Y_o position of the instrument carriage and bring the principal point (cross) onto the mark by using ω and ϕ elements. This will give the ω_o and ϕ_o positions.

Step 3: The inclination of the stage plate (interior orientation) can be determined from grid observation in one plane. The pattern of distortion can be seen in a plot of the residuals and the magnitude of rotations can be calculated by using the following equations:

$$\left.\begin{aligned} dx &= \frac{x^2}{f}d\varphi - \frac{xy}{f}d\omega \\ dy &= \frac{xy}{f}d\varphi - \frac{y^2}{f}d\omega \end{aligned}\right\} \qquad (2.10)$$

These are reduced from Eq. 2.9 after assuming all other parameters to be zero. The coordinates *x, y* are reduced to the principal point as origin and scaled to photo-scale (e.g., by using a symmetrical pair of grid lines (in the model) which are not affected by a rotation of the grid plate.

Step 4: Rotations $d\omega$ and $d\phi$, when found, can be applied to the instrument (being rotations around the respective axes passing through the perspective center) with additional adjustments of the principal point (dx_o and dy_o).

Step 5: Repetition of Step 3 along with iterative observations can be continued until satisfactory results are finally obtained.

Note: The parameters, bx, by and bz, as also their necessary components (*by*', *by*", *bz*' and *bz*") may be derived from basic considerations of the particular instrument.

BIBLIOGRAPHY

Bertram, S.; The Universal Automatic Map Compilation Equipment *PE* 31, No. 2; 1965.

Brown, Duane; Computational Trade-offs in the Design of a Comparator; *PE* 35, No. 2; 1969.

Chamard, R. R.; The MPS-2 Microanalytical Photogrammetric System; A Small-format system for close-range photogrammetry; *Proceedings of Int. Conf. and Workshop on Analytical Instrumentation,* ASPRS, Washington: 1987.

Chitayat, A.; Interference Comparators for Coordinate Measurement of Ballistic Plates,; *Photographic Science and Engineering* 4. No. 5; 1960.

Dowman, I.J.; A Working Method for the Calibration of Plotting Instruments Using Computers; *PR* 7, No. 42; 1973.

Eisenhart, Churchill; Realistic Evaluation of the Precision and Accuracy of Instrument Calibration System; *Journal of Research,* NBS - C - Engineering and Instrumentation, Vol. 67c, No. 2; 1963.

Eisenhart, Churchill, *Precision Measurement and Calibration*; NBS Special Publication 300, Vol. 1; 1969.

Ghosh, Sanjib K.; *Theory of Stereophotogrammetry* (2nd Ed); The Ohio State University Bookstores, Columbus, Ohio; 1972.

Ghosh, Sanjib K,; *Phototriangulation*; Lexington Books, Lexington, Massachusetts; 1975.

Ghosh, Sanjib K.; Some Thoughts on Instrument Calibration; *Proceedings* of ASPRS, Fall Convention, Seattle, Washington; 1976.

Ghosh, Sanjib K.; Standards for three-dimensional mensuration with electron micrographs; Optical Testing and Meteorology, *SPIE Proceedings*, Vol. 661; 1986.

Gugel, R.A.; Comparator Calibration; *PE* 31, No. 5; 1965.

Hallert, Bertil P.; Test Measurements in Comparators and Tolerances for Such Instruments; *PE* 29, No. 2; 1963.

Helava, U.V. and R.H. Seymour; US-1 Universal Stereoplotter; *ISP Archives,* XIII Congress; Helsinki, Finland; 1976.

Hempenius, S.A.; Physical Investigations on Pricked Points Used in Aerial Triangulation: *Photogrammetria* 19, No. 7; 1962-64.

Herda, Klaus, : The Performance Capability of the TRANSMARK Laser Point Transfer Machine; *ISP Archives,* XIII Congress,: Helsinki, Finland; 1976.

Hobbie, D.; C100 Planicomp — The Analytical Stereoplotting System; *ISP Archives,* XIII Congress; Helsinki, Finland,; 1976.

Jeyapalan, K.; Calibration of a Comparator; PE38, No. 5; 1972.

Kern Instrument, Inc.; *Generalized Program for the Calibration of Monocomparators and Coordinatographs;* Aarau, Switzerland, Undated.

Klein, K.E.; PC power in analytical photogrammetry; *Proceedings of Int. Conf. and Workshop on Analytical Instrumentation*; ASPRS; 1987.

Konecny, G.; Software Aspects of Analytical Plotters; *ISPRS Archives,* XIII Congress; Helsinki, Finland; 1976.

Ladouceur, G.; P. Trotier and R. Allard; Zeiss Stereotope Modified into an Analytical Stereoplotter; *PERS* 48, No. 10; 1982.

Marckwardt, W.; Geometrical Checking and Testing Methods for Precision Coordinatorgraphs; *Vermessungs Informationen,* No. 26; Jena, Germany; 1973.

Okang, Joseph P.; Errors in Point Marking; *PE* 37, No. 10; 1971.

Okang, Joseph P.; *Comparative Study of Point Marking Devices and Their Suitability for Photogrammetric Problems*; Ph.D. Dissertation, The Ohio State Univ., Columbus, Ohio; 1972.

Roelofs, R.; The Future of Radial Triangulation; *Photogrammetria* 12, No. 4, 1956.

Roos, Maurits; The Automatic Réseau Measuring Equipment (ARME); *PERS* 41, No. 9; 1975.

Schenk, Toni; *Digital Photogrammetry*: Terra Science, Laurelville, Ohio; 1999.

Schut, G.H.; Methods and Fortran Programs for Self-calibration of Position Measuring Devices; *NRC of Canada Div. of Physics Pub.* No. P-PR 45; Ottawa, Canada; 1974.

Wildi, Theodore; *Units and Conversion Charts;* IEEE Press; Piscataway, N. J., 1991.

Yzerman, H.; The APY system for interpolation, compilation and revision of geographical data: *Proceedings of Int. Conf. and Workshop on Analytical Instrumentation*; ASPRS, Washington; 1987.

3

COORDINATE SYSTEMS

A coordinate system is one of reference for defining point, lines or geometric objects in space by means of distances or angles or both. This reference can be made with respect to designed axes, planes or surfaces. In Surveying and Mapping, two general types of references are distinguished:

1. *Rectangular.* This can be two or three dimensional, where points are defined by linear distances from two mutually perpendicular axes (in two dimensions) or from three mutually perpendicular planes (in three dimensions).
2. *Spherical.* In this, points in space or on a spherical or spheroidal surface are defined in terms of angles subtended at specific points with respect to specified directions or planes.

There are, however, instances where features of one are combined with the features of another to develop a special system of coordinates, for example:

A. *Plane-polar system*, which is much used in land surveying. In this, points in a plane (two-dimensional) are defined by distances from a point of reference (pole) along direction angles (with regard to a reference direction).

B. *Geographical system*, in which two direction angles (latitude and longitude) are combined with one distance (height above a reference surface (whose dimensions and form are fixed).

C. *Cylindrical system*, in which two distances (radial distance from an axis of reference and height above a reference plane) are combined with one direction angle (with regard to a reference direction). Ghosh (1966) used this system in calibrating solar collectors.

A spherical system by itself alone (i.e., by considering direction angles only) suffers from the lack of dimensional information. A well known example is its use in astronomy with regard to Altitude and Azimuth or Declination and Hour Angle. A rectangular system by itself does not suffer from any such drawback because directions are always derivable from dimensional data.

Directly associated with a coordinate system is often the necessity of defining the direction to a point or of a line (camera axis, etc.). For this, one usually finds it convenient to use a *Roll-*

Pitch-Yaw (or *Tilt-Tip - Swing)* sequence. In this, roll (Ω or ω) is the rotation around the *X*-axis, pitch (Φ or ϕ) is around the *Y*-axis and yaw (K or κ) is around the *Z*-axis, (see Section 3.3). In earth-related aerial photography, one may also use a variation, such as the *Tilt-Swing-Azimuth* sequence, where tilt is the angle from the nadir direction, swing is the rotation around the camera axis and azimuth is the angle from the north direction.

The use of a coordinate system in analytical photogrammetry can be with regard to a photograph, a stereo-model or the corresponding object. Accordingly, one may refer to photographic, model or object space coordinate systems. We shall study these in detail and in terms of their variations.

3.1 PHOTOGRAPHIC COORDINATE SYSTEM

It is a three-dimensional, orthogonal and right-handed system. Ideally, the origin of the system lies at the perspective center (Fig. 3.1) and the plane of the photograph is the *x, y* plane, *z* being a constant.

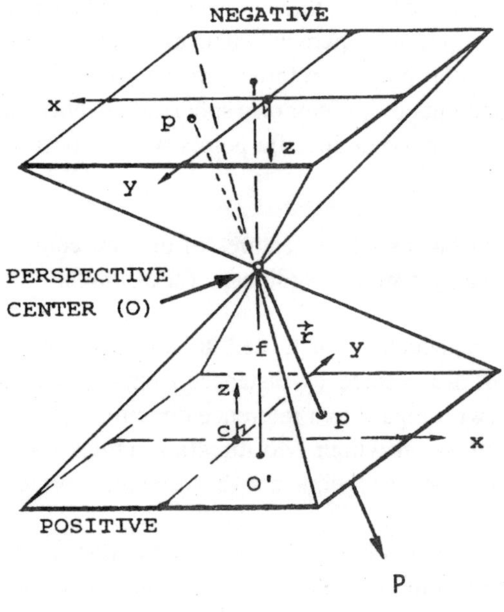

Fig. 3.1: Photographic coordinate system

The optical axis of the camera lens is considered to be normal to the plane of the photograph at the 'principal point' (see Chap. 5 for the definition), O′. In the physical reality, there being no reference direction or plane of reference at the perspective center, one has to relate to the obtainable references on the photograph. The set of fiducial or collimation marks provide the *x, y* reference in which the *x*-axis is customarily considered along the direction of flight or the camera-base. The principal point (O′) in the fiducial system has coordinates.

$$x_o, y_o, 0$$

The perspective centre (O) of the the objective lens lies on the optical axis. Its distance from the plane of the photograph is the focal length (*f*). Therefore, the perspective center has coordinates,

$$x_o, y_o, f$$

Any image point (*p*) on the photo, in this fiducial reference system, is definable by its coordinates,

$$x_p, y_p, 0$$

Therefore, the vector ($\vec{r}$) defining the location of point *p* with respect to the perspective center is

$$\vec{r} = \begin{bmatrix} x_p & -x_o \\ y_p & -y_o \\ 0 & -f \end{bmatrix}$$

In a well built and properly adjusted camera, the *x, y* fiducial coordinates of the principal point are practically zero. Then the image location vector $\vec{r}$ can be written as

$$\vec{r} = \begin{bmatrix} x_p \\ y_p \\ -f \end{bmatrix}$$

In some cameras, the fiducial marks are located in the corners of the image format. This corresponds to either a rotation or translation or both in the *x, y* coordinates of the image point as will be obvious. Another variation is present when the photograph negatives (instead of positives) are utilized. Associated with this coordinate system are the rotations, ω, ϕ and κ, around *x*–, *y*– and *z*– axes, respectively. Variations are provided by the sequence in which they are considered in operation — giving 'primary', 'secondary' and 'tertiary' rotations, being different in different cases.

3.2 MODEL COORDINATE SYSTEM

It refers to the spatial coordinates of points imaged in a stereoscopic model (established mathematically or analogically at a stereoplotting instrument), which usually relates its position with reference to the camera base or to the instrument axes. Coordinates are defined in terms of *X, Y, Z; X, Y, H* (Height); Easting, Northing, Elevation; or any other set of 3-D reference.

The most used (and preferred) system is the one agreed upon at the International Congresses of Photogrammetry in 1956 and 1960 (see ISP Archives, 1957 and 1961). It is right-handed and orthogonal (Fig. 3.2). The origin is at the projection center of the left side photograph. The *X* direction coincides with the camera base (or, general flight direction in the aerial case), and the *Z* direction coincides with the camera axis in the zero position. The base components, *bx*, *by*, and *bz*, coincide with the *X, Y* and *Z* directions, respectively. The model rotations, Ω (around *X*-axis), Φ (around *Y*-axis) and K (around *Z*-axis) are analogous to ω, ϕ and κ rotations,

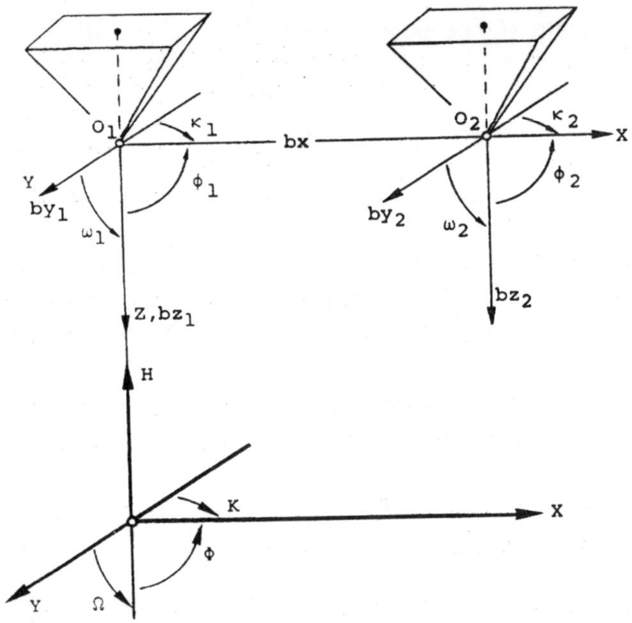

Fig. 3.2: Model coordinate system (International)

respectively, for single photographs. The positive directions are indicated by arrowheads on the respective lines (for the coordinates or linear dimensions) or on the respective planes (for realisation of rotations). See Ghosh (1972) for a more detailed description of this system and several other systems used by many organizations.

In phototriangulation, for convenience, sometimes one works with *Strip coordinates,* which are nothing but extensions of the coordinates of the first model in the strip, i.e., any point in the strip is referred to the origin and axes of the coordinate system of the first stereo-mode. Similarly, strip coordinates may be extended into *Block coordinates,* the origin of which would refer to an arbitrary model in the block.

3.3 OBJECT SPACE COORDINATE SYSTEMS

These refer to coordinate systems used to define the positions of points in the object space, as distinguished from the image or the model. In the context of the earth as the object, broadly speaking, we may consider one of three coordinate systems: (a) The Geodetic coordinates of Latitude, Longitude and Height above the particular ellipsoid (Φ, λ, H); (b) The Geocentric Universal (Space Rectangular) system explained later in detail; and (c) The Local Space Rectangular system (X,Y, Z), also explained later. Of these, the Geodetic system is not used in analytical photogrammetry directly due to the inherent inconvenience of having to express the values in non-linear units (of degrees, grades, etc.). These are generally converted into one of the rectangular systems. For many applications, however, where, the earth's curvature is of very minor importance, one may use a plane coordinate system, e.g., one of the 'state' coordinate systems, one of the standard map projections, or any 'local' surveyors' system.

3.3.1 Geocentric Universal System

This system is extensively utilized for phototriangulation, particularly when a large portion of the earth's surface is involved. The system is shown in Fig. 3.3. This is an orthogonal system whose origin is at the center of the earth. The $\bar{X}\bar{Y}$-plane contains the Equator, the $\bar{X}$-axis passes through the zero (Greenwich) meridian and the $\bar{Z}$-axis passes through the North pole. The $\bar{Y}$-axis coincides with 90° east longitude in a right-handed system.

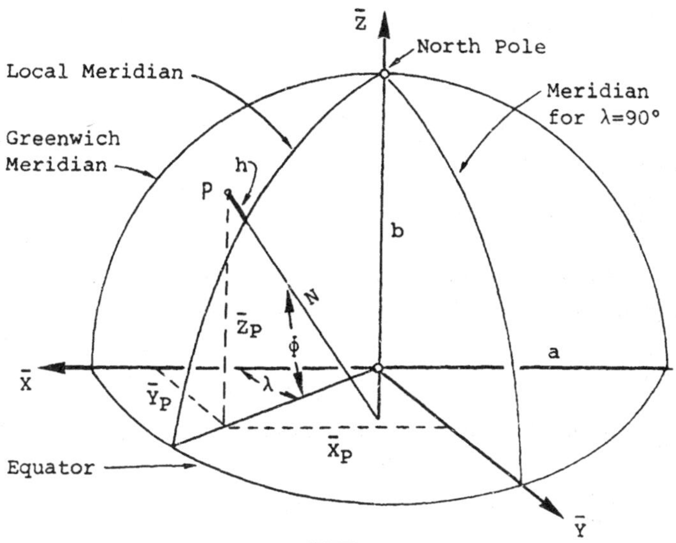

Fig. 3.3: Geocentric Universal system and its relationship with the Geodetic system

The earth can be considered to be represented by a pre-determined rotational ellipsoid, which is determined by two quantities (*a* and *b*, Fig. 3.3), where *a* is the semi-major axis and *b* is the semi-minor axis.

Further, the first eccentricity, $e = \sqrt{\{(a^2 - b^2)/a^2\}}$

and the second eccentricity, $e' = \sqrt{\{(a^2 - b^2)/b^2\}}$

Any point p (e.g., an object point on ground or a camera station in space) has the following geodetic coordinates: Latitude (Φ) Longitude (λ) and Elevation or Height above the ellipsoid (*h*).

Additional, derived, parameters are given here for their possible uses in practice. For details of such geodetic systems and derivation of the equations, one may refer to any standard book on Geodesy, e.g., Bomford (1971), Jordan-Eggert (1962), Zakatov (1962), etc.

The Fundamental Quantities:

$$\left.\begin{aligned} W &= \sqrt{(1 - e^2 \sin^2 \Phi)} \\ V &= \sqrt{(1 - e'^2 \cos^2 \Phi)} \end{aligned}\right\} \qquad (3.1)$$

The radius of curvature at a point along the meridian:

$$M = \frac{a(1-e^2)}{W} \tag{3.2}$$

The radius of Curvature at a point along the prime vertical:

$$N = \frac{a}{W} \tag{3.3}$$

The universal Geocentric coordinates may be expressed as functions of the geodetic coordinates and may be computed by using the following formulas (known as the *Direct Formulas)*:

$$\left.\begin{aligned} \bar{X} &= (N+h)\cos\Phi\cos\lambda \\ \bar{Y} &= (N+h)\cos\Phi\sin\lambda \\ \bar{Z} &= \left\{N(1-e^2)+h\right\}\sin\Phi \end{aligned}\right\} \tag{3.4}$$

The *Inverse Formulas* to obtain geodetic coordinates from the universal geocentric coordinates, are given below:

$$\lambda = \text{arc tan}\frac{\bar{Y}}{\bar{X}} \tag{3.5}$$

Note: for λ near 90^0 where the tangent function discontinues,

$$\lambda = \text{arc cos}\frac{\bar{X}}{R} = \text{arc sin}\frac{\bar{Y}}{R} \tag{3.6}$$

where $R = \sqrt{\left(\bar{X}^2 + \bar{Y}^2\right)}$

The values of Φ and h cannot be determined explicitly in the same way as of λ because of the strong correlation between them. The initial value of Φ is given by

$$\begin{aligned} \Phi &= \text{arc tan}\frac{\bar{Z}(N+h)}{R\left\{(1-e^2)N+h\right\}} \\ &= \text{arc tan}\frac{\bar{Z}\left\{a^2 + ah\sqrt{(1-e^2\sin^2\Phi)}\right\}}{R\left\{b^2 + ah\sqrt{(1-e^2\sin^2\Phi)}\right\}} \end{aligned} \tag{3.7}$$

A value of h has to be estimated in order to use Eq. 3.7, which is effective when Φ is less than 45°. In case Φ is larger than 45°, the cotangent function is more effective. After Φ has been calculated, h can be obtained by using Eq. 3.8:

$$h = \frac{\bar{Z}}{\sin\Phi} - \frac{a(1-e^2)}{\sqrt{(1-e^2\sin^2\Phi)}} \tag{3.8}$$

Note that near the Equator, both $\bar{Z}$ and Φ have values close to zero. Therefore, in practice,

Eq. 3.8 should not be used for points where $3° > \Phi > -3°$. In such cases an alternate formula can be used:

$$h = \frac{R}{\cos\Phi} - \frac{a}{\sqrt{\left(1 - e^2 \sin^2 \Phi\right)}} \tag{3.9}$$

A variation geocentric system is important for satellite triangulation where, of necessity, a reference to the astronomic system of coordinates is imperative. This is similar to the one discussed above (illustrated in Fig. 3.3), with the $\bar{X}$ -axis passing through the Vernal Equinox, λ is replaced by Right Ascension (R.A.) and Φ is replaced by Declination (δ). The two systems are mutually related through local Sidereal Time.

3.3.2 Local Coordinate System

This one is another much favoured object space coordinate system often used in phototriangulation. This system, illustrated in Fig. 3.4, is also right-handed and orthogonal. It has the *Z*-axis normal to the selected ellipsoid at an origin (O) in the area. The *Y*-axis coincides with the north direction and the elevation (h_0) of the origin is usually considered negative for the sake of convenience, such that all points on the ground and camera stations will automatically have positive values. Note, the origin (O) may be below one camera station, one of the control points, the origin of a superimposed grid system of the local mapping or any other convenient point.

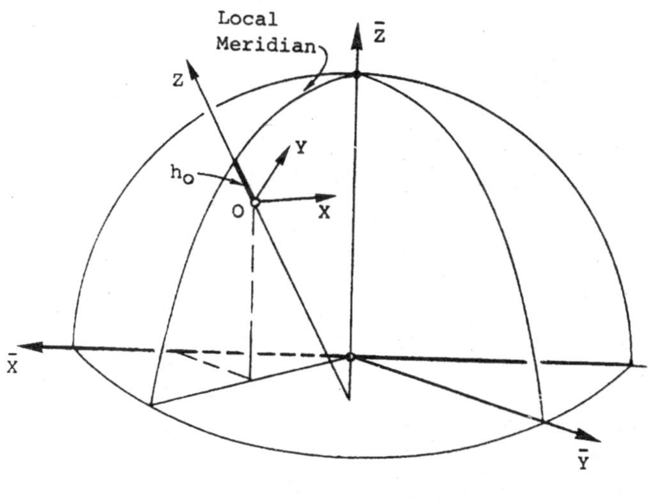

Fig. 3.4: Local Coordinate system in relation to the Geocentric Universal system

This system, while retaining all features of the Geocentric system, contains two advantages, Firstly, because it is local, one need not carry too many digits. This would often permit the computations to be performed in "single precision" with considerable saving in computer utilization. Secondly, the *Z*-axis parallels the local vertical, which further simplifies the work by permitting a separation of planimetry from elevation values.

The local coordinates are easily obtainable from the geocentric coordinates by a three-dimensional transformation, which contains a translation, a rotation and, possibly, a scale change (explained later in Section 3.4). Further simplifications or variations of such a local system can be made when coordinates need not relate to the earth. Such systems may be arbitrary and may be job related, e.g., a system referred to the object for non-topographic mapping or a local survey system for engineering projects.

3.4 TRANSFORMATION OF COORDINATES

It is often necessary to establish the relationship between two coordinate systems in order to transfer a number of points from one to the other. There are numerous methods of transformation for use in three-dimensional problems, simplified versions of which are applicable to two-dimensional space. The effect of transformation of a body can be a simple change in location and attitude (i.e., without any change in shape and size) or a complex one (i.e., change in both shape and size) or something in between, e.g., variation in size (scale) with no change in shape or location or attitude.

3.4.1 General Three-dimensional Transformation

Also known as *Similarity Transformation*, it involves translations, rotations and a scale change. Referable to the same object, consider two systems of coordinates, X, Y, Z, and $\bar{X},\bar{Y},\bar{Z}$ and both being rectangular. The three-dimensional transformation involving no change in shape is symbolized by:

$$\boldsymbol{X} = k\boldsymbol{M}^T \bar{X} + X_0 \tag{3.10}$$

where

$\boldsymbol{X} = [X\ Y\ Z]^T$ coordinates after transformation

$\bar{X} = [\bar{X},\bar{Y},\bar{Z}]^T$ coordinates before transformation

$\boldsymbol{X}_0 = [X_0\ Y_0\ Z_0]^T$ vector of three shifts indicating the X,Y,Z coordinates of the origin of the $\bar{X},\bar{Y},\bar{Z}$ system.

M = an orthogonal three-angle rotation matrix (of three sequential rotations) and

k = scale factor.

In order to study these in detail, consider first only the rotations, sequentially, Ω around $\bar{X}$, Φ around $\bar{Y}$ and K around $\bar{Z}$ axes.

The *Primary Rotation* (Ω) transforms the axes $\bar{Y}$ and $\bar{Z}$ into the positions Y_Ω and Z_Ω respectively (see Fig. 3.5). This is expressed by the rotation matrix

$$M_\Omega = \begin{bmatrix} 1 & 0 & 0 \\ 0 & \cos\Omega & \sin\Omega \\ 0 & -\sin\Omega & \cos\Omega \end{bmatrix} \tag{3.11}$$

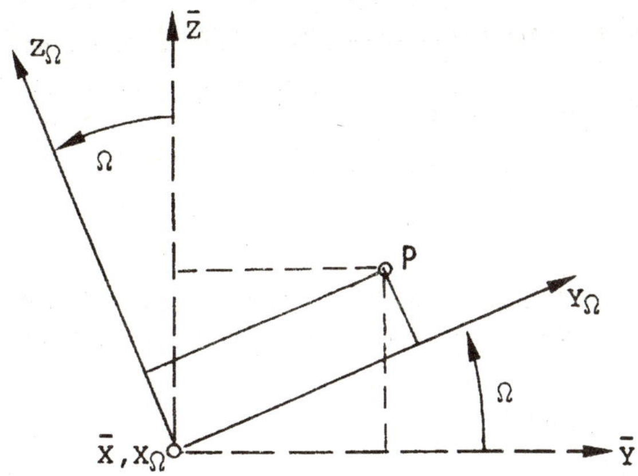

Fig. 3.5: Primary roatation, Ω

The coordinates of any point P in this, primary rotated, X_Ω, Y_Ω, Z_Ω systems are:

$$\left.\begin{aligned} X_\Omega &= \bar{X} \\ Y_\Omega &= \bar{Y}\cos\Omega + \bar{Z}\sin\Omega \\ Z_\Omega &= -\bar{Y}\sin\Omega + \bar{Z}\cos\Omega \end{aligned}\right\} \tag{3.12}$$

The Secondary Rotation (Φ) transforms the axes X_Ω and Z_Ω into the position $X_{\Omega\Phi}$ and $Z_{\Omega\Phi}$, respectively (see Fig. 3.6). This is expressed by the rotation matrix

$$M_\Phi = \begin{bmatrix} \cos\Phi & 0 & -\sin\Phi \\ 0 & 1 & 0 \\ \sin\Phi & 0 & \cos\Phi \end{bmatrix} \tag{3.13}$$

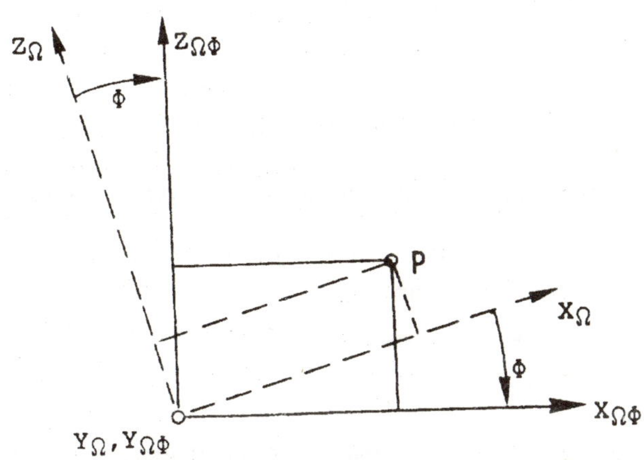

Fig. 3.6: Secondary rotation, Φ

The coordinates of the same point P in the twice rotated $X_{\Omega\Phi}$, $Y_{\Omega\Phi}$, $Z_{\Omega\Phi}$ system are:

$$\left.\begin{aligned} X_{\Omega\Phi} &= X_{\Omega}\cos\Phi - Z_{\Omega}\sin\Phi \\ Y_{\Omega\Phi} &= Y_{\Omega} \\ Z_{\Omega\Phi} &= X_{\Omega}\sin\Omega + Z_{\Omega}\cos\Omega \end{aligned}\right\} \tag{3.14}$$

The *Tertiary Rotation* (K) next transforms the axes $X_{\Omega\Phi}$ and $Y_{\Omega\Phi}$ into the positions $X_{\Omega\Phi K}$, and $Y_{\Omega\Phi K}$, respectively (see Fig. 3.7). This is expressed by the rotation matrix

$$M_K = \begin{bmatrix} \cos K & \sin K & 0 \\ -\sin K & \cos K & 0 \\ 0 & 0 & 1 \end{bmatrix} \tag{3.15}$$

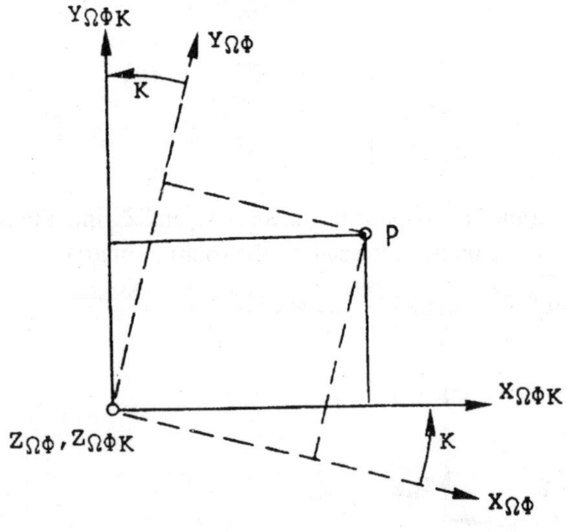

Fig. 3.7: Tertiary rotation, K

The coordinates of the same point P now in the final, thrice rotated, $X_{\Omega\Phi K}$, $Y_{\Omega\Phi K}$, $Z_{\Omega\Phi K}$ system are:

$$\left.\begin{aligned} X_{\Omega\Phi K} &= X_{\Omega\Phi}\cos K + Y_{\Omega\Phi}\sin K \\ Y_{\Omega\Phi K} &= -X_{\Omega\Phi}\sin K + Y_{\Omega\Phi}\cos K \\ Z_{\Omega\Phi K} &= Z_{\Omega\Phi} \end{aligned}\right\} \tag{3.16}$$

It may be noted that $\bar{X}$ remained unchanged in the primary rotation because the $\bar{X}$ and X_{Ω} axes remained coincident in this rotation. Similarly, the Y and Z axes remained unchanged in the secondary and tertiary rotations, respectively.

The final effect of all the three rotations is then expressed by the *rotation matrix* (***M***) as used in Eq. 3.10, $\boldsymbol{M}^{T}$ being its transpose.

$$\boldsymbol{M} = \boldsymbol{M}_{\Omega} \bullet \boldsymbol{M}_{\Phi} \bullet \boldsymbol{M}_{K} \tag{3.17}$$

In view of mathematical procedures, i.e., the order of matrix multiplications, it is better written as follows:

$$\boldsymbol{M} = \boldsymbol{M}_{K} \bullet \boldsymbol{M}_{\Phi} \bullet \boldsymbol{M}_{\Omega} \tag{3.18}$$

The elements of this rotation matrix can be expressed in various ways:

$$\boldsymbol{M}^{T} = \begin{bmatrix} m_{11} & m_{21} & m_{31} \\ m_{12} & m_{22} & m_{32} \\ m_{13} & m_{23} & m_{33} \end{bmatrix} \tag{3.19a}$$

or,

$$\boldsymbol{M}^{T} = \begin{bmatrix} \cos\Phi\cos K & -\cos\Phi\sin K & \sin\Phi \\ \cos\Omega\sin K & \cos\Omega\cos K & -\sin\Omega\cos\Phi \\ +\sin\Omega\sin\Phi\cos K & -\sin\Omega\sin\Phi\sin K & \\ \sin\Omega\sin K & \sin\Omega\cos K & \cos\Omega\cos\Phi \\ -\cos\Omega\sin\Phi\cos K & +\cos\Omega\sin\Phi\sin K & \end{bmatrix} \tag{3.19b}$$

The rotation matrix *M* can also be considered as composed of the direction-cosines, which relate to the angles between the corresponding axes in the two systems, *X, Y, Z* and $\bar{X}, \bar{Y}, \bar{Z}$. These nine matrix elements, expressed in terms of the direction cosines, are:

$$\boldsymbol{M}^{T} = \begin{bmatrix} \cos X\bar{X} & \cos Y\bar{X} & \cos Z\bar{X} \\ \cos X\bar{Y} & \cos Y\bar{Y} & \cos Z\bar{Y} \\ \cos X\bar{Z} & \cos Y\bar{Z} & \cos Z\bar{Z} \end{bmatrix} \tag{3.19c}$$

The rotation matrix being orthogonal, the normal rules for such matrices apply here also, i.e., $\boldsymbol{M}^{-1} = \boldsymbol{M}^{T}$ or, $\boldsymbol{M}\boldsymbol{M}^{T} = \boldsymbol{M}\boldsymbol{M}^{-1} = I$, the Identity matrix. In this respect, for easy solution of the rotation-translation-scaling problem, it has been suggested (see, Sanso, 1973, for example) to use the quaternion algebra. That approach holds some potential.

3.4.2 Affine Transformation in Three Dimensions

The general transformation as described in the previous section assumes that the scale in the three dimensional space is the same in any direction. If one can assume that there exist three different scales along the three directions, *X, Y* and *Z*, and affine relationship is thereby assumed. Often, due to various reasons, such a situation may persist (e.g., in a stereo model due to the introduction of a focal length different from the correct one, oft-quoted in literature discussing the use of 'super-wide-angle' photography). In such cases, the Eq. 3.10 of the general case may be modified by using $k = 1$ and

$$\bar{\boldsymbol{X}} = \begin{bmatrix} \kappa_{\bar{x}}\bar{X} & \kappa_{\bar{y}}\bar{Y} & \kappa_{\bar{z}}\bar{Z} \end{bmatrix}^T \tag{3.20}$$

where $\kappa_{\bar{X}}$, $\kappa_{\bar{Y}}$ and $\kappa_{\bar{Z}}$ are the respective scales along $\bar{X}, \bar{Y}$ and $\bar{Z}$ axes. See also Ghosh (1972, 1975) for further discussions related to this aspect.

3.4.3 Polynomial Transformation in Three Dimensions

In view of the propagated error or orderly and systematic deformation in a stereo model or the final output (as done in a map projection, for example), often a polynomial transformation is found to be convenient. Polynomials of various types are used, depending on the most appropriate "mathematical model" the photogrammetrist may find adequate. Two typical sets of polynomials used in three-dimensional transformation are presented in Eqs 3.21 and 3.22. Here also, as before, *X, Y, Z,* are considered coordinates after transformation, and $\bar{X}, \bar{Y}, \bar{Z}$ are those before transformation.

A. General polynomials in three-dimensions (see Ghosh, 1975):

$$\begin{aligned} X &= a_o + a_1\bar{X} + a_2\bar{Y} + a_3\bar{Z} + a_4\bar{X}^2 + a_5\bar{Y}^2 + a_6\bar{Z}^2 + a_7\bar{X}\bar{Y} + a_8\bar{Y}\bar{Z} \\ &\quad + a_9\bar{Z}\bar{X} + a_{10}\bar{X}\bar{Y}^2 + a_{11}\bar{X}^2\bar{Y} + a_{12}\bar{X}\bar{Z}^2 + \ldots \\ Y &= b_o + b_1\bar{X} + b_2\bar{Y} + b_3\bar{Z} + b_4\bar{X}^2 + b_5\bar{Y}^2 + b_6\bar{Z}^2 + b_7\bar{X}\bar{Y} + b_8\bar{Y}\bar{Z} \\ &\quad + b_9\bar{Z}\bar{X} + b_{10}\bar{X}\bar{Y}^2 + b_{11}\bar{X}^2\bar{Y} + b_{12}\bar{X}\bar{Z}^2 + \ldots \\ Z &= c_o + c_1\bar{X} + c_2\bar{Y} + c_3\bar{Z} + c_4\bar{X}^2 + c_5\bar{Y}^2 + c_6\bar{Z}^2 + c_7\bar{X}\bar{Y} \\ &\quad + c_8\bar{Y}\bar{Z} + c_9\bar{Z}\bar{X} + c_{10}\bar{X}\bar{Y}^2 + c_{11}\bar{X}^2\bar{Y} + c_{12}\bar{X}\bar{Z}^2 + \ldots \end{aligned} \tag{3.21}$$

B. Three-dimensional polynomials which are conformal in the three planes (see Mikhail, 1964):

$$\begin{aligned} X &= A_o + A_1\bar{X} + A_2\bar{Y} - A_3\bar{Z} + A_5\left(\bar{X}^2 - \bar{Y}^2 - \bar{Z}^2\right) + 0 \\ &\quad + 2A_7\bar{Z}\bar{X} + 2A_6\bar{X}\bar{Y} + \ldots \\ Y &= B_o - A_2\bar{X} + A_1\bar{Y} + A_4\bar{Z} + A_6\left(-\bar{X}^2 + \bar{Y}^2 - \bar{Z}^2\right) + \\ &\quad + 2A_7\bar{Y}\bar{Z} + 0 + 2A_5\bar{X}\bar{Y} + \ldots \\ Z &= C_o + A_3\bar{X} - A_4\bar{Y} + A_1\bar{Z} + A_7\left(-\bar{X}^2 - \bar{Y}^2 + \bar{Z}^2\right) \\ &\quad + 2A_6\bar{Y}\bar{Z} + 2A_5\bar{X}\bar{Y} + 0 + \ldots \end{aligned} \tag{3.22}$$

Note: In Eqs. 3.21 and 3.22, the *a*'s, *b*'s, *c*'s, *A*'s, B_0 and C_0 are certain constant terms. The *O*'s in Eqs. 3.22 are put there with the purpose of indicating zeros as the coefficients for terms, $\overline{YZ}$ in X, $\overline{ZY}$ in Y and $\overline{YZ}$ in *Z*. These polynomials, however, do not give conformal transformations and should, therefore, be used only when rotation angles are sufficiently small.

3.4.4 Projective Transformation in Three Dimensions

Any two coordinate systems are in *projective relation* and are said (in mathematical language) to form a projectivity if a one-to-one correspondence exists between the elements of the two such that each four harmonic elements of one correspond to four harmonic elements of the other.

One can correctly assume in practice that there exists a one-to-one correspondence between the space to be transformed from and the space to be transformed into. This concept is fundamental to the problems of mensuration. If that is not so, one may have, for example, a line in one space (say, ground) corresponding to only one point in the other space (say, stereo-model). That is, mathematically, speaking, two different functions (*F* and *f*) in two different spaces are related to each other (considering that *X, Y, Z* and $\overline{X}, \overline{Y}, \overline{Z}$ convey the same sense as in the previous section):

$$F(X, Y, Z) = f(\overline{X}, \overline{Y}, \overline{Z}) \tag{3.23}$$

In this relationship, no variable would stay in second or higher degree by itself or even in conjunction with other variables. In that case, one can express the relation as:

$$\frac{A_1X + A_2Y + A_3Z + A_4}{D_1X + D_2Y + D_3Z + D_4} = \frac{a_1\overline{X} + a_2\overline{Y} + a_3\overline{Z} + a_4}{d_1\overline{X} + d_2\overline{Y} + d_3\overline{Z} + d_4} \tag{3.24}$$

Note: In Eq. 3.24 through 3.30, the *A*'s...*D*'s and the *a*'s ...*g*'s indicate certain coefficients having unique values in each case.

Equation 3.24 has 16 unknown terms (coefficients and constants), not all of which are independent. The expression with only independent unknowns (eleven) has the form of Eq. 3.25a (see Ghosh and Das, 1966 for derivation):

$$\frac{Y + A_3Z + A_4}{A_1X + A_2Z + 1} = \frac{a_1\overline{X} + a_2\overline{Y} + a_3\overline{Z} + a_4}{d_1\overline{X} + d_2\overline{Y} + d_3\overline{Z} + 1} \tag{3.25a}$$

The one-to-one correspondence could be established if only eleven points are known and identified in both systems (e.g., stereo-model and ground). One requires three independent equations to solve for all unknown in order to transform values of *X, Y* and *Z* into $\overline{X}, \overline{Y}$ and $\overline{Z}$ or vice versa, i.e., in addition to Eq. 3.25a, one needs the following two also:

$$\frac{Z + B_3X + B_4}{B_1Y + B_2X + 1} = \frac{b_1\overline{X} + b_2\overline{Y} + b_3\overline{Z} + b_4}{e_1\overline{X} + e_2\overline{Y} + e_3\overline{Z} + 1} \tag{3.25b}$$

$$\frac{X + C_3Y + C_4}{C_1Z + C_2Y + 1} = \frac{c_1\bar{X} + c_2\bar{Y} + c_3\bar{Z} + c_4}{f_1\bar{X} + f_2\bar{Y} + f_3\bar{Z} + 1} \tag{3.25c}$$

A special case of the degenerated form of the above transformation is obtained by assuming $A_1 = A_2 = B_1 = B_2 = C_1 = C_2 = 0$ in Eq. 3.25. This gives :

$$\left.\begin{aligned} Y + A_3Z + A_4 &= \frac{a_1\bar{X} + a_2\bar{Y} + a_3\bar{Z} + a_4}{d_1\bar{X} + d_2\bar{Y} + d_3\bar{Z} + 1} \\ Z + B_3X + B_4 &= \frac{b_1\bar{X} + b_2\bar{Y} + b_3\bar{Z} + b_4}{e_1\bar{X} + e_2\bar{Y} + e_3\bar{Z} + 1} \\ X + C_3Y + C_4 &= \frac{c_1\bar{X} + c_2\bar{Y} + c_3\bar{Z} + c_4}{f_1\bar{X} + f_2\bar{Y} + f_3\bar{Z} + 1} \end{aligned}\right\} \tag{3.26}$$

From these, if one solves for *X, Y* and *Z* separately, one gets:

$$\left.\begin{aligned} X &= \lambda_1\left\{\frac{a_1\bar{X} + \ldots}{d_1\bar{X} + \ldots}\right\} + \lambda_2\left\{\frac{b_1\bar{X} + \ldots}{e_1\bar{X} + \ldots}\right\} + \lambda_3\left\{\frac{c_1\bar{X} + \ldots}{f_1\bar{X} + \ldots}\right\} \\ Y &= \mu_1\left\{\frac{a_1\bar{X} + \ldots}{d_1\bar{X} + \ldots}\right\} + \mu_2\left\{\frac{b_1\bar{X} + \ldots}{e_1\bar{X} + \ldots}\right\} + \mu_3\left\{\frac{c_1\bar{X} + \ldots}{f_1\bar{X} + \ldots}\right\} \\ Z &= \upsilon_1\left\{\frac{a_1\bar{X} + \ldots}{d_1\bar{X} + \ldots}\right\} + \upsilon_2\left\{\frac{b_1\bar{X} + \ldots}{e_1\bar{X} + \ldots}\right\} + \upsilon_3\left\{\frac{c_1\bar{X} + \ldots}{f_1\bar{X} + \ldots}\right\} \end{aligned}\right\} \tag{3.27}$$

where λ's, μ's, and υ's are certain constants.
A careful inspection of Eq. 3.27 would reveal that the situation is complex, for example,

$$Z = \frac{\text{one cubic expression in } \bar{X}, \bar{Y}, \bar{Z}}{\text{another cubic expression in } \bar{X}, \bar{Y}, \bar{Z}}$$

This, however, is simplified if one considers all the coefficients, except the constant term, in the denominator to be zero. Then one obtains, as a particular case, for example, Z=one cubic polynomial expression in $\bar{X}, \bar{Y}, \bar{Z}$. Here, if for example, one considers Z = a constant, (i.e., say, a horizontal plane in the ground space), one obtains a curved surface in the corresponding space (say, the one in the instrument model space). In a strict linear or projective transformation, the degree of the surface should remain the same, i.e., a plane should transform into a plane, or a quadratic surface into a quadratic surface, and so on.

In view of the above, with regard to "error surfaces" to represent 3-D error propagations (for example, in phototriangulation), one may consider a compromise solution, as follows: In the polynomial expression, Z = two constants, k_1, and k_2, would give the same error surface but with a parallel shift, i.e., the surfaces obtained due to this parallel shift (corresponding to the different values of *Z*) are identical in nature but the change is continual. Such a concept may be desirable in treating the surface deformations when one is working, for example, on phototriangulation in an extremely mountainous terrain.

In such a transformation, one would need nine points. This means that, although cubic in nature, the expression may be degenerated into a general quadratic form (since there are nine unknown coefficients also in a general quadratic polynomial) e.g.,

$$g_1X^2 + g_2Y^2 + g_3Z^2 + g_4XY + g_5ZX + g_6YZ + g_7X + g_8Y + g_9Z = \text{a constant}$$

This could, further, be simplified for use in practice. For example, peculiar to the uses of stereoplotters where axial planes (viz., X = a constant, Y = another constant and Z = a third constant) would remain planes. With this consideration, Eq. 3.26 would become (Okamoto, 1981):

$$\left.\begin{aligned} X &= \frac{c_1\bar{X} + c_2\bar{Y} + c_3\bar{Z} + c_4}{f_1\bar{X} + f_2\bar{Y} + f_3\bar{Z} + 1} \\ Y &= \frac{a_1\bar{X} + a_2\bar{Y} + a_3\bar{Z} + a_4}{d_1\bar{X} + d_2\bar{Y} + d_3\bar{Z} + 1} \\ Z &= \frac{b_1\bar{X} + b_2\bar{Y} + b_3\bar{Z} + b_4}{e_1\bar{X} + e_2\bar{Y} + e_3\bar{Z} + 1} \end{aligned}\right\} \tag{3.28}$$

It may be noted here that even this expression is neither linear nor projective. They are "bi-projective" (Das, 1952b). An arbitrary plane in one (say, ground) space, $\ell X + mY + nZ = p$, where p is a constant, would become (considering Eq. 3.28):

$$\ell\left\{\frac{c_1\bar{X} + \dots}{f_1\bar{X} + \dots}\right\} + m\left\{\frac{a_1\bar{X} + \dots}{d_1\bar{X} + \dots}\right\} + n\left\{\frac{b_1\bar{X} + \dots}{e_1\bar{X} + \dots}\right\} = p \tag{3.29}$$

which is another cubic expression in $\bar{X}$, $\bar{Y}$, $\bar{Z}$. It is interesting to note further that although $Z = k_1$ is a plane, $Z = k_1, k_2, k_3$...etc. family of axial planes get transformed (in the other space) into another family of planes (non-parallel) and the degree of freedom of this envelope is seven. Thus, a seven-point transformation would serve the purpose practically in small units. This means that in hilly areas where a polynomial expression may fail, we may safely use 7, 9 or 11 points and obtain satisfactory results by using the continually varying family of surfaces. This transformation, further degenerated, would give the following expressions (Okamoto, 1981):

$$\left.\begin{aligned} X &= \frac{a_1'\bar{X} + a_2'\bar{Y} + a_3'\bar{Z} + a_4'}{d_1'\bar{X} + d_2'\bar{Y} + d_3'\bar{Z} + 1} \\ Y &= \frac{b_1'\bar{X} + b_2'\bar{Y} + b_3'\bar{Z} + b_4'}{d_1'\bar{X} + d_2'\bar{Y} + d_3'\bar{Z} + 1} \\ Z &= \frac{c_1'\bar{X} + c_2'\bar{Y} + c_3'\bar{Z} + c_4'}{d_1'\bar{X} + d_2'\bar{Y} + d_3'\bar{Z} + 1} \end{aligned}\right\} \tag{3.30}$$

where

$$\begin{vmatrix} a_1' & a_2' & a_3' & a_4' \\ b_1' & b_2' & b_3' & b_4' \\ c_1' & c_2' & c_3' & c_4' \\ d_1' & d_2' & d_3' & d_4' \end{vmatrix} \neq 0$$

The denominators here are the same in each of the expressions for *X, Y* and *Z*. This is the 'projective' transformation used so frequently by the photogrammetrists. For interesting ideas in this, see Novakovskiy (1974) and Okamoto (1981).

It was first observed by G.B. Das of Survey of India while working on a strip of aerial photographs over a highly mountainous terrain (with ruggedness of more than 10,000 ft in almost each model) that the height differences play a very important role in correctly adjusting a triangulated strip. In such a case, different sets of error profile curves drawn for varying ground elevations give a better adjustment than a single set of profiles (corresponding to a single error surface) as are expressed in one set of polynomials (Ghosh, 1975), which are customarily used. Furthermore, Eqs. 3.28 can be used in other applications. The first two (*X, Y*) can establish a relationship between 2-D photocoordinates and 3-D ground coordinates ($\bar{X}, \bar{Y}, \bar{Z}$). In case the two photos in a stereo-overlap are coplanar, the equations become projective (by having the denominators as constant for a particular point). In such a case they can be used to derive the ground height of a fifth point if the heights of four points in the overlap are known. See Das (1952a) for further interesting ideas on this.

3.4.5 Two-dimensional Transformations

Two-dimensional cases may be viewed as the simplified versions of the three-dimensional ones in which the third coordinate (dimension) is constant and may not appear at all in practice. The ones mostly used are listed below:

A. From *Plane-Polar to a Rectangular* (Cartesian) system:

$$\left. \begin{aligned} X &= r \cdot \cos\theta \\ Y &= r \cdot \sin\theta \end{aligned} \right\} \qquad (3.31)$$

where r is the distance of the point from the origin (pole) and θ is the angle subtended by its direction with the *X*-axis.

Note: For example, certain instruments like Kern PG2 use this form of transformation in principle to obtain planimetric coordinates in a model.

B. From one Rectangular system to another *(Regular, Similarity transformation):*

Consider Eq. 3.10 with all elaborations subsequently discussed in Section 3.4.1. Also consider Z = a constant and $\Omega = \Phi = 0$. This gives:

$$\begin{bmatrix} X \\ Y \end{bmatrix} = k \begin{bmatrix} \cos K & \sin K \\ -\sin K & \cos K \end{bmatrix} \begin{bmatrix} \bar{X} \\ \bar{Y} \end{bmatrix} + \begin{bmatrix} X_o \\ Y_o \end{bmatrix} \tag{3.32}$$

or,

$$\left.\begin{aligned} X &= k \cdot \cos K \cdot \bar{X} + k \cdot \sin K \cdot \bar{Y} + X_o \\ Y &= -k \cdot \sin K \cdot \bar{X} + k \cdot \cos K \cdot \bar{Y} + Y_o \end{aligned}\right\} \tag{3.33}$$

or,

$$\left.\begin{aligned} X &= a_1\bar{X} + a_2\bar{Y} + a_o \\ Y &= -a_2\bar{X} + a_1\bar{Y} + b_o \end{aligned}\right\} \tag{3.34}$$

This has four unknown parameters, viz., a_1, a_2, a_o and b_o.

Note: For example, one would use this type of transformation to obtain observed (at a comparator) photo coordinates referred to the fiducial marks.

C. Affine Transformation in Two-Dimensions

Considering Eq. 3.32 and the affinity (note, Eq. 3.20) in two-dimensions, i.e. $k = \begin{bmatrix} k_{\bar{x}} & k_{\bar{y}} \end{bmatrix}^T$

$$\begin{bmatrix} X \\ Y \end{bmatrix} = \begin{bmatrix} \cos K & \sin K \\ -\sin K & \cos K \end{bmatrix} \begin{bmatrix} k_{\bar{x}}\bar{X} \\ k_{\bar{y}}\bar{Y} \end{bmatrix} + \begin{bmatrix} X_o \\ Y_o \end{bmatrix} \tag{3.35}$$

This gives:

$$\left.\begin{aligned} X &= k_{\bar{x}} \cdot \cos K \cdot \bar{X} + k_{\bar{y}} \cdot \sin K \cdot \bar{Y} + X_o \\ Y &= -k_{\bar{x}} \cdot \sin K \cdot \bar{X} + k_{\bar{y}} \cdot \cos K \cdot \bar{Y} + Y_o \end{aligned}\right\} \tag{3.36}$$

or,

$$\left.\begin{aligned} X &= a_1\bar{X} + a_2\bar{Y} + a_o \\ Y &= b_1\bar{X} + b_2\bar{Y} + b_o \end{aligned}\right\} \tag{3.37}$$

This has six unknown parameters, the *a*'s and the *b*'s, although the real unknowns are only five, viz., $k_{\bar{X}}$, $k_{\bar{Y}}$, K, X_0 and Y_0.

Note: For example, this type of transformation would be effective in two typical cases, (1) Non-orthogonality of axes in a comparator inspite of their having the same scale factor, or (2) Linear stretching of film causing scale affinity on the photo.

D. Polynomial Transformation in Two-Dimensions

Considering Z = a constant, one obtains from Eqs 3.21, the following general, two-dimensional polynomials:

$$\left.\begin{aligned} X &= a_o + a_1\bar{X} + a_2\bar{Y} + a_3\bar{X}^2 + a_4\bar{Y}^2 + a_5\bar{X}\bar{Y} + \ldots \\ Y &= b_o + b_1\bar{X} + b_2\bar{Y} + b_3\bar{X}^2 + b_4\bar{Y}^2 + b_5\bar{X}\bar{Y} + \ldots \end{aligned}\right\} \tag{3.38}$$

The conformal version in two-dimensions will be obtained by considering Z = a constant in Eq. 3.22:

$$\left.\begin{aligned} X &= A_o + A_1\bar{X} + A_2\bar{Y} + A_3\left(\bar{X}^2 - \bar{Y}^2\right) + A_4\left(2\bar{X}\bar{Y}\right) + \ldots \\ Y &= B_o + A_2\bar{X} + A_1\bar{Y} + A_4\left(\bar{X}^2 - \bar{Y}^2\right) + A_3\left(2\bar{X}\bar{Y}\right) + \ldots \end{aligned}\right\} \tag{3.39}$$

Note: For example, this type of transformation would be effective in say, (1) establishing the effect of non-linear distortion due to the objective lens on a photograph, or (2) Calibrating a comparator (note Eq. 2.7).

E. Projective Transformation in Two-Dimensions

For single image photogrammetric works, the projectivity between planes may be of special interest sometimes. It is a case of two dimensions in each space, and the number of coordinates per point is two. For such cases, Eqs 3.30 lead into the following:

$$\left.\begin{aligned} X &= \frac{a_1'\bar{X} + a_2'\bar{Y} + a_3'}{d_1'\bar{X} + d_2'\bar{Y} + d_3'} = \frac{a_1\bar{X} + a_2\bar{Y} + a_3}{d_1\bar{X} + d_2\bar{Y} + 1} \\ Y &= \frac{b_1'\bar{X} + b_2'\bar{Y} + b_3'}{d_1'\bar{X} + d_2'\bar{Y} + d_3'} = \frac{b_1\bar{X} + b_2\bar{Y} + b_3}{d_1\bar{X} + d_2\bar{Y} + 1} \end{aligned}\right\} \tag{3.40}$$

This indicates that the projectivity between two planes is uniquely determined if a total of eight coefficients are known. This requires at least four points whose both X and Y coordinates in both the spaces are known. After computing the coefficients, they may be used for calculating all X, Y values of the other points in one plane whose coordinates in the other plane are known. The only condition to validate these expressions is that three of the points used in the transformation in either plane be not collinear, i.e.,

$$\begin{vmatrix} a_1' & a_2' & a_3' \\ b_1' & b_2' & b_3' \\ d_1' & d_2' & d_3' \end{vmatrix} \neq 0$$

Note: These equations are of use in the problems of rectification of single photos.

F. Cross (or, Anharmonic) Ratio

The general concept of projectivity, the theory of cross ratio, is illustrated in Fig. 3.8. Consider a bundle of rays originating from the photo image points, a, b, c, and d, passing through the perspective center (O), are located on plane 1 at A_1, B_1, C_1 and D_1 and on plane 2 at A_2, B_2, C_2

and D_2, respectively. By considering the inherent linearity of the rays, the following relationships of cross ratio can be established:

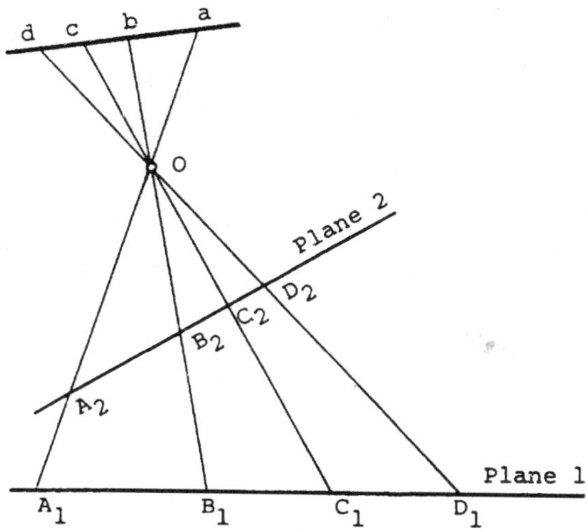

Fig. 3.8: Projectivity and cross-ratio

$$\frac{A_1C_1}{B_1C_1} : \frac{A_1D_1}{B_1D_1} = \frac{\sin A_1OC_1}{\sin B_1OC_1} : \frac{\sin A_1OD_1}{\sin B_1OD_1} = \text{a constant}$$

In the same way, one can prove that the same constant value is true for the corresponding points A_2, B_2, C_2 and D_2 and also for every other corresponding point sequences. In this context, one can state that two figures are projective when their elements correspond to each other and when the cross ratio between any four elements in one figure equals the corresponding cross ratio in the other figure. Therefore, projective elemental figures can be arranged in a perspective configuration. One can now say (see Fig. 3.8) that

$$\frac{A_1C_1}{B_1C_1} : \frac{A_1D_1}{B_1D_1} = \frac{A_2C_2}{B_2C_2} : \frac{A_2D_2}{B_2D_2} \tag{3.41}$$

If the coordinates of points A_1, B_1, C_1 and D_1 in plane 1 are x_1, x_2, x_3 and x_4 and of points A_2, B_2, C_2 and D_2 in plane 2 are x'_1, x'_2, x'_3 and x'_4, respectively, from Eq. 3.41,

$$\frac{x_3 - x_1}{x_3 - x_2} : \frac{x_4 - x_1}{x_4 - x_2} = \frac{x_3' - x_1'}{x_3' - x_2'} : \frac{x_4' - x_1'}{x_4' - x_2'} \tag{3.42}$$

By using this equation, if one coordinate, e.g., x_4 is unknown, it can be determined from the rest of the known coordinates. The general expression can be derived from the above:

$$X = \frac{a_1'\overline{X} + a_2'}{d_1'\overline{X} + d_2'} = \frac{a_1\overline{X} + a_2}{d_1\overline{X} + 1} \tag{3.43}$$

The number of coefficients here is three. The coefficients are functions of the reciprocal positions of the point sequences and the perspective center (see also Hallert, 1960). To make the operation possible, there should be one condition that the determinant

$$\begin{vmatrix} a_1' & a_2' \\ d_1' & d_2' \end{vmatrix} \neq 0$$

3.5 DIFFERENTIAL FORMS

In computer programming such transformations, the partial derivatives of the orientation (or, rotation) matrix $\boldsymbol{M}$ are required frequently. Consider the sequential rotations giving $\boldsymbol{M} = \boldsymbol{M}_{\Omega} \bullet \boldsymbol{M}_{\Phi} \cdot \boldsymbol{M}_{\mathrm{K}}$ (Eq. 3.17). The partial derivatives of $\boldsymbol{M}$ with respect to Ω, Φ and K, respectively can be shown to be:

$$\frac{\partial \boldsymbol{M}}{\partial \Omega} = \boldsymbol{M}_{\mathrm{K}} \bullet \boldsymbol{M}_{\Phi} \frac{\partial \boldsymbol{M}_{\Omega}}{\partial \Omega} = \boldsymbol{M} \begin{bmatrix} 0 & 0 & 0 \\ 0 & 0 & +1 \\ 0 & -1 & 0 \end{bmatrix}$$

By using Eq. 3.19b, one now obtains the detailed differential form with regard to the element Ω :

$$\frac{\partial \boldsymbol{M}}{\partial \Omega} = \begin{vmatrix} 0 & \begin{matrix} -\sin\Omega\sin\mathrm{K} \\ +\cos\Omega\sin\Phi\cos\mathrm{K} \end{matrix} & \begin{matrix} \cos\Omega\sin\mathrm{K} \\ +\sin\Omega\sin\Phi\cos\mathrm{K} \end{matrix} \\ 0 & \begin{matrix} -\sin\Omega\cos\mathrm{K} \\ -\cos\Omega\sin\Phi\sin\mathrm{K} \end{matrix} & \begin{matrix} \cos\Omega\sin\mathrm{K} \\ -\sin\Omega\sin\Phi\sin\mathrm{K} \end{matrix} \\ 0 & +\cos\Omega\cos\Phi & \sin\Omega\cos\Phi \end{vmatrix} \tag{3.44}$$

By comparing the terms in this with the terms in the $\boldsymbol{M}^{\mathrm{T}}$ matrix of Eq. 3.19b, one obtains:

$$\frac{\partial \boldsymbol{M}}{\partial \Omega} = \begin{bmatrix} 0 & -\mathrm{m}_{13} & \mathrm{m}_{12} \\ 0 & -\mathrm{m}_{23} & \mathrm{m}_{22} \\ 0 & -\mathrm{m}_{33} & \mathrm{m}_{32} \end{bmatrix} = \begin{bmatrix} \mathrm{M}_{\Omega_1} \\ \mathrm{M}_{\Omega_2} \\ \mathrm{M}_{\Omega_3} \end{bmatrix} \tag{3.45}$$

Similarly,

$$\frac{\partial \boldsymbol{M}}{\partial \Phi} = \boldsymbol{M}_{K} \frac{\partial \boldsymbol{M}_{\Phi}}{\partial \Phi} \boldsymbol{M}_{\Omega} = \boldsymbol{M} \begin{bmatrix} 0 & \sin\Omega & \cos\Omega \\ -\sin\Omega & 0 & 0 \\ \cos\Omega & 0 & 0 \end{bmatrix}$$

$$= \begin{bmatrix} 0 & 0 & -\cos K \\ 0 & 0 & \sin K \\ \cos K & -\sin K & 0 \end{bmatrix} M$$

$$= \begin{bmatrix} -\sin \Phi \cos K & \sin \Omega \cos \Phi \cos K & -\cos \Omega \cos \Phi \cos K \\ \sin \Phi \sin K & -\sin \Omega \cos \Phi \sin K & \cos \Omega \cos \Phi \sin K \\ \cos \Phi & \sin \Omega \sin \Phi & -\cos \Omega \sin \Phi \end{bmatrix} = \begin{bmatrix} M_{F1} \\ M_{F2} \\ M_{F3} \end{bmatrix} \qquad (3.46)$$

Further,

$$\frac{\partial M}{\partial K} = \frac{\partial M_K}{\partial K} M_\Phi \cdot M_\Omega = \begin{bmatrix} 0 & +1 & 0 \\ -1 & 0 & 0 \\ 0 & 0 & 0 \end{bmatrix} M$$

$$= \begin{bmatrix} -\cos \Omega \sin K & \begin{matrix} \cos \Omega \cos K \\ -\sin \Omega \sin \Phi \sin K \end{matrix} & \begin{matrix} \sin \Omega \cos K \\ +\cos \Omega \sin \Phi \sin K \end{matrix} \\ -\cos \Phi \cos K & \begin{matrix} -\cos \Omega \sin K \\ -\sin \Omega \sin \Phi \cos K \end{matrix} & \begin{matrix} -\sin \Omega \sin K \\ +\cos \Omega \sin \Phi \cos K \end{matrix} \\ 0 & 0 & 0 \end{bmatrix}$$

$$= \begin{bmatrix} m_{21} & m_{22} & m_{23} \\ -m_{11} & -m_{12} & -m_{13} \\ 0 & 0 & 0 \end{bmatrix} = \begin{bmatrix} M_{K_1} \\ M_{K_2} \\ M_{K_3} \end{bmatrix} \qquad (3.47)$$

Note: The rotations Ω, Φ and K in a stereo-model are analogous to rotations ω, ϕ and κ in a single photograph. Therefore, such differential forms can be used with respect to an orientation matrix whose rotations are ω, ϕ and κ in that same order. In case a change in the sequence is necessary, the matrix can be appropriately formed for use in practice.

3.6 OTHER CAPABILITIES WITH 3-D COORDINATES

The use of 3-D coordinates data for mensuration has been the unique strength of analytical photogrammetric procedures. Although the following topics are beyond the general scope of this book, they are briefly mentioned here as certain examples in view of their growing importance in the fields where photogrammetry may be applied:

A. Digital Terrain Modelling (DTM)

A Digital Terrain Model (DTM) is regarded as a numerical description of the surface of an object based on measured or derived coordinates of numerous scattered points on this surface. The concept of DTM has been widely used in many engineering applications since its inception in 1955 at the Massachusetts Institute of Technology. Such applications have been exemplified by solutions related to highway planning, automatic profile construction, etc. In recent years, DTM has been used in contouring algorithms to find efficient two-dimensional graphical displays of three-dimensional topographical surfaces. The importance of three-dimensional rectangular systems of coordinates in such applications is unsurpassed (see, for example, ISPRS Archives, 1976, 1980, 1984).

B. Differential Mapping

By Differential Mapping is meant the mapping of an object-surface relative to itself, in view of changes in time and space or relative to another object with which it may bear some physical dimensional relationship. Qualitative and quantitative studies of dynamic objects are best made with photogrammetric (space or aerial, terrestrial, microscopic, etc.). procedures. Selected studies like those on shoreline erosion problems, changes in glacial patterns, growth patterns in urban areas, etc. can be made better in terms of the time the photographs are taken and the changes occurring observed through the use of repetitive photographic coverage. This is comparative photogrammetry. Techniques of handling numerical data involving conversion of three-dimensional stereo-photogrammetric models into digital information for subsequent treatments at a high speed computer have been developed in numerous agencies.

The DTM and differential mapping procedures have two essential components, viz., a set of scattered points measured in three-dimensions and interpolation algorithms for finding new (unobserved or derived) points also in three-dimensions. Three-dimensional transformation of one type or the other is esentially involved in all such works. Various interpolation techniques (surface fitting and prediction) are inherent in such works also. The interested reader would benefit from the work of numerous authors and from the proceedings of numerous recent conferences in this general area, in particular the Auto Carts symposia organized under the auspices of the ASPRS.

C. Polylateration

A simple method of deriving 3-D coordinates of unknown points in terms of their direct distances to five or more known points has been developed by Das (1973). This brings not only in geodetic measurements the full potentialities of Electronic Distance Measurements (EDM) but also in photogrammetry the tremendous possibilities in view of the use of modern electronic calculators.

The entire theory is based on the simple analytical expression of the distance between two points: P (p_1, p_2, p_3) and A (a_1, a_2, a_3). The subscripts 1, 2 and 3 here refer to the X, Y and Z coordinates respectively. The distance can be expressed by

$$(PA)^2 = (p_1 - a_1)^2 + (p_2 - a_2)^2 + (p_3 - a_3)^2 \tag{3.48}$$

Similarly, for a second point, B

$$(PB)^2 = (p_1 - b_1)^2 + (p_2 - b_2)^2 + (p_3 - b_3)^2 \tag{3.49}$$

Hence,

$$\begin{aligned}(PA)^2 - (PB)^2 = &-2(a_1 - b_1)\mathrm{p}_1 - 2(a_2 - b_2)\mathrm{p}_2 - 2(a_3 - b_3)\mathrm{p}_3 \\ &+ \left[\left(a_1^2 + a_2^2 + a_3^2\right) - \left(b_1^2 + b_2^2 + b_3^2\right)\right]\end{aligned} \tag{3.50}$$

Eq. 3.50 is a linear expression in p_1, p_2, p_3 of the form

$$S_{\mathrm{AB}} = \ell_1 p_1 + \ell_2 p_2 + \ell_3 p_3 + \ell_4$$

where $S_{\mathrm{AB}} = (PA)^2 - (PB)^2$

From the above, it would be seen that if the origin is shifted to A i.e., if $a_1 = a_2 = a_3 = 0$ then the parameters $\ell_1 = 2b_1$; $\ell_2 = 2b_2$ and $\ell_3 = 2b_3$ are really twice the coordinates of B.

If, therefore, five points are known then the four independent quantities S_{AB} can be related to four of the points in terms of the fifth point considered as the ad hoc origin, and the four parameters ℓ_1, ℓ_2, ℓ_3, ℓ_4 can be derived from the four linear equations. In case more than five points are known, then the method of least squares can be utilised for an acceptable solution.

With regard to the expected error propagation, to quote Das (1973), "If the unknown points fall inside the space covered by the known points, the deducted coordinates will be more reliable than for points falling outside the space. The error will vary directly as the distance of the unknown point from this space and inversely as the separation between the extreme points in a particular direction."

The concept can be obviously simplified in 2-D space also, for example, with regard to obtaining photo coordinates being derived from observed distances; such as could be possible with the calibrated data on four fiducial marks and the principal point.

BIBLIOGRAPHY

American Society of Photogrammetry; *Manual of Photogrammetry* (4th Ed.), ASP Falls Church, Virginia; 1980.

Bomford, G.; *Geodesy*; The Clarendon Press, Oxford, U.K.; 1971.

Buchholtz, A. by Rüger, W. et al; *Photogrammetrie*; VEB Verlag für Bauwesen, Berlin, Germany; 1973.

Das, G. B.; *Deformation of a Stereogram*; PE 18, No. 1; 1952a.

Das, G.B.; *Supplementary Height Control*; PE 18, No. 1; 1952b.

Das, G.B.; *Poloylateration*; Academia Scientiarum Bulgarica; Vol. Vladimiro K. Hristov - Septuagenario; 1973.

Ghosh, Sanjib K.; *Solar Collector Calibration*; PE Vol. 32, No. 2; 1966.

Ghosh, Sanjib K.; and Gouri B. Das; Some New Ideas in Aerotriangulation; *Proceedings of ISP Symposium in Commission III;* Urbana, Illinois; 1966.

Ghosh, Sanjib K.; *Theory of Stereophotogrammetry* (2nd Ed.); The Ohio State Univ. Bookstores, Columbus, Ohio; 1972.

Ghosh, Sanjib K.; *Phototriangulation;* Lexington Books, Lexinton, Massachusetts; 1975.

Hallert, Bertil; *Photogrammetry;* McGraw-Hill; 1960.

International Society for Photogrammetry; Archives, Vol. 13, 1957; Vol. 14, 1961; Vol. 15, 1965; Vol. 16, 1969; Vol. 17, 1974; Vol. 21, 1976; Vol. 22, 1978; Vol. 23, 1980; Vol. 24, 1982; Vol. 25, 1984.

Jordan-Eggert; *Jordan's Handbook of Geodesy*; Translation of 8th Edition, 1941 by Martha W. Carta; US Army Map Service, Washington, DC; 1962.

Kratky, V.; *Image Transformations*; PE 28, No. 5; 1972.

Light, D.L.; *The Orientation Matrix*; PE 32, No. 3; 1966.

Mikhail, E.M.; *Simultaneous Three-dimensional Transformation of Higher Degrees*; PE 30, No. 4; 1964.

Moffitt, F.H. and Mikhail, E.M.; *Photogrammetry* (3rd Ed.); International Text-Book Co.; 1980.

Novakovskiy, B.A.; Stereophotogrammetric Processing of Photographs of Nontopographical Types of Surveys with Unknown Orientation Elements; *Geodesy, Mapping and Photogrammetry 16*, No. 1; 1974.

Okamoto, Atsushi; *Orientation and Construction of Models*. Parts I, II, III, Respectively PERS 47, Nos 10, 11 and 12; 1981.

Sanso, Fernando; An Exact Solution of the Roto-translation Problem; *Photogrammetria* 29, No. 6; 1973.

Schut, G. H.; Construction of Orthogonal Matrices and Their Application in Analytical Photogrammetry; *Photogrammetria* 15; 1958/59.

Schut, G.H.; Similarity *Transformation and Least Squares*; PE 39, No. 6; 1973.

Zakatov, P.S.; *A Course in Higher Geodesy;* Translated from Russian by Israel Program for Scientific Translation for National Science Foundation; No. OTS-6 1-31212; 1962.

4

GEOMETRY OF PHOTOGRAPHS

Photographs taken with a camera of known internal geometry permit reconstruction of the bundle of rays with which the object is projected on the negative. They, in turn, permit reconstruction of the object-model, which is used for measurements. The various phases of such reconstructions are denoted with the general term "Orientation". The orientation of a bundle or rays can be considered in two parts, Interior and Exterior. The exterior orientations of two conjugate bundles are considered sequentially in Relative and Absolute orientations. The following definitions and elaborations would be pertinent.

Orientation is defined as the determination of the position and attitude of a camera, photograph, model, triplet or such a unit in space relative to a system of coordinate reference.

Orientation, Interior: The recovering of a projected cone of rays geometrically identical with the cone of rays that entered the camera lens to make the original exposure. The parameters that define this relationship are the *elements of interior orientation.* which include: (a) The *camera constant* (also known as focal length or principal distance); (b) *location of principal point* with respect to the fiducial marks; and (c) all *distortion parameters* (for the interior of the photographic system referenced to the principal point and the fiducial marks). Interior orientation, at the plotting instrument, is an attempt to duplicate the cone of rays by setting the elements. This is achieved by the measurement of several reference marks (fiducial marks) on the photograph and the susequent computation of the coordinate transformation which relates the coordinates of these points in the instrument carrier system to their known coordinates in the photo system. In view of possible stretching of film in the camera during film transport and film development (negatives and diapositives), a six-parameter affine transformation (see Chap. 3) would be preferred since it incorporates separate scaling parameters for the X and Y directions. This requires that at least four fiducials be measured in the image. Modern aerial cameras are typically equipped with either four or eight fiducials. Most analytical plotters are programmed to automeasure (carriage movements in a sequential manner) upto eight fiducials with options for aborting, rejecting and backtracking measurements. The quality of interior orientation can be checked with standard errors displayed on the monitor on-line.

Orientation, Exterior: The exterior orientation of a single bundle (or cone) consists of two sets of parameters (elements): (a) Coordinates (3-D) giving the location of the perspective center; and (b) Orientation angles defining the attitude of the camera at the instant of exposure.

Orientation, Relative: The reconstruction of the same perspective relative situation between photographs of a pair, which existed when the photographs were taken. This is achieved when all pairs of conjugate rays are coplanar with the base; i.e., all y-parallaxes are eliminated. In establishing the spatial relative relationship between the two photographs at a typical analytical plotter (like Zeiss P3 Planicomp) the method of *Dependent* Relative Orientation is used. Here the right photograph is oriented to the left one which is assumed to be vertical. Hence the unknowns to be determined are the base components b_y and b_z plus the three rotation angles of the right camera (ω, ϕ and κ). Such programs are based on analogical *Y*-parallax equation (correction equation; see Ghosh, 1972):

$$-Py = -dby + \frac{Y}{Z}dbz + Z\left(1 + \frac{Y^2}{Z^2}\right)d\omega - \frac{(X-2b)Y}{Z}d\phi - (X-2b)\,d\kappa$$

where *X, Y* and *Z* are the model-coordinates of the point; *b* is the model base and *Py* is the observed *Y*-parallax (determined by way of elimination) at the observed point. Observations are made at six standard locations (two principal points and four corners of the model, also known as "von Gruber points"). With five unknowns and six observations one obtains a least square solution. Most programs, however permit at least two additional points for a better solution, as may be desired. Automeasure with options for aborting, rejecting and backtracking are also routinely possible in relative orientation. The quality of relative orientation can be checked with standard deviation of residual *Y*-parallaxes by considering all the observed points.

Orientataion, Absolute: Following relative orientation, the process of absolute orientation establishes the relationship between the model and ground control coordinate systems. This is performed by using a 3-D similarity transformation (with seven parameters): three rotation angles (Ω, Φ and κ), three translation parameters (*dX, dY* and *dZ*) and the model scale. This requires at least three non-collinear control points. At an analytical plotter, point identification and their coordinates having been stored in the memory, after two points are observed, the automeasure mode brings the carriage sequentially to all points available in the model. Options for aborting, rejecting and backtracking (correcting) are also possible. Residual errors in each coordinate at each point are displayed at the monitor in order to evaluate the quality of orientation.

Beyond the above adaptations of concepts of analogical photogrammetry into modern analytical plotters, computational photogrammetry consists of mathematical modelling of the relationships between different systems (like, photo and ground, photo and model, model and ground). Such relationships are virtually independent of the applications, i.e., the same formulation may be valid for aerial, spatial, terrestrial or microscopic cases. To arrive at a solution, one may have to use a set of *condition equations* to establish the relationship between the observed values and the unknown parameters for the specific case. The condition equations most commonly used are: (i) Collinearity Condition, (ii) Coplanarity Condition, and (iii) Scale-restraint Condition. Each condition equation has specific functions, scopes and limitations. The choices of condition equations, may, therefore, lead to different approaches to the solution of any specific problem. Representative characteristics of the various condition equations are given in Table 4.1 Depending on the circumstances, any condition equation may have to be modified in order to make it adaptable to the working system in view of the desired results.

Table 4.1
Various Conditions and their Characteristics

(Representative examples)

	Applications	Observation Data	Parameters	
			Knowns	Unknowns
COLLINEARITY CONDITION	Camera Calibration	$x'\ y'$	$X_O\ Y_O\ Z_O\ \omega_p\ \phi_p\ \kappa_p$	$x_O\ y_O\ f\ \omega_O\ \phi_O\ \kappa_O$
	Space Resection	$x'\ y'$	$x_O\ y_O\ f\ \ X_p\ Y_p\ Z_p$	$X_O\ Y_O\ Z_O\ \omega\ \phi\ \kappa$
	Space Intersection	$x'\ y'\ x''\ y''$	$x_0 y_0 f$ $X'_0\ Y'_0\ Z'_0\ \ X''_0\ Y''_0\ Z''_0$ $\omega'\ \varphi'\kappa'\ \ \omega''\ \varphi''\kappa''$	$X_p\ Y_p\ Z_p$
	Strip Photography (stereo)	$x'\ y'\ x''\ y''$	$X'_O Y'_O Z'_O f$ $X''_O Y''_O Z''_O v_F$	$X_p\ Y_p\ Z_p$
	Panoramic Photography (Stereo)	$x'\ y'\ x''\ y''$	$X'_O Y'_O Z'_O f$ $X''_O Y''_O Z''_O \theta$	$X_p\ Y_p\ Z_p$
COPLANARITY CONDITION	Relative Orientation (Dependent)	$x'\ y'\ x''\ y''$	$x_O\ y_O\ f\ by'\ bz'$ $\omega'\ \phi'\ \kappa'\ bx$	$by''\ bz''$ $\omega''\ \phi''\ \kappa''$
	Relative Orientation (Independent)	$x'\ y'\ x''\ y''$	$x_O\ y_O\ f\ bx$ $by\ bz\ \omega'$	$\kappa'\ \phi'$ $\kappa''\ \phi''\ \omega''$
SCALE RESTRAINT CONDITION	Scale Transfer	——	$k_{i-1}\ \ k_i$ $x_{Oi-1}\ y_{Oi-1}\ z_{Oi-1}$ $x_{Oi}\ y_{Oi}\ z_{Oi}$	$x_{Oi+1}\ y_{Oi+1}\ z_{Oi+1}$ $bx_i\ by_i\ bz_i$ k_{i+1}
ANGULAR (CHURCH) CONDITION	Space Resection	$x'\ y'$	$x_O\ y_O\ f\ \ x_p\ y_p\ z_p$	$X_O\ Y_O\ Z_O$

Note : See the List of Symbols for their explanations. Single prime refers to one photo or the one on the left side and double prime refers to the photo on the right side (or photo-pair). Subscripts *o*, *i*, *p* and *P* refer to the center of perspectivity, the photo, the point on photo and the point on ground, respectively.

4.1 COLLINEARITY CONDITION

The basic transformation (projective) equation describing the relationship between two mutually associated three-dimensional systems of coordinates is (see Fig. 4.1 and *cf.* Eq. 3.10):

$$\begin{bmatrix} x \\ y \\ z \end{bmatrix} = kM \begin{bmatrix} X & - & Xo \\ Y & - & Yo \\ Z & - & Zo \end{bmatrix} \tag{4.1}$$

where *x, y, z* are the coordinates in the system to be transformed into
k is the scale factor
M is the rotation matrix
Xo, Yo, Zo are the coordinates of the origin (O) in the *X, Y, Z* system which is to be transformed from.

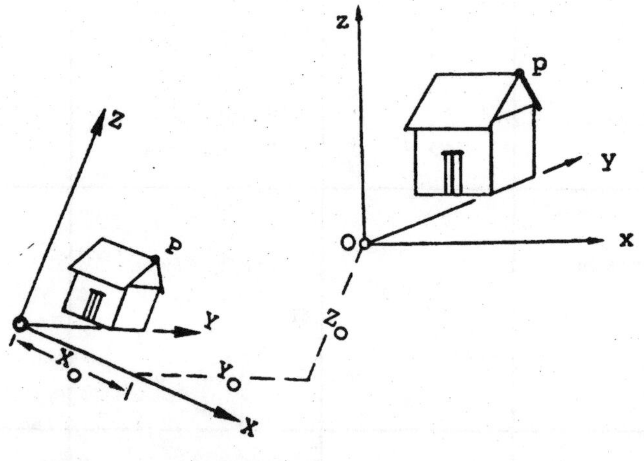

Fig. 4.1: Transformation of coordinates in three dimensions

As described in Chapter 3, the rotation matrix ***M*** is a 3 × 3 orthonormal matrix and is made up of three independent rotations around the three axes. It is usually expressed in one of the following forms:

$$M = \begin{bmatrix} m_{11} & m_{12} & m_{13} \\ m_{21} & m_{22} & m_{23} \\ m_{31} & m_{32} & m_{33} \end{bmatrix} = \begin{bmatrix} \cos Xx & \cos Yx & \cos Zx \\ \cos Xy & \cos Yy & \cos Zy \\ \cos Xz & \cos Yz & \cos Zz \end{bmatrix} \tag{4.2}$$

Here cos *Xx*, cos *Yx*, etc. are the cosines of the space angles between the respective, *x, y, z* axes of the system to be transformed into and the *X, Y, Z* axes of the system to be transformed. Various authors have selected different directions and sequences for these rotations. Nonetheless, the numerical values of the nine elements of ***M*** are identical, regardless of the choice of the angles involved therein. Because of the peculiar nature of the rotation matrix ***M***, its inverse and its transpose are identical.

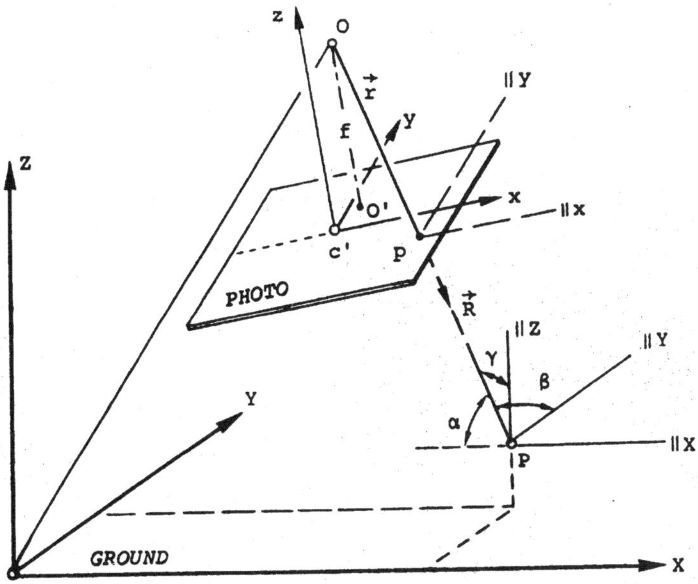

Fig. 4.2: Collinearity condition and exterior orientation

Considering a diapositive, any image point *p* (see Fig. 4.2) may be located in the photograph by its coordinates: x_p, y_p (the third dimension being zero). The optical (camera) axis intersects the diapositive plane at *O'* whose coordinates are: x_o, y_o (the third dimension is also zero). The optical axis being normal to the plane of the diapositive and parallel to the *z*-axis (of the photograph system), one gets the coordinates of the perspective center; x_o, y_o, *f*.

In the photographic system of coordinates, the vector defining the location of the point p is

$$\vec{r} = \begin{bmatrix} x_p & - & x_o \\ y_p & - & y_o \\ 0 & - & f \end{bmatrix} \tag{4.3}$$

In the ground system of coordinates, the perspective center (*O*) is located at X_o, Y_o, Z_o, and the corresponding ground point (*P*) is located at X_p, Y_p, Z_p. Thus, the vector defining the location of the ground point *P* is

$$\vec{R} = \begin{bmatrix} X_P & - & X_0 \\ Y_P & - & Y_0 \\ Z_P & - & Z_0 \end{bmatrix} \tag{4.4}$$

When the exterior orientation of the photograph is correctly established, the two location vectors $\vec{r}$ and $\vec{R}$ are collinear. The two vectors differ only in length, one being a scalar multiple of the other. This gives the scale factor:

$$k = \frac{|r|}{|R|} \tag{4.5}$$

In keeping with the fundamental relationship expressed in Eq. 4.1, the collinearity condition may be written as:

$$\vec{r} = \begin{bmatrix} x_p & - & x_o \\ y_p & - & y_o \\ & - & f \end{bmatrix} = k \cdot \boldsymbol{M} = \begin{bmatrix} X_p & - & X_o \\ Y_p & - & Y_o \\ Z_p & - & Z_o \end{bmatrix} = k \cdot \boldsymbol{M} \cdot \vec{R} \tag{4.6}$$

or,
$$\vec{R} = \frac{1}{k} \cdot \boldsymbol{M}^{\mathrm{T}} \cdot \vec{r} \tag{4.7}$$

4.1.1 Standard Form

The matrix multiplication indicated in Eq. 4.6 may be carried out by the components along rows and columns. If the first and second rows are divided by the third row and the resulting expressions are multiplied by $-f$, one obtains the Collinearity condition equations with respect to the two photo coordinates:

$$x = (x_P - x_O) = -f \frac{(X_P - X_O)m_{11} + (Y_P - Y_O)m_{12} + (Z_P - Z_O)m_{13}}{(X_P - X_O)m_{31} + (Y_P - Y_O)m_{32}(Z_P - Z_O)m_{33}} \tag{4.8}$$

$$y = (y_P - y_O) = -f \frac{(X_P - X_O)m_{21} + (Y_P - Y_O)m_{22} + (Z_P - Z_O)m_{23}}{(X_P - X_O)m_{31} + (Y_P - Y_O)m_{32} + (Z_P - Z_O)m_{33}}$$

These two equations imply that the two vectors, $\vec{r}$ and $\vec{R}$ are collinear, i.e., the object point (*P*), the perspective center (or, the exposure station, *O*), and the image point (*p*) lie on the same straight line.

This assumed condition, however, does not hold true always in the physical reality. A variety of disturbances, (e.g., lens distortion, atmospheric refraction, and others) may cause the actual ray to deviate from the collinearity situation. However if these disturbances are known and can be determined in advance, one can apply appropriate corrections and use refined data before imposing the collinearity condition. In certain cases, one can compensate for such disturbances by way of augmenting the collinearity equations also. Chapter 5 deals with such refinement considerations.

Each measured point on the photograph leads to two condition equations, one for each of the *x* and *y* coordinates. These equations, contain practically all the elements of the problem (viz., of interior orientation and exterior orientation). They contain the image coordinates as well as the object space coordinates and are sufficient in themselves for the solution of any problem in conventional photogrammetry. They can be used in various other forms also as discussed below.

4.1.2 Matrix Form

Eq. 4.8, in matrix form are

$$x = -f\frac{M_1\bar{X}}{M_3\bar{X}} \text{ and } y = -f\frac{M_2\bar{X}}{M_3\bar{X}} \tag{4.9}$$

where f is calibrated focal length of the camera, as before.

$$\boldsymbol{M} = \begin{bmatrix} M_1 \\ M_2 \\ M_3 \end{bmatrix} \text{ and } \bar{X} = \begin{bmatrix} X_p & - & X_o \\ Y_p & - & Y_o \\ Z_p & - & Z_o \end{bmatrix}$$

The elements M_1, M_2 and M_3 are the corresponding row matrices which, in general notations, are

$$M_i = [m_{i1}, m_{i2}, m_{i3}]$$

Collinearity condition equations in such forms are conveniently used for various expressions.

4.1.3 Direction Cosine Form

Consider that the location vector $\vec{R}$ (*OP* in Fig. 4.2) subtends angles α, β and γ with the *X*, *Y* and *Z*-axes, respectively. These define the direction cosines of this vector in the *X-Y-Z* system. In Eq. 4.8, the quantities $(X_P - X_O)$, $(Y_P - Y_O)$ and $(Z_P - Z_O)$ are proportional to the direction cosines of the vector from *O* to *P* ($\vec{R}$). Therefore, with proper substitutions, one gets the Collinearity condition equations in the form:

$$\begin{aligned}(x_P - x_o) &= -f\frac{m_{11}\cos\alpha + m_{12}\cos\beta + m_{13}\cos\gamma}{m_{31}\cos\alpha + m_{32}\cos\beta + m_{33}\cos\gamma} \\ (y_P - y_o) &= -f\frac{m_{21}\cos\alpha + m_{22}\cos\beta + m_{23}\cos\gamma}{m_{31}\cos\alpha + m_{32}\cos\beta + m_{33}\cos\gamma}\end{aligned} \tag{4.10}$$

The condition equations in this form are useful in certain special problems when scale of the object is no considerations, e.g., for camera calibration using photographs of collimator-banks or stars. When the directions to some points used as control are known, equations in such forms permit numerical evaluations of their corresponding direction cosines, which help in determining the angular orientation of the photograph and the interior orientation of the camera.

Most of the agencies using the computational methods with the conventional frame cameras have programs involving the collinearity equations, which are almost routinely applied in aerial mapping jobs. However, in un-conventional applications, where the concept of a simple central projection is no longer adequate to describe the geometry of the physical characteristics, it becomes a problem. Cases in point are, for example, Continuous Strip Photography, Panoramic Photography, etc. Simple modifications of the computer programs can be used in such cases.

4.1.4 Linearization of Collinearity Equations

In theory, the solution of any problem (wherein this condition is applicable) is obtained by inserting the known quantities in the equations and enough image points must be observed to permit a solution for the remaining (unknown) parameters. There are, however, two problems in this. Firstly, the condition equations, are non-linear. Secondly, in usual cases, more image points are observed than are necessary for explicit and closed solutions. To obtain a practical and statistically acceptable solution, therefore, linearized forms of the condition equations are developed first and, next, the method of Least Squares is applied to account for the extra (redundant) data. Generally, the equations are linearized by using a 'Taylor' expansion and (in view of an interative solution) only the first order terms are retained.

The condition equation may be written as a function (F) of observation and parameters equated to zero:

$$F(O, X) = 0 \tag{4.11}$$

where O Symbolizes the observations, (or, directly related quantities)
and X Symbolizes the variable parameters.

If the observations and a set of approximate values of the parameters are substituted, the equations, cannot be satisfied exactly. They can, however, be satisfied by adding (to this function) terms involving the residual errors in the observations and the corrections to the approximate values of the parameters. This gives:

$$(F_0) + [A]\,(V) + [B]\,(\Delta) = 0 \tag{4.12}$$

where F_0 is the function, F, evaluated with the observations and the approximate values (initial values in an interative procedure) of the parameters
A is a row matrix composed of the partial derivatives of F with respect to each of the observed quantities, i.e., $\partial F/\partial$ (observations)
V is a column vector composed of the residuals to the observations
B is a row matrix composed of the partial derivatives of F with respect to each of the parameters, i.e., $\partial F/\partial$ (parameters)
Δ is a column vector composed of the corrections (or, alterations) to the approximate values of the parameters.

The partial derivatives (see the Appendix) in A and B are with respect to the approximate values of the parameters and hence become the coefficients in a linear equation in which F_0 is the constant term. The partial derivatives of the collinearity condition equations with respect to their application in aerial triangulation (interior orientation elements considered as known) cases are given in the Appendix.

By way of substituting the quantities containing the rotation angles, transposing and clearing fractions, one obtains from Eq. 4.8 (for the m elements, one may refer to Eqs. 3.17 and 3.19).

$$
\begin{aligned}
& x\,[(X-X_o)\sin\phi + (Y-Y_o)(-\sin\omega\cos\phi) + (Z-Z_o)\cos\omega\cos\phi] \\
& \quad + f\,[(X-X_o)\cos\phi\cos k + (Y-Y_o) + (\cos\omega\sin k + \sin\omega\sin\phi\cos k) \\
& \quad + (Z-Z_o)(\sin\omega\sin k - \cos\omega\sin\phi\cos k)] = 0 \qquad (4.13) \\
& y\,[(X-X_o)\sin\phi + (Y-Y_o)(-\sin\omega\cos\phi) + (Z-Z_o)\cos\omega\cos\phi] \\
& \quad + f\,[(X-X_o)(-\ldots\cos\phi\sin k) + (Y-Y_o) + (\cos\omega\cos k - \sin\omega\sin\phi\sin k) \\
& \quad + (Z-Z_o)(\sin\omega\cos k + \cos\omega\sin\phi\sin k)] = 0
\end{aligned}
$$

Eqs 4.13 are 'transcendental' and in most general cases all of the twelve terms within the square brackets are considered unknowns. They simply represent another form of the same collinearity condition. If per chance the condition does not exist, it is desirable to allow incremental corrections (differentials) to the observed coordinates x,y such that they fulfil the principles of Least Squares. Harris *et al.*, (1963) used a form of Newton's method (see Eshbach, 1957) to solve them. This considers an iterative method based on initial approximations, which are easily obtainable in any problem for all unknowns. After partial differentiations and rearranging the terms, one may consider $dx = v_x$ and $dy = v_y$.

Note: dx and dy are corrections or deviations to measured photo coordinates x and y. They may be interpreted as residual errors in the measurements.

One obtains now the following simplified forms of the linearized observation equations for the case where all of the interior orientation elements are known:

$$
\left.
\begin{aligned}
v_{x_{ij}} &= (p_{11ij} + p_{12ij}d\omega_i + p_{13ij}d\phi_i + p_{14ij}d\kappa_i - p_{15ij}dX_{oi} - p_{16ij}dY_{oi} \\
&\quad - p_{17ij}dZ_{oi} + p_{15ij}dX_j + p_{16ij}dY_j + p_{17ij}dZ_j)/A_{ij} \\
v_{y_{ij}} &= (p_{21ij} + p_{22ij}d\omega_i + p_{23ij}d\phi_i + p_{24ij}d\kappa_i - p_{25ij}dX_{oi} - p_{26ij}dY_{oi} \\
&\quad - p_{27ij}dZ_{oi} + p_{25ij}dX_j + p_{26ij}dY_j + p_{27ij}dZ_j)/A_{ij}
\end{aligned}
\right\} \qquad (4.14)
$$

where subscripts i and j refer to the photograph and to the point, respectively;

p_{11} and p_{21} are the residual errors (misclosures) in x and y, respectively (i.e., the observed value minus the value computed by using the approximate values of the unknowns);

$p_{12} \cdots p_{17}$, $p_{22} \cdots p_{27}$ are the partial derivatives of Eqs 4.8 or 4.13, evaluated by using the approximate values of the unknowns;

$d\omega$, $d\phi$, dk are the small corrections to be applied to the approximate (initial) values of the unknowns ω, ϕ and κ;

dX_o, dY_o, dZ_o are the small corrections to be applied to the approximate (initial) values of X_o, Y_o and Z_o;

dX, dY, dZ are the small corrections to be applied to the approximate (initial) values of $X, Y,$ and Z;

and A_{ij} is a constant for the point observed and the photo containing it.

Harris et al. (1963) have given convenient equations for computing the p coefficients. These equations are in a sense 'universal'. They can be used to solve different problems, e.g., Relative Orientation, Resection, Block Triangulation, etc. However, they have to be adapted to the requirements of specific problems. In the case of *Block Triangulation,* the presence of all nine terms (dω...dZ) is necessary. In *Space Resection* computations, where *X, Y* and *Z* ground coordinates of all points are known, one would use the first six terms ($d\omega ... dZ_0$) because the terms dX, dY and dZ would be zero in this case. The equations can be further simplified in the case of a *Relative Orientation* problem because one of the two photos (say, the left side one) can be considered 'fixed' as in a 'dependent' method, that perspective center can be selected as the origin (of the system of coordinates) and the distance to the second perspective center can be selected as unity (whereby dX_0 has then no significance). The terms, dX, dy and dZ can be eliminated by substitution and expressed in terms of other unknowns $d\omega$, $d\phi$, $d\kappa$ and dZ_0). This will give the special observation equations for a 'dependent' case of Relative Orientation:

$$\left.\begin{aligned} v_x &= a_1 d\omega + a_2 d\phi + a_3 d\kappa + a_4 dY_o + a_5 dZ_o \\ v_y &= d_1 d\omega + d_2 d\phi + d_3 d\kappa + d_4 dY_o + d_5 dZ_o \end{aligned}\right\} \tag{4.15}$$

The pair of Eqs 4.15 occurs for each image point on each photograph. See also Harris *et al*., (1963) for the full meanings of the coefficients, *a*'s and *d*'s. Corresponding to the use of the *Y*-parallaxes, only the *y*-equation is significant. Nevertheless, some organizations utilize both*x*- and *y*-equations for programming uniformity, even in the relative orientation cases. The *x*-equations by themselves can be used profitably only in some special cases where the use of *Y*-parallaxes may be prohibitive or impossible, e.g., problem models with 'critical surface' in which the element ω may be unsolvable, or models with difficulty in stereo-vision at one or more of the standard locations. See Ghosh (1972) for further ideas on this.

Such iterative solutions are best made with a clear indication as to when to terminate the iterations. A sound and realistic logic is to terminate when the incremental corrections to the parameters (linear or angular) are smaller than their observational precisions. The NOS, for example, terminates such interactions when each of the elements, $d\omega$, $d\phi$ and $d\kappa$ is less than 10^{-5} radian. In an interesting study, Pope (1972) suggested that quantities related to both the parameters and the observations should be updated for each such iteration.

The collinearity condition being applicable in various cases of diverse nature, the solution of the corresponding equations are also of different types. These are discussed in detail in the respective chapters 6, 8 and 9.

4.2 COPLANARITY CONDITION

The Coplanarity condition (see Fig. 4.3) implies that the two perspective centers, any object point and the corresponding image points on the two photographs of the stereo-pair, must all lie in a common plane. This condition is fundamental to *Relative Orientation* or *Space Intersection.* When relative orientation is achieved, the vector $\vec{R}_{1i}$ (from O_1 to P_i) will have an intersection with the vector $\vec{R}_{2i}$ (from O_2 to P_i) and these two vectors together with the air-base vector $\vec{b}$ will be coplanar. This means that their scalar triple product is zero. The function (mathematical model) F_i is

$$F_i = \vec{b} \cdot \vec{R}_{1i} \times \vec{R}_{2i=} = 0 \tag{4.16}$$

This, written in a determinant form is:

$$\boldsymbol{F}_1 = \begin{vmatrix} b_X & b_Y & b_Z \\ X_{1i} & Y_{1i} & Z_{1i} \\ X_{2i} & Y_{2i} & Z_{2i} \end{vmatrix} = 0 \tag{4.17}$$

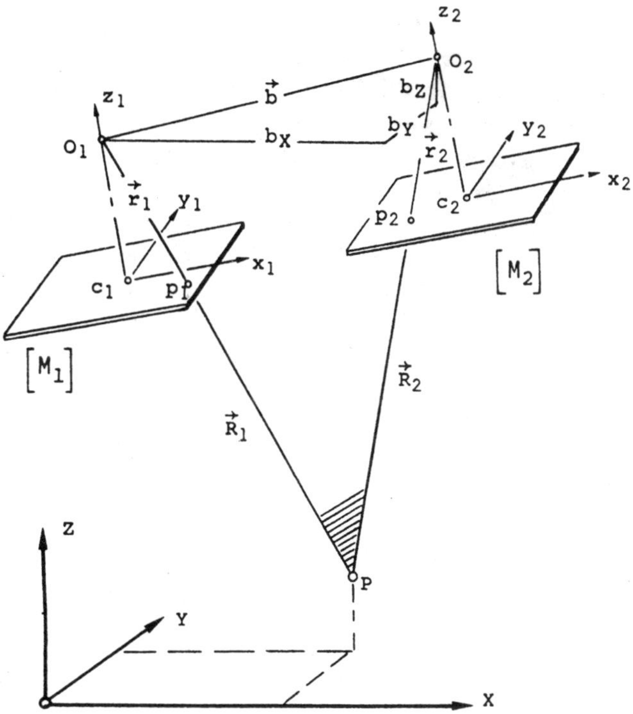

Fig. 4.3: Coplanarity condition and intersection for relative orientation

Also, in view of expressions 4.6 and 4.7,

$$\vec{b}' = \begin{bmatrix} b_X \\ b_Y \\ b_Z \end{bmatrix}; \ \vec{R}_{1i} = k_1 \boldsymbol{M}_1^{\mathrm{T}} \vec{r}_{1i} \ \ \textit{and} \ \ \vec{R}_{2i} = k_2 \boldsymbol{M}_2^{\mathrm{T}} \vec{r}_{2i}$$

where

k_1 and k_2 are the scale factors of the corresponding location vectors $\vec{r}_1$ and $\vec{r}_2$ within the camera spaces

$\boldsymbol{M}_1$ and $\boldsymbol{M}_2$ are the orientation matrices for photographs 1 and 2, respectively.

One coplanarity condition equation may be written for each of the object points used in a solution. It has the main advantage that the coordinates of the points in the object space may be avoided in its application. Modifications of Eq. 4.17 are utilized to express the condition in different forms:

(a) *Y*-parallax of a point in the image space (with certain conditions, e.g., alignment of the photo bases in the pair) equal to zero;
(b) *Y*-parallax of a point in the model space equal to zero (as is usual in analogical procedures with a stereoplotter); or
(c) The minimum distance between corresponding rays equal to zero (discussed later).

These concepts are extended in incorporating linear features into the computation of relative orientation in digital photogrammetric approaches.

The intersection of five pairs of rays $\vec{R}_1$ and $\vec{R}_2$ is the requirement for a relative orientation (Ghosh, 1972). Since the coordinates of points in object space are not included, the coplanarity condition equations by themselves (without scale and model orientation considerations) are not sufficient for a complete solution of any phototriangulation problem. It has, however, been used for systems involving simultaneous intersection solution of all photographs in the triangulation. Like the Collinearity condition equations, these are also non-linear and need to be linearized. The partial derivatives in this respect are given in the Appendix.

In the simplest procedure of its application, consider a *Dependent* method of *Relative Orientation* and the same scale factor (equated to unity) for all points in the two photos of a stereopair. Also consider the left hand side photo being fixed, i.e.,

$$k_1 = k_2 = 1 \text{ and } \omega_1 = \phi_1 = \kappa_1 = by_1 = bz_1 = 0$$

also $\quad b_Y = by_2 - by_1$ and $b_Z = bz_2 - bz_1$

The vectors $\vec{R}_{1i}$ and $\vec{R}_{2i\,i}$ are then reduced to

$$R_{1i} = \begin{bmatrix} X_{1i} \\ Y_{1i} \\ Z_{1i} \end{bmatrix} = \begin{bmatrix} 1 & 0 & 0 \\ 0 & 1 & 0 \\ 0 & 0 & 1 \end{bmatrix} \begin{bmatrix} x_{1i} \\ y_{1i} \\ -f \end{bmatrix} = \begin{bmatrix} x_{1i} \\ y_{1i} \\ -f \end{bmatrix} \tag{4.18}$$

$$R_{2i} = \begin{bmatrix} X_{2i} \\ Y_{2i} \\ Z_{2i} \end{bmatrix} = \begin{bmatrix} x_{2i} \cos\phi \cos\kappa - y_{2i} \cos\phi \sin\kappa - f \sin\phi \\ x_{2i} (\cos\omega \sin\kappa + \sin\omega \sin\phi \cos\kappa) + y_{2i} (\cos\omega \cos\kappa \\ -\sin\omega \sin\phi \sin\kappa) + f \sin\omega \cos\phi \\ x_{2i} (\sin\omega \sin\kappa - \cos\omega \sin\phi \cos\kappa) + y_{2i} (\sin\omega \cos\kappa \\ +\cos\omega \sin\phi \sin\kappa) - f \cos\omega \cos\phi \end{bmatrix} \tag{4.19}$$

Here, ω, ϕ and κ ares for the right-hand side camera (i.e., number 2). Now, with substitutions, of Eqs 4.18 and 4.19 into Eq. 4.17, and also rearranging, one gets the mathematical model:

$$\begin{aligned} F_i = & \{b_X y_{1i} - by_2 x_{1i}\}\{x_{2i}(\sin\omega\ \sin\kappa - \cos\omega \sin\phi \cos\kappa) \\ & + y_{2i}(\sin\omega \cos\kappa + \cos\omega\ \sin\phi\ \sin\kappa) - f\cos\omega\cos\phi\} \\ & + \{b_x f + bz_2 x_{1i}\}\{x_{2i}(\cos\omega\ \sin\kappa + \sin\omega \sin\phi \cos\kappa) \\ & + y_{2i}(\cos\omega\cos\kappa - \sin\omega\ \sin\phi \sin\kappa) + f\sin\omega\cos\phi\} \\ & + \{by_2 f + bz_2 y_{1i}\}\{y_{2_i} \cos\phi \sin\kappa - x_{2_i} \cos\phi\cos\kappa + f\sin\phi\} \\ = & \ 0 \end{aligned} \tag{4.20}$$

4.2.1 Linearization of Coplanarity Equation

The same concept as applicable to the linearization of the collinearity condition equations and expressed in Eq. 4.12 is valid in this case also. The observed quantities are the image coordinates, x_{1i}, y_{1i} and x_{2i}, y_{2i}, refined for the systematic errors (distortions) as discussed in Chap. 5. The general form here, therefore, is also

$$(F_0) + [A](V) + [B](\Delta) = 0 \tag{4.21}$$

where, with explanations, of the terms similar to Eq. 4.12, one gets:

$$[A_i] = \begin{bmatrix} \frac{\partial F_i}{\partial x_{1i}} & \frac{\partial F_i}{\partial y_{1i}} & \frac{\partial F_i}{\partial x_{2i}} & \frac{\partial F_i}{\partial y_{2i}} \end{bmatrix} \tag{4.22}$$

$$[B_i] = \begin{bmatrix} \frac{\partial F_i}{\partial by_2} & \frac{\partial F_i}{\partial bz_2} & \frac{\partial F_i}{\partial \omega_2} & \frac{\partial F_i}{\partial \phi_2} & \frac{\partial F_i}{\partial k_2} \end{bmatrix} \tag{4.23}$$

$$(V_i) = \begin{bmatrix} v_{x_1} \\ v_{y_1} \\ v_{x_2} \\ v_{y_2} \end{bmatrix}_i \tag{4.24}$$

$$(\Delta) = \begin{bmatrix} \delta by_2 \\ \delta bz_2 \\ \delta\omega_2 \\ \delta\phi_2 \\ \delta\kappa_2 \end{bmatrix} \tag{4.25}$$

The partial derivatives are given in Appendix B. For full derivations and ideas of the sizes and forms of these matrices, see Ghosh (1975) Appendix A.

4.2.2 Solution of Coplanarity Equation

For basic ideas on adjustment computations one may refer to several books, e.g., Hirvonen (1971) or Mikhail (1976). With regard to the application of the principle of Least Squares, in this case, one obtains the solution vector (of corrections to the approximate parameters):

$$\Delta = -(B^T M^{-1} B)^{-1} B^T M^{-1} F_o \tag{4.26}$$

where

$$M = AW^{-1}A^T$$

Note : This M is not to be confused with M used for the Rotation matrix used elsewhere in the book.

W = Weight matrix associated with the observations.

$$V^T WV = -K^T_L Fo \tag{4.27}$$

where

$$K_L = -M^{-1}(B\Delta + F_o)$$

The unit variance, m^2_o, is given by

$$m^2_o = \frac{V^T WV}{r-u} \tag{4.28}$$

where $(r - u)$ is the *degrees of freedom; r* being the number of condition equations, and u being the number of unknown quantities. The variance-covariance matrix of unknown parameters is

$$\Sigma_\Delta = m^2_0 Q_\Delta \tag{4.29}$$

and the weight coefficient matrix of Δ can be expressed as

$$Q_\Delta = (B^T M^{-1} B)^{-1} \tag{4.30}$$

The corrections (Δ) are added to the approximate (initial for the particular iteration) values of the parameters used in computing the coefficients of F_i, A_i and B_i. The number of iterations would depend on the initial approximations, the parameters, the geometric strength of the stereo-model and the desired precision. As was discussed in Section 4.1, a good method is to terminate the iterations when the incremental corrections to the parameters are smaller than their observational precision.

4.2.3 Intersected Point and Parallax

The condition for relative orientation of a photo-pair is the intersection of five (evenly distributed) pairs of rays, $\vec{R_1}$ and $\vec{R_2}$. It is quite possible that some rays fail to intersect, giving thereby residual *parallaxes*. One must, therefore, consider an acceptable point which will represent the location of intersection for the purpose of mensurations. Generally, the point midway along the vector $\vec{D}$ representing the parallax (see Fig. 4.4) in the region where the rays come closest, is chosen. The direction (but not the length) of $\vec{D}$ which is perpendicular to both $\vec{R_1}$ and $\vec{R_2}$ is

$$\vec{D} = \vec{R_1} \times \vec{R_2} \tag{4.31}$$

It will follow directly from Fig. 4.4 that

$$k_1.\vec{R_1} - k_2.\vec{R_2} + d.\vec{D} = \vec{b} \qquad (4.32)$$

where k_1, k_2 and d are three unknown scalar multipliers. Eq. 4.32 can be solved for the three scalars.

Note: From the principles of vector analysis (see for example, Coxeter, 1969), any four vectors, *a, b, c,* and *d* in three-dimensional space can be related to each other through

$$(a \times b) \times (c \times d) = (a.c \times d)b - (b.c \times d)\,a \;=\; (a.b \times d)\,c - (a.b \times c)d$$

This gives,

$$(a.b \times c)d - (b.c \times d)a + (c.d \times a)b - (d.a \times b)c = 0 \qquad (4.33)$$

Consider equating vectors, *a, b, c* and *d* with $\vec{b}, \vec{R_1}, \vec{D}$ and $\vec{R_2}$. While Eq. 4.33 is valid for any four vectors, Eq. 4.32 is valid for unique values of k_1, k_2 and d. These considerations give (see Ghosh, 1975 for explanations):

$$k_1 = \frac{\vec{b}\,\vec{D} \times \vec{R_2}}{\vec{R_1}\,\vec{D} \times \vec{R_2}}; \qquad k_2 = \frac{\vec{R_1}\,\vec{D} \times \vec{b}}{\vec{R_1}\,\vec{D} \times \vec{R_2}} \quad \text{and} \quad d = \frac{\vec{R_1}\,\vec{b} \times \vec{R_2}}{\vec{R_1}\,\vec{D} \times \vec{R_2}} \qquad (4.34)$$

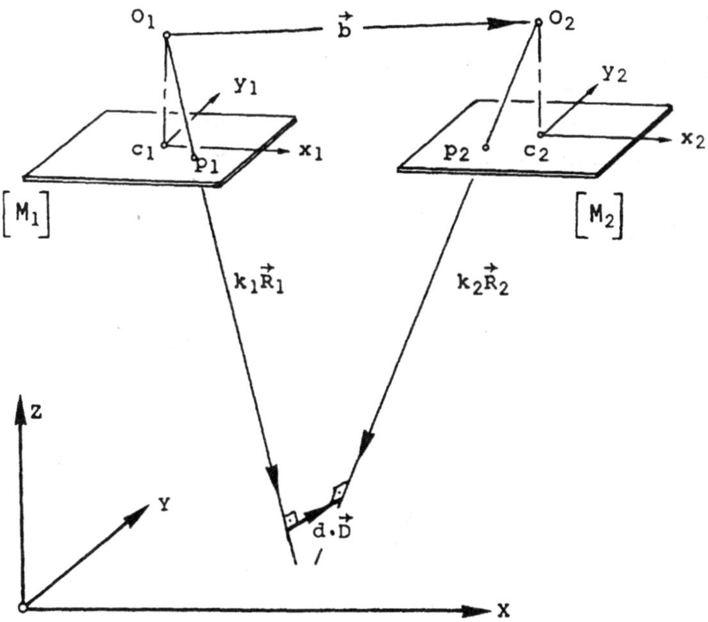

Fig. 4.4: Parallax in a stereo-model

The vectors $\vec{R_1}$ and $\vec{R_2}$ are determined by using Eqs 4.18 and 4.19 after orientation matrices $\boldsymbol{M}_1$ and $\boldsymbol{M}_2$ are finally evaluated. The base components *bx, by* and *bz* are determined after the relative orientation solution. the coordinates of each model point are determined next from

$$\begin{bmatrix} X \\ Y \\ Z \end{bmatrix} = \begin{bmatrix} X_{01} \\ Y_{01} \\ Z_{o1} \end{bmatrix} + k_1 \begin{bmatrix} R_{1X} \\ R_{1Y} \\ R_{1Z} \end{bmatrix} + (0.5)d \begin{bmatrix} D_X \\ D_Y \\ D_Z \end{bmatrix} \tag{4.35}$$

The coordinates of the perspective center O_1 in the case of a single model could be assumed to be (0,0,0). In the case of a strip formation they are equal to the perspective center O_2 of the preceding model, and by way of adding the components of the base to the previous perspective center coordinates, one can obtain the coordinates of the new perspective center:

$$\begin{bmatrix} X_{O2} \\ Y_{O2} \\ Z_{O2} \end{bmatrix} = \begin{bmatrix} X_{O_1} \\ Y_{O1} \\ Z_{O1} \end{bmatrix} + \begin{bmatrix} bx \\ by \\ bz \end{bmatrix} \tag{4.36}$$

An expression for the vector $\vec{D}$ (Eq. 4.31) can be written in the form

$$\vec{D} = \begin{bmatrix} D_X \\ D_Y \\ D_Z \end{bmatrix} = \begin{bmatrix} Y_1Z_2 & - & Z_1Y_2 \\ Z_1X_2 & - & X_1Z_2 \\ X_1Y_2 & - & Y_1X_2 \end{bmatrix} \tag{4.37}$$

The residual spatial parallax at each model point is computed as follows:

$$\text{Parallax} = (d \cdot (D^2_x + D^2_y + D^2_z)^{1/2} \tag{4.38}$$

Because the line of flight is along the X = axis, it is possible as a harmless approximation to choose for $\vec{D}$ the unit vector along the Y direction. With such a simplification one obtains the following working expressions (see Fig. 4.5 for a simple explanation):

$$k_1 = \frac{R_{2Z}.bx - R_{2X}.bz}{R_{2Z}.R_{1X} - R_{2X}.R_{1Z}} = \frac{Z_2.bx - X_2.bz}{Z_2.X_1 - X_2.Z_1} \tag{4.39}$$

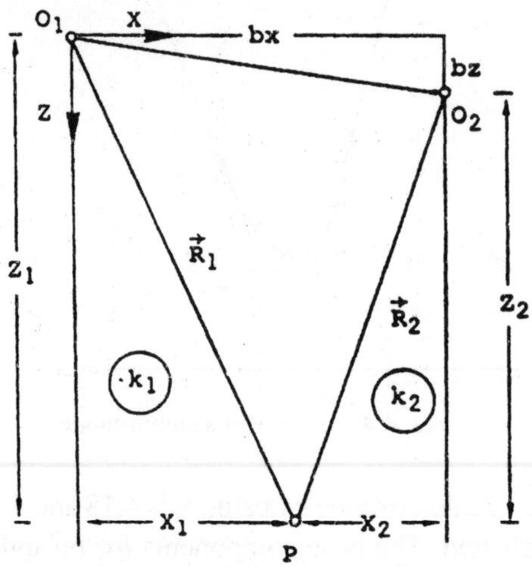

Fig. 4.5: Situation on *X-Z* plane, explanation of scale factors

$$k_2 = \frac{R_{1X}.bz - R_{1Z}.bx}{R_{2Z}.R_{1X} - R_{2X}.R_{1Z}} = \frac{X_1.bz - Z_1.bx}{Z_2.X_1 - X_2.Z_1} \tag{4.40}$$

$$d = (Y_{O2} + k_2.R_{2Y}) - (Y_{O1} + k_1.R_{1Y}) = (Y_{O2} + k_2.Y_2) - (Y_{O1} + k_1.Y_1) \tag{4.41}$$

The coordinates of the required point in the model are, in view of the simplifications (*cf.* Eq. 4.35):

$$\left.\begin{aligned} X &= X_{O1} + k_1.X_1 \\ Y &= (0.5)\,[(Y_{O2} + k_2.Y_2) + (Y_{O1} + k_1.Y_1)] \\ Z &= Z_{O1} + k_1.Z_1 \end{aligned}\right\} \tag{4.42}$$

A further practical simplification would be to consider $k_1 = k_2$ in each model. It is now apparent that the Coplanarity Condition involves both interior and exterior orientations of each of the two photographs without considering the object-space coordinates. Such information may be included any time if an indentifiable control point appears on two or more photos in the block or strip.

4.3 SCALE RESTRAINT CONDITION

This condition is generally applicable in sequential photo-triangulation procedure. It corresponds to *scale transfer* as performed in the aeropolygon method of phototriangulation (Ghosh, 1975). In the Independent Models method of photo-triangulation, this is automatically applied through the three-dimensional transformation of adjacent models.

The geometry of this condition is illustrated in Fig. 4.6. The three model- (or object-) space vectors $\vec{R}_1, \vec{R}_2$ and $\vec{R}_3$ to a point *P* may fail to intersect at a common point due to scale

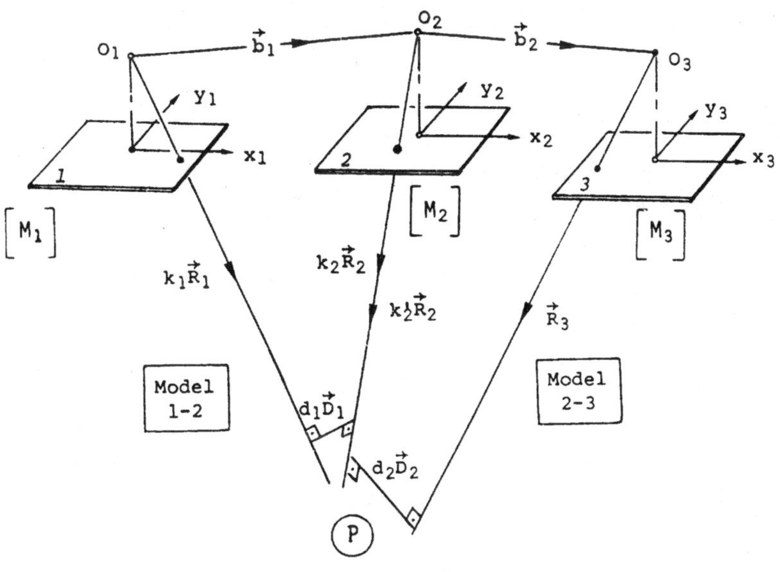

Fig. 4.6: Scale restraint condition geometry

variations even though the two adjacent models have been otherwise properly oriented. The vector R_1 and R_2 intersect in stereomodel 1-2 while R_2 and R_3 intersect in model 2-3. Therefore, one may consider two scalar multipliers k_2 and k_2' for the same vector R_2 in the first and second models, respectively. By applying Eq. 4.34 in stereomodel 1-2,

$$k_2 = \frac{\vec{R}_1 \vec{D}_1 \times \vec{b}_1}{\vec{R}_1 \vec{D}_1 \times \vec{R}_2} \tag{4.43}$$

Similarly, in stereo-model 2-3, for the same vector $\vec{R}_2$ (which corresponds to k_1 in Eq. 4.34), one gets here,

$$k'_2 = \frac{\vec{b}_2 \vec{D}_2 \times \vec{R}_3}{\vec{R}_2 \vec{D}_2 \times \vec{R}_3} \tag{4.44}$$

In order to obtain the two intersections in the two models at the same point, these two scalar multipliers must match, i.e., they must be equal in magnitude but opposite in sign, i.e.,

$$k_2 + k'_2 = 0 \quad \text{...(4.45)}$$

Eq. 4.45, expressing the scale restraint condition, is always used in conjunction with the coplanarity equations. There may arise a question whether a third coplanarity equation assuring an intersection between vectors $\vec{R}_1$ and $\vec{R}_3$ and would accomplish the same result. However, in normal strips with straight line flights, it is possible that the three vectors $\vec{R}_1, \vec{R}_2$ and $\vec{R}_3$ lie on the same plane. Consequently, the vectors may mutually intersect at three different points, on the same plane. Thus, the coplanarity equation by itself is not enough.

During the strip formation in a sequential phototriangulation process, it is required that the coplanarity and scale restraint conditions (i.e., corresponding to relative orientation and scale transfer, respectively) are applied successively in each model. The practical steps suggested by Ghosh (1975) are as follows:

Step 1: At the (i-1)th model (i.e., with photographs i-1 and i): $k_{i-1} = k_i$ (i.e., k_1 and k_2 are both known). Compute X, Y, Z coordinates of all points in this model. Also known in this model are, X_{01}, Y_{01}, Z_{01} and X_{02}, Y_{02}, Z_{02} i.e., the perspective centers of photographs i-1 and i.

Step 2: At the ith model (i.e., with photographs i and i+1): Perform co-orientation (coplanarity equation) considering $k_{1i} = k_{2i-1}$ (i.e., the same scale as of the previous model). With this k, obtain Z of the points common with the previous model.

Also compute, bx, by and bz of this model (i.e., vector $\vec{b}_i$). If now, $Zp_{i-1} = Zp_i$ within permissible limits, it is all right. If it is not,obtain corrections to k_{1i} (i.e., k_1 of this model). Then correct bx, by and bz proportionately.

Next, obtain the coordinates of the perspective center for the (i+1)th photograph i.e.,

$$X_{O_{i+1}} = X_{O_i} + bx_i; Y_{O_{i+1}} = Y_{O_i} + by_i \text{ and } Z_{O_{i+1}} = Z_{O_i} + bz_i$$

Now, by using Eqs 4.39 and 4.40, check if $k_{1_i} = k_{2_{i-1}}$. If not, repeat Step 2.

If yes, compute finally *X, Y, Z* coordinates of all points in this model.

Step 3: At the (*i*+1)th model (i.e., with photographs *i*+1 and *i*+2): Repeat the operations of Step 2.

4.4 ANGULAR RELATIONSHIP CONDITION

It was first observed by Church (Church and Quinn, 1944) that in order to maintain correct perspectivity, the angles subtended at the perspective center between points in the object space must equal the corresponding angles in the camera space. By imposing this condition of angular relationship (also known by the name of Church, as the *Church Condition),* one can solve the space resection and other problems (also see, Chap. 6).

By obtaining the photo coordinates (x', y') from observation data and considering the focal length (f) along with the photo coordinates of the principal point (x_o, y_o), one can establish the location vector ($\vec{r}$) of any point observed on the photo (Eq. 4.3). Subsequently, the angles (∇) between the vectors subtended at the perspective center are easily obtained.

In Fig. 4.7, *a, b* and *c* are images of object points *A, B* and *C* respectively, giving the corresponding camera-space location vectors $\vec{r}_a, \vec{r}_b$ and $\vec{r}_c$. Angles ∇_{ab}, ∇_{bc} and ∇_{ca} are subtended at the perspective center, *O*, between the points as indicated in the subscripts. In view of three components (*x, y* and *f*) of these vectors, by using the principles of *'dot product'*, one can compute the space-angles between two vectors from the following, for example,

$$\cos \nabla_{ab} = \frac{x_a x_b + y_a y_b + f^2}{|r_a| \cdot |r_b|} \tag{4.46}$$

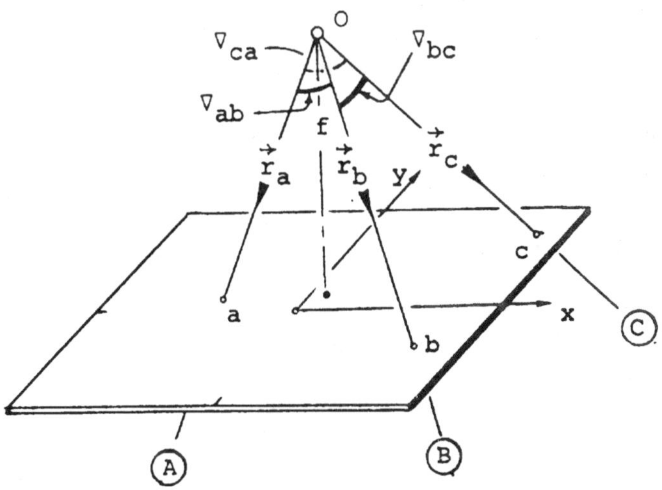

Fig. 4.7: Angular configuration at perspective center

where $|r_a|$ and $|r_b|$ are the absolute values of the corresponding vectors, i.e.

$|r_a| = (x_a^2 + y_a^2 + f^2)^{1/2}$ and $|r_b| = (x_b^2 + y_b^2 + f^2)^{1/2}$

Similar expressions can be written for cos ∇_{bc} and cos ∇_{ca}.

All parameters in Eq. 4.46 are know, either from camera calibration (*f*), or from observations (*x, y* photo coordinates: refined in view of various known distortion corrections). With regard to the corresponding location vectors for the object points, considering coordinates in the object space,

$$\cos \nabla_{ab} = \cos \nabla_{AB}$$

$$= \frac{(X_A - X_O)(X_B - X_O) + (Y_A - Y_O)(Y_B - Y_O) + (Z_A - Z_O)(Z_B - Z_O)}{|R_A|.|R_B|} \quad (4.47)$$

where

$$|R_A| = [(X_A - X_O)^2 + (Y_A - Y_O)^2 + (Z_A - Z_O)^2]^{1/2}$$

and

$$|R_B| = [(X_B - X_O)^2 + (Y_B - Y_O)^2 + (Z_B - Z_O)^2]^{1/2}$$

Similar expressions can be written for cos∇_{BC} and cos∇_{CA} also. Depending on the circumstances, the angular relationship between the camera and object spaces can be utilized to solve various problems. One case is that of space resection where X_O, Y_O, Z_O coordinates of the perspective center are to be determined (Section 6.1.3). Another typical case is its application in camera calibration where all coordinates in the object space may be known but the camera focal length (*f*) and the associated lens distortion affecting observed photo coordinates are to be determined.

It may be pertinent to comment here on the relationship between the corresponding location vectors in the camera and object spaces, viz.,

$$\vec{r_a} = \lambda_a . \vec{R_A} \; ; \vec{r_b} = \lambda_b . \vec{R_B} \text{ and } \vec{r_c} = \lambda_c . \vec{R_C} \quad (4.48)$$

where λ_a λ_b and λ_c are scalar multipliers (scale factors) which are different, but have the same value only if the terrain is perfectly flat and if the photo plane is parallel to the other plane (i.e., no camera tilt).

Another form of Eq. 4.47 can be obtained by inserting the direction cosines for respective directions. For example, with regard to points *A* and *B*, Eq. 4.47 can be written as follows (*cf.* α, β and γ in Fig. 4.2)

$$\cos\nabla_{AB} = \cos \alpha_A \cos \alpha_B + \cos \beta_A \cos \beta_B + \cos \gamma_A \cos \gamma_B \quad (4.49)$$

Similar amplifications can be made with respect to the camera space also.

4.5 CRITICAL GEOMETRY

The concept of critical geometry has one-, two- or three-dimensional implications in photogrammetry. One very well-known two-dimensional analogy is obtained from the problem of planimetric resection, in surveying, where if the observer's station (unknown) falls on a circle passing through three or more known stations, the solution for the observer's station is indeterminable. This is known as the *critical circle.* Such critical geometric circumstances may arise in photogrammetry even with an added spatial dimension and are known as *critical surfaces*.

Mathematically speaking, a critical condition arises when there exist dependent variables indicating correlations.

Note: *Mathematical dependency:* A matrix $Y = c_1X_1 + c_2X_2 + ... + c_mX_m$ is said to be a linear combination of the m matrices $X_1, X_2, ... X_m$ of the same order, where $c_1, c_2 ... c_m$ are scalars. If a linear combination, in which not all scalars are zero, is equal to the null matrix, then the matrices are said to be "linearly dependent", (Faddeeva, 1959) i.e., when

$$c_1X_1 + c_2X_2 + ... + c_mX_m = \bar{0}$$

The significance of such linear dependency can be studied from a simple example of a set of linearized condition equations for two parameters:

$$[a_1, a_2...a_m]^T . \delta X + [b_1, b_2...b_m]^T.\delta Y = [c_1, c_2...c_m]^T \tag{4.50}$$

A solution of these equations is possible by an arbitrary choice of one of the values (say, δX). A consistent solution of all equations is possible then by one appropriate but correspondingly incorrect value for δY. Therefore, a check in this respect for such dependencies will be of worthwhile significance. One such test would be provided through an analysis of the $\dot{B}$ matrix for linearly dependent columns. In this respect, the Normal Equations provide a means for isolating critical geometries also. Consider e.g., the (above) two-parameter problem. Assuming that normal equations are formed (X being the solution vector and U being the constant vector),

$$NX + U = \bar{0} \tag{4.51}$$

Using Gaussian notations, $|N| = \begin{bmatrix} \Sigma aa & \Sigma ab \\ \Sigma ba & \Sigma bb \end{bmatrix}$

The test for singularity of N is: $|N| = 0$, in which case no solutions of the normal equations is possible because N^{-1} is not defined. However, considering $ka = b$, where k is a scalar, one gets

$$|N| = (\Sigma aa)\ (\Sigma bb) - (\Sigma ab)\ (\Sigma ba) = (\Sigma aa)\ k^2\ (\Sigma aa) - (\Sigma aa)\ k\ (\Sigma aa)\ k = \bar{0} \tag{4.52}$$

Therefore, $|N|$ is singular for linearly dependent (condition) equations. Several representative examples are given below as illustrations.

A. Single photo case (one-dimensional implication)

Consider a vertical photo taken on a flat terrain, where the focal length (f) and the flying height (h) above ground, both, are not known. It would be apparent from Fig. 4.8 that if the same photo can be considered with respect to two different locations of the perspective center (O' and O''), and accordingly, two different focal lengths (f' and f'') would correspond with two different flying heights (h' and h''). The perspective geometry would be maintained to give direct one-to-one correspondence between all points on each location of the photo and their respective ground locations. This indicates a correlation between f and h and indicates a direct dependency, f/h being a constant. The correct value of one of the two would remain indeterminable without the knowledge of the other. On the other hand, in so far as the 2D photo- or ground-coordinates are concerned, this correlation situation has no effect, f/h being the constant scale factor.

From the point of view of mathematical considerations, consider here the application of the collinearity condition (general projective) equation in the partial differential form giving the B matrix (i.e., the total array of partials with respect to unknown parameters). Since the photo is vertical, $\omega = \phi = \kappa = 0$. The flying height h corresponds to $(Z - Z_0)$. In this case, the elements of the B matrix are as in Table 4.2. The terrain being flat, $(Z - Z_0)$ is a constant. Table 4.2 indicates a strong correlation between f and $(Z - Z_0)$ to involve the factor $f/(Z - Z_0)$, a scalar multiple, whereby it will not be possible to separate x_0, y_0 and f from X_0, Y_0 and Z_0, respectively. In case the terrain is flat yet sloping, it may not change the fundamental geometry problem; however, in this case the tilt (ω) may be considered to be exchanged for the slope and then

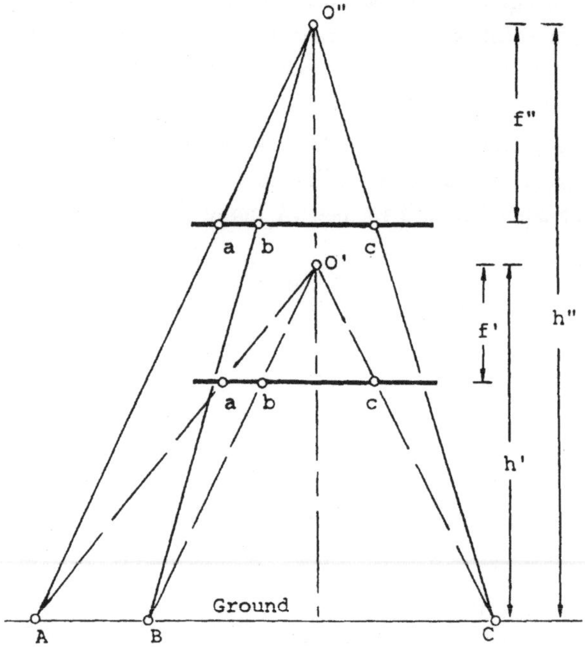

Fig. 4.8: Correlation between focal length and flying height

$\omega \neq 0$, hence some correlations are avoidable. This demonstrates a fundamental problem in calibrating a camera with photographs taken over a test area of flat terrain. Part of the problem is avoided by tilting the camera heavily, but the best would be to use for the test range a terrain where $(Z - Z_0)$ is not constant since f remains a constant with a photogrammetric camera.

Table 4.2

Elements of the coefficient matrix, B, of parameters (single photo resection)

	x_0	y_0	f	x_0	y_0	z_0
$f(x)$	−1	0	$\frac{(X - X_0)}{(Z - Z_0)}$	$\frac{f}{(Z - Z_0)}$	0	$-f\frac{(X - X_0)}{(Z - Z_0)^2}$
$f(y)$	0	−1	$\frac{(Y - Y_0)}{(Z - Z_0)}$	0	$\frac{f}{(Z - Z_0)}$	$-f\frac{(Y - Y_0)}{(Z - Z_0)^2}$

B. Arrangement of fiducial marks (two-dimensional implication)

In one experiment on the use of additional fiducial marks towards improved accuracy (McIntosh, 1972), the arrangement of eight fiducial marks was as in Fig. 4.9(a). Considering all significant terms, the resulting equations were:

$$\Delta x = a_0 + a_1x + a_2y + a_3x^2 + a_4y^2 + a_5xy + a_6x^2y + a_7xy^2$$
$$\Delta y = b_0 + b_1x + b_2y + b_3x^2 + b_4y^2 + b_5xy + b_6x^2y + b_7xy^2$$

where Δx, Δy are the differences between the 'known' x, y and the 'observed' x, y values. and a's and b's are the instrumental constants (coefficients).

a
Erroneous arrangement of fiducial marks

b
Correct arrangement of fiducial marks

Fig. 4.9: Studies in arrangement of fiducial marks in excess

In this case, the least squares solution yielded a standard deviation of 122 μm which was considered unacceptable as the system was known to be capable of giving a standard deviation of ~2 μm. An analysis of the N^{-1} matrix in the adjustment revealed strong correlations, and thus proved to be unreliable due to instability. The cause of this was discovered to be that the fiducial points were on or nearly close to a circle with the origin at the center. This situation establishes the relationship $x^2 + y^2 = R^2$. Furthermore, in this case obviously, R^2 is a constant and establishes a dependency of terms. Such a problem could be avoided by one or both of the following two ways:

(i) Consider the arrangement of fiducial marks as in Fig. 4.9 (b) such that they do not fall on the critical circle.
(ii) Consider a ninth point (say, the centroid of all the eight points, indicated by a cross in Fig. 4.9 (a) and use this extra point in the least squares adjustment procedure.

C. Relative Orientation (three-dimensional implication)

Consider a dependent relative orientation (coplanarity condition) by using the elements of the right hand side camera expressed by

$$Py - dby_{\text{II}} + \frac{Y}{Z}dbz_{\text{II}} + z\left(1 + \frac{Y^2}{Z^2}\right)d\omega_{\text{II}} - \frac{(X-b)Y}{Z}d\phi_{\text{II}} - (X-b)d\kappa_{\text{II}} = 0$$

A solution of this equation requires Py (Y-parallax) observations at five points. There may arise a situation when the equations cannot be solved because of a constant ratio between at least two of the elements. Consider a point b (Fig. 4.10) in the middle of the model such that $Y_b = 0$ and $Z_b = Z_0$. For a point c at the edge of model, $Y_c = Y$ and $Z_c = Z$. Then with respect to the

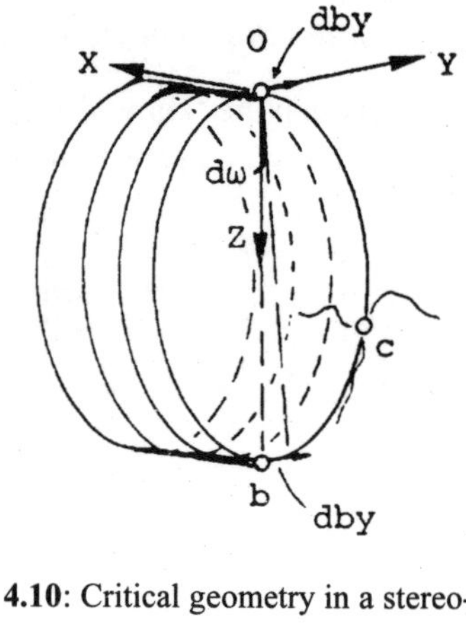

Fig. 4.10: Critical geometry in a stereo-model

coefficient of $d\omega$, considering points b and c, we get: $Z_0 = Z\,(1 + Y^2/Z^2)$, i.e., $Y^2 = Z_0 Z - Z^2$, which is the equation of a circle in the Y-Z plane. The movement for the element by is applied at the perspective center (O) where $Y = Z = 0$ and this by-movement is in a direction tangential to a circle passing through points b, c and O on the Y-Z plane. If the terrain is formed in such sectional profiles containing circles, one would have a critical geometry with correlation between the elements dby and $d\omega$. The meaning of this critical geometry is that a parallax-free model surface can be obtained in such a situation without being able to correctly solve for the elements (i.e., at the stereo-instrument, without being able to correctly set the particular elements). Thus, in such a case, the relative orientation is indeterminable. Such a sectional profile may extend into a critical surface for the stereo-model. Furthermore, such a surface may degenerate into a critical cylinder or a critical cone. For further interesting ideas on such surfaces, see Ghosh (1972). Real critical surfaces in nature are rare. However, a closeness to a critical surface may affect accuracy and should be avoided (Brandenberger, 1947) with proper prior planning of the job, or certain possible manipulations during the process.

BIBLIOGRAPHY

American Society of Photogrammetry; *Manual of Photogrammetry* (4th Ed,), ASPRS, Falls Church, Virginia; 1980.

Brandenberger, A.J.; *Fehlertheorie der äussern Orientierung von Steilaufnahmen;* Diss., ETH, Zürich; 1947.

Church, E. and A. Quinn; *Elements of Photogrammetry;* Syracuse University Press, Syracuse, N.Y.; 1944.

Coxeter, H. S. M.; *Introduction to Geometry*; John Wiley & Sons, Inc., N.Y.; 1969.

Eshbach, O. W.; *Handbook of Engineering Fundamentals* (2nd Ed); John Wiley & Sons, Inc., N.Y.; 1959.

Faddeeva, V. N.; *Computational Methods of Linear Algebra;* Dover Publications, Inc., N.Y.; 1959.

Ghosh, Sanjib K.; *Theory of Stereophotogrammetry* (2nd Ed); Ohio State University Bookstores, Columbus, Ohio; 1972.

Ghosh, Sanjib K.; *Phototriangulation*, Lexington Books, Lexington, Mass; 1975.

Harris, W. D., G.C. Tewinkel and C.A. Whitten; *Analytic Aerotriangulation*; Technical Bulletin No. 21 (Corrected), U. S. Departmemt of Commerce, Coast and Geodetic Survey; 1963.

Hirvonen, R.A.; *Adjustment by Least Squares;* F. Unger Publishing Co.; N.Y.; 1971.

McIntosh, Bernard W.; *Investigation of Aerial Film Distortion Compensation Techniques Based on Fiducial Marks;* M.Sc. Thesis, Ohio State University; 1972.

Mikhail, E. M.; *Observations and Least Squares;* IEP-A Dun-Donnelley Publisher, N.Y.; 1976.

Pope, A. J.; *Some Pitfalls to be Avoided in the Iterative Adjustments of Nonlinear Problems;* Presented paper at annual convention, ASP; 1972.

Schut, G. H.; *An Introduction to Analytical Strip Triangulation with a Fortran Program* (Revised Ed); NRC, Canada, Division of Physics, Publication No. NRC 13148; Ottawa, Canada; 1973.

5

REFINEMENT OF PHOTO COORDINATES

At a photogrammetric measuring instrument the location of an image point is measured in a rectangular 2-D coordinate system having ranges in both directions which are sufficiently large to cover the entire photograph. The origin of this, instrument coordinate system, may be outside the photograph and, depending on the initial settings, is arbitrarily located.

Most of the analytical procedures require the photo coordinates with the *Principal Point* as the origin. Therefore, such photo coordinates are to be obtained by subtracting the 'instrument coordinates' of the principal point from those of the image points. Various principal points used in practice may be noted (see also ASPRS Manual of Photogrammetry, 1980):

1. *Principal Point (Photogrammetry)*: The foot of the perpendicular from the interior perspective center to the plane of the photograph.
2. *Principal Point (optics)*: The point on the optical axis where it intersects the principal plane (from principles of optics).
3. *Principal Point of Autocollimation:* The point where a ray which in the object space is perpendicular to the plane of the photograph intersects that plane (used by NRC, Canada).
4. *Principal Point of Symmetry:* The point in the focal plane of the camera about which all lens distortions are symmetrical.

Usually, the principal point cannot be measured directly because it is not marked on the photograph. Furthermore, the photographic coordinates need to be established in a system of reference provided by the *fiducial marks*. The coordinates of the principal point are derived from those of the *fiducial center* (in the fiducial axes system) by way of using the camera calibration data. In practice, however, the fiducial center and the principal point are usually considered to be identical.

Corrections for comparator calibration effect (see Chap. 2) and for the réseau (discussed in Section 5.6) are to be applied before any corrections due to all external influences are considered. Usually, these are contained in the transformation equations used for the reduction of the photo coordinates. The errors due to the approximations in the mathematical models applied at various stages may be significant at times. The physical sources inherent in the system are discussed in this chapter. Analogically applied corrections and the computational refinement of data should give appreciably correct photo coordinates. It is imperative that these corrections are applied sequentially in the order reverse to that of their occurrence during the data acquisition procedure.

5.1 EMULSION CARRIER

The emulsion and its carrier (film or glass) may be subjected to dimensional distortions, which are functions of the material, environment (e.g., temperature and humidity), aging and treatment (e.g., chemical processing). The effect may sometimes be complicated. Such dimensional distortions can be of three categories:

A. Uniform (systematic) distortion

Shrinkage or expansion of uniform nature would produce a scale error, dl/l = a constant, for length ℓ measured on the photograph (see Fig. 5.1) in any direction. Such a distortion may be considered, for the sake of corrections, being radial from any point on the photo (say, the fiducial center). In the absence of a register glass with grid (réseau), measurement of the fiducial marks can give an indication of the distortion. The observed distances between such marks are compared with the corresponding true distances (obtained from the calibration information). This can be applied as a scale correction to all the observed coordinates.

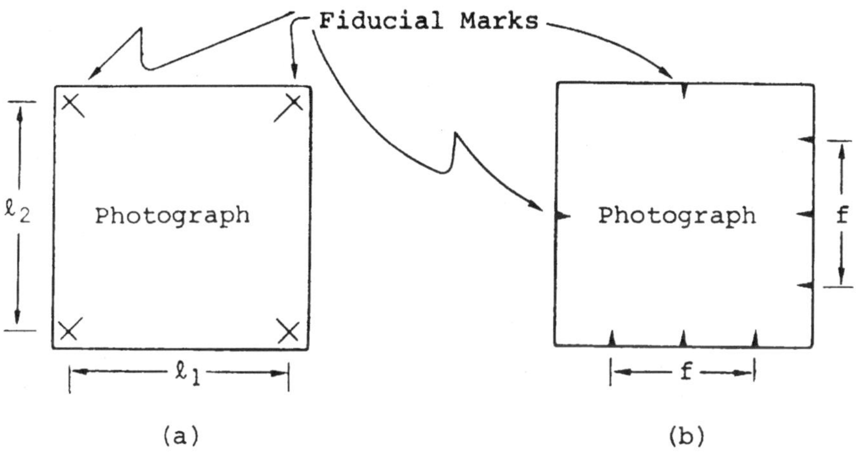

Fig. 5.1: Dimensional distortion checks in a photograph

B. Differential (systematic) distortion

One may often notice one systematic distortion along the length of the film and a different systematic distortion along the width of the film (note ℓ_1 and ℓ_2 in Fig. 5.1), giving an affine deformation of the photograph. This can be compensated by performing an affine transformation of the photocoordinates (see Section 3.3). Unfortunately, most cameras have only four fiducial marks. That is not sufficient for determination of non-linear dimensional distortion over the whole area of the photograph. Additional fiducial marks (e.g., combining the pattern in Figs. 5.1a and 5.1b) or réseau photography are other possible answers to such a problem.

C. Irregular (systematic) distortion

This may affect the photo-coordinates, being effected by various causes, e.g., varying elastic properties of the material, lack of flatness of the emulsion surface or localized emulsion creep. Such errors can be complex and do not follow any linear distribution pattern. These errors can be minimized only by using réseau photography.

In using four fiducial marks and considering systematic distortions, the effects can be compensated by using correction equations (after Keller and Tewinkel, 1965) as below:

$$\left.\begin{aligned} x' &= x + a_1 + b_1 x + c_1 y + d_1 xy \\ y' &= y + a_2 + b_2 x + c_2 y + d_2 xy \end{aligned}\right\} \tag{5.1}$$

where

x', y'	are the corrected photo coordinates;
x, y	are the observed photo coordinates; and
a's, d's	are certain coefficients, to be determined.

These coefficients can correct for several effects at the same time, viz., provide the translations to the origin (a_1, a_2); accomplish rotation and affine scale-corrections (b_1, b_2, c_1, c_2); and provide a quadratic or curvilinear correction (d_1, d_2) for film (i.e., emulsion base) distortion.

In this connection, it will be good to note that it is necessary for precision mensural work to have the image surface (surface of emulsion) absolutely flat. Lack of flatness may cause unsharpness or deviation or both. This, however, does not pose any great problem in the observational work if the instrument has an orthogonal (to the image surface) viewing. Furthermore, image unsharpness caused by movement of the camera during exposure (i.e., image smear) and the image quality parameters of the system (e.g, limiting resolving power) can be two causes of concern sometimes. While the former can be compensated by an appropriate Image Motion Compensation (IMC) device in the camera, the latter imposes limitation to the photogrammetric procedure. The difference in the sharpness of the two conjugate images comprising the stereoscopic model may contribute towards irregular pointing accuracies in the model. In jobs demanding very high precision, one has to consider all such factors very carefully.

5.2 LENS (OBJECTIVE) DISTORTION

All lenses in use now-a-days have measurable distortions and other optical defects (aberrations). The aberrations (viz., spherical and chromatic aberrations, coma, astigmatism and curvature of field) degrade the quality or the sharpness of image. Lens distortion, on the other hand, causes displacement of the image, which is unfavourable to precision measurements. It can have *radial* and *tangential* components. It is essential, therefore, that all camera objectives (lenses) be tested (calibrated) carefully. The *camera calibration* procedure determines the focal-length, the location of the principal point and all distortion parameters.

5.2.1 Radial Distortion

One must first assure the use of the intended principal point. The center of the perspective bundle of rays in the image space is considered along the perpendicular at the assumed principal point and at a distance equal to the calibrated focal length (f) from the photo plane. Let α be the field angle made by a ray with the perpendicular and let r be the distance of the image point from the principal point (Fig. 5.2). The radial distortion Δr is the radial distance between the actual and the ideal locations of the image point. This can be expressed by

$$\Delta r = r - f.\tan\alpha \tag{5.2}$$

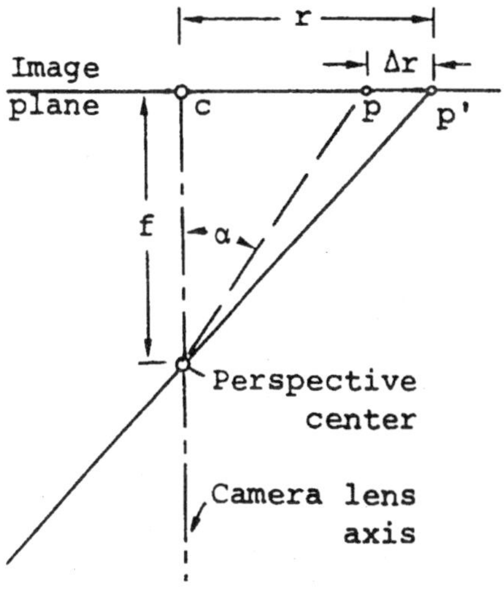

Fig. 5.2: Radial lens distortion

Eq. 5.2 shows that the radial distortion is a function of the assumed value of the focal length. In practice, one determines that value of the focal-length which makes the maximum difference between the values of the radial distortion and the standard reference values for the lens as small as possible. In case the reference values for the camera are not available, one determines that value of the focal length which makes the maximum value of the distortion as small as possible (by balancing the positive and the negative maximum values of Δr). This value is known as the Calibrated Focal Length. Consider the aberrations (Klein, 1970) and the following general hypotheses (after Conrady, 1919 and Washer, 1957):

(a) The axial ray passes undeviated through the lens;
(b) The distortion can be represented by a continuous function; and
(c) The sense of the distortion should be positive for all outward displacement of the image.

Accordingly, the following polynomial may be considered to approximate the radial lens distortion curve:

$$\Delta r = a_0 r + a_1 r^3 + a_2 r^5 + a_3 r^7 + a_4 r^9 + \ldots \tag{5.3}$$

The 'a' coefficients define the shape of the curve. They may be obtained through a least squares curve fitting computation during the camera calibration procedure. The radial distortion is considered in terms of two components (Δx and Δy, see Fig. 5.3). The radial distance (r) being equal to $\sqrt{(x^2 + y^2)}$, , the distortions and their components are related to each other as follows:

$$\frac{\Delta r}{r} = \frac{\Delta x}{x} = \frac{\Delta y}{y} \qquad ...(5.4)$$

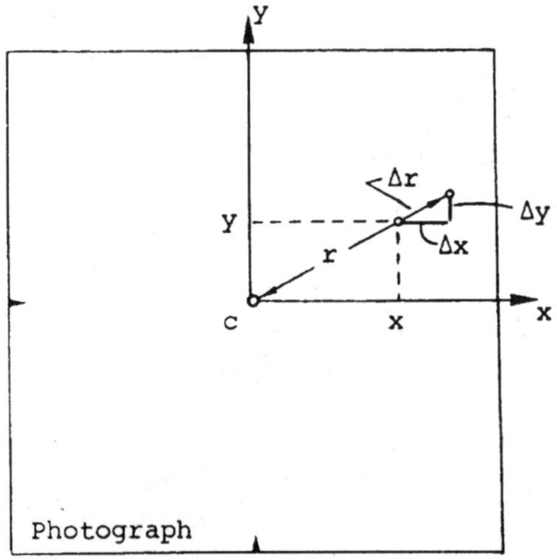

Fig. 5.3: Components of radial distortion

The corrected Photo coordinates (x', y') are given by

$$x' = x - \Delta x = x\left\{1 - \frac{\Delta r}{r}\right\} = x(1 - a_0 - a_1 r^2 - a_2 r^4 - ...)$$

$$y' = y - \Delta y = y\left\{1 - \frac{\Delta r}{r}\right\} = y(1 - a_0 - a_1 r^2 - a_2 r^4 - ...) \qquad (5.5)$$

In using Eq. 5.5., at least five to six terms in the series can be taken to express the correction adequately. In some organization (Harris *et al.*, 1962), such uniform lens distortion is corrected along with that for atmospheric refraction through the use of Eqs 5.6, in which the terms k_1 and k_2 relate to atmospheric refraction (see also Section 5.3):

$$x' = x\left\{1 + \frac{rd}{r^2} + k_1 + k_2 r^2\right\}$$

$$y' = y\left\{1 + \frac{rd}{r^2} + k_1 + k_2 r^2\right\} \qquad (5.6)$$

The value rd is obtained in the computer from tabulated values and interpolation based on r^2 as the independent argument as in Eq. 5.5. It may be recommended that the numerical precision of such data should be better than the precision obtainable from the consideration of the distortion alone. This is generally of the order of 0.1 μm with modern photogrammetric systems.

5.2.2 Decentering Distortion

This is due to imperfect centering of the lens components and other manufacturing defects in a compound lens. The consequences, occurring in many lenses, is roughly equal to the effect of adding a small prism to the lens. As a result, the distortion is asymmetric with respect to the principal point of autocollimation and the resulting effect is called *Tangential Distortion.* There is, however, always one radial line (called the axis of zero tangential distortion), which remains straight. Washer (1957) called it *Prism Effect.* The distortion can be referred to a different principal point. This implies that the center of the perspective bundle in the image space is shifted. As a result of this shift (also involving a rotations), the pattern of the distortion in the photo plane is changed. With narrow projective bundles, this shift of the principal point is very nearly the projective equivalent of a small tilt of the camera axis. This distortion pattern can be expressed (according to Brown, 1966; after Conrady, 1919) as below:

$$\left.\begin{aligned} \Delta x &= \{P_1\,(r^2 + 2x^2) + 2P_2xy\}\ \{1 + P_3r^2 + P_4r^4 + \ldots \\ \Delta y &= \{2P_1\,xy + P_2(r^2 + 2y^2)\}\ \{1 + P_3r^2 + P_4r^4 + \ldots \end{aligned}\right\} \tag{5.7}$$

where
$$\begin{aligned} P_1 &= -J_1 \,.\, \sin f_O \\ P_2 &= J_1 \,.\, \cos \phi_O \\ P_3 &= J_2/J_1 \\ P_4 &= J_3/J_4 \text{ etc.} \end{aligned}$$

J_1, J_2 etc., are the coefficients of the profile function of the decentering distortion;
ϕ_O is the angle subtended by the axis of maximum tangential distortion with the photo x-axis (see Figs. 5.4 and 5.5.);
and P's represent the tangential profile function, i.e., the tangential distortion at radial distance r along axis of maximum tangential distortion.

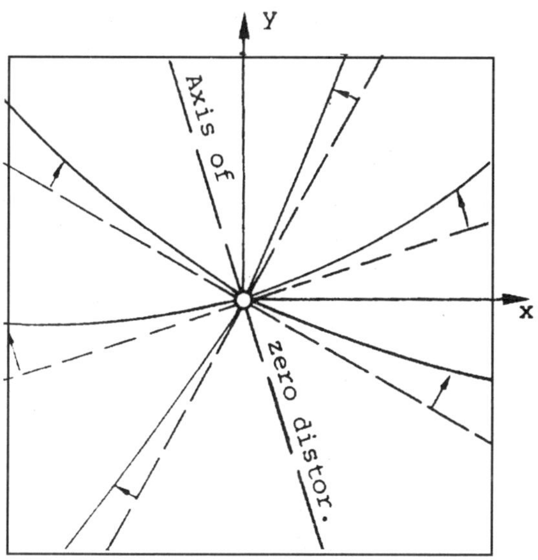

Fig. 5.4: Tangential distortion pattern

Decentering distortion can be effectively determined through calibration. But also it can be tolerated to the extent that it does not affect the accuracy to any considerable extent.

If one considers the shift and rotation (due to decentering distortion) made in such a way that the asymmetries in the radial distortion become as small as possible, the new principal point is called the principal point of best symmetry. If a shift of the perspective center parallel to a radial direction is a_1, the rotation associated to it is a_1/f, and the shift perpendicular to the plane of the photo is a_2 (Fig. 5.6). the resulting radial shift of a point of intersection of a ray and the radial is

$$dr = \underline{a}_1 - \frac{r^2 + f^2}{f^2}\underline{a}_1 + \frac{r}{f}\underline{a}_2 = -\frac{r^2}{f^2}\underline{a}_1 + \frac{r}{f}\underline{a}_2 \tag{5.8}$$

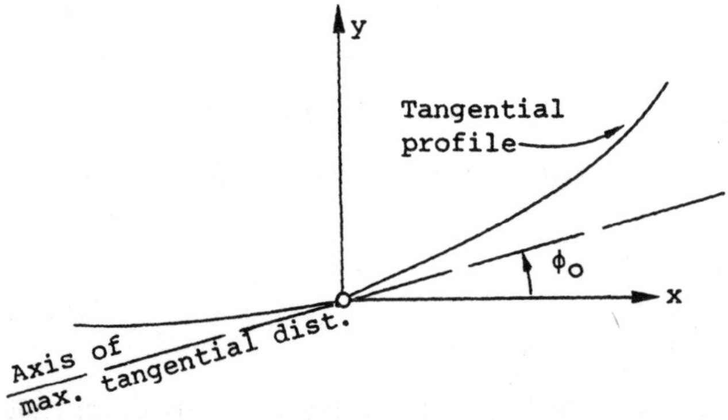

Fig. 5.5: Geometric significance of tangential distortion

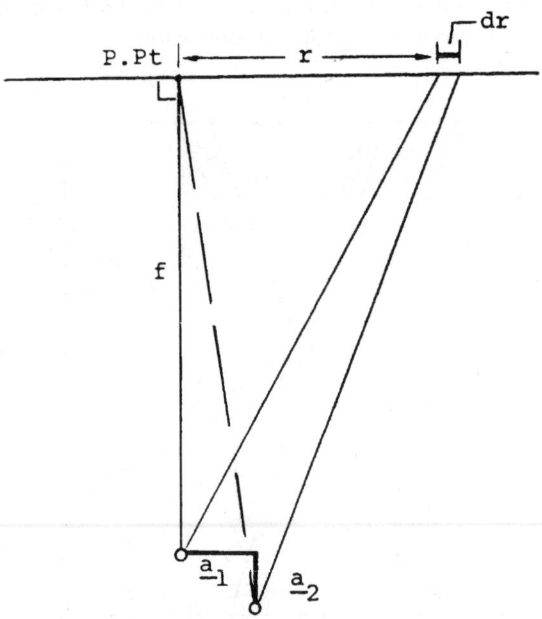

Fig. 5.6: Effect of change in the choice of principal point on radial distortion

For two points at equal distances on opposite sides of the principal point, the shifts (*dr*) must cancel the radial distortions valid for the principal point of autocollimation. By definition, the radial distance (*r*) is always positive, while the radial distortion (*dr*) is positive in the direction away from the principal point.

Therefore, for two such points (on opposite sides of the principal point), the required radial shifts dr_1 and $-dr_2$ give, by using Eq. 5.8:

$$dr_1 - dr_2 = -2\frac{r^2}{f^2}\underline{a}_1$$

$$dr_1 + dr_2 = 2\frac{r}{f}\underline{a}_2 \qquad (5.9)$$

The shifts a_1 and a_2 can thus be computed for each pair of radial distortions at equal distances on opposite sides of the principal point. The computation of the shifts can be performed for numerous point pairs on the two principal diagonals of the photo by using Eqs 5.9. This would help obtain the location of the principal point of best symmetry with regard to the previously used principal point. With most modern cameras, such shifts are seldom >10 μm. Some organizations (e.g., the National Research Council of Canada) maintain computer programs to provide such corrections.

The nature of asymmetry of radial distortion being complex, generally no effort is made in practice to compensate for the irregular part of such errors. This is particularly true of the tangential distortion, which is seldom more than one-seventh of the radial distortion at the same point.

5.3 ATMOSPHERIC REFRACTION

5.3.1 Vertical Photography

On its path from the ground to the camera, a light ray passes through air of decreasing density. This causes a continuous bending of the ray due to refraction. It is a function of the refractive index of the air at all the points along the ray path. The refractive index depends on temperature, pressure and composition (humidity, dust, carbon-dioxide, etc.) of the atmosphere. Since these quantities cannot be measured along the entire ray, it is customary to generalize the path (see Fig. 5.7). The radial displacement (*dr*) corresponds to the angular deviation (ψ) of the ray path.

The light ray from the ground point (*P*) reaches the lens (at *O*) as it passes through the atmosphere, which may be considered to be composed of numerous layers of refractive indices decreasing from the ground upwards. Between any two such successive layers, the angles of incidence an refraction are β_i and $\beta_i + d\alpha$, respectively. Their refractive indices are $n_i + d_n$ and n_i, respectively (along the upward direction). According to the law of refraction,

$$(n_i + d_n) . \sin \beta_i = n_i . \sin (\beta_i + d_\alpha)$$

The angle d_α being very small, this gives, after appropriate generalization and simplification.

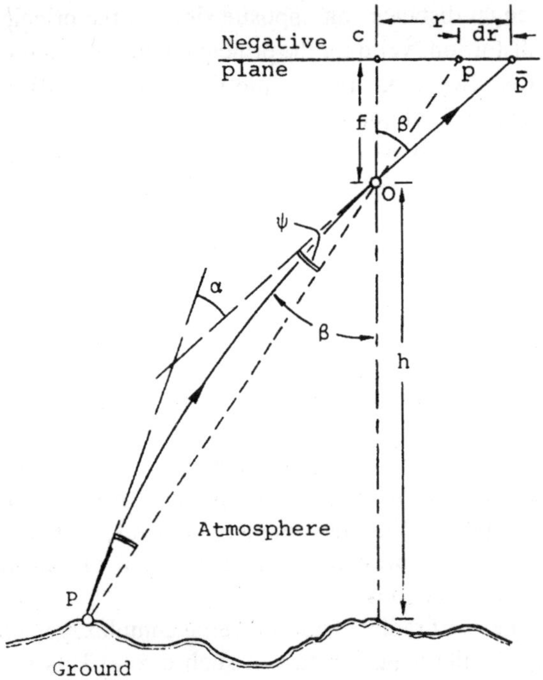

Fig. 5.7: Atmospheric refraction in vertical aerial photography

$$d\alpha = \frac{dn}{n}\tan\beta \tag{5.10}$$

By integrating, from Eq. 5.10,

$$\alpha = \int_{\alpha_P}^{\alpha_0} d\alpha = \tan\beta \int_{n_P}^{n_0} \frac{dn}{n} = \tan\beta .\ \ell n(n)\Big|_{n_p}^{n_0} \tag{5.10a}$$

where ℓn indicates natural logarithm;
and O,P (subscripts) refer to the camera station (O) and the ground point (P).
In view of the generalization,

$$\psi = \frac{\alpha}{2} = K.\tan\beta = K.\frac{r}{f} \tag{5.11}$$

In these expressions, all variables except β are considered constant for a given photograph and contained in the factor K. Based on the derivations made (Bertram, 1969) with respect to the ARDC Standard atmosphere, for example,

$$K = \frac{1}{H_c - H_g}\left[I(H_c) - I(H_g)\right] - R(H_c) \qquad \text{...(5.11a)}$$

where H_c and H_g are the camera and ground elevations, respectively;
ρ is the atmospheric density as a function of altitude;

$$R = 226\,\rho\,; \qquad \text{and}$$

$$I(H) = 226\int_0^H \rho\,.\,dH$$

Bertram (1969) gives an example of calculating *K*, for $H_c = 5\ km$ *and* $H_g = 1\ km$, where he obtains a value of $K = 40.4$ micro-radians. Using an abbreviated table and ρ for the ARDC Standard atmosphere (after Minzner *et al.*, 1959), one gets the following values, for example:

H(km)	ρ	*R*	*I*
0	1.225	276.8	0
1	1.112	251.3	264.0
3	0.909	205.4	719.9
5	0.736	166.3	1090.8

Furthermore, the radial displacement (*dr*) of the image point is

$$dr = f.\ \sec^2\beta\ .\ \psi$$

This gives, from aforementioned considerations,

$$dr = \frac{(r^2 + f^2)r}{2f^2}[\ln(n_0) - \ln(n_P)] \qquad \text{...(5.12)}$$

where

r = the radial distance of the point from photo center; and
f = the focal length of the camera.

Note: The refractive index at any point in the atmosphere is given by

$$n = 1 + \frac{(n'-1)B}{(1+ta)760}$$

where

n' = the refractive index at 0°C temperature and 760 mm air pressure, and $n' = 1.0002926$;
a = the expansion coefficient of air due to temperature;
t = the temperature (in °C) at the location in question;and
B = the air pressure (in mm of mercury) at the location in question.

In normal practice, one of the various standard atmospheres is assumed, e.g.,

1. The US Standard Atmosphere, 1962; of the US Committee on Extension to the Standard Atmosphere (obtainable from the US Government Printing Office);
2. The ARDC Standard Atmosphere, 1959 (Minzner *et al.*, 1959); or
3. The ICAO Standard Atmosphere, 1952 (NASA Report 1235, 1955).

These three atmospheres are practically the same upto about 20 km height. In view of a standard atmosphere, a particular flying height and a particular focal-length, Eq. 5.12 can be simplified into a power series:

$$dr = k_1 r + k_2 r^3 + k_3 r^5 + \ldots \tag{5.12a}$$

where k_1, k_2, etc. are certain constants. In practice, the series is considered upto two terms (see Harris *et al*, 1962). dr, k_1 and k_2 can be pretabulated for a standard atmosphere with respect to the particular camera. A brief example, after Harris *et al.*, (1962) is given in Table 5.1.

The x and y components of such radial displacement (dr) are often obtained and applied as corrections to the photo coordinates along with the uniform radial lens distortion as indicated in Eqs 5.6.

Table 5.1 : Radial image distortion due to atmospheric refraction
(*dr* in μm for a focal length of 153 mm and ICAO standard atmosphere; after Harris *et al.*, 1962)

Flying Ht in m	*For Radial Distance r of Image Point from photo center, in mm*									*Coefficients*	
	12	24	50	63	78	94	111	131	153	$k_1.10^{-2}$	$k_2.10^{-6}$
	For ground elevation – 0 m above sea level										
3000	0.4	0.9	1.9	2.6	3.4	4.5	5.9	7.9	10.7	3.4	1.53
6000	0.7	1.5	3.3	4.4	5.9	7.7	10.1	13.5	18.3	6.1	2.50
9000	0.9	1.9	4.2	5.7	7.5	9.9	13.0	17.3	23.4	7.7	3.23
	For ground elevation – 500 m above sea level										
3000	0.3	0.7	1.6	2.1	2.8	3.7	4.9	6.4	8.8	2.8	1.25
6000	0.7	1.3	3.0	4.0	5.3	6.9	9.1	12.2	15.4	5.4	2.30
9000	0.9	1.8	3.9	5.3	7.0	9.2	12.0	16.0	21.7	7.2	2.99
	For ground elevation – 1000 m above sea level										
3000	0.3	0.6	1.3	1.7	2.2	2.9	3.9	5.1	6.9	2.2	0.99
6000	0.6	1.2	2.7	3.6	4.8	6.3	8.2	10.9	14.5	4.8	2.08
9000	0.8	1.6	3.6	4.9	6.5	8.5	11.2	14.9	20.1	6.7	2.76
	For ground elevation – 1500 m above sea level										
3000	0.2	0.4	0.8	1.2	1.6	2.2	2.8	3.8	5.1	1.6	0.74
6000	0.5	1.1	2.4	3.2	4.2	5.5	7.3	9.7	13.1	4.2	1.87
9000	0.7	1.5	3.4	4.5	6.0	7.8	10.3	13.8	18.6	6.1	2.59

5.3.2 Tilted Photography

If the camera is tilted, the image displacement due to refraction is different from that of the vertical case. The difference is maximum along the direction of the greatest tilt. Table 5.2 (after Schut, 1969) gives refraction errors for an exactly vertical photo and those along the direction of greatest tilt for a tilt of 2°. This table demonstrates that the error due to neglecting the tilt of an aerial photograph may, in practice, be negligibly small. Schut (1969) noted that the positional errors introduced by 'real' (as against 'standard') atmosphere can differ upto 10 per cent from those calculated with regard to a standard atmosphere. This, however, is a negligible quantity because of the small size of the refraction error itself.

Table 5.2 : Radial atmospheric refraction errors in tilted photographs (values in μm, after Schut, 1969)

Field Angle from camera axis	*Standard Angle Camera Focal length : 152.4 mm Flying height : 6000 m*		*Super Wide Angle Camera Focal length : 88.2 mm Flying height : 6000 m*	
	Tilt 0°	*Tilt 2° max*	*Tilt 0°*	*Tilt 2° max*
9°	1.5	1.8	0.9	1.0
18°	3.2	3.6	1.9	2.1
27°	5.7	6.2	3.3	3.6
36°	9.9	10.7	5.7	6.2
45°	17.9	19.2	10.4	11.1
59°	–	–	32.5	35.2

Interesting ideas on various aspects of refraction have been presented by numerous researchers, for example, Bertram (1966), Leijonhufvud (1953) and Saastamoinen (1972 and 1974).

In the case of excessive tilt, the consideration of atmospheric refraction as in a vertical photograph may not be adequately valid. Consideration of a fictious Instantaneous Equivalent Vertical Photograph (IEVP) would conveniently adapt to existing computer program for such cases. The rotation matrix (***M***, see Chap. 4) is assumed to have been known with some approximation, e.g., from previous cycle of adjustment (or, iteration). The photo coordinates of the points in the 'real' photograph are projected to the IEVP by considering a unit focal length by way of utilizing Eqs. 5.13.

$$\left.\begin{aligned} x_F &= f' \frac{a_{11}x + a_{21}y + a_{31}f}{a_{13}x + a_{23}y + a_{33}f} \\ y_F &= f' \frac{a_{12}x + a_{22}y + a_{32}f}{a_{13}x + a_{23}y + a_{33}f} \end{aligned}\right\} \tag{5.13}$$

where x_F and y_F are the photo coordinates on the IEVP (by considering $f' = 1$)
x,y and f refer to the real photograph;
and the "a" elements refer to the inverse of the orientation matrix for the real photo.

The coordinates of the IEVP may now be refined as with vertical photos to correct for the effects of atmospheric refraction. The final step then is to project from the IEVP back to the real (tilted) photo plane, also recognizing that $f' = 1$.

5.4 EARTH CURVATURE

If the photogrammetric work is performed in a rectangular three-dimensional coordinate system (e.g., universal geocentric or local space rectangular), the earth curvature effect as a contributing distortion does not exist. If conditions permit, this approach is to be preferred. If, however, the work is performed in a geodetic reference system or a plane coordinate system with respect to a reference surface, it may then be necessary to account for image distortion (apparent) caused by the curvature of the earth.

The aerial photograph is a central projection on a plane, but the points on the earth's surface are referenced to one or the other of the following reference surfaces:

Geoid: By definition, every point on the geoid is horizontal. Spirit levelling refers to the geoid.

Reference Ellipsoid: A regular ellipsoid of revolution; different ellipsoids are considered according to various assumptions.

Earth Sphere: The best fitting sphere, approximated, under various different considered criteria.

None of these reference surfaces can be portrayed by the photograph without any apparent distortion. The correction may be applied either to individual photos or to the stereo-models. While the latter is used traditionally in analogical (instrumental) work, the former may sometimes be more convenient in computational work.

This displacement (*ds*) due to earth curvature (p′p in Fig. 5.8) is negative by convention, being towards the photograph nadir point (*n*). Assuming the Earth Sphere, one obtains (Ghosh, 1975):

$$ds = \frac{hs^3}{2Rf^2} = \frac{fS^3}{2Rh^2} \tag{5.14}$$

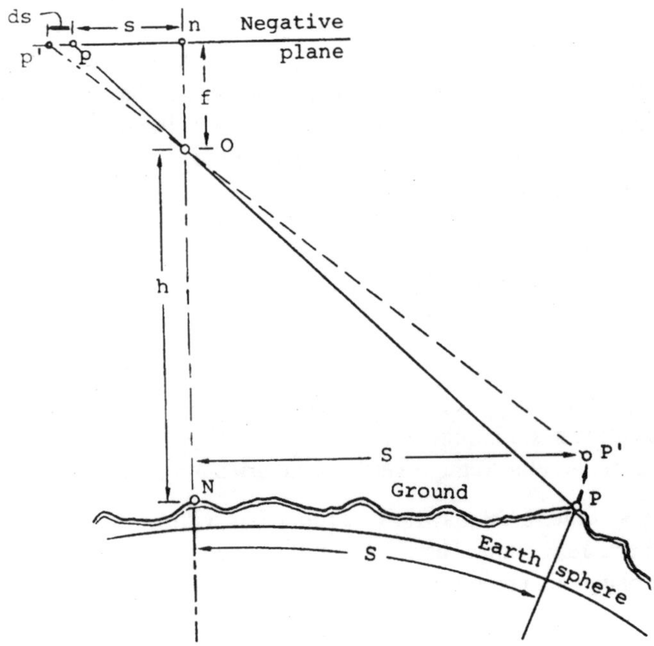

Fig. 5.8: Effect of earth curvature

where

h = flying height above the ground nadir point;

R = radius of the earth sphere;

s = radial distance of the image point from the nadir point on the photo;

S = distance of the ground point from the nadir point (N) along the earth sphere surface; and

f = focal length of the camera.

The earth curvature displacement being radial with respect to the nadir point, on a vertical photograph this correction may be added to the corrections due to the radial lens distortion and atmospheric refraction. Earth curvature correction, by itself, may be of sizable dimension sometimes (see Table 5.3). In case the photo is not vertical, this effect may exceed other image errors.

If the earth curvature correction is not applied, a strip triangulation will develop an elevation misclosure corresponding to the difference in elevation between the curved earth and a plane tangent to the earth at the nadir point of the first photograph of the strip. Consider, as an example, a standard camera (f = 152 mm; format: 230 × 230 mm) and flying height of 6 km. Points in the corners of the photograph are 3.2 m below the plane which is tangent to the earth sphere in the center. If the strip is 100 km long, points ar the end of the strip are 800 m below this plane. It follows that even for a single photograph this displacement may not be negligible. The direct transformation of the strip in such a case would produce correct map coordinates and elevations only if it is preceded or accompanied by a deformation of the triangulated strip that is identical with the deformation in that system.

Table 5.3 : Radial displacement due to earth curvature
(Vertical photo, f = 150 mm; values, negative, in μm)

At *s* (mm)	*For Flying Heights in km*						
	0.5	1	2	4	6	8	10
10	0	0	0	0	0	0	0
20	0	0	0.1	0.1	0.2	0.2	0.3
40	0.1	0.2	0.4	0.9	1.3	1.8	2.2
60	0.4	0.8	1.5	3.0	4.5	6.0	7.6
80	0.9	1.8	3.6	7.2	10.8	14.3	17.9
100	1.8	3.5	7.0	14.0	21.0	28.0	35.0
120	3.1	6.0	12.1	24.2	36.3	48.4	60.5
140	4.9	9.6	19.2	38.4	57.6	76.8	96.0
160	7.1	14.3	28.6	57.2	85.7	114.3	142.9

5.5. IMAGE MOTION

Image motion of various types has been known to be one primary cause of degradation of the space or air photography (NASA publication SP-193, 1969). It is the most frequent and at the same time most damaging form of distortion likely to appear in images relating to the space exploration. Aircraft (or spacecraft) motion, rotation (roll, pitch or yaw) and vibration during the opening of the camera shutter may cause the image blur. This may result in resolution degradation and displacement of the image point. Camera magazines have been designed to provide film movement during exposure by using the Image Motion Compensation (IMC) device. Since the advent of jet aircrafts and the use of slow-speed, fine-grained, high-resolution photographic emulsions, the need for IMC became more profound. As an example, consider vertical photography with a focal length of 152 mm, shutter speed 1/100 sec., aircraft speed of 800 km per hour, and flying height of 12 km. The image smear in this case will be 28 μm in the direction of flight.

There are three basic methods of accomplishing IMC, viz., (a) By moving the platen-film assembly, (b) By moving the lens cone (tilting), and (c) By using a focal plane shutter. Often the third method is combined with the first or the second. Whereas the first or the second method tends to disturb the interior geometry of the camera system, the third one creates a situation somewhat similar to the strip camera i.e., instead of giving a central perspective of a frame photograph, it represents an infinite number of line photographs with respect to a continuously changing perspective center (a locus). Devices such as electro mechanical *V/h* sensor cam correlator have been successfully used in obtaining comparatively sharp images (e.g., in the Lunar Orbiter Systems, see NASA publication SP-193, 1969); although their intrinsic metric qualities are not yet fully assessed.

The aircraft vibration causes blur of another kind. The vibration can be internal to the camera (because of the required use of various devices associated with the camera) or can be external (due to the vehicle and the various mechanisms of the vehicle). Anti-vibration devices are used but a fully vibration-free system has not been developed.

Optical and photoelectric restoration of the images degraded by atmospheric turbulence have been attempted. The experiments have shown results that show sharp imagery, whose metric quality remain doubtful. In all these attempts, if the type of the error source is known from prior information, the quality of the image can be improved. But the post facto removal of the degradation is yet imperfect and is unworkable for high precision work. Improvements with somewhat successful results have been obtained with both digital and non-digital processing techniques (see, NASA, 1969 publication for details). However, considerable scope exists for further improvements in all these and motion degradation remains as one of the most important areas of concern in space photography. In normal use of vertical aerial photography for medium and large scale mapping, however, in most cases IMC may not be necessary at all. In special cases of high precision works, one may consider the image motion of two kinds, viz., (a) Due to linear motions and (b) Due to rotational motions.

5.5.1 Due to Linear Motions

With constant flying height, constant aircraft speed and no rotation of the camera, one may consider the following relations:

$$\text{Speed of film} = v_F = \frac{fV}{h} \quad \text{and Speed of image} = v_I = \frac{fV}{(h-H)}$$

where f is the camera focal length, h is the flying height above datum, H is the height of the ground above datum and V is the ground speed of the aircraft. From these, the relative speed Δv may be obtained,

$$\Delta v = f.V \frac{H}{(h-H)h} \tag{5.15}$$

If the effective exposure time is t_e, then the blurring (b), contributing an image error in the x direction (but nothing in the y direction) is:

$$b = \Delta v.t_e \tag{5.16}$$

It may be pointed out that the IMC devices are meant to compensate for this kind of image blur in the regular photogrammetric cameras.

5.5.2 Due to Rotationalotions

The image velocities from rotational motions, roll, pitch and yaw (ω, ϕ and κ) for various cases are as in Table 5.4 (after Kawachi, 1965). One needs first to determine the rotational velocities from available data; next, these values are substituted into the appropriate equations (Table 5.4); next, the image velocity has to be multiplied by the exposure time to get the approximate distance of blur due to rotational motions. This procedure assumes that there are no other sources of image motion. The image motion from other sources is often not readily known. In such a case, the loss of resolution, assuming that rotational motions are just the only causes of the blur, is the single information which may be estimated (or computed). Often, this information may be sufficient, because it may show that the rotational motions have either very large or very small effect. Table 5.5, after Kawachi (1965) gives an example of such possibilities.

Table 5.4 : Image velocity from rotational motions, various cases (after Kawachi, 1965)

Special Case	*Velocity from Aircraft*		
	Roll Rate	*Pitch Rate*	*Yaw Rate*
Vertical Frame Camera	$\dot{x}_\omega = \frac{xy}{f}\dot{\omega}$ $\dot{y}_\omega = \left(\frac{f^2+y^2}{f}\right)\dot{\omega}$	$\dot{x}_\phi = \left(\frac{f^2+x^2}{f}\right)\dot{\phi}$ $\dot{y}_\phi = \frac{xy}{f}\dot{\phi}$	$\dot{x}_\kappa = y\dot{\kappa}$ $\dot{y}_\kappa = x\dot{\kappa}$
Forward Oblique Frame Camera	$\dot{x}_\omega = y(\sin\varphi - \frac{x}{f}\cos\varphi)\dot{\omega}$ $\dot{y}_\omega = \left[\left(\frac{f^2+y^2}{f}\right)\cos\varphi + x.\sin\varphi\right]\dot{\omega}$	$\dot{x}_\phi = \left(\frac{f^2+x^2}{f}\right)\dot{\phi}$ $\dot{y}_\phi = \frac{xy}{f}\dot{\phi}$	$x_\kappa = y\left(\cos\phi + \frac{x}{f}\sin\phi\right)\dot{\kappa}$ $\dot{y}_\kappa = \left[\left(\frac{f^2+y^2}{f}\right)\sin\phi - x.\cos\phi\right]\dot{\kappa}$
Side Oblique Frame Camera	$\dot{x}_\omega = \frac{xy}{f}\dot{\omega}$ $\dot{y}_\omega = \left(\frac{f^2+y^2}{f}\right)\dot{\omega}$	$\dot{x}_\phi = \left[\left(\frac{f^2+x^2}{f}\right)\cos\omega + y.\sin\omega\right]\dot{\phi}$ $\dot{y}_\phi = x\left(\sin\omega - \frac{y}{f}\cos\omega\right)\dot{\phi}$	$\dot{x}_\kappa = \left[\left(\frac{f^2+x^2}{f}\right)\sin\omega - y.\cos\omega\right]\dot{\kappa}$ $\dot{y}_\kappa = x\left(\cos\omega + \frac{y}{f}\sin\omega\right)\dot{\kappa}$
Vertical Panoramic Camera	$\dot{x}_\omega = 0$ $\dot{y}_\omega = f.\dot{\omega}$	$\dot{x}_\phi = \left(\frac{f^2+x^2}{f}\right)\cos\theta.\dot{\phi}$ $\dot{y}_\phi = x.\sin\theta.\dot{\phi}$	$\dot{x}_\kappa = \left(\frac{f^2+x^2}{f}\right)\sin\theta.\dot{\kappa}$ $\dot{y}_\kappa = x.\cos\theta.\dot{\kappa}$

Note: The symbols in this table are as follows (dots indicating velocities):

f = camera focal length;
x,y = photo coordinates, along and perpendicular to the flight direction;
ω = angle of roll, positive in the right-side direction;
ϕ = angle of pitch, positive in the forward direction:
κ = angle of yaw, positive in the right-handed sense;
$\dot{\omega}, \dot{\phi}, \dot{\kappa}$ = respective angular velocities in radians per second, and
θ = sweep-angle of panoramic camera, positive in the left-side direction.

Table 5.5 : Examples of resolution degradation due to rotational motions, vertical camera (after Kawachi, 1965)

Focal lengh	*Static resolution*	*Exposure time*	*Rotational velocity*	*Photo coordinates x*	*y*	*Degradation*
mm	*lines/mm*	*sec*	*° per sec*	*mm*	*mm*	*%*
152	20	1/500	1	0	0	0.6
			10	0	0	0.6
			10	115	115	50.0
		1/2000	1	0	0	0.0
			10	0	0	4.0

The above approach, credited to Kawachi (1965), is nicely applicable in refining the photo coordinates data. However, the formulas do not interconnect the image and the object spaces directly, which possibility exists by using the collinearity condition. Therefore, another approach, by the procedure of augmentation of the collinearity condition equation may be considered when a mathematical relationship incorporating direct connection between the object and image spaces is desired.

5.5.3 Augmentation of Collinearity Equations

Consider the collinearity condition equations (see Chapter 4) in the following form:

$$x_P - x_O = -f\left\{\frac{M_1\,(X_P - X_O)}{M_3\,(X_P - X_O)}\right\}$$

$$y_P - y_O = -f\left\{\frac{M_2\,(X_P - X_O)}{M_3\,(X_P - X_O)}\right\} \tag{5.17}$$

where f is the calibrated focal length of the camera;

x_p, y_p = photo coordinates of a point;
x_o, y_o = coordinates of the principal point;
M_i = i-th row of the general rotation matrix $\boldsymbol{M}$
X_P = vector of object space coordinates, i.e., $X_P = [X \quad Y \quad Z]^T{}_P$ and
X_o = vector of coordinates representing the perspective center (camera station), i.e., $X_o = [X \quad Y \quad Z]^T{}_o$

In view of a moving camera over a stationary object, photo point 1 is taken at X_o, X'_o and yields coordinates x'_p, y'_p and photo 2 is taken at X_o, X''_o and yields coordinates x''_p, y''_p for the same object point represented by X_P. Assume the camera (photo platform) to move with a three-dimensional velocity V. This will give $X''_o - X'_o = V\bullet\Delta t$, where Δt is the exposure time responsible for creating the blur. Therefore, alternative expressions for x''_p, y''_p are:

$$x''_P - x_O = -f\left\{\frac{M_1(X_P - X'_O - V.\Delta t)}{M_3\,(X_P - X'_O - V.\Delta t)}\right\}$$

$$y''_P - y_O = -f\left\{\frac{M_2(X_P - X'_O - V.\Delta t)}{M_3\,(X_P - X'_O - V.\Delta t)}\right\} \tag{5.18}$$

Then, the displacement of the image causing the blur may be computed as below:

$$\Delta x = x''_P - x'_P \text{ and } -f\left\{\frac{M_1(X_P - X'_O - V.\Delta t)}{M_3\,(X_P - X'_O - V.\Delta t)}\right\} + f\left\{\frac{M_1(X_P - X'_O)}{M_3\,(X_P - X'_O)}\right\}$$

$$\Delta y = y''_P - y'_P \text{ and } -f\left\{\frac{M_2(X_P - X'_O - V.\Delta t)}{M_3\,(X_P - X'_O - V.\Delta t)}\right\} + f\left\{\frac{M_2(X_P - X'_O)}{M_3\,(X_P - X'_O)}\right\} \tag{5.19}$$

The image velocities due to the translation of the perspective center can be obtained from the above expressions as

$$v_x = \Delta x/\Delta t \quad \text{and} \quad v_y = \Delta y/\Delta t \tag{5.20}$$

We shall next describe the velocities due to the rotational motions. we know,

$$\boldsymbol{M} = \begin{bmatrix} M_1 \\ M_2 \\ M_3 \end{bmatrix} = \boldsymbol{M}\kappa.\boldsymbol{M}\phi.\boldsymbol{M}\omega$$

The corresponding augmented rotation matrix is

$$\boldsymbol{N} = \boldsymbol{M}_{(\kappa + \dot{\kappa}.\Delta t)}\,\boldsymbol{M}_{(\phi + \dot{\phi}.\Delta t)}\,\boldsymbol{M}_{(\omega + \dot{\omega}.\Delta t)} \tag{5.21}$$

This, by virtue of the 'double angle' formulas, gives,

$$\boldsymbol{N} = \begin{bmatrix} N_1 \\ N_2 \\ N_3 \end{bmatrix} = \boldsymbol{M}_\kappa\,\boldsymbol{M}_{\dot{\kappa}.\Delta t}\,\boldsymbol{M}_\phi\,\boldsymbol{M}_{\dot{\phi}.\Delta t}\,\boldsymbol{M}_{\dot{\omega}.\Delta t} \tag{5.22}$$

where $\dot{\kappa}$, $\dot{\phi}$ and $\dot{\omega}$ are the respective angular velocities in radians per second of time and Δt, as before, is the exposure epoch.

The general expression for image coordinates of a moving system with respect Δt a defined epoch are, then,

$$x_P - y_O = -f\left\{\frac{N_1(X_P - X_O - V.\Delta t}{N_3\,(X_P - X_O - V.\Delta t}\right\}$$

$$y_P - y_O = -f\left\{\frac{N_2(X_P - X_O - V.\Delta t}{N_3\,(X_P - X_O - V.\Delta t}\right\} \tag{5.23}$$

In a way similar to Eq. 5.19 obtained from Eq. 5.18 (for the translation case), one can obtain expression for Δx and Δy, by differentiating which with respect to Δt, one gets the following expressions for the image velocities from rotational motions:

$$
\begin{aligned}
v_x = \dot{x}_P = -f \Big\{ & \left[\dot{N}_1 (X_P - X_O - V.\Delta t) - N_1 V\right]\left[N_3 (X_P - X_O - V.\Delta t)\right] \\
& - \left[\dot{N}_3 (X_P - X_O - V.\Delta t) - N_3 V\right]\left[N_1 (X_P - X_O - V.\Delta t)\right]\Big\} \\
& \bullet \left[\dot{\underline{N}}_3 (X_P - X_O - V.\Delta t)\right]^{-2}
\end{aligned}
$$

and

$$
\begin{aligned}
v_y = \dot{y}_P - f \Big\{ & \left[\dot{N}_2 (X_P - X_O - V.\Delta t) - N_2 V\right]\left[N_3 (X_P - X_O - V.\Delta t)\right]\Big\} \\
& - \left[\dot{N}_3 (X_P - X_O - V.\Delta t) - N_3 V\right]\left[N_2 (X_P - X_O - V.\Delta t)\right] \\
& \bullet \left[N_3 (X_P - X_O - V.\Delta t)\right]^{-2}
\end{aligned}
\tag{5.24}
$$

where $\dot{\underline{N}}_1 = \dfrac{d\underline{N}_1}{d\Delta t}$; and $\dot{\underline{N}}_2, \dot{\underline{N}}_3''$ are obtained similarly.

Equations 5.24 are without restrictions as to the initial orientation of the camera, the terrain ruggedness, the time interval (Δt) or the magnitude of the rates of motion. The only restriction remains in the assumption that the rates are constant. It can be demonstrated by expanding the N and $\dot{N}$ matrices and using specific values that the expressions 5.24 would, by degeneration, yield the values as presented in Table 5.4. The ideas has been further elaborated in Ghosh (1985).

5.6 RÉSEAU PHOTOGRAPHY

Réseau (focal plane grid) photography has been used for precision photogrammetric work for quite some time. Prior to the Second World War, the British mapping organizations used réseau in various aerial film camera applications (in the U.K., India and South Africa). In these, a grid plate (glass) was interposed between the lens and the emulsion at the focal plane and was used as a registration plate (see Lawrence method, Chap. 2). More recent developments in various countries have taken basically two forms. Accordingly, those two types are discussed below.

5.6.1 Réseau Mounted in Focal Plane

This type (e.g., Wild Modified RC-8 Aviogon, Zeiss RMK-AR or Hasselblad 500 EL Data cameras) is similar to the British pattern but is somewhat modified. The Modification is basically in the use of a plano-convex glass plate (with the convex side facing the camera lens), in order to reduce another source of distortion error due to the plate acting as a lens, as the film support. The réseau crosses are on the plane side of the plate. In this case, the coordinates of each réseau intersection are determined from camera calibration. These calibrated coordinates are referred to the principal point as origin and may be already corrected for lens distortion. There are three possibilities:

(i) The simplest method of using them is to read the coordinates x_i, y_i of the réseau intersection nearest to each observed image point. Then the image point coordinated are given by:

$$x' = x'_i + (x - x_i)$$
$$y' = y'_i + (y - y_i) \quad (5.25)$$

where subscript i refers to the réseau point number;

x'_i, y'_i = réseau point coordinates obtained from calibration;
x, y = observed coordinates of the image point; and
x_i, y_i = the observed coordinates of the réseau point.

In this approach, it is assumed that the comparator axes are coinciding with the réseau axes during observations. The principal drawback here is that this procedure ignores any non-linear deformation within the réseau interval.

(ii) An alternate method is to read the grid intersections around the image point. Then a projective transformation is applied by using the following equations:

$$x' = \frac{a_1 x + a_2 y + a_3}{c_1 x + c_2 y + 1}$$

$$y' = \frac{b_1 x + b_2 y + b_3}{c_1 x + c_2 y + 1} \quad (5.26)$$

where the a's, b's and c's are certain constants. By using the observed and calibrated coordinates of the four réseau points, one may obtain the eight constants. A variation of this approach would be to use an affine transformation,

$$x' = a_1 x + a_2 y + a_3$$
$$y' = b_1 x + b_2 y + b_3 \quad (5.27)$$

Here on has six unknown constants: therefore, three grid points would be adequate. However, with four points, a least squares fit is pertinent.

(iii) A third alternative method will be to observe all réseau points on each photograph along with all of the image points. The differences between the calibrated coordinates and the observed coordinates are used to determine the coefficients in the polynomials which express the corrections to the measured coordinates as functions of the positions of the images on the photo,

$$x' = x + a_0 + a_1 x + a_2 x^2 + a_3 y + a_4 y^2 + a_5 xy + a_6 x^2 y + \ldots$$
$$y' = y + b_0 + b_1 x + b_2 x^2 + b_3 y + b_4 y^2 + b_5 xy + b_6 x^2 y + \ldots \quad (5.28)$$

The number of terms in the polynomials will have to be decided upon separately in each case (arbitrarily, depending on factors such as desired precision, computer capability, etc.). This is, however, generally done without much basic understanding or scientific justifications. In case of redundant data, it would be appropriate to have a least squares adjustment.

5.6.2 Réseau from the Pressure Plate

In some cameras (like Fairchild KC-6A camera) light coming through tiny holes arranged in a grid pattern in the pressure plate is superposed from the rear during the film exposure. In this case, the pressure platen cannot be expected to occupy precisely the same position for each exposure. This means that the relationship between the réseau and fiducial marks must be established freshly every time. The images of the fiducial marks, therefore, should be treated as other images and are corrected for film distortion according to the observed coordinates of the réseau. In this case, an orthogonal transformation (with or without any scale-change, i.e., affine) may be applicable, e.g.,

$$\begin{aligned} x' &= a_1x + a_2y + a_3 \\ y' &= b_1x + b_2y + b_3 \end{aligned} \quad \text{or,} \quad \begin{aligned} x' &= a_1x + a_2y + a_3 \\ y' &= a_2x - a_1y + a_3 \end{aligned} \tag{5.29}$$

Recently developed automatic réseau measuring equipment (see Roos, 1975) is also capable of reading coordinates with standard deviations below 1 μm. In such equipment, if at any time the accuracy becomes too low, a new calibration can be performed to obtain a new set of coefficients for using at the computer for subsequent operations/applications. The measurement of réseau points on a comparator means considerable extra work. The Oberschwaben Test (performed by OEEPE during the early 1970's) compared the results of final practical applications of non-réseau and réseau cameras. It revealed no significant difference between them. This can be interpreted as a definitive establishment of the fact that errors of interior (top camera) geometry after corrections are of secondary importance compared to the external influences. Perry (1978) concludes that back-lighted réseau is not as accurate as the glass réseau. However, its low cost, ease of calibration and extreme flexibility outweigh its lower accuracy and it would be a useful tool in photogrammetry.

BIBLIOGRAPHY

American Society of Photogrammetry; *Manual of Photogrammetry* (4th Ed.) (ASPRS, Falls, Church, Virginia; 1980).

Arthur, D.W.G.; *A Stereocomparator Technique for Aerial Triangulation* (Ordnance Survey Professional Paper, New Series No. 20, London: 1966).

Bertram, S.; "Atmospheric Refraction", *PE* 35, No. 6 (1969).

Brown, D. C.; *The Simultaneous Determination of the Orientation and Lens Distortion of a Photogrammetric Camera* (Technical Report No. 33, RCA Data Reduction: 1956).

Brown, D. C.: "Decentering Distortion of Lenses', *PE* 32, No. 3 (1966).

Conrady, A.E.; "Decentered Lens Systems" *Monthly Notices of the Royal Astronomical Society* 79, No. 5; London (1919).

Ghosh, Sanjib K.; *Phototriangulation* (Lexington Books, Lexington, Mass.; 1975).
Ghosh, Sanjib K.: "Image Quality versus Metric Capability," *PE* 39, No.11 (1973).
Ghosh, Sanjib K., "Image motion compensation through augmented collinearity equations," *Optical Engineering* 24, No. 6 (1985).
Harris, W. D., G.C. Tewinkel and C.A. Whitten; *Analytic Aerotriangulation* Technical Bulletin No. 21; US Department of Commerce, C & G S: 1968).
Kammerer, Joachim; " The Moon Camera and Its Lenses," *PE* 39, No. 1 (1973).
Kawachi, D.A., "Image motion and its compensation for the oblique frame camera, *PE* 31, No. 1 (1965).
Kawachi, D.A.; "Image Motion Due to Camera Rotation", *PE* 31, No. 5 (1965).
Keller, M. and G.C. Tewinkel,: *Aerotriangulation, Image Coordinate Refinement* (Technical Bulletin No. 25; US Department of Commerce, C&GS; 1965).
Klein, Miles V.; *Optics*; (John Wiley and Sons, Inc.: 1970).
Lampton, B. Frank; "Film Distortion Compensation, *PE* 31, No. 5 (1965).
Leijonhufvud, Axel; "On Photogrammetric Refraction, *Photogrammetria* 9, No. 3 (1953).
Minzner, R.A.; K.S.W. Champion and H.L. Pond; *The ARDC Model Atmosphere, 1969* (Air Force Surveys in Geophysics No. 115, USAF Cambirdge Research Center: 1969).
NASA; *Evaluation of Motion-Degraded Images* (Publications No. NASA SP-193: 1969).
Perry, Leslie H.; "An NOS-Developed Backlight Réseau and Its Effect on Coordinate Refinement," *Proceedings of the ASP, Fall Technical Meeting* (1978).
Roos, Maurits; "The Automatic Réseau Measuring Equipment (ARME)", *PERS* 41, No. 9 (1975).
Saastamoinen, J.; "Refraction," *PE* 38, No. 3 (1972).
Saastamoinen, J. "Local Variation of Photogrammetric Refraction," *PE* 40, No. 3 (1974).
Schöler, Horst "On Photogrammetric Distortion," *PERS* 41, No. 6 (1975).
Schut, G.H.; "Photogrammetric Refraction," *PE* 35, No. 1 (1969).
Trachsel, Arnold F.; "Réseau Techniques," *PE* 31, No. 5 (1965).
Trott, T.; "The Effects of Motion on Resolution," *PE* 26, No. 5 (1960).
US Standard Atmosphere Supplements (US Government Printing Office: 1966).
Van Roessel, J.: "Estimating Lens Distortion with Orthogonal Polynomials," *PE* 36, No. 6 (1970).
Vlcek, J.; "Systematic Errors of Image Coordinates," *PE* 35, No. 6 (1969).
Washer, F.E.' "Prism Effect, Camera Tipping and Tangential Distortion," *PE* 23, No. 4 (1957).
Washer, F.E.' "Calibration of Airplane Cameras", *PE* 25, No. 5 (1957).
Wolfe, R.N. and R.L. Lamberts; "The Effects of Image Motion on Resolving Power', *PE* 11, No. 4 (1955).
Ziemann, H.; "Economics of Image Deformation Correction", *PE* 38, No. 2 (1972).

6

RELATIONSHIP BETWEEN OBJECT AND PHOTO

The fundamental relationship between the object and the corresponding photograph can be formulated by utilizing the geometry of the imaging process (Chap. 4). The related problems are considered as different, according to the parameters that are known directly from observations (measured data), those obtained from sources other than direct observations (accepted as known data) and those to be determined from the computational or other solution process (considered as unknown data). The corresponding conditions (equations) can thereby be established.

The most obvious and usually the simplest approach is to treat the image coordinates as the observed values. A number of standard problems (and the corresponding conditions) are listed in Table 4.1. If some of the known parameters are also observed quantities and are subject to observational errors, it is possible to incorporate them in the solution as constrained parameters. The techniques of considering such constraints are discussed in Chap. 9. Some practical uses of the geometric relations where the data are straightforward will be discussed in this chapter. These are the standard and most frequently solved problems. Other problems, which may be considered as extensions of the discussed ones, are easily derivable in view of the purposes under specific circumstances.

With regard to a single photograph, its *exterior orientation* (with respect to the object space) consists of two easily separable sets of parameters. The first set involves *angular orientation data,* whereby the attitude of the photograph (or, better, the camera axis) at the time of exposure is defined in terms of the angles of rotation (ω, ϕ and κ). The second set contains the *positional data* of the exposure station in terms of the three-dimensional coordinates of the perspective center (X_0, Y_0 and Z_0). The solution is known as *space-resection.*

With the knowledge of the exterior orientation parameters of two or more photographs taken of the same object, one may perform *space-intersection* to obtain the locations of unknown object points.

Another typical problem is the *inverse problem* giving *fictitious photographs*, where the image coordinates are derived after the corresponding object points and the camera parameters are known. This may be found useful in various applications (for example, camera calibration, establishing the effects of atmospheric refraction, in handling some un-conventional imaging systems, etc.).

6.1 EXTERIOR ORIENTATION

6.1.1 Complete, by Use of Collinearity Equations

A method very frequently used in obtaining the exterior orientation data of one photograph is by applying the collinearity condition. Equations 4.8 provide the basis for this condition here.

The unknown (required) data being six (viz., X_o, Y_o, Z_o, ω, ϕ, and κ), one requires at least six equations, which are provided by three ground control points. In view of the non-linearity of the equation, a linearized form of the condition equations is necessary and the solution should, therefore, be iterative.

In Eqs 4.8 or Eqs 4.9, consider the first function as F_1 and the second one as F_2 (see also Appendix A). Starting with approximate (or estimated) values of the unknown parameters and, thereafter, the terms of the partial derivatives with respect to the variables being added, one would establish the mathematical models concerning the corrected (or updated) photo-coordinates:

$$\left.\begin{aligned} x_i &= \frac{\partial F_1}{\partial \omega}\Delta\omega + \frac{\partial F_1}{\partial \phi}\Delta\phi + \frac{\partial F_1}{\partial \kappa}\Delta\kappa - \frac{\partial F_1}{\partial X_O}\Delta X_O - \frac{\partial F_1}{\partial Y_O}\Delta Y_O - \frac{\partial F_1}{\partial Z_O}\Delta Z_O + F_1 \\ y_i &= \frac{\partial F_2}{\partial \omega}\Delta\omega + \frac{\partial F_2}{\partial \phi}\Delta\phi + \frac{\partial F_2}{\partial \kappa}\Delta\kappa - \frac{\partial F_2}{\partial X_O}\Delta X_O - \frac{\partial F_2}{\partial Y_O}\Delta Y_O - \frac{\partial F_2}{\partial Z_O}\Delta Z_O + F_2 \end{aligned}\right\} \tag{6.1}$$

The observation equations obtained from the above, in general form, can be written as:

$$\left.\begin{aligned} v_{xi} &= x_i - \underline{x}_i \\ v_{yi} &= y_i - \underline{y}_i \end{aligned}\right\} \tag{6.2}$$

where x_i, y_i are the observed photo coordinates and v_{x_i}, v_{y_i} are the discrepancies (or observational errors). Alternately, one may consider only the pertinent terms of Eqs 4.14 for such a solution. Table 6.1 provides an example.

Table 6.1 : Exterior orientation at Wild Aviolyt BC-1

Note : One step solution; NASA-USA Large Format Camera
f = 305.88 mm; Approximate flying height : 244.8 km.
Two photographs over littoral Morocco were used.
Points *P1*, *P3*, *P11* and *P13* are at sea level. Program PMO

	RESIDUALS ON							
	Photo coordinates (μm)					*Ground coordinates (m)*		
Point No.	*DXL*	*DYL*	*DXR*	*DYR*	*PY*	*DXG*	*DYG*	*DZG*
P1	–.0	–.9	–.1	.9	1.8			
P2	.0	–1.1	–.1	1.4	2.6			
P3	–.6	1.9	.7	–1.9	4.0	4.58	–9.71	3.70
P5	–.0	–1.6	.1	1.4	2.9			
P7	–.1	–1.9	–.2	1.9	3.7			
P9	2.7	1.8	–3.1	–2.1	7.0	–4.94	–18.98	–20.42
P10	–.1	.6	.0	–.7	1.3			–.01
P11	–.4	6.7	.2	–6.7	13.4			.44
P12	–.1	–.8	–.1	.8	1.7			
P13	–.2	–.6	.4	.7	1.4	.56	17.59	
P14	–.1	–3.3	.2	3.6	6.9	–13.97	12.73	
P15	–1.6	–.6	1.7	.5	3.5			14.05
P16	.0	1.8	.2	–1.9	3.6			
P18	.8	–1.8	–.3	1.4	3.4	33.18	5.50	
P20	–2.3	–.9	2.2	.9	4.9			19.42
P21	–.5	–1.3	.4	1.3	2.7			4.44
P22	1.8	1.7	–2.1	–1.4	5.0	–19.42	–7.09	–21.61
R.M.S.					4.1	16.93	12.95	13.66

Table 6.1 : *(Contd.)*

Orientation elements and their standard deviations :

Photo No.	X_O	Y_O	Z_O	Omega	Phi	Kappa
CM1	491181.48	512759.98	244876.19	–.086	.120	–146.237
	82.46	79.50	42.14	.020	.021	.011
CM2	476158.37	484022.86	244737.94	.265	–.281	–146.229
	82.62	80.02	43.02	.020	.021	.011

Normalized standard deviation : 1.2 m.

Data redundancy : 25

There are various ways of simplifying the process. With near vertical aerial photographs, one may consider the initial values of ω, φ and κ to be zero, which give the following ***M*** matrix:

$$\boldsymbol{M} = \begin{bmatrix} 1 & 0 & 0 \\ 0 & 1 & 0 \\ 0 & 0 & 1 \end{bmatrix}$$

In order to compute Eqs 6.2, the partial derivatives must first be evaluated. These are given in Appendix A. The equations can be solved for ΔX_o, ΔY_o, ΔZ_o, Δω, Δφ and Δκ. Next, they are iterated until the changes are minimized to acceptable values close to zero.

6.1.2 Angular Orientation Only

As indicated in Chapter 4, the collinearity condition (of vectors $\vec{r}$ and $\vec{R}$) establishes the exterior orientation of the photograph. The situation becomes simple when the coordinates of the perspective center (i.e., the camera station) are known along with an adequate number of ground stations whose photo coordinates are observed. The required (i.e., considered unknown) data here being the rotation angles only, the scalar multiple, *k* (i.e., the scale factor) need not be considered and one can work with unit vectors.

The unit vector ($\vec{r^o}$) corresponding to $\vec{r}$ has 3 components in the photographic coordinate system, i.e.,

$$\vec{r^o} \text{ and} = \left\{ \frac{(x_P - x_O)}{\left[(x_P - x_O)^2 + (y_P - y_O)^2 + f^2\right]^{1/2}};\ \frac{(y_P - y_O)}{\left[(x_P - x_O)^2 + (y_P - y_O)^2 + f^2\right]^{1/2}};\ \frac{-f}{\left[(x_P - x_O)^2 + (y_P - y_O)^2 + f^2\right]^{1/2}} \right\} \quad (6.3)$$

However, each component can be expressed as a direction cosine of the vector $\vec{r}$, i.e., the unit vector can be expressed by:

$$\vec{r}^{\circ} = (\cos xpO;\ \cos ypO;\ \cos zpO) \tag{6.4}$$

Similarly, the unit vector $\vec{R}^{\circ}$ corresponding to the vector $\vec{R}$ in the object space can be expressed by:

$$\vec{R}^{\circ} = (\cos XPO\ ;\ \cos YPO\ ;\ \cos ZPO) \tag{6.5}$$

The unit vectors, $\vec{r}^{\circ}$ and $\vec{R}^{\circ}$ represent the same line. However, they have been defined above in two different coordinate systems; viz., $\vec{r}^{\circ}$ in the photographic system and $\vec{R}^{\circ}$ in the object space system. Therefore, in order to provide the correspondence, one must be rotated to coincide with the other, i.e.,

$$\boldsymbol{M}^{\mathrm{T}}.\vec{r}^{\mathrm{O}} = \vec{R}^{\mathrm{O}} \tag{6.6}$$

where the rotation matrix $\boldsymbol{M}$ is the same as the one expressed in Eq. 4.2. This matrix has nine terms. Consequently, three control points must be known for determining all the terms. Consider, therefore, three known object points, P_1, P_2 and P_3 corresponding to which the photo points are p_1, p_2 and p_3, respectively. Then Eq. 6.6 can be expressed as :

$$\boldsymbol{M}^{T}.\left[\vec{r}_1^{\mathrm{O}}\ \ \vec{r}_2^{\mathrm{O}}\ \ \vec{r}_3^{\mathrm{O}}\right] = \left[\vec{R}_1^{\mathrm{O}}\ \ \vec{R}_2^{\mathrm{O}}\ \ \vec{R}_3^{\mathrm{O}}\right] \tag{6.7a}$$

i.e.,

$$\begin{bmatrix} m_{11} & m_{12} & m_{13} \\ m_{21} & m_{22} & m_{23} \\ m_{31} & m_{32} & m_{33} \end{bmatrix} \begin{bmatrix} \cos xp_1^{\mathrm{O}} & \cos xp_2^{\mathrm{O}} & \cos xp_3^{\mathrm{O}} \\ \cos yp_1^{\mathrm{O}} & \cos yp_2^{\mathrm{O}} & \cos yp_3^{\mathrm{O}} \\ \cos zp_1^{\mathrm{O}} & \cos zp_2^{\mathrm{O}} & \cos zp_3^{\mathrm{O}} \end{bmatrix}$$

$$= \begin{bmatrix} \cos XP_1^{\mathrm{O}} & \cos XP_2^{\mathrm{O}} & \cos XP_3^{\mathrm{O}} \\ \cos YP_1^{\mathrm{O}} & \cos YP_2^{\mathrm{O}} & \cos YP_3^{\mathrm{O}} \\ \cos ZP_1^{\mathrm{O}} & \cos ZP_2^{\mathrm{O}} & \cos ZP_3^{\mathrm{O}} \end{bmatrix} \tag{6.7b}$$

From this, the orientation matrix ($\boldsymbol{M}$) can be solved:

$$\boldsymbol{M} = \left[\vec{R}_1^{\mathrm{O}}\ \ \vec{R}_2^{\mathrm{O}}\ \ \vec{R}_3^{\mathrm{O}}\right]^{-1} \left[\vec{r}_1^{\mathrm{O}}\ \ \vec{r}_2^{\mathrm{O}}\ \ \vec{r}_3^{\mathrm{O}}\right] \tag{6.8}$$

The angles of rotation in the object space can, next, be individually obtained from the elements of this rotation matrix (see Eq. 3.18 for the details).

6.1.3 Space Resection Only

Several different approaches to this problem are in use. One very frequently used method only will be discussed here. This method uses the angular relationship criterion (see Chap. 4).

Consider Fig. 4.7 which illustrates the situation. The known ground control points *A, B* and *C* have the corresponding image points *a, b,* and *c*. Consider also that the camera focal length (f) is known. The purpose here is to obtain the coordinates of the perspective center (X_0, Y_0 and Z_0) in the object (ground) system.

As has been discussed in Chapter 4 (see Eq. 4.47), the angles subtended by the point location vectors in the camera space must be equal to the corresponding angles in the object space, i.e.,

$$\left.\begin{aligned} \cos \nabla_{ab} &= \cos \nabla_{AB} \\ \cos \nabla_{bc} &= \cos \nabla_{BC} \\ \cos \nabla_{ca} &= \cos \nabla_{CA} \end{aligned}\right\} \tag{6.9}$$

Expanding the first one, for example (see Eqs 4.46 and 4.47), one gets:

$$\frac{x_a.x_b + y_a.y_b + f^2}{|r_a|.|r_b|} = \frac{(X_A - X_O)(X_B - X_O) + (Y_A - Y_O)(Y_B - Y_O) + (Z_A - Z_O)(Z_B - Z_O)}{|R_A|.|R_B|} \tag{6.10}$$

The other two relations can be expanded similarly. In these, whereas all parameters in the camera space are known either through observation (photo coordinates) or from a priori knowledge (focal length from camera calibration data), the expressions for the object space contain the unknowns (X_0, Y_0 and Z_0). However, a direct solution of these unknowns in this case is difficult because of the non-linear nature of these equations. Therefore, usually a Newton method of approximation is applied. This is done by first assuming:

$$\left.\begin{aligned} X_O &= X'_O + \Delta X \\ Y_O &= Y'_O + \Delta Y \\ Z_O &= Z'_O + \Delta Z \end{aligned}\right\} \tag{6.11}$$

where X'_0, Y'_0, Z'_0 are the initial approximate coordinates of the exposure station (e.g., estimated from an available map and flight data);

and ΔX, ΔY, ΔZ are the corrections to the initial approximate values.

A set of approximate values of the angles, ∇'_{AB}, ∇'_{BC} and ∇'_{CA}, can be obtained by using these approximate coordinates. Subsequently, one can write, for example:

$$\cos \nabla_{ab} = \cos\nabla'_{AB} + \frac{\partial \cos\Delta'_{AB}}{\partial X'}\Delta X' + \frac{\partial \cos\nabla'_{AB}}{\partial Y'}\Delta Y' + \frac{\partial \cos\nabla'_{AB}}{\partial Z'}\Delta Z' \tag{6.12}$$

It may be noted that $\Delta X'$, $\Delta Y'$ and $\Delta Z'$ here are approximate values in view of the differentiation. Similar expressions can be written for $\cos \nabla_{bc}$ and $\cos\nabla_{ca}$. Now, rearranging these equations,

$$\left.\begin{aligned} \cos \nabla_{ab} - \cos \nabla'_{AB} &= \Delta_1 \\ \cos \nabla_{bc} - \cos \nabla'_{BC} &= \Delta_2 \\ \cos \nabla_{ca} - \cos \nabla'_{CA} &= \Delta_3 \end{aligned}\right\} \tag{6.13}$$

in which

$$\left.\begin{aligned}\Delta_1 &= \frac{\partial \cos\nabla'_{AB}}{\partial X'}\Delta X' + \frac{\partial \cos\nabla'_{AB}}{\partial Y'}\Delta Y' + \frac{\partial \cos\nabla'_{AB}}{\partial Z'}\Delta Z' \\ \Delta_2 &= \frac{\partial \cos\nabla'_{BC}}{\partial X'}\Delta X' + \frac{\partial \cos\nabla'_{CA}}{\partial Y'}\Delta Y' + \frac{\partial \cos\nabla'_{BC}}{\partial Z'}\Delta Z' \\ \text{and}\quad \Delta_3 &= \frac{\partial \cos\nabla'_{CA}}{\partial X'}\Delta X' + \frac{\partial \cos\nabla'_{CA}}{\partial Y'}\Delta Y' + \frac{\partial \cos\nabla'_{CA}}{\partial Z'}\Delta Z'\end{aligned}\right\} \tag{6.14}$$

The three unknowns, $\Delta X'$, $\Delta Y'$ and $\Delta Z'$, can now be obtained by solving Eq. 6.14. Accordingly, the coordinates of the camera station after the initial corrections are:

$$\left.\begin{aligned}X''_O &= X'_O + \Delta X' \\ Y''_O &= Y'_O + \Delta Y' \\ \text{and}\quad Z''_O &= Z'_O + \Delta Z'\end{aligned}\right\} \tag{6.15}$$

This approach implies an iterative procedure because of the computations of ∇'_{AB} etc. and the involved differentiations. Therefore, such computations must be continued through successive iterations, each time with updated values and executed until corrections are acceptably small and close to zero. For example, after the second iteration, one obtains:

$$\left.\begin{aligned}X'''_O &= X''_O + \Delta X'' \\ Y'''_O &= Y''_O + \Delta Y'' \\ Z'''_O &= Z''_O + \Delta Z''\end{aligned}\right\} \tag{6.16}$$

In order to compute ΔX, ΔY and ΔZ from Eq. 6.14, the partial derivatives are to be evaluated. By using Eq. 4.47 (which expresses the cosine function of the subtended angle as a function of ground coordinates), the partials are:

$$\frac{\partial \cos\nabla_{AB}}{\partial X} = \frac{(X_A - X_O)}{|R_A|}\left\{\frac{1}{|R_B|} - \frac{1}{|R_B|}\cos\nabla_{ab}\right\} + \frac{(X_B - X_O)}{|R_B|}\left\{\frac{1}{|R_A|} - \frac{1}{|R_B|}\cos\Delta_{ab}\right\}$$

i.e.,
$$\frac{\partial \cos\nabla_{AB}}{\partial X} = \cos\alpha_A\left\{\frac{1}{|R_B|} - \frac{1}{|R_A|}\cos\nabla_{ab}\right\} + \cos\alpha_B\left\{\frac{1}{|R_A|} - \frac{1}{|R_B|}\cos\nabla_{ab}\right\} \tag{6.17a}$$

Further, similarly

$$\frac{\partial \cos\nabla_{AB}}{\partial Y} = \cos\beta_A\left\{\frac{1}{|R_B|} - \frac{1}{|R_A|}\cos\nabla_{ab}\right\} + \cos\beta_B\left\{\frac{1}{|R_A|} - \frac{1}{|R_B|}\cos\nabla_{ab}\right\} \tag{6.17b}$$

and
$$\frac{\partial \cos\nabla_{AB}}{\partial Z} = \cos\gamma_A\left\{\frac{1}{|R_B|} - \frac{1}{|R_A|}\cos\nabla_{ab}\right\} + \cos\gamma_B\left\{\frac{1}{|R_A|} - \frac{1}{|R_B|}\cos\nabla_{ab}\right\} \tag{6.17c}$$

The other derivatives may be obtained similarly. The partial derivatives may be evaluated also as follows:

$$\frac{\partial \cos\nabla_{AB}}{\partial X} = (X_A - X_O)\, T_{BA} + (X_B - X_O)\, T_{AB} \qquad \text{...(6.18a)}$$

where

$$T_{AB} = \left\{ 1 - \frac{\dfrac{|R_A|.\cos\nabla_{ab}}{|R_B|}}{|R_A|.|R_B|} \right\}$$

and

$$T_{BA} = \left\{ 1 - \frac{\dfrac{|R_B|.\cos\nabla_{ab}}{|R_A|}}{|R_A|.|R_B|} \right\}$$

Similarly,

$$\frac{\partial \cos\nabla_{AB}}{\partial Y} = (Y_A - Y_O)\, T_{BA} + (Y_B - Y_O)\, T_{AB} \qquad (6.18b)$$

$$\frac{\partial \cos\nabla_{AB}}{\partial Z} = (Z_A - Z_O)\, T_{BA} + (Z_B - Z_O)\, T_{AB} \qquad (6.18c)$$

and so on.

This approach requires at least three known ground control points. In case there are more than three points, the least squares method of adjustment by using observation equations may be applied to obtain unique solutions. An observation equation based on Eq. 6.12 may be written as follows:

$$v_{ij} = \frac{\partial \cos\nabla'_{IJ}}{\partial X'}\Delta X' + \frac{\partial \cos\nabla'_{IJ}}{\partial Y'}\Delta Y' + \frac{\partial \cos\nabla'_{IJ}}{\partial Z'}\Delta Z' - (\cos\nabla_{ij} - \cos\nabla'_{IJ}) \qquad (6.19)$$

where *ij* or *IJ* refers to the point-pair subtending angle at the perspective center (capital letter subscripts refer to the object space and lower case letters refer to the camera space); and v_{ij} is the deviation between the cosines of the corresponding angles in the image (camera) and object spaces.

These deviations (v_{ij}) should be minimized by the Least Squares adjustment. Considering unit weight in the observations, this means Σvv = a minimum. However, the real observations being the photo coordinates, one may consider that the use of these v's is unrealistic. In practice, however, in view of desirable assessment of the quality of the work, this is permissible even though this assessment could be interpreted as being indirect.

6.2 SPACE INTERSECTION

The problem of spatial intersection will be discussed here in terms of three different approaches. In the first case, the camera station coordinates and the orientation angles are treated as measured (known) quantities and may be regarded as fixed. The second case is based on the collinearity equations, which can be combined with the space resection program, resulting in a unified, resection-cum-intersection solution. In the third case, simplified approaches with regard to terrestrial photography are studied to illustrate the needs of various parameters in view of various modes of obtaining data.

6.2.1 Direct Solution

The objective is to obtain three-dimensional coordinates of points on the object. The situation is illustrated in Fig. 6.1 where P is an intersected point, whose coordinates X, Y, Z are unknown. The known quantities are the two orientation matrics $\boldsymbol{M}_1$ and $\boldsymbol{M}_2$ for the two overlapping photos. The camera station (i.e., perspective center) coordinates for both photographs are also known either from space resection or from direct measurements, i.e., X_{01}, Y_{01}, Z_{01}, X_{02}, Y_{02} and Z_{02} are known. The observed quantities are the photo-coordinates (x_1, y_1 and x_2, y_2). the focal length (f) is also known, say, from the camera calibration data.

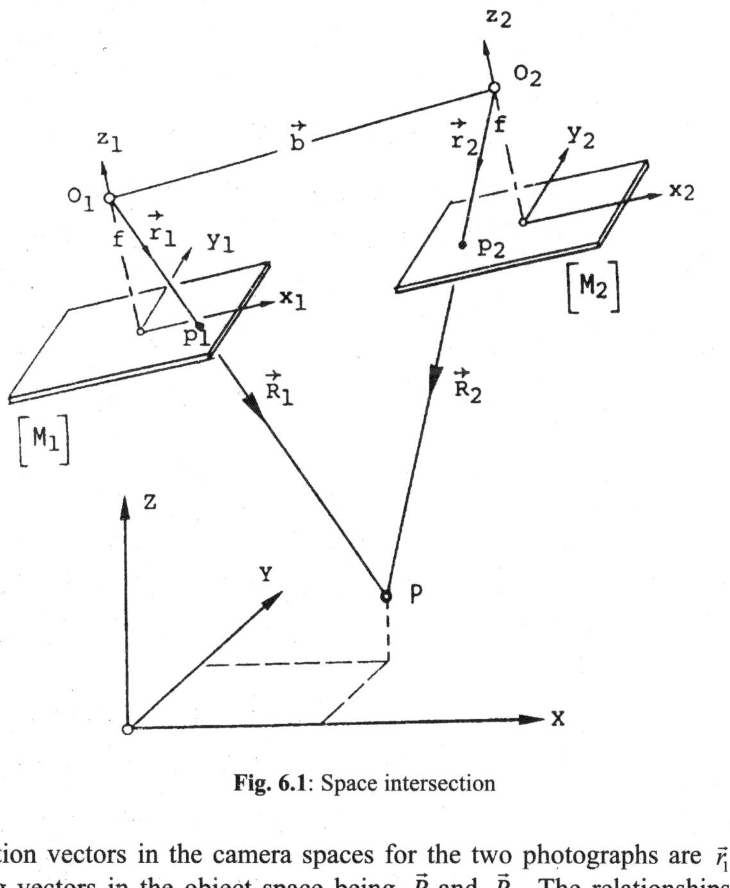

Fig. 6.1: Space intersection

The location vectors in the camera spaces for the two photographs are $\vec{r}_1$ and $\vec{r}_2$, their corresponding vectors in the object space being $\vec{R}_1$ and $\vec{R}_2$. The relationships between the respective unit vectors are (as in Eq. 6.6) :

$$M_1^{\mathrm{T}} . \vec{r}_1^{\,o} = \vec{R}_1^{o}$$

and $$M_2^{\mathrm{T}} . \vec{r}_2^{\,o} = \vec{R}_2^{o} \qquad (6.20)$$

The equations of the $\vec{R}_1$ and $\vec{R}_2$ lines can be written (after Eq. 6.5 in the pattern of Eq. 6.3) as :

$$\left.\begin{aligned} \frac{X - X_{O1}}{\cos XPO_1} = \frac{Y - Y_{O1}}{\cos YPO_1} = \frac{Z - Z_{O1}}{\cos ZPO_1} \\ \text{and} \quad \frac{X - X_{O2}}{\cos XPO_2} = \frac{Y - Y_{O2}}{\cos YPO_2} = \frac{Z - Z_{O2}}{\cos ZPO_2} \end{aligned}\right\} \qquad (6.21)$$

The three unknown coordinates (*X, Y, Z*) of the intersected point *P* can be obtained from these equations. A practical procedure will be to first solve for only *X* and *Y* coordinates by using the portions of Eq. 6.21 involving *X* and *Y*, i.e.,

$$\left.\begin{aligned} \frac{X - X_{O1}}{\cos XPO_1} = \frac{Y - Y_{O1}}{\cos YPO_1} \\ \text{and} \quad \frac{X - X_{O2}}{\cos XPO_2} = \frac{Y - Y_{O2}}{\cos YPO_2} \end{aligned}\right\} \qquad (6.22)$$

Thereafter, by substituting the values of *X* and *Y* in the rest of Eqs 6.21, one can obtain two separate values of *Z* for the same point. This provides a check on the computations and the difference between the two values would provide an assessment of the quality of the work.

There can be other interesting applications of Eqs 6.21. For example, if the *Z* coordinate of a point is known from a ground survey or otherwise, its *X* and *Y* coordinates can be determined from a single photograph by using one equation in parts:

$$\left.\begin{aligned} X = X_{O1} + (Z - Z_{O1})\frac{\cos XPO_1}{\cos ZPO_1} \\ \text{and} \quad Y = Y_{O1} + (Z - Z_{O1})\frac{\cos YPO_1}{\cos ZPO_1} \end{aligned}\right\} \qquad (6.23)$$

Furthermore, in such a case, if two or more photographs containing the same points are available, a Least Squares solution will be appropriate.

6.2.2 Use of Collinearity Equations

The collinearity equations (Eq. 4.8) contain three groups of parameters for the space exterior to the camera, viz., rotation elements (contained in the rotation matrix), the coordinates of the camera station, and the coordinates of the ground point. Consequently, if the first two groups of parameters are known, the third group (i.e., the ground coordinates) can be obtained by using the collinearity equations. Equations 4.8 can be rearranged for any point *i* as follows:

$$\left.\begin{aligned} x_i\ \{X_i - X_O)m_{31} + (Y_i - Y_O)m_{32} + (Z_i - Z_O)m_{33}\} \\ = -f\ \{(X_i - X_O)m_{11} + (Y_i - Y_O)m_{12} + (Z_i - Z_O)m_{13}\} \\ y_i\ \{(X_i - X_O)m_{31} + (Y_i - Y_O)m_{32} + (Z_i - Z_O)m_{33}\} \\ = -f\ \{(X_i - X_O)m_{21} + (Y_i - Y_O)m_{22} + (Z_i - Z_O)m_{23}\} \end{aligned}\right\} \tag{6.24}$$

In these X_i, Y_i and Z_i are the unknowns (being the coordinates of point P, see Fig. 6.1). The rest are known quantities, either through direct observations (x_i, y_i photo coordinates), or otherwise (f, focal length from camera calibration data; X_0, Y_0, Z_0 and the m's from, say, space resection or phototriangulation). In view of the unknowns, Eqs 6.24 can be rearranged with respect to one photograph:

$$\left.\begin{aligned} X_i\,(x_i m_{31} + f.m_{11}) + Y_i(x_i m_{32} + f.m_{12}) + Z_i\,(x_i m_{33} + f.m_{13}) \\ = x_i\,(X_O m_{31} + Y_O m_{32} + Z_O m_{33}) + f\,(X_O m_{11} + Y_O m_{12} + Z_O m_{13}) \\ X_i\,(y_i m_{31} + f.m_{21}) + Y_i(y_i m_{32} + f.m_{22}) + Z_i\,(y_i m_{33} + f.m_{23}\} \\ = y_i\,(X_O m_{31} + Y_O m_{32} + Z_O m_{33}) + f\,(X_O m_{21} + Y_O m_{22} + Z_O m_{23}) \end{aligned}\right\} \tag{6.25}$$

With two photographs of known exterior orientations, one gets two sets (i.e., four) of Eqs 6.25, where all the parameters except X_i, Y_i and Z_i for the specific point are known. Any suitable computational solution can be used, e.g., the method of determinant or of the Least Squares. It may be pertinent to mention here that a similar arrangement of the Collinearity equations can also be applicable to the problem of Exterior Orientation. This may be found to be, in some cases, simpler than the approach discussed in Section 6.1.1 earlier.

6.2.3 Simple Intersection with Terrestrial Photos

For the sake of simplicity and convenience in work, photographs with terrestrial cameras (like photo-theodolites or stereometric cameras or even amateur cameras) would be planned so that the horizontal collimating (fiducial) line in each photo remains horizontal while the vertical collimating line may not always remain vertical due to the inherent tilt. A point on ground (object) is defined in terms of 3-D coordinates, X, Y, Z while the corresponding points in the photographs are in terms of their photo-coordinates, x', y' for point p' on the left side photograph and x'', y'' for point p'' on the right side photograph (see Fig. 6.2).

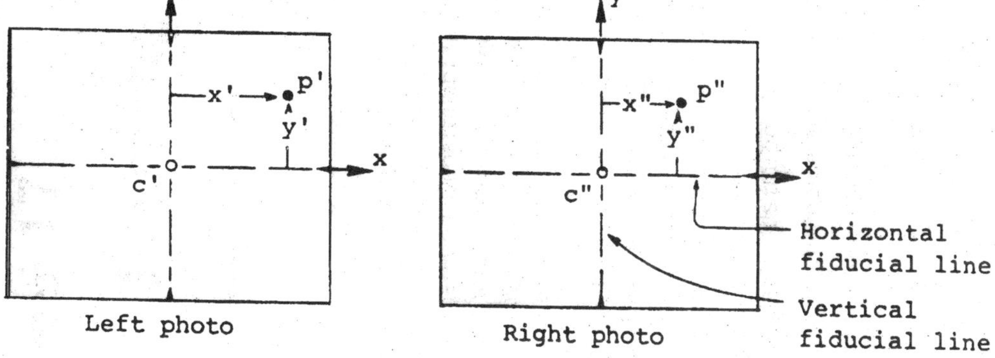

Fig. 6.2: Coordinate determination on terrestrial stereophotos

The ground coordinates (*X, Y, Z*) are in a system of which the perspective center of the left side camera is the origin and the left side camera axis (assumed horizontal) indicates the direction of the *Y*-axis in a right-handed system with the *X*-axis pointed in the general direction of the camera-base (see Figs. 6.3 and 6.4).

Two typical cases can be studied, viz, (1) the normal case where both camera axes are parallel and perpendicular to the terrestrial (camera) base (case *A*) and (2) the camera axes are arbitrarily convergent (case *B*).

Case A: Normal Case

This is illustrated in Fig. 6.3.

The photo coordinates, x', y' and x'', y'' are measured quantities. The horizontal projection of the camera base ($\bar{b}$) is assumed known and so is the focal length (*f*). The following relationship can be established from simple geometric consideration:

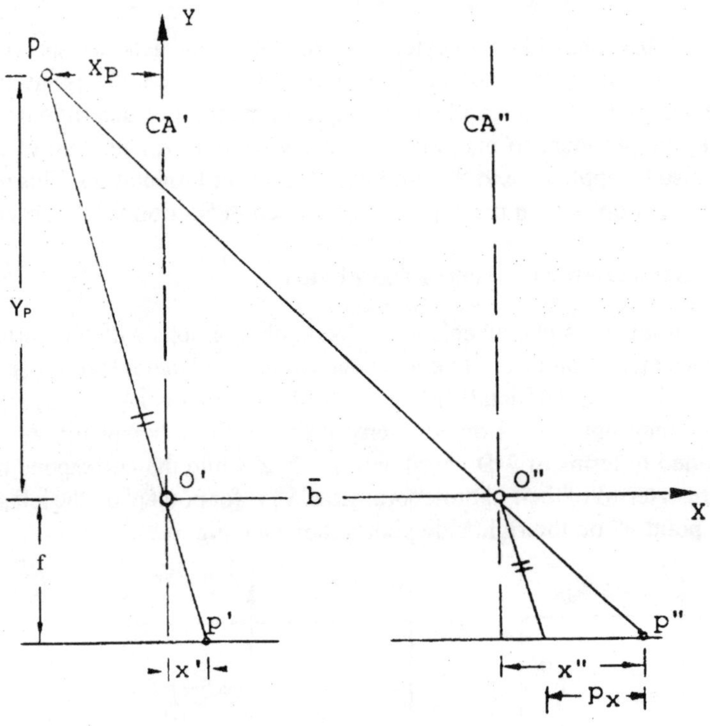

Fig. 6.3: Intersection with terrestrial photos, Normal case

$$\frac{\bar{b}}{x'' - x'} = \frac{Y_P}{f}$$

i.e. $$Y_P = \frac{\bar{b}.f}{P_X} \tag{6.26}$$

where $P_X = x'' - x'$ = the x-parallax

Similarly, $X_p = -\dfrac{Y_P.x'}{f}$

with substitution from Eq. 6.26,

$$X_p = -\frac{Y_P.x'}{f} \tag{6.27}$$

and $$Z_P = Z_{O'} - \frac{Y_P . y'}{f} = Z_{O'} - \frac{\bar{b} . y'}{px} \tag{6.28}$$

where $Z_{O'}$ is the elevation of the camera position O' for the left photographs.

An expression similar to Eq. 6.28 can be written also where $Z_{O''}$ of the right side camera position is used. It is interesting to note here that Eqs. 6.27 and 6.28 i.e. expressions for X and Z coordinates of the ground point are independent of the focal length in this, Normal case. A normal case would be the simplest and is recommended if the situation permits.

Case B: Convergent Case

This is illustrated in Fig. 6.4 where, as in the Normal Case, $\bar{b}$ is the horizontal projection of the camera base.

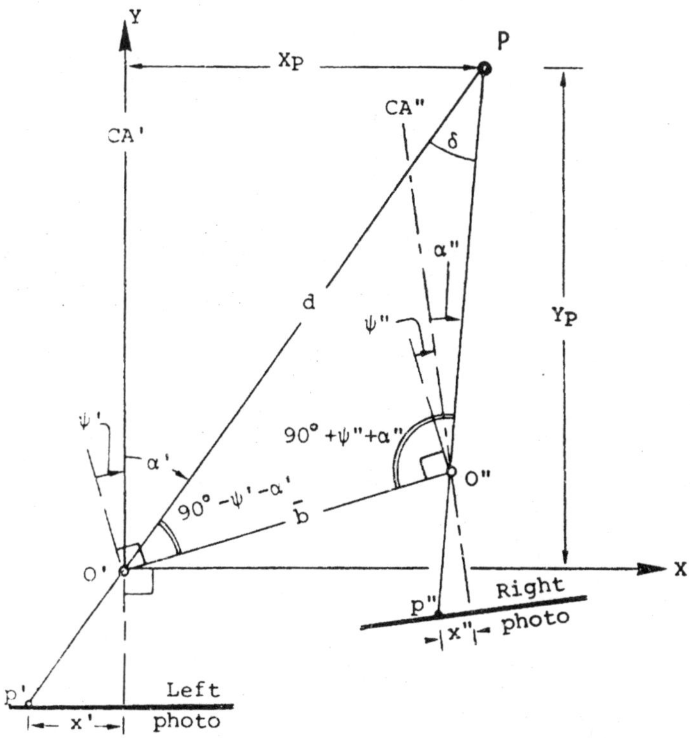

Fig. 6.4: Intersection with terrestrial photos, Convergent case

The angles ψ' and ψ'', the angles subtended by the camera axes with the directions of the perpendiculars to the camera base on the horizontal planes, define the convergence of the left and right camera, respectively. These two angles of convergence are assumed known as also b and f. Consider the horizontal distance of a ground point P from the left camera position, $O'P = d$. The photo coordinates x', y' and x'' y'' are measured quantities. Consider α' and α'' being the directions to the point P with regard to the respective camera axes (CA' and CA''). Furthermore,

$$\alpha' = \arctan\left(-\frac{x'}{f}\right) \text{ and } \alpha'' = \arctan\left(-\frac{x''}{f}\right)$$

Then; $\delta = (\psi' - \psi'' + \alpha' - \alpha'')$

also, from sine conditions in triangle $O'PO''$,

$$\frac{d}{\bar{b}} = \frac{\sin(90^\circ + \psi'' + \alpha'')}{\sin\delta}$$

i.e.
$$d = \frac{\bar{b}\,.\cos(\psi'' + \alpha'')}{\sin(\psi' - \psi'' + \alpha' - \alpha'')}$$

These give,
$$Y_P = d.\cos\alpha' = \frac{\bar{b}.\cos(\psi'' + \alpha'')\cos\alpha'}{\sin(\psi' - \psi'' + \alpha' - \alpha'')} \tag{6.29}$$

Now,
$$X_P = -\frac{Y_P\,.\,x'}{f} \tag{6.30}$$

and
$$Z_P = Z_{O'} - \frac{Y_P\,.\,y'}{f} \tag{6.31}$$

Similar expression can be written with regard to $Z_{O''}$.

If $\psi' = \psi''$ one obtains a case with no convergence but a case with camera axes turned and parallel to each other. On the other hand if $\psi' = -\psi''$ one obtains a case of symmetrical convergence. In these two cases the situations become somewhat less complex and are recommended if the Normal case cannot be worked out adequately.

6.3 INVERSE PROBLEM

In case the three-dimensional ground coordinates of certain points and the camera orientation data (both Interior and Exterior) are known, one would be able to obtain the corresponding photo coordinates of those points. These would represent the theoretically obtained locations of those image points. In case the photographic coordinates of those points are also measured, the difference between the measured (actual) and computed (theoretically correct) locations are obtained. Such information can be of help in various problems. For example, assuming that such differences are due to the (unaccounted for) lens distortion, one could use this in calibrating the camera lens.

One way of doing this will be by using the collinearity equations (Eqs 4.8) directly. In this, all parameters in the right hand side of the equations being known, the photo-coordinates (x, y) are computed directly.

Alternatively, in view of Eqs 6.4, 6.5 and 6.6, with respect to the corresponding unit vectors $\vec{r}^{\circ}$ and $\vec{R}^{\circ}$,

$$\begin{bmatrix} \cos xpO \\ \cos ypO \\ \cos zpO \end{bmatrix} = M \cdot \begin{bmatrix} \cos XPO \\ \cos YPO \\ \cos ZPO \end{bmatrix} \tag{6.32}$$

This gives the direction cosines within the camera space. The equation of the line from the image point to the perspective center (camera station) is:

$$\frac{x_P - x_o}{\cos xpO} = \frac{y_P - y_o}{\cos ypO} = \frac{-f}{\cos zpO} \tag{6.33}$$

Now, assuming that the coordinates of the principal point are $x_0 = y_0 = 0$, one obtains simple expressions for the photo-coordinates:

$$x_p = -f\,\frac{\cos xpO}{\cos zpO}$$

and

$$y_p = -f\,\frac{\cos ypO}{\cos zpO} \tag{6.34}$$

For further ideas, see Chapter 10 (concept of IEFP).

BIBLIOGRAPHY

Brown, Duane C.; *A Solution to the General Problem of Multiple Station Analytical Stereo-Triangulation* (R.C.A. Data Reduction Technical Report, No. 43: 1958).

Keller, M. and G.C. Tewinkel; *Space Resection in Photogrammetry* (ESSA Technical Report, C. & G.S. No. 32, U. S. Department of Commerce: 1966).

Merritt, E.L.; *Analytical Photogrammetry* (Pittman Publishing Company, New York: 1958).

Rapp, R. H.; "Comparison of Space Resection Adjustment," *Journal of the Surveying and Mapping Division,* ASCE 92 (1966).

Tewinkel, G.C.; *Analytical Absolute Orientation in Photogrammetry;* (C & GS Technical Bulletin No. 19, U.S. Department of Commerce: 1962).

7

DESIGN OF PROJECTS

Technological, circumstantial and competitive factors interact in a very complicated fashion in today's economy. It is not easy to design a project that is both realistic and economical. Another reason for complexity is that sometimes the organizations may pursue inconsistent goals. The responsibility for making decisions may be diffused often. There is often no clear line of demarcation between the work of the photogrammetrist and that of the user of photogrammetric data. Such an user can be from any field, e.g., space science, industrial engineering, metallurgy, surgery, etc. Because of such diversities, the photogrammetrist cannot always follow any standard procedure. Moreover, there are generally several ways to approach any problem. Therefore, careful planning and designing of any project is necessary.

A project development may become ineffective and inefficient if its cost-effectiveness is inadequate. Cost-effectiveness considerations are also complex (for an introduction to this, see Ghosh, 1976). This book emphasizes the technical aspects only and, therefore, the socio-economic aspects will not be discussed. However, the working photogrammetrist must keep in mind that decisions concerning the utilization of the end product of photogrammetry are often economic rather than technical.

Some basic and fundamental yet important technical considerations necessary for designing and/or evaluating any project will be discussed in this chapter. There are some differences between aerial (also spatial) and terrestrial applications and yet there are aspects common to every case. In view of these, the discussions will be in general terms. The reader will be able to apply the concepts easily to the specific cases.

7.1 SCALE AND CAMERA CONSIDERATIONS

For topographical mapping, most of the countries in the world are switching from graphical (by direct tracing) mapping to instrumental and automated (analytic) map compilation. Analytical/computational generation of control data to assist such map compilations is also pursued extensively now. Between the aerial photograph and the finished map, there are two operational steps involving possibilities of changing the scales. In this respect, one considers Photo-, Model-, Compilation- (at instrument), and Map-Publication-Scales. These are symbolized by $M_{B'}$ $M_{M'}$ $M'_{K'}$ and $M_{K'}$ respectively. The specific values of such scale factors are valid for a certain stage (operational step) for specific man-machine-technique combination in order to meet certain tolerances of mensural qualities. The computational part being only a portion of the entire operation, one cannot ignore the other implications. The general aspects have been broadly discussed by Ghosh (1971 and 1988). For general planning, however, the photogrammetrist may consider the two extremes, viz., M_B and M_K. Based on the currently available hardware and expertise, one may consider their relationships as presented in Fig. 7.1 This figure is based on 1988 data collected under the UN auspices and as reported by Brandenberger and Ghosh (1990).

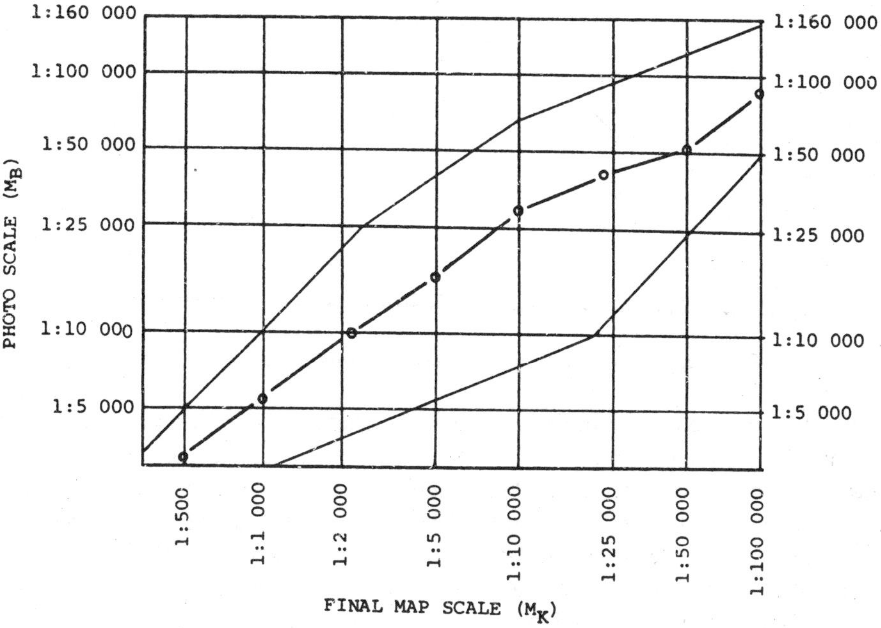

Fig. 7.1: Reasonable photo-to-map scale relations

Here the upper line corresponds to the best possible situation, i.e., when excellent cameras and instruments (best precision) are used. The lower line corresponds to average situations such as are available to almost all mapping organizations. Most cases are expected to stay within the ranges indicated by the two lines. The central line indicates the optimum on the average for cadastral and topographic mapping in general. The graph is limited to Map Scales 1:500 and 1:100,000. This is because in common practice, direct mapping (as against derived mapping) from aerial photographs is done within this range. Both scales being logarithmic (used for the sake of convenience), the figure indicates linear relationships.

Associated with the above is the problem of selecting the camera and the mode of its use. This is governed by two basic aspects, viz., (1) the ground coverage (for overall economy, see Fig. 7.2), which is inversely proportional to the focal length; and (2) the geometry of intersection (discussed in Section 7.2), which is associated with the stereo-coverage (for overall obtainable accuracy). The two, however, are not always compatible. With a wider field-angle of the camera, one would expect fewer stereo models which would require fewer control points and, in some cases, would give better intersection geometry. On the other hand, this may cause stereo-gaps on rugged (mountainous) terrain or may have masking effects locally.

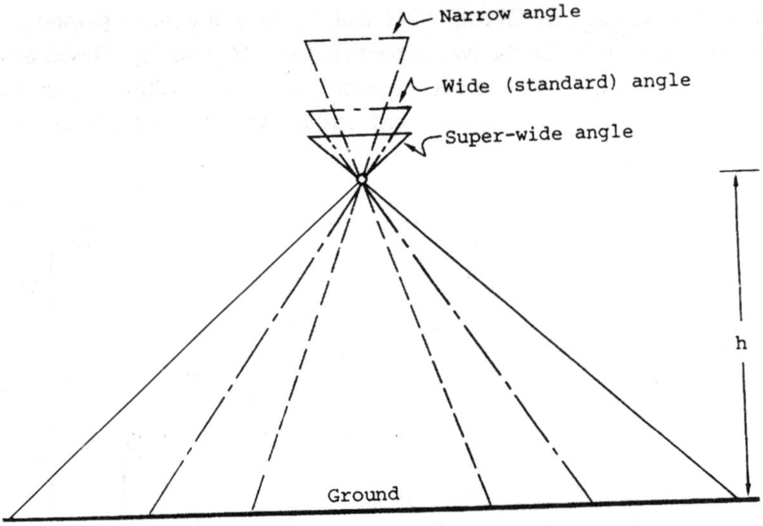

Fig. 7.2: Comparison of ground coverage with different camera angles

Further points to consider in these regards are whether or not the photography is meant to be used in other jobs (e.g., orthophotography, mosaicing, etc.); whether or not unusual lack of flatness of the emulsion/ film is expected; whether or not critical geometry is involved, etc. In depth discussions on these are given in the Manual of photogrammetry (1980).

In general, unless economy at the expense of some accuracy (in spite of some other problems) is desired, it will be advisable to use a camera with smaller field angle, provided sufficiently large intersection angle is obtained.

7.2 GEOMETRIC CONSIDERATIONS

Three-dimensional mensuration is essentially dependent on the quality of the spatial intersection of the conjugate rays. In order to establish formulation for assessing the quality of such intersection, one can consider a two-dimensional analogy from ground survey (see Fig. 7.3). Consider an intersected point (P) of two rays, $1P$ and $2P$, originating from stations 1 and 2, respectively. Here γ is the angle of intersection (parallactic angle, b is the base (distance between the stations, α's are included angles at the stations, ν's are the azimuths, and d's are the distances from the stations. The subscripts refer to the specific points or directions. One can state, for the coordinates of the intersected point (P),

$$\begin{aligned} X &= X_1 + d_1 \sin n_{1P} \\ Y &= Y_1 + d_1 . \cos n_{1P} \end{aligned} \tag{7.1}$$

also,

$$\begin{aligned} \gamma &= 180^\circ - (\alpha_1 + \alpha_2) \\ \nu_{1P} &= \nu_{12} - \alpha_1 \end{aligned} \tag{7.2}$$

$$d_1 = \left(\frac{\sin \alpha_2}{\sin \gamma}\right) b$$

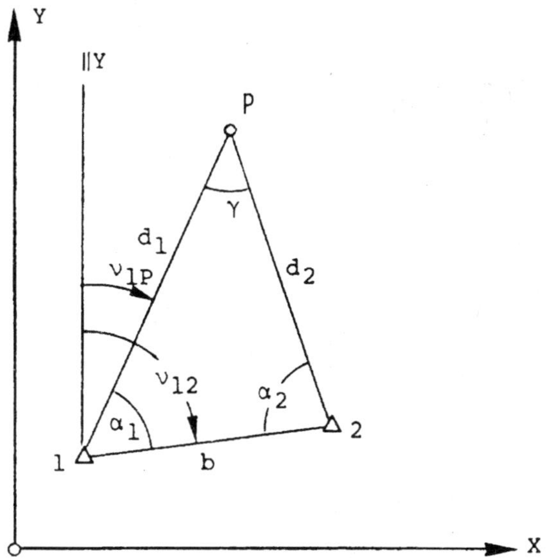

Fig. 7.3: Geometry of intersection

Considering Eqs. 7.2 and substituting appropriate values, one gets from Eqs. 7.1:

$$X = X_1 + \frac{b.\sin\alpha_2.\sin\,(\nu_{12} - \alpha_1)}{\sin\,(\alpha_1 + \alpha_2)}$$

$$Y = Y_1 + \frac{b.\sin\alpha_2.\sin\,(\nu_{12} - \alpha_1)}{\sin\,(\alpha_1 + \alpha_2)} \tag{7.3}$$

Equations 7.3 contain information obtainable from the two base stations and the base length. The partial derivatives of Eqs 7.3 give:

$$\frac{\partial X}{\partial \alpha_1} = -\frac{b.\sin\alpha_2.\sin\,(\nu_{12} + \alpha_2)}{\sin^2\gamma} \tag{7.4a}$$

$$\frac{\partial X}{\partial \alpha_2} = \frac{b.\sin\alpha_1.\sin\,(\nu_{12} - \alpha_1)}{\sin^2\gamma} \tag{7.4b}$$

$$\frac{\partial Y}{\partial \alpha_1} = -\frac{b.\sin\alpha_2.\cos\,(\nu_{12} + \alpha_2)}{\sin^2\gamma} \tag{7.4c}$$

and $$\frac{\partial Y}{\partial \alpha_2} = \frac{b.\sin\alpha_1.\cos\,(\nu_{12} - \alpha_1)}{\sin^2\gamma} \tag{7.4d}$$

The standard error in planimetry of intersection at point *P* can be expressed:

$$m_S^2 = m_X^2 + m_Y^2 \tag{7.5}$$

where

$$m_X^2 = \left(\frac{\partial X}{\partial \alpha_1}\right)^2 m_{\alpha 1}^2 + \left(\frac{\partial X}{\partial \alpha_2}\right)^2 m_{\alpha 2}^2$$

and $$m_Y^2 = \left(\frac{\partial Y}{\partial \alpha_1}\right)^2 m_{\alpha 1}^2 + \left(\frac{\partial Y}{\partial \alpha_2}\right)^2 m_{\alpha 2}^2 \tag{7.6}$$

Considering that the angles are obtained with equal reliability (in consideration of the same instrument, same observer, etc.) i.e.,

$m_{\alpha 1} = m_{\alpha 2} = m_\alpha$; one gets from Eqs 7.5 and 7.6;

$$m_S^2 = \left\{\left(\frac{\partial X}{\partial \alpha_1}\right)^2 + \left(\frac{\partial X}{\partial \alpha_2}\right)^2 + \left(\frac{\partial Y}{\partial \alpha_1}\right)^2 + \left(\frac{\partial Y}{\partial \alpha_2}\right)^2\right\} . m_\alpha^2 \tag{7.7}$$

From the above, with appropriate substitutions and rearrangements,

$$m_S^2 = \frac{d_1^2 + d_2^2}{sin^2 \gamma} m_\alpha^2 \tag{7.8}$$

Considering that the working system is constant, the mensural reliability of all angles will be the same. Hence, consider m_α as unity (or, a constant). This gives the expression of the weight or the degree of reliability of the planimetry of the intersection (P_s being the weight):

$$P_S \propto \frac{1}{m_S^2} = \frac{sin^2 \gamma}{d_1^2 + d_2^2} \tag{7.9}$$

The above analogy from land surveying can be appropriately applied to a stereomodel where the perspective centers are the "stations" for the originating rays and the intersections are in the epipolar planes (i.e., these are spatial intersection cases), the perspective centers being the epipoles. Equation 7.9 can be expressed in terms of 'model' data (see Ghosh, 1972):

$$P_S \propto \frac{\sin^2\gamma}{d_1^2 + d_2^2} = \frac{b^2 (R^2 - X^2)}{R^2 (R^2 + b^2 - 2bx)(2R^2 + b^2 - 2bX)} \tag{7.10}$$

where γ is the space-angle of intersection (parallactic angle);
d_1, d_2 are the distances of the model point from the perspective centers;
b is the model base;
$R^2 = X^2 + Y^2 + Z^2$
and X, Y, Z are the model coordinates of the point in the International system of coordinates (the left side perspective center being the origin, the system being right handed with X-axis coinciding with the base and the Z-axis pointing downwards).

Equation 7.10 can be used in principle in designing or planning a photogrammetric project consisting of stereo models, in one way or the other.

The denominator in Eq. 7.10 (i.e., $d_1^2 + d_2^2$) will give, generally speaking, better values when the object distances are smaller, which also corresponds to larger scale photographs. The numerator indicates that the best possible situation with regard to the angle of intersection is when $\gamma = 90^0$. However, from practical considerations, this is not always realistic. Usually, if the parallactic angle is very large, stereo vision may be difficult. Unless the instrument is equipped with continuously zooming optics, there could be serious problems in stereo observation. In extreme cases, detail point identification may be impossible.

For planning purposes, it is customary to express the parallactic angle in terms of base-distance ratio (or, base-height ratio in the aerial case). This, at the middle of the model (considering $d_1 = d_2$) is: $b/Z = 2 \tan (\gamma/2)$. The obtainable accuracy of coordinates in the stereo model (expressed in terms of error-ellipsoids or variance-covariance matrix, see Ghosh, 1972) can be related to the average of all base-distance ratios in the model or the average parallactic angle for the purpose of designing a project. The actual values may be obtained empirically with regard to the camera, photograph material, instrument, etc. An example is illustrated in Fig. 7.4, where a standard photography situation (i.e., $f = 15$ cm, 23×23 cm format) has been used. The standard errors of measuring the Z coordinates (m_z) were obtained at a Wild A7 Autograph instrument with precision grid stereo models.

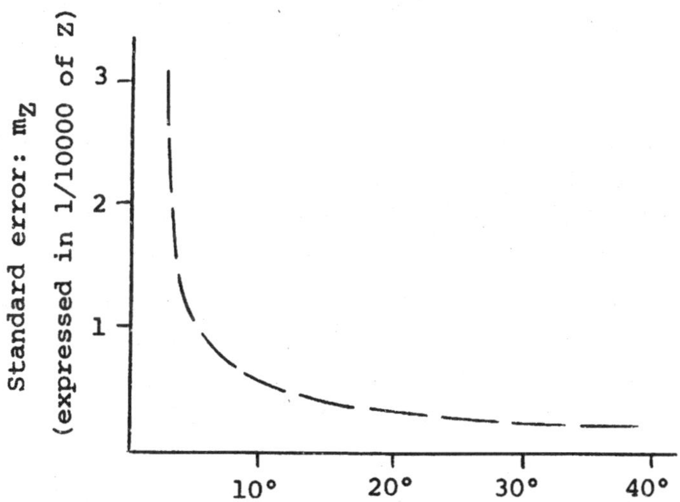

Fig. 7.4: Relation between height error and Parallactic angle
Note: Z is the projection distance.

An earlier study by Harpe (1965) with Zeiss Stereoplanigraph C8 instrument also gave similar results. Such graphs can be used for successful planning of a project. The optimum with regard to required accuracy and suitable stereo coverage of the object can be decided upon very easily.

7.3 TARGET DESIGN

Photogrammetric precision work often demands pre-signalization of points. The particular situation of the camera relative to the object would influence the shape and size of such targets. Other influencing factors are the imaging quality of the camera, the capability of the instrument (size of measuring marks, in particular), resolving capacity of the photographic material and the scale of the photograph. Targets must be provided in cases where lack of good stereo vision (say, due to extreme geometry) or lack of desirable natural features pose identification problems.

Because of the involved perspectivity, the targets may appear irregularly distorted in shape and in varying sizes on different photographs taken over the same object area in a stereo or multiple image situation. The resulting problems of image matching and accurate pointing are considerably minimized (practically eliminated) if symmetrical shaped targets (e.g., circles, concentric rings, crosses, triangles, or squares) are designed for use. The center of the target should, of course, refer to the point to be located and measured. Fortunately, all measuring instruments have symmetrical (usually circular) shaped measuring marks. The placement of such marks on the target image can be made with great reliability if the target appears larger than the measuring mark. In this light, considering a circular target, its minimum apparent diameter should not be smaller than that of the measuring mark. This would depend on the photo-scale. Accordingly, the following relationship holds:

$$d_{\min} = \frac{d'}{M_B} = \frac{D.d'}{f} \tag{7.11}$$

where d and d' are the diameters of the circular target and the measuring mark, respectively;
f is the focal length of the camera;
D is the object distance from camera base (flying height in aerial);
and M_B is the photo scale.

On the other hand, if the target appears as unusually large, placement of the measuring mark may not be made with sufficient reliability. In practice, therefore a very logical maximum diameter of such a target may be suggested:

$$\mathrm{d}_{\max} = \frac{2D.d'}{f} \tag{7.12}$$

In terrestrial work, one may expect D to vary considerably. Therefore, careful individual designing of such targets is imperative. In general, targets of concentric rings giving several contrasty bands are favoured. These seem to be universal in their applications.

Often one may require targets/marks used for identification purpose only and not for measurements. These have no consequences on the mensural accuracy; hence are not discussed here. However, mensural targets can always be used in such jobs.

7.4 REQUIRED ACCURACIES AND RESULTS

Each job being different from any other, its accuracy requirements need to be separately specified at the time of planning/designing with due consideration of the final objectives. Accordingly, on the completion of the project, the results should be assessed to see if the accuracy specifications are realized. For this also there should be acceptable criteria (of standards and specifications) and testing procedures.

Standard accuracy specifications and testing criteria can be and usually are established for standard (regular) jobs. Topographical mapping is one good example of such standard work. However, even in topo-mapping, accuracy specifications and testing procedures cannot be so clear and without controversy that they would give only one answer to the problem of evaluating the accuracy of a given map. Furthermore, a map may pass or fail, according to how the accuracy specifications are applied or interpreted.

The United States National Map Accuracy Standards, as drawn up by the Congress and issued by the office of Management and Budget (formerly, the Bureau of the Budget) in June 1947 states, among other points:

1. *Horizontal Accuracy*

For maps on publication scales larger than 1:20,000, not more than 10 per cent of the points tested shall be in error by more than 1/30 inch, measured on the publication scale; for maps on publication scales of 1:20,000 or smaller, 1/50 inch. These iimits of accuracy shall apply in all cases to positions of well defined points only. "Well defined" points are those that are easily visible or recoverable on the ground, such as the following: monuments or markers, such as bench marks, property boundary monuments; intersection of roads, railroads, etc.; corners of large buildings or structures (or center points of small buildings); etc. In general what is "well defined" will also be determined by what is plotable on the scale of the map within 1/100 inch. Thus while the intersection of two roads or property lines meeting at right angles would come within a sensible interpretation, identification of the intersection of such lines meeting at an acute angle would obviously not be practicable within 1/100 inch. Similarly, features not identifiable upon the ground within close limits are not considered as test points within the limits quoted, even though their positions may be scaled closely upon the map. In this class would come timber lines, soil boundaries, etc.

2. *Vertical Accuracy*

As applied to contour maps on all publication scales, will be such that not more than 10 per cent of the elevations tested shall be in error more than one-half the contour interval. In checking elevations taken from the map, the apparent vertical error may be decreased by assuming a horizontal displacement within the permissible horizontal error for a map of that scale.

3. *The accuracy of any map*

It may be tested by comparing the positions of points whose locations or elevations are shown upon it with corresponding positions as determined by surveys of a higher accuracy. Tests shall be made by the producing agency, which shall also determine which of its maps are to be tested, and the extent of such testing.

Similar specifications are existing or are being developed in other countries and organizations. They indicate several important aspects, viz.,

(a) There is a general agreement on the desirability of using "standard deviation (or error)" or "root mean square error", directly or indirectly to express accuracy.
(b) In estimating accuracy on a map, there is a widespread agreement of separating planimetry (*X* and *Y* coordinates being combined) from elevation (*Z* coordinates); i.e., horizontal (planimetric) accuracy from vertical (height) accuracy.
(c) For planimetry, it is debatable whether its accuracy should be expressed as a univariate or a bivariate (i.e., consisting of two variables, *X* and *Y*) entity.
(d) Another question remains, whether correct statistical theory is used in such expressions; e.g., whether or not the 90 percent rule is appropriate in evaluating topo maps.

7.4.1 Accuracy in Planimetry

In keeping with common practices, the linear standard errors for planimetric parameters are expressed as below:

$$\sigma_X = \left\{ \frac{\sum_{i=1}^{n} (\Delta X_i)^2}{n} \right\}^{1/2}$$

and

$$\sigma_Y = \left\{ \frac{\sum_{i=1}^{n} (\Delta Y_i)^2}{n} \right\}^{1/2} \tag{7.13}$$

where ΔX_i and ΔY_i are the coordinate discrepancies between accepted (as true or absolutely correct) and mapped positions at each test point;

and n is the total number of points used for checking.

Note: It is debatable if n (or, rather $n-1$) should be used in the denominators. For large values of n, the difference is not significant.

The planimetric standard error (σ_p) is expressed by:

$$\sigma_P^2 = \sigma_X^2 + \sigma_Y^2 \tag{7.14}$$

Some, however, favour using in such cases the *two-dimensional* (i.e., circular or elliptical) *standard error*, which is the error in a quantity defined by two random variables. With a fundamental assumption that planimetric errors are expected with equal probability in any direction with equal magnitude, the circular standard error concept is popular in many quarters. The circular standard error (σ_c) would represent the bivariate distribution level of 39.35 per cent probability.

A comparative study made by Crombie (1967), reported in Thompson and Rosenfield (1971), of three approximate method against the exact solution for determining the radius of a 90 per cent probability circle indicates that the radius that most closely approximates the correct values under all conditions of $\sigma_{min}/\sigma_{max}$ where σ_{min} is the smaller linear standard error of the two gives:

$$\sigma_c = \left\{\frac{\sigma_X^2 + \sigma_Y^2}{2}\right\}^{1/2} = \frac{\sigma_P}{\sqrt{2}} \tag{7.15}$$

7.4.2 Accuracy in Elevation

The elevation accuracy in a map may be expressed by using the Koppe (1905) formula directly or indirectly. This formula, expressed for any point on a contour line is:

$$\sigma_{HC} = \sigma_{H'} + \sigma_P.\tan\alpha \tag{7.16}$$

where σ_{HC} is the standard error in the elevation of a point on the contour line;
$\sigma_{H'}$ is the standard error of the determination of the spot height of a point (a measure of the working system and procedure);
σ_p is the standard planimetric error of a point (also a measure of the system and procedure);
and α is the local slope of the terrain.

This formula is usually adapted for expressing permissible elevation accuracy of points in a map:

$$\sigma_{\bar{H}} = 0.3\cdot\bar{C} + \sigma_P.\tan\alpha \tag{7.17}$$

where $\sigma_{\bar{H}}$ is the permissible standard error in elevation;
$\bar{C}$ is the contour interval;
and σ_P, α are as above.

In practice, this can be applied when the ground slope is uniform over the entire area. In case there is considerable ruggedness, the formula should be applied point by point. This means that, for test points, the formula needs to be somewhat modified and rewritten (after Thompson, 1979):

$$\sigma_H = 0.3\cdot\bar{C} \tag{7.18}$$

where

$\sigma_H = \left\{\frac{\sum e_{\bar{H}}^2}{n}\right\}^{1/2}$ = permissible standard error in elevation (or, height) based on residual errors at each point;

$e_{\bar{H}} = e - \sigma_P.\tan\alpha$ = residual error at each point;

and e is the elevation error before horizontal shift allowance.

7.4.3 Contour Interval

The choice of a contour interval, the obvious expression of the form of a surface is not an easy task. The contour intervals are practically always equal-step sequences.

The contour interval depends basically, on two considerations, viz., the map-scale and the amount of relief. In areas of high relief, the interval needs to be large because primarily of the inability to accommodate numerous lines in a small space. The same argument holds with regard to smaller map-scales. Smaller intervals would mean more work and thus certainly a factor of economic reality also. On the other hand, in order to depict landform in the best possible way one would use the smallest possible interval. This has also a direct relation to the permissible tolerances in the vertical accuracy desired of the map. The contour interval represented on a map should be consistent with the map scale and the intend use of the map.

Based on the UN Studies (1990) a study of the frequency of contour intervals with regard to specific map scales was made by Ghosh (1988). In view of this, one can make a list of recommended contour intervals (Table 7.1)

Table 7.1 : Reasonable contour intervals and elevation accuracies

		Contour intervals (in metre)				
			According to Imhof			
Map scale *M_K*		*Recommended in general (UN study)*	*Mountain-ous terrain ($\alpha = 45°$)*	*Medium terrain ($\alpha = 26°$)*	*Flat terrain ($\alpha = 9°$)*	*Standard error at control points : m_H (in metre)*
1 : 500	Large-Scale group	0.5	1	0.46	0.15	± 0.15
1 : 1 000	Large-Scale group	1	1	0.5	0.25	± 0.30
1 : 2 000	Large-Scale group	2	2	1	0.5	± 0.40
1 : 5 000	Large-Scale group	5	5	2	1	± 0.60
1 : 10 000	Large-Scale group	5, 10	10	5	2	± 0.70
1 : 20 000	Small-Scale group	10, 20	20	10	2.5	± 0.80
1 : 25 000	Small-Scale group	10, 20	20	10	2.5	± 1.00
1 : 50 000	Small-Scale group	10, 20, 40	20, 30	10, 20	5	± 1.25
1 : 100 000	Small-Scale group	20, 50	50	25	5, 10	± 2.00

Note : Usually the cost of mapping varies inversely as the square of m_H for the same map-scale. Therefore, accuracy requirements should be established with care.

Associated with the contour-intervals vis-a-vis the map-scale is the consideration of elevation accuracy. Following the practice in the U.S.A. and most of the NATO countries, the à posteriori standard height error (m_H) required in most countries is that 90% of the elevations tested should be accurate within half the contour interval. On the other hand, the obtainable accuracy in photogrammetric mapping depends on the photography, the camera, the intersection geometry (overlap) and the instrument used, amongst others. Assuming a good quality wide angle (standard) aerial camera, 60% forward overlap and a precision plotter, one would expect m_H to be always better than 0.1% of the flying height. These two accuracy criteria often do not agree in the results.

In view of the above, certain confusion exists with the people involved in planning for topographical mapping. In particular, since the obtainable accuracy depends on the ground control, it is the accuracy desired of such ground control that is often of immediate concern to the planner. In this regard, a list of reasonable average elevation accuracies for ground control as provided in Table 7.1 can be suggested.

With regard to contour intervals (C.I.) one of the most authoritative ideas was presented by Imhof (1965) suggesting the following equation, irrespective of the accuracy requirements:

$$\text{C.I.} = \text{n.log n. tg } \alpha \tag{7.19}$$

where $n = \sqrt{\dfrac{K}{100} + 1}$

α = Slope of terrain

and K = map scale number

Imhof considered in general $\alpha = 45°$ to represent highly mountainous terrain (for example, in countries like Nepal, Switzerland or Equador), $\alpha = 26°$ for medium mountainous terrain (for example, in countries like Burma or Greece) and $\alpha = 9°$ for flat terrain (for example in countries like Bangladesh, Egypt or Holland). For the sake of technical interest, Imhof's ideas may be studied against the values recommended here.

There is also a current tendency, however, to promote variable contour intervals in a map—this based on the terrain ruggedness and other demands made from the map. Even contour intervals combined with shading has been attempted. These indicate newer tendencies. The future would show the possibilities. However, these are beyond the scope of this book.

For further interesting ideas with respect to contour lines and contour intervals, see Richardus (1973).

In assessing test data, one must avoid blunders. An appropriate and statistically acceptable method of detecting blunders (so that one can eliminate them) should be used. Furthermore, in most organizations, coordinatographs are used for reading map coordinates as necessary in such assessments. The positional accuracy of points is evaluated by measurements of graticule (or map grid) marks or lines and well-defined points. In this respect, the use of a calibrated precision coordinatograph is imperative. The use of an on-line computer would allow the evaluation as a real-time operation.

The map grid or graticule points need to be evaluated first in accordance with the used map-projection since the grid represents the geometric foundation of the map. The plan positions of the grid points must be corrected first according to the coordinatograph calibration. The corrected data are then to be fitted by an acceptable transformation (with due consideration of the Least Squares adjustment). The residuals of this adjustment (of grid points) would give an idea of the overall reliability of the map. Only after an evaluation of the map grid points should one work for the evaluation of the detail points for both planimetry and elevation.

Two other tables (Tables 7.2 and 7.3) are presented here with a view to providing answers to other remaining questions with regard to the control on which such map complications are based. These two tables were prepared in 1967 by the ASP Photogrammetry for Highway Committee.

Table 7.2 : Specifications for basic control in aerial surveys and mapping (Maximum error of closure for basic ground control)

Order of accuracy	*Unadjusted horizontal distances*	*Unadjusted horizontal angles*			*Unadjusted vertical distances*
		Traverse	*Triangulation*		
			Average	*Maximum*	
First	1 : 25 000	2" $\sqrt{N}$	1"	3"	4.0 mm $\sqrt{K}$
Second	1 : 10 000	10" $\sqrt{N}$	3"	5"	8.4 mm $\sqrt{K}$
Third	1 : 5 000	30 " $\sqrt{N}$	5"	10"	12.0 mm $\sqrt{K}$
Fourth	1 : 2 500	60" $\sqrt{N}$	15"	30"	120.0 mm $\sqrt{K}$

Note : N is the number of stations in the traverse circuit.
and K is the number of kilometres in the level circuit.
[After the Highway Committee, ASP, 1967]

Table 7.3 : Specifications for error tolerances in control extension by photo-triangulation

Classification		*Absolute error as a fraction of flying height*		
		Planimetry		*Elevation*
		X	*Y*	*Z*
Maximum (±)	(1)	1 : 2 700	1 : 2 700	1 : 1 800
	(2)	1 : 2 100	1 : 2 100	1 : 1 500
Average	(1)	1 : 18 000	1 : 18 000	1 : 12 000
	(2)	1 : 14 000	1 : 14 000	1 : 10 000
Standard (rms)	(1)	1 : 9 000	1 : 9 000	1 : 6 000
	(2)	1 : 7 000	1 : 7 000	1 : 5 000

Note : (1) Refers to Super-wide-angle ($f \sim 9$ cm) photography
(2) Refers to Standard-angle ($f \sim 15$ cm) photography
[After the Highway Committe, ASP, 1967]

It is, however, assumed that with improving technology one would expect to improve on the presented 'specifications'. Individual organizations would consider their own criteria with regard to specific work circumstances. Therefore, the ideas presented in this chapter should be taken in the spirit of a broad guiding outline, of which details could not be provided here.

BIBLIOGRAPHY

American Society of Photogrammetry; *Manual of Photogrammetry,* (4th Ed.) (ASPRS, Falls Church, Virginia: 1980)

Crombie, M.A.; *Note on Circular Errors* (Unpublished, Autometric Operations, Raytheon Corporation: 1967).

Ghosh, Sanjib K.; "Photo/Model/Map Scales", *PE* 37, No. 11 (1971).

Ghosh, Sanjib K.; *Theory of Stereophotogrammetry* (The Ohio State University Bookstores; Columbus, Ohio: 1972).

Ghosh, Sanjib K.; "Economic Aspects in Special Applications of Photogrammetry", *ISP Archives (Invited Paper)* Helsinki Congress; Helsinki, Finland (1976).

Ghosh, Sanjib K.; "Some thoughts on Photo-scale, Map-scale and Contour intervals in topographic mapping", *Photogrammetria* 42, No. 1 (1988).

Harpe, R.W.; "Experiments with Minimum to Optimum Base-Height Ratios" *Proceedings of ASP Semi-Annual Convention;* Dayton, Ohio (1965).

Imhof, Eduard; *Kartographische Gelände-Darstellung* (Walter de Gruyter & Co., Berlin; 1965).

Richardus, P.; "The Precision of Contour Lines and Contour Intervals of Large and Medium Scale Maps", *Photogrammetria* 29, No. 3 (1973).

Thompson, M. M. and G. H. Rosenfield; "On Map Accuracy Specifications", *Surveying and Mapping* 31, No. 1 (1971).

Thompson, M.M.; *Maps for America* (US Geological Survey: 1979).

United Nations (Brandenberger, A.J. and Ghosh, S. K. for the UN); *World Cartography* [Vol. XX, UN Sales No. E. 90. I. 8 (No. ST/TCD/14) : 1990].

8

MULTIPLE-PHOTO APPLICATIONS

The utilization of more than two photographs is nothing but the synthesis of certain photogrammetric principles that are applied to a single photo or simple extension of stereophotogrammetric principles. The user of photogrammetric services can be from various fields of science and engineering. Nevertheless, one major use of analytical photogrammetry has been in the field of control provision for topographic mapping. This is known as *Photo-triangulation* (or, Aerial Triangulation). There are numerous photo-triangulation procedures depending on the instrumental or computational solutions of various involved operations (Ghosh, 1975). These are illustrated in Figs. 8.1 and 8.1a. Depending on the extent of use of an instrument or a computer, one may consider a particular procedure as *analogical* or *analytical.*

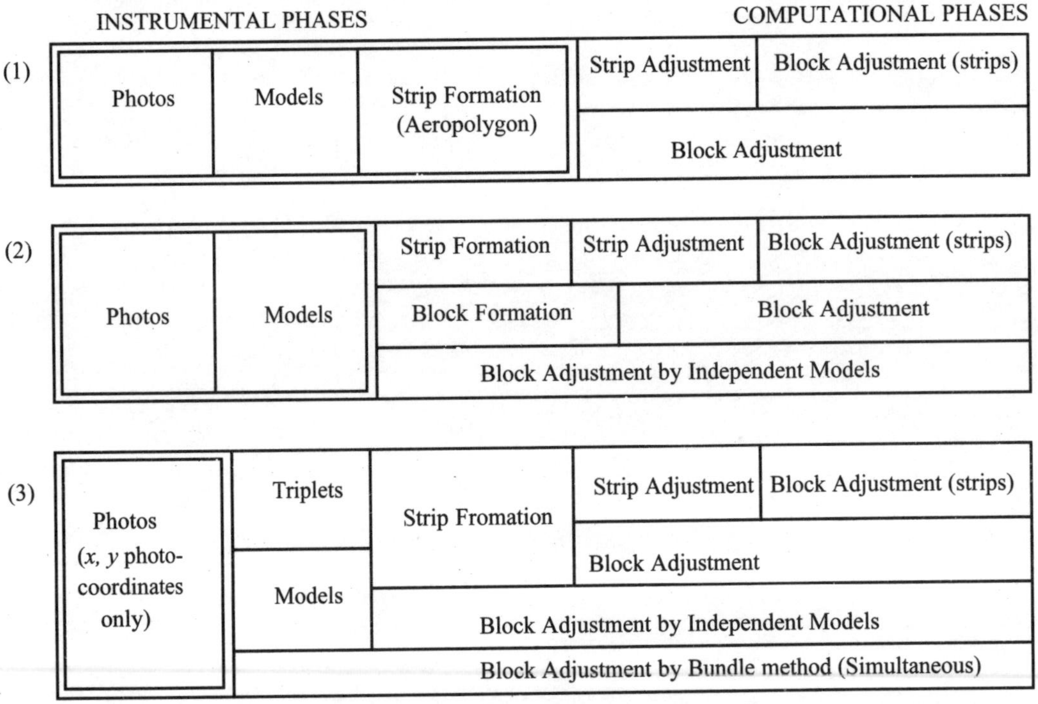

Fig. 8.1: Outline of phototriangulation procedures : [1] Analogical procedures; [2] Semi-analytical procedures; and [3] Analytical procedures

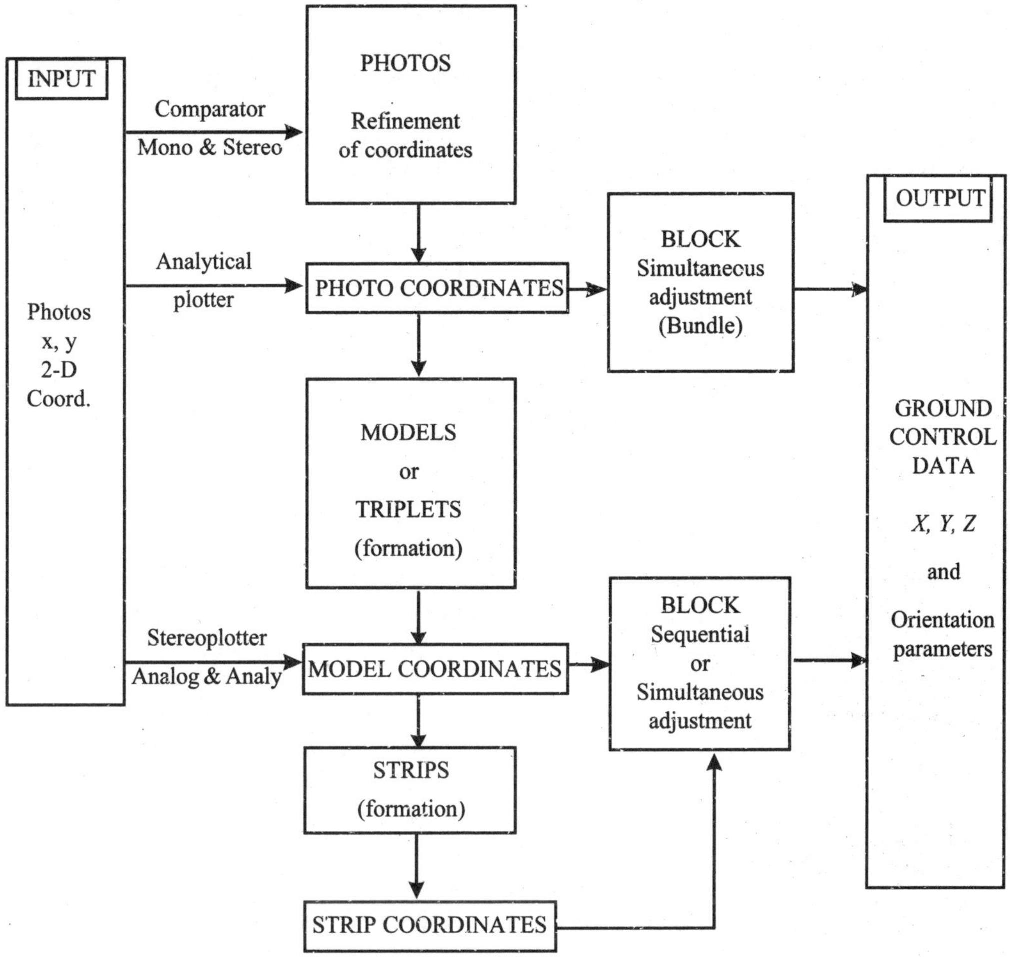

Fig. 8.1a: Flowchart showing various possibilities of analytical phototriangulation

There are usually many ways to approach a problem. It is not easy to prepare a schedule that is both economical and realistic. With regard to data acquisition and data processing, problems related to single photos or stereo models have been presented in Chaps 3, 4 and 5. Multiple photographs pose different and unique data-handling procedures and may even require supplementary mathematical modelling. In this chapter will be discussed only the computational procedures where the instrumental work is limited to the reading of only the x, y photo coordinates, the rest being done at a computer, on-line or off-line. These would illustrate certain procedures which are utilized with success in various organizations.

It may be noted that multiple photographs may also be used in applications other than control extension, like in self-calibration (Chap. 9) or in enhancing intersection accuracies. The triangulation procedures are grouped in two categories, sequential and simultaneous.

8.1 SEQUENTIAL PROCEDURE

This procedure can be visualized as analogous to the instrumental process of photo-triangulation. It consists of the following three computational steps:

(a) Relative Orientation of individual basic units in arbitrary coordinate systems (*Note:* A basic unit can be a stereo-pair, a triplet or a sub-block of limited number of photographs);
(b) Assembly of the basic units to form the full block (of all the photographs);
(c) Adjustment of the assembled block to known control.

There are two variations in this approach:

1. *Aeropolygon*: The procedure somewhat follows the routine of an analog stereoplotter by performing co-orientations (relative orientation by dependent method) in second and subsequent models in each strip. Next, without affecting the co-orientation, the resulting model's scale (say, by utilizing the scale restraint condition) is adjusted to that of the preceding model. One strip is formed and possibly adjusted initially. Other strips are subsequently formed, adjusted and connected one after the other (sequentially) to form the block which is finally adjusted to the ground control. The method of Independent Models (Ackermann *et al.*, 1973; Ghosh, 1975), in principle is basically this approach, performed also with analog stereo plotters.
2. *Three-photo (Triplet) Analytic:* In this procedure, all six orientation elements of the photograph are computed simultaneously (by applying the Collinearity condition) and, in the presence of redundant observations, adjusted by utilizing the principles of Least Squares. For rays to points which are common with the preceding stereo pair, the condition of intersection with the corresponding ray from the first photograph in that model is used for adjusting all exterior orientation elements (see details given later).

In these procedures, in spite of using more than one common point between models, the deformation of one model (Ghosh, 1972) may cause the next and other subsequent models to deform also. Consequently, the results of the triangulation would depend on the initial model (or the basic unit) and the propagation of error through the strip.

A typical example of the various stages of a sequential method of triangulation is as follows (as practiced at the NOS; Keller and Tewinkel, 1967):

Phase I : Data Acquisition
1. Photo preparation and stereo marking of necessary points;
2. Coordinate measurements of all points on the photographs;

Phase II : Data Processing:
1. Coordinate refinement
   a. Correction for comparator calibration (Chap. 2);
   b. Correction for film distortion with reduction to perspective center (Chap. 5);
   c. Correction for lens distortion (Chap. 5);

d. Correction for atmospheric refraction (Chap. 5);
e. Correction for Earth's curvature (Chap. 5), if applicable;
f. Corrections for image motion and réseau (Chap. 5) as may be applicable;

2. Solution
   a. Iterative coorientations (or three-photo orientations, explained later);
   b. Cantilever assembly (with or without scale restraint, Chap. 4);
   c. Earth curvature correction, if applicable and not performed earlier;
   d. Strip (or Block) transformation to the ground control system (Chap. 3);
3. Solution refinement
   a. Further transformation as necessary (e.g., to Geocentric system);
   b. Block adjustment (explained later) in case necessary.

Most strip triangulations would terminate at Phase II2b (Keller and Tewinkel, 1967). However, depending on the degree of required accuracy, one may continue with the subsequent steps. Step II2a, alternately, may be performed by (i) Relative orientation using coplanarity condition (Chap. 4) and (ii) Scale-transfer, by using the scale-restraint condition (Chap. 4). Some of these steps are elaborated briefly below:

Iterative Coorientation

This is entirely independent of any ground control data. The three-photo orientation is also coorientational. At the end of the strip, one obtains the positions of all pertinent points in a three-dimensional coordinate system at the approximate photo scale (unless a particular scale is considered). The residual errors can be analyzed at this stage with the help of a computer. Data with blunders may be removed to obtain 'clean' data for subsequent work.

Strip Transformation to Ground System

This is the transformation of model coordinates into the prevailing ground control by fitting, through the application of polynomials (Ghosh, 1975). The principle of Least Squares may be applicable here also. The result of this step is a set of provisional three-dimensional coordinates of all points in the strip. Large residual discrepancies may be detected by human inspection to provide another step of freeing the data of blunders prior to entering the solution refinement program.

Block Adjustment

This would involve: (a) Simultaneous solution of the parameters of absolute orientation (viz., dX_0, dY_0, dZ_0 $d\omega$, $d\phi$ and $d\kappa$) for all the photos; and (b) Corrections to the provisional coordinates (X, Y, Z) of all the points. In the US National Oceanic Survey practice (Keller and Tewinkel, 1967), this consists of three stages:

1. *Space Resection.* It starts with reading into storage the known ground coordinates (duly weighted) of control points and also the provisional ground coordinates of all points. The space resection routine fits the image coordinates data from each photograph

to the corresponding provisional ground data in order to determine the initial exterior orientation parameters. This leads to the solution of the sets of equations (one set for each photograph) having the six incremental corrections to the unknown parameters and solving iteratively until further corrections are insignificant (see also Chaps. 4 and 6).

2. *Block Orientation.* The solution of absolute orientation of all the photographs and the obtaining of the ground coordinates (final) of each point. The output of this stage contains:
   (a) The maximum angular correction required by each program pass;
   (b) The ground coordinates of all *pass points* used in relative orientation;

   Note: Pass points are of two types: (1) *Transfer points,* used for connecting adjacent models in the same strip; and (2) *Tie* or *Wing points*, used for connecting adjacent or crossing strips (Ghosh, 1975).

   (c) The misfits at the weighted control points;
   (d) The residual discrepancies of all photo coordinates on each photograph and the standard (RMS) values for the entire block;
   (e) The sine and cosine values of the final rotation angles (ω, ϕ, κ) of each photograph; and
   (f) The final three coordinates of each camera station (X_0, Y_0, Z_0).
3. *Object Intersection.* This gives the points other than pass points and the control points for which accurate ground coordinates are to be computed (e.g., the points for low-flown models from high-flown photographs). Because these points are non-uniformly distributed, they are generally not included in the stage of orientation, since their very presence could weight the solution unduly in view of their locations. An unlimited number of points may be determined in this stage because of their separate treatments.

Three-Photo Analytic (or, Triplet) Method

One requires only two photographs for a relative orientation. The use of three photographs, combining aspects of relative orientation and scale transfer in a simultaneous solution, may be considered as a computational advantage toward a stronger geometry. The scheme is set for basic unit of three photographs (hence the name, Triplet), e.g., 1-2-3, 2-3-4, 3-4-5, and so on. Each triplet is oriented separately. By using three photographs in the triple overlap area, one obtains a double check on the y-parallax (relative orientation) and a check on the x-parallax (scale transfer). This scheme is illustrated in Fig. 8.2. This arrangement helps tie one stereopair (say 3-4) to the adjacent ones (say, here, 2-3 and 4-5) with considerable strength. This is because one has a complete stereopair consisting of two rows of pass-points for connecting adjacent triplets (e.g., in Fig. 8.2, points *d, e, f,* and *g, h, i,* are common to the triplets I and II). The working procedure is to consider the middle photograph of a triplet as fixed and the adjacent photographs are tied to it simultaneously on both sides. Also, a value for one stereo base (bx) is assigned initially. For example, one may consider the following in triplet I:

Photo #1 : $X_{01} = 0$ and ω_1, ϕ_1, κ_1, Y_{01}, Z_{01} are assumed to be zero initially.
Photo #2 : $X_{02} = 1$ and $\omega_2 = \phi_2 = \kappa_2 = Y_{02} = Z_{02} = 0$ kept fixed; and
Photo # 3: X_{03}, Y_{03}, Z_{03}, ω_3 ϕ_3 and κ_3 are assumed to be zero initially.

Each photograph having six exterior orientation elements, this scheme gives seven out of the total eighteen elements as fixed initially. In order to avoid negative values, for practical convenience, it is advisable to consider $X_{01} = 0$ and $X_{02} = 1$. This means that, in this triplet, in view of one collinearity equation for each photo coordinate and the standard pass points, the following situation exists :

Photo no.	*Number of Points*	*Number of Unknowns*	*Number of Equations*
1	6	5	12
2	9	0	18
3	6	6	12

Thus, in this triplet, there are 11 unknowns and 42 observation equations, which can be reduced to eleven normal equations (in order to solvė for the eleven unknowns by applying the principles of Least Squares). The method of obtaining model coordinates of points and the associated details are discussed in Ghosh (1975).

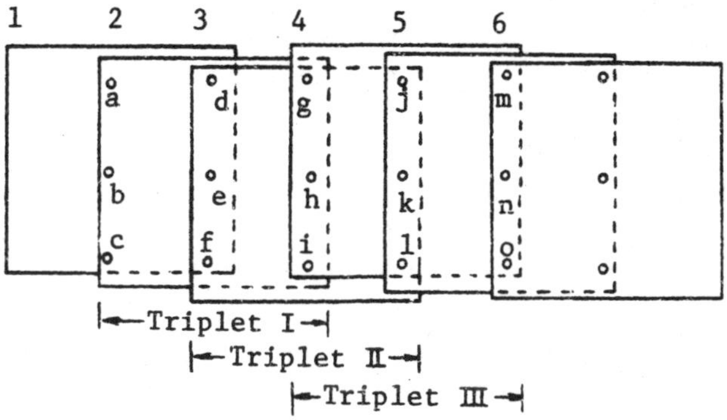

Fig. 8.2: Schematic arrangement of triplets

When triplet II is connected to triplet I, the Z values at points d, e, f are first taken from triplet I; at points g, h, i are taken from triplet II; while the X and Y values are checked together from both triplets. This procedure follows to the end of the strip. Circumstances permitting, two-directional (i.e., along X- and Y-axes) triplets are of considerable help in block formation and adjustment.

The basic condition equations in this case are of the form of Eqs 4.8 for photographs 1 and 3 (2 being fixed), by linearizing which the set of observation equations of the form of Eqs 4.14 is obtained:

For the first stereogram (i.e., photo pair 1-2):

$$\left.\begin{aligned} v_{x1j} &= P_{11} + P_{12}d\omega_1 + P_{13}d\phi_1 + P_{14}d\kappa_1 - P_{15}dX_{01} - P_{16}dY_{01} \\ &\quad - P_{17}dZ_{01} + P_{15}dX_{1j} + P_{16}dY_{1j} + P_{17}dZ_{1j} \\ v_{y1j} &= P_{21} + P_{22}d\omega_1 + P_{23}d\phi_1 + P_{24}d\kappa_1 - P_{25}dX_{01} - P_{26}dY_{01} \\ &\quad - P_{27}dZ_{01} + P_{25}dX_{1j} + P_{26}dY_{1j} + P_{27}dZ_{1j} \end{aligned}\right\} \qquad (8.1)$$

For the second stereogram (i.e., photo pair 2-3):

$$\left.\begin{aligned} v_{x3j} &= Q_{11} + Q_{12}d\omega_3 + Q_{13}d\phi_3 + Q_{14}d\kappa_3 - Q_{15}dX_{O1} - Q_{16}dY_{O3} \\ &\quad - Q_{17}dZ_{O3} + Q_{15}dX_{3j} + Q_{16}dY_{3j} + Q_{17}dZ_{3j} \\ v_{y3j} &= Q_{21} + Q_{22}d\omega_3 + Q_{23}d\phi_3 + Q_{24}d\kappa_3 - Q_{25}dX_{O3} - Q_{26}dY_{O3} \\ &\quad - Q_{27}dZ_{O3} + Q_{25}dX_{3j} + Q_{26}dY_{3j} + Q_{27}dZ_{3j} \end{aligned}\right\} \quad (8.2)$$

Where the coefficients $P_{11} \ldots P_{27}$ and $Q_{11} \ldots Q_{27}$ are derived by partial differentiation of the basic pairs of equations of the form of Eqs 4.8. Subscript j refers to the point, subscripts x and y refer to the respective photo coordinates, and subscripts 1, 2 and 3 refer to the respective photographs. The coefficients obtained in this way have initially only preliminary values, which are changed in the iterative procedure of computation to add corrections to the respective variables.

The unknown parameters here are of two groups, viz, (a) The Exterior orientation parameters, $d\omega$, $d\phi$, $d\kappa$, dX_0, dY_0 and dZ_0, all of which remain constant for one photograph; and (b) the Model coordinates, dX_j, dY_j and dZ_j, each of which differ for each point. Because X, Y, Z are variables that differ with each photograph, an elimination of these variables is necessary for the solution of Eqs 8.1 and 8.2. This can be done by substituting their values in terms of the variables that are fixed in value for every photograph (i.e., ω, ϕ, κ, X_0, Y_0 and Z_0). For interesting ideas on these, see Harris *et al*., (1963), Anderson and McNair (1966), and Ghosh (1975).

The most used sequential procedure is not fully computational. It may be considered as a variation where the relative orientation of the stereo models is performed at a stereo plotter (can be an analytical plotter), simply because of convenience and overall efficiency. In this procedure, model connection, scale-transfer, strip or block formation and adjustments are subsequently performed at a computer. Because of this combination of analytical and anological processes, often this is called a "Semi-analytical" method of photo triangulation.

Some specific methods of sequential photo-triangulation procedure as currently available in the world are listed below:

1. *The Ohio State University Method:* For strip or block triangulation at a stereo plotter or an analytical plotter by the collection of Independent Models (see Ghosh, 1975 for details and the computer programs). Philip (1973) made an interesting error study of this method and Strahle (1971) made a comparative study of this method by utilizing an analytical plotter.
2. *National Research Council of Canada Method*: For strip triangulation, with a possibility of extension into a block by using only comparator data. In this the basic unit is the stereo model. See Schut (1973) for details.
3. *National Oceanic Survey of the USA Method*: For strip or block triangulation by using triplets as basic units and by utilizing only comparator data. See Harris *et al*., (1963), Keller and Tewinkel (1966, 1967) for details and various aspects of the procedure.
4. *University of Stuttgart Method*: For strip or block triangulation with Independent Models with a stereo plotter or a comparator, the basic unit being the stereo model. See Ackermann *et al*., (1973) for details. The software contains a simultaneous adjustment of models in the block.

5. *Rapid Analytical Block Aerial Triangulation System (RABATS) Method*: This is a comprehensive strip or block triangulation software package developed by J. F. Kenefick, Photogrammetric Consultant, Inc., Florida, USA. The basic unit here is a stereo model formed either at a stereo plotter or with comparator data. Private communications with the author indicates that this has various features; e.g., as a by-product of fully analytical solutions, relative and absolute orientation elements are calculated for a number of stereo plotters. A group of 'support' programs are provided for computation peripheral to the aerial triangulation solution itself. An auxiliary program allows readjustment of a provisional horizontal solution for a strip or block to independently measured distances and azimuths. Some interesting features of this method are presented in Ghosh (1975).This has since been updated by using GPS capabilities.

8.2 SIMULTANEOUS PROCEDURE

This procedure (also known as "Bundle" solution) offers another approach whereby the desired parameters are also adjusted as a result of one simultaneous least squares solution of all the photographs by an iterative method. The iteration is involved because of the fact that the associated condition equations are non-linear. However, one can also form non-linear 'normal equations', in which case the solution can be considered as 'direct'. From a theoretical point of view, such a simultaneous procedure should provide the most accurate results.

The fundamental requirements in this procedure are the estimates of the exterior orientation parameters. Furthermore, depending on the specific approach taken, the estimates for coordinates of all pass points may also be needed. Thus, a simultaneous, procedure should include a feasible method of obtaining the necessary estimated (approximate) values initially.

The basic equations used in this are the ones establishing the collinearity condition (see Eqs. 4.8, 4.9, 4.10). These are non-linear functions relating the parameters (unknowns) to the observed and given (known) data:

$$f(L) = F(O, X) \tag{8.3}$$

where L represents the observed (x, y) photo coordinates, already refined for all systematic distortions;
O represents the exterior orientation parameters;
and X represents the object space coordinates.

Considering that the observation data (albeit refined) may have discrepancies or residual errors (represented by V), one gets:

$$L + V = F(O_0 + \Delta O, X_0 + \Delta X) \tag{8.4}$$

where O_0, X_0 are the approximate values;
and $\Delta O, \Delta X$ are the successive corrections.

Linearization of Eq. 8.4 by a Taylor expansion would give :

$$f(L) + \frac{\partial f}{\partial L}\Delta L = F(O_0, X_0) + \frac{\partial F}{\partial O}\Delta O + \frac{\partial F}{\partial X}\Delta X \tag{8.5}$$

This, compactly stated and utilizing the commonly used notations, with respect to the image point *j* on photograph *i*, is :

$$\underset{(2,1)}{v_{ij}} + \underset{(2,6)}{\dot{B}_{ij}}\ \underset{(6,1)}{\dot{\delta}_i} + \underset{(2,3)}{\ddot{B}_{ij}}\ \underset{(3,1)}{\ddot{\delta}_j} = \underset{(2,1)}{\epsilon_{ij}} \tag{8.6}$$

where $v_{ij} = [v_x\ v_y]_{ij}$ = residuals of measured photo-coordinates;

$\dot{B}_{ij} = \begin{bmatrix} a_1\ a_2 \ldots\ a_6 \\ b_1\ b_2 \ldots b_6 \end{bmatrix}$ = coefficient matrix, in which the elements are partial differentials of the collinearity equations with respect to the unknown, exterior orientation, parameters of the photograph;

$\dot{\delta}_i = \left[\delta_\omega, \delta_\phi \ldots z_O\right]_i$ = corrections to estimates for the unknown exterior orientation parameters;

$\ddot{B}_{ij} = \begin{bmatrix} a_7\ a_8 \ldots\ a_9 \\ b_7\ b_8 \ldots b_9 \end{bmatrix}_{ij}$ = coefficient matrix, in which the elements are partial differentials of the collinearity equations with respect to the unknown, object point, coordinates;

$\ddot{\delta}_h = \left[\Delta X\ \ \Delta Y\ \ \Delta Z\right]_j$ = corrections to estimates for the unknown object point, coordinates;

and $\epsilon_{ij} = \left[f(x)\ \ f(y)\right]_{ij}$ = the value of Eq. 8.3 with estimated values being substituted for the unknown parameters.

Equivalently, $\bar{V} + \bar{B}\,\bar{\delta} = \epsilon$ (8.7)

Equations 8.6 or 8.7 are the 'condition' equations, from which the 'Normal' equations (see for example, Mikhail, 1976) are formed:

$$N.\,\delta = C \tag{8.8}$$

where $\boldsymbol{N} = \boldsymbol{\bar{B}}^{\mathrm{T}} \boldsymbol{P}\, \boldsymbol{\bar{B}}$

$C = \boldsymbol{\bar{B}}^{\mathrm{T}} \boldsymbol{P} \epsilon$

and $\boldsymbol{P}$ is the weight (inverse of the covariance) matrix.

The solution of the normal equations is expressed by:

$$\delta = N^{-1}C \tag{8.9}$$

Further consideration of the comparative reliability of various parameters can be made in the adjustment procedure by enforcing "weight constraints" (discussed in Chap. 9). The weight matrics of the exterior orientation parameters and of the object point coordinates can be determined. Their utilization in a simultaneous solution of a block of aerial photographs (after Brown, 1974, 1976) modifies the set of normal equations (Eq. 8.8), by making use of partitioning, to give:

$$\begin{bmatrix} \dot{N}+\dot{P} & \bar{N} \\ \bar{N}^T & \ddot{N}+\ddot{P} \end{bmatrix} \begin{bmatrix} \dot{\delta} \\ \ddot{\delta} \end{bmatrix} = \begin{bmatrix} \dot{C}-\dot{P}_{\in} \\ \ddot{C}-\ddot{P}_{\in} \end{bmatrix} \tag{8.10}$$

in which, for a block of m photographs containing n object points, the respective dimensions are given below:

$\dot{\delta}$: 6m × 1 $\dot{\text{P}}$: 6m × 6m $\in$: 6m × 1

$\ddot{\delta}$: 3n × 1 $\ddot{\text{P}}$: 3n × 3n $\in$: 3n × 1

Note, as before, single dots refer to the exterior orientation parameters and double dots refer to the object point coordinates. $\dot{\mathbf{P}}$ and $\ddot{\mathbf{P}}$ are the inverse covariance matrices. $\in$ and $\in$ are the vectors of discrepancies between *a priori* (or, observed) values of exterior orientation parameters and object point coordinates, respectively, and their corresponding values used in linearization of projective equations. $\dot{N}, \ddot{N}, \bar{N}, \dot{C}$ and $\ddot{C}$ are the contributions to normal equations resulting from the observed (and refined) photo-coordinates of the points.

The feasibility of a solution in practice depends on the augmentation of the weight matrices, their becoming diagonal matrices of dimension 6 × 6 for each photograph. This hinges on the assumption that the exterior orientation elements of different photographs are uncorrelated. Likewise, the coordinates of different object points are also assumed to be uncorrelated. For those parameters which are treated as completely unknown, the appropriate positions of the augmented weight matrices are filled with zero elements. The augmented supplementary discrepancy vectors $\in$ and $\in$ also would contain zero elements in the appropriate locations for the unknown quantities. Thus, $\ddot{P}_j$ and $\in_j$ for points used in relative orientation for example, would reduce to null matrics.

8.3 SOLUTION OF NORMAL EQUATIONS

It will be of interest to note that the normal equations of the form given below (Eq. 8.11) are indeterminate if one holds the working assumption that all of the three coordinates of each of the ground points as well as six of the exterior orientation parameters of each photograph, both, are unknowns unless some other additional considerations (as in self-calibration) are made. The matrics are defined directly by the linearized pair of projective equations (Eq. 8.6).

$$\begin{bmatrix} \underset{(6,6)}{\dot{N}_{ij}} & \underset{(6,3)}{\bar{N}_{ij}} \\ \underset{(3,6)}{\bar{N}^{T}_{ij}} & \underset{(3,3)}{\ddot{N}_{ij}} \end{bmatrix} \begin{bmatrix} \underset{(6,1)}{\dot{\delta}_i} \\ \underset{(3,1)}{\ddot{\delta}_j} \end{bmatrix} = \begin{bmatrix} \underset{(6,1)}{\dot{C}_{ij}} \\ \underset{(3,1)}{\ddot{C}_{ij}} \end{bmatrix} \tag{8.11}$$

where $\dot{N} = \dot{B}^{T} P \dot{B}$; $\ddot{N} = \ddot{B}^{T} P \ddot{B}$; $\bar{N} = \dot{B}^{T} P \ddot{B}$

$\dot{C} = \dot{B}^{T} P \dot{I}$; $\ddot{c} = \ddot{B}^{T} P \ddot{I}$;

and P is the weight matrix of the measured photo coordinates.

This difficulty of indeterminacy can be removed by deleting from this system each row and column corresponding to a known quantity. Furthermore, whenever a point (*j*) fails to appear on a photo (i), the weight matrix (***P***) can be set to a zero matrix. This yields two alterations of the general normal equations, viz. (a) All corresponding $\bar{N}_{ij}$ submatrices become null matrices; and (b) All indicated summations along the principal diagonal are limited either to the points appearing on a given photograph (upper semidiagonal) or to the photographs containing a given point (lower semi-diagonal).

In view of above, for an aerial block triangulation, the overall $\bar{N}$ submatrix tends to be rather sparse in the final structure. This is illustrated in Fig. 8.4, which shows the structure of the coefficient matrix of the general system of normal equations generated from the photo block schematically presented in Fig. 8.3.

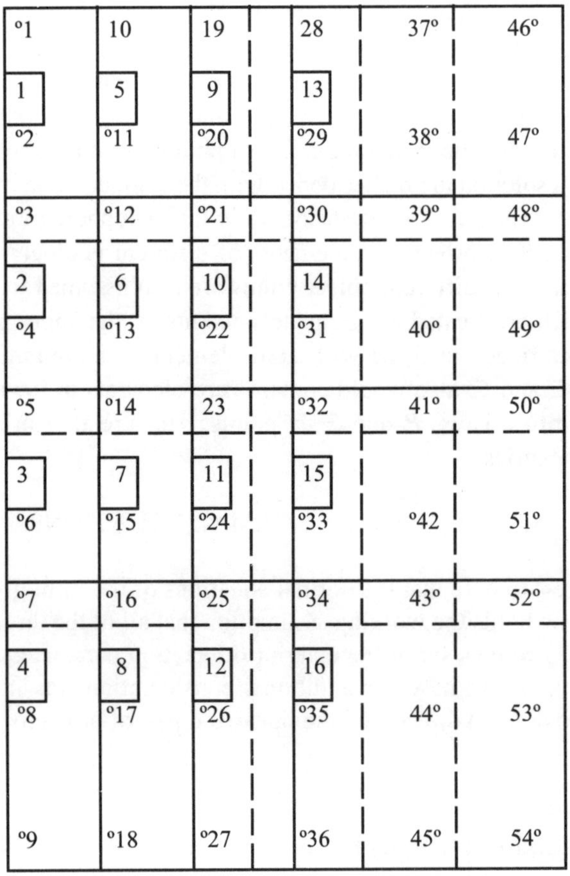

Fig. 8.3: Schematic diagram of a block of 4 × 4 photographs (with cross-strip ordering of points and photographs, after Brown, 1976)

Brown *et al.*, (1964), in taking advantage of the sparseness characteristics of the matrix, utilized the indirect method of *Block Successive Over-Relaxation* (BSOR). The unique characteristic of this approach lies in the use of an indexing scheme whereby, (a) only the non-zero submatrices of the normal equations would be formed, and (b) these would be stored and operated on in a collapsed form (see Fig. 8.4). This process drastically reduces storage requirements in the computer and facilitates the formation and solution of the normal equations. Davis (1966) demonstrated the effectiveness of this approach. The BSOR approach is somewhat sensitive to the number and distribution of absolute control points in the block. If there are more control points, the convergence of the solution is faster (i.e., fewer iterations). In the extreme cases of very sparse control, the slowness of convergence may create confusion in otherwise satisfactory reduction of data. Another drawback of this approach is that it does not produce the inverse of the coefficient matrix of the normal equations. Thus, the assessment of the quality of the adjustment (in terms of computations of the covariance matrices of triangulated coordinates) is not accomplished efficiently.

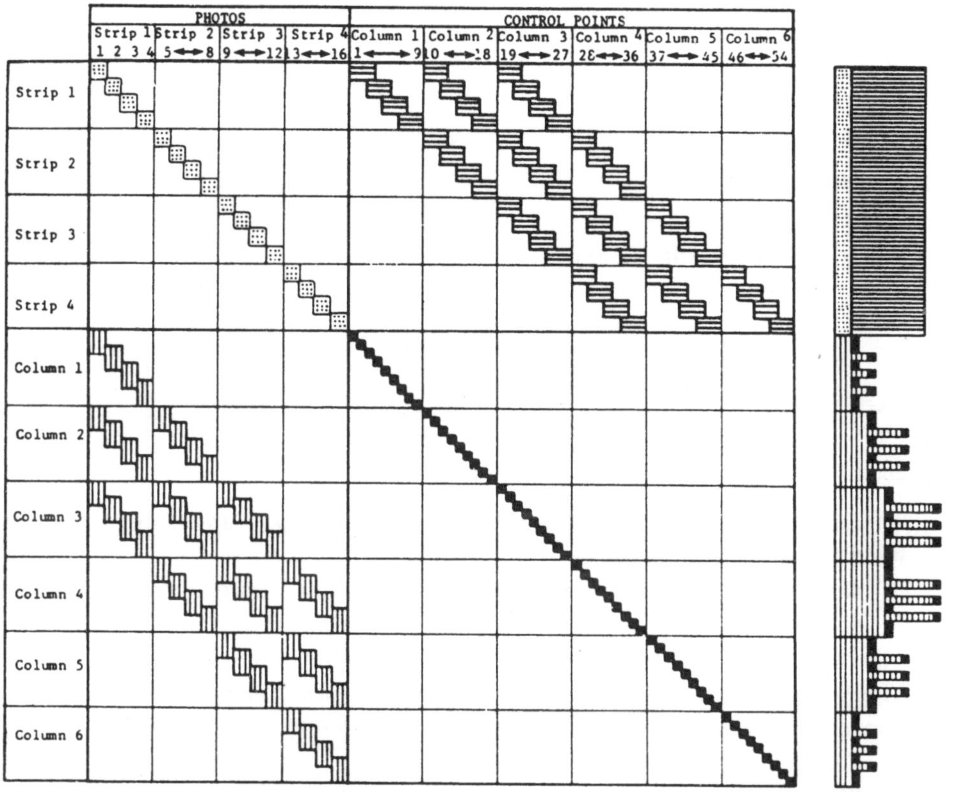

(a) The Full Cofficient Matrix

(b) The collapsed Matrix

Fig. 8.4: Structure of general normal equations for simultaneous adjustment of the block shown in Fig. 8.3 (after Brown, 1976)

The shortcomings of the BSOR reduction are avoided by utilizing an algorithm called *Recursive Partitioning,* first published by Gyer (1967). This is performed by exploiting the banded structure of the reduced normal equations generated in the block triangulation with appropriately ordered photographs (see Fig. 8.4, note the $\bar{N}$ matrix for example, conforming to the cross-strip ordering scheme of Fig. 8.3). With cross-strip ordering, all non-zero elements of the coefficient matrix are confined to a diagonal band. The width of the band depends on the number of strips forming the block, but is independent of the number of photographs in the strips.

Recursive partitioning is also applicable to banded-bordered system as illustrated in Fig. 8.5, which shows one $N \times N$ coefficient matrix having bandwidth q and borderwidth r. Following Brown (1976), one may start with the quadruply partitioned banded-bordered system as illustrated in Fig. 8.5. The number of elements in the first partition (s) is arbitrary except that $s \leq q$. In the second partition, the number of elements correspond to the bandwidth q. The third partition contains $t = N - (s + q + r)$ and the fourth partition is equal to the borderwidth r. In view of this partitioning, the submatrics N_{13} and $N^T{}_{13}$ are both composed of zeroes.

Furthermore, the subvector δ_1 is eliminated by applying the method of partitioning. This process gives the system (mathematical model) as expressed in Eq. 8.12.

$$\left\{\begin{vmatrix} N_{22} & N_{23} & N_{24} \\ N_{23}^T & N_{33} & N_{34} \\ N_{24}^T & N_{34}^T & N_{44} \end{vmatrix} - \begin{vmatrix} N_{12}^T \\ N_{13}^T \\ N_{14}^T \end{vmatrix} N_{11}^{-1} \begin{bmatrix} N_{12} & N_{13} & N_{14} \end{bmatrix}\right\} \begin{bmatrix} \delta_2 \\ \delta_3 \\ \delta_4 \end{bmatrix} = \begin{bmatrix} c_2 \\ c_3 \\ c_4 \end{bmatrix} - \begin{bmatrix} N_{12}^T \\ N_{13}^T \\ N_{14}^T \end{bmatrix} N_{11}^{-1} c_1 \tag{8.12}$$

The N_{13} and $N^T{}_{13}$ matrices being zero matrices, Eq. 8.12 reduced to :

$$\begin{bmatrix} N_{22} - N_{12}^T N_{11}^{-1} N_{12} & N_{23} & N_{24} - N_{12}^T N_{11}^{-1} N_{14} \\ N_{23}^T & N_{33} & N_{34} \\ N_{24}^T - N_{14}^T N_{11}^{-1} N_{12} & N_{34}^T & N_{44} - N_{14}^T N_{11}^{-1} N_{14} \end{bmatrix} \begin{bmatrix} \delta_2 \\ \delta_3 \\ \delta_4 \end{bmatrix} = \begin{bmatrix} c_2 - N_{12}^T N_{11}^{-1} c_1 \\ c_3 \\ c_4 - N_{14}^T N_{11}^{-1} c_1 \end{bmatrix} \tag{8.13}$$

This reduced system (Eq. 8.13) would demonstrate the following:

1. The original banded-bordered form is preserved with the same band- and border-widths (viz., q and r, respectively in Fig. 8.5);
2. N_{11} N_{12} and $N^T{}_{12}$ are eliminated with their contributions absorbed into N_{22};
3. N_{14} and $N^T{}_{14}$ are eliminated with their contributions absorbed into N_{24}, $N^T{}_{24}$ and N_{44};
4. The remainder, N_{34} and $N^T{}_{34}$ remain unaltered; and importantly enough,
5. There is no change in the basic structure of the coefficient matrix although the dimensions are reduced from $N \times N$ to $(N - s) \times (N - s)$.

The above indicates a simple repetitive reduction process which can be formulated as one recurring, and thus the name *Recursive Partitioning.* The number of arithmetic operations required in the reduction of an $N \times N$ banded-bordered system is much reduced. With a bandwidth q and a borderwidth r, assuming $q >> r$ (which is the case in practice), the number of arithmetic operations required in reducing one $N \times N$ system is approximately proportional to $(q+r)^2N$ as against N^3 in a conventional reduction by Gaussian elimination procedure. This indicates considerable computational efficiency when $(q + r) << \mathbf{N}$, which is common with aerial photo block-triangulation. Further interesting ideas on these can be obtained in the publications of Gyer (1967) and Brown (1976). Mikhail and Helmering (1973) have presented interesting discussions on the application of recursive methods in photogrammetric data reduction in general.

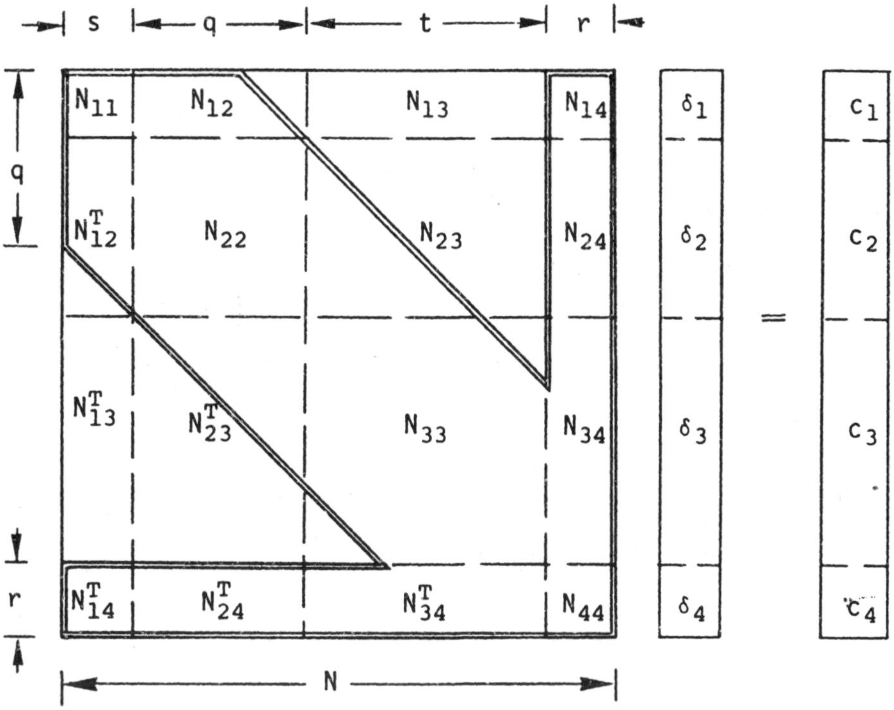

Fig. 8.5: An example of $N \times N$ banded-bordered coefficientmatrix with bandwith q and borderwidth r (after Brown, 1976)

Some specific examples of simultaneous procedure of photo-triangulation programs as currently available in the world are briefly discussed below:

1. *The Ohio State University Method*: Coded FORTBLOCK (Fortran Block-triangulation) consists of the main section and five sub-routines as follows:
   (a) MAIN program has all of the storage allocated for those arrays whose size is data dependent. It arrays documentation.
   (b) BLKTN (for block) subroutine handles actual numerical computation in three steps; viz., (i) Formation of normal equations, (ii) Call subroutine COFEI to compute partials with respect to exterior orientation and survey coordinate parameters, and (iii) Residuals of photo coordinates are computed and printed prior to adjustment.
   (c) COFEI subroutine computes partials with respect to elements and survey coordinates as mentioned above.
   (d) MATINV subroutine computers increase of matrix using a border technique;
   (e) MERGE subroutine receives control and forms the data base to be used. It provides

a means to combine the input data (e.g., exposure station, survey coordinates, etc.) into a form acceptable to the BLKTN subroutine.

(f) OUTPOS subroutine computes the elements of the rotation matrices.

Note : A simpler version of this program has been presented in Ghosh (1975).

2. *SAPGO* (an acronym for Simultaneous Adjustment of Photogrammetric and Geodetic Observations) *Method*: It was developed by Wong and Elphingstone (1972) and gives a solution to include geodetic measurements such as distances, horizontal angles, Laplace azimuths, longitudes, latitudes and elevations. It has been coded in Fortran IV language and has been tested for both strips and blocks. The SAPGO package consists of separate programs as follows:
   (a) *Image refinement:* for correcting the image coordinates for lens distortion, atmospheric refraction and film shrinkages;
   (b) *The Principal program:* for performing photo triangulation; and
   (c) *Error Propagation program:* for computing the standard deviations of the computed ground coordinates. The inverse of the normal equations matrix is stored on disc for use in this program.
3. *MUSAT* (an acronym for Multiple Station Analytical Triangulation) *Method*: It was developed by the US Army Engineer Topographic Laboratories (see Matos, 1971) and provides a technique for the triangulation and adjustment of a model, strip or block of aerial photographs in a single computer run. Two variations of the MUSAT program have been completed by the Raytheon Corporation under contract of the US-ATL. The first, called MUSAT, employs the coplanarity condition for forming the stereo pairs; and the second, called Expanded MUSAT, uses the collinearity condition. This latter version also includes data editing, blunder elimination, and a technique for rapid solution and inversion of large systems of normal equations. The MUSAT programs are coded to run in the IBM 7094 with Fortran IV language. They have also been coded to run in the UNIVAC 1108 computer. The programs are capable of some statistical analyses of results and propagation of errors. The Expanded MUSAT is claimed to be capable of triangulating up to 2000 photos in one run. Position data output may be in UTM (Universal Transverse Mercator), Geographic, Geocentric or Local coordinate systems. The program has been modified to include the functional constraints of air and ground distance measurements to supplement required standard ground control.
4. *Schmid Method*: It is based on the work of Schmid (1959). It uses the so called "bundles" of rays in each photograph simultaneously. A program documented by Schenk (1972) was written in Fortran IV language for the CDC 6400/6500 computer. The initial program can handle upto 500 photographs in the block to a maximum of 49 points per photograph and to a maximum of 2048 points in the block. The method, however, somewhat resembles the system developed in the US National Oceanic Survey as discussed by Keller and Tewinkel (1967).
5. *Brown Method*: It has been developed by the DBA System Inc., Melbourne, Florida. The solution is based on a pair of collinearity condition equations for each point as in

the other methods. In the words of Brown "In the solution, a duality exists between all quantities associated with the unknown elem^nts of orientation and the corresponding quantities associated with the unknown coordinates of the control points. Hence, there exists two forms of the solution, depending upon the interpretation assigned to the primary matrices and their associated indices" . The solution is iterative as the other programs and provides a simultaneous adjustment of an entire strip or block. Brown claims considerable versatility in the entire program, which was originally written for the CDC 1604-B computer complex of the Rome Air Development Center of the US Air Force. It consists of a direct formation of the "collapsed" system of normal equations and utilization of the iterative method of "Block Successive Overrelaxation". For the initial program, which is understood to have been considerably modified since then, see Brown *et al.*, (1964).

6. *Bundle Refinement Aerial Triangulation Solution (BRATS) Method*: Developed by J. F. Kenefick, Photogrammetric Consultants, Inc., Florida, U.S.A. Nearly all of BRATS input data are collected from files generated by RABATS (Sec. 8.1). Like RABATS, it is comprised of a series of program modules. BRATS is a fully rigorous bundle solution in which individual control points may be appropriately weighted. All BRATS modules contain their own data validation checks and it is possible to edit data or even to iterate the solution which is not often required.

It has been demonstrated during the 1980s that Block Triangulation (by the Bundle method even without self-calibration or by the Independent Model method) can reach a precision level of 3 μm or better for image coordinates. This is indicative of the high geometrical quality fidelity of modern aerial photography and measuring instruments. The efficiency, however, depends also on sequential algorithm, required computer facilities, method of analyses and degree of interactions in the computation procedures (Gruen, 1985; Julia, 1986).

An interesting study by Forstner (1985) supports the views given in Ghosh (1975) to emphasize good preparation and project planning for Block Aerotriangulation. Such a project planning should consist of appropriate choice of block parameters like overlap and of the distribution of control and pass points. These would lead to not only a homogeneous precision but also to a high reliability of such a triangulation.

These ideas can be extended to imagery other than direct aerial or spatial photography. McGlone and Mikhail (1985) obtained very satisfactory results with aircraft multispectral scanner data by using modified collinearity equations, constrained segmentation of strips, *a priori* weighting of parameters and constraints, and editing and evaluation statistics.

Camera orientation data and all other supplementary data available from modern computer controlled systems for photo-flight navigation provide extended auxiliary data, the processing of which in simultaneous block adjustment would permit considerable reduction of ground control (Ackermann, 1984).

The widespread availability and utilization of Personal Computers (PC) made PC-compatible triangulation softwares adaptable to the needs of users in the world. An outstanding example is the J.F. Kenefick developed PC-RABATS/BRATS program. This is compatible to IBM PC, XT, AT, PS/2 or True compatible. The operating systems usable are: PC-DOS 3.1,

Windows for Workgroups, Windows 95 and Windows NT. It requires a memory of 512 Kb, can use Floppy discs of 5¼" or 3½" or Hard disc with 10Mb and a monitor having 80-column or wider display. A parallel port printer would be required but printer is optional (output is to print files). The software package comprises various features including even an auxiliary module to accomodate all State Plane coordinate Systems on NAD27 or NAD83 for the USA and the entire suite of worldwide UTM projections. Its capacities are limited to 100 strips consisting 2400 photos, 400 bandwidths, 12000 photos per job and 1500 control points per job. Numerous service programs for several analytical compilers/data collection modules are developed for systems manufactured by Intergraph, Kern & Wild (Leica), Qasco and Zeiss, amongst others (Kenefick, 1999).

BIBLIOGRAPHY

Ackermann F.; "Utilization of Navigation Data for Aerial Triangulation," *ISPRS Archives Commission III* (15th Congress, Rio-de-Janeiro, Brazil: 1984).

Ackermann, F., H. Ebner and H. Klein; "Block Triangulation with Independent Models," *PE* 39, No. 9 (1973).

Ackermann, F.; "Results of Recent Experimental Investigations in Aerial Triangulation," *Proceedings of the 40th Annual Meeting of ASP;* St-Louis, Mo. (1974).

Anderson, James M. and A. J. McNair; "Analytic Aerotriangulation-Triplets and Sub-Blocks," *Photogrammetria* 21, No. 6 (1966).

Antipov, I.T.; "Automated System of Processing Photogrammetric Measurements," Presented Paper, *ISP Archives, Commission III,* 13th Congress; Helsinki, Finland (1976).

Brown, D.C., R. G. Davis and F.C. Johnson; *The Practical and Rigorous Adjustment of Large Photogrammetric Nets* (Publication No. RADC-TRD-64-092; Rome Air Development Center; Rome, New York: 1964).

Brown, D.C.; "Evolution, Application and Potential of the Bundle Method of Photogrammetric Triangulation," Presented Paper, *Proceedings of ISP Commission III Symposium;* Stuttgart, West Germany (1974).

Brown, D.C.; "The Bundle Adjustment— Progress and Prospects," Invited Paper, *ISP Archives, Commission III*, 13th Congress; Helsinki, Finland (1976).

Davis, R.G. ;"Analytical Adjustment of Large Blocks", *PE* 32, No. 1 (1966).

Förstner, Wolfgang; "The Reliability of Block Triangulation," *PERS* 51, No. 6 (1985).

Ghosh, Sanjib K.; *Theory of Stereophotogrammetry,* (2nd Ed) (The Ohio State University Bookstores; Columbus, Ohio: 1972).

Ghosh, Sanjib K.; *Phototriangulation* (Lexington Books; Lexington, Mass.: 1975).

Gruen, A. W.; "Algorithm Aspects in On-line Triangulation," *PERS* 51, No. 4 (1985).

Gyer, M.S.; *The Inversion of the Normal Equations of Analytical Aerotriangulation by the Method of Recursive Partitioning* (Publication No. RADC-TR-67-69; Rome Air Development Center; Rome, New York: 1967).

Harris, W.D., G.C. Tewinkel and C.A. Whitten; *Analytic Aerotriangulation* (Technical Bulletin No. 21 [corrected]; US Department of Commerce, C & GS, Washington, D.C.: 1963).

Inghilleri, G., and R. Galetto; "Further Developments of the Method of Aerotriangulation by Independent Models," *Photogrammetria 22,* No. 1 (1967).

Julia, J. E.,"Developments with the COBLO Block Adjustment Program," *PR* 12, No. 68 (1986).

Keller, M. and G.C. Tewinkel: *Three-photo Aerotriangulation* (Technical Bulletin No. 29; US Department of Commerce, C & GS, Washington, D.C.; 1966).

Keller, M. and G.C. Tewinkel; *Block Analytic Aerotriangulation* (Technical Bulletin No. 35; US Department of Commerce, C & GS, Washington, D.C.: 1967).

Kenefick, J. F.; Personal Communications (1999).

Kratky, V.; "On the Solution of Analytical Aerotriangulation by Means of an Iterative Procedure", *Photogrammetria 22,* No. 5 (1967).

Lobanov, A. N.; Analytical Aerotriangulation and its Application in the U.S.S.R.; Presented Paper, *ISP Archives, Commission III,* 13th Congress; Helsinki, Finland (1976).

McGlone, J.C. and E.M. Mikhail; "Evaluation of Aircraft MSS Analytical Block Adjustment," *PERS* 51, No. 2 (1985).

Mikhail, Edward M.; *A New Approach to Analytical Aerotriangulation— Two Directional Triplets in Sub-block* (Ph.D. Thesis, Cornell University; Ithaca, New York: 1963).

Mikhail, Edward M. and R.J. Helmering; "Recursive Methods in Photogrammetric Data Reduction", *PE* 39, No. 9 (1973).

Mikhail, Edward M.; *Observations and Least Squares* (IEP-A Dun-Donnelley Publishers, New York: 1976).

Matos, Robert A.; "Multiple Station Analytical Triangulation," *PE* 37, No. 2 (1971).

Philip, Aldwyn; *Independent Model Aerial Triangulation Refinement and Error Studies* (Ph. D. Dissertation, The Ohio State University; Columbus, Ohio: 1972).

Schmid, Hellmut H.; *A General Analytical Solution to the Problem of Photogrammetry* (US Ballistic Research Laboratories Report No. 1065; Aberdeen Proving Ground, Maryland: 1959). (Also, Bildmessung and Luftbildwesen, Heft 4 (1958) und Heft 1 (1959).

Schenk, Anton; *Fortran Program for Photogrammetric Block Triangulation with the Bundles Method* (Institut für Geodasie und Photogrammetry; E.T.H., Zurich, Switzerland: 1972).

Schut, G.H.; *Adjustment of Bundles* (National Research Council of Canada, Publication No. P-PR-47; Ottawa, Canada: 1978).

Schut, G.H.; *An Introduction to Analytical Strip Triangulation with a Fortran Program* (National Research Council of Canada Publication No. P-PR-44; Ottawa, Canada: 1973).

Strahle, John A.; *Comparison of Semi-analytical and Aeropolygon Stereo-triangulation on the Analytical Stereoplotter AP/C* (M.Sc. Thesis, The Ohio State University; Columbus, Ohio: 1971).

Wong, K. W. and G. Elphingstone; "Aerotriangulation by SAPGO," *PE* 38, No. 8 (1972).

Wood, R.; "Analytical Aerial Triangulation with Angular Measurements," PR 6, No. 36 (1970).

9

SELF-CALIBRATION AND CONSTRAINTS

Thus far, the universality of the projective equations has been established. These equations are amenable to practically any case of photogrammetry, aerial, spatial or terrestrial. These imply also, in a sense, completely rigorous techniques. Most of these techniques are limited to cases where the camera and the object related parameters are either exactly known or completely unknown.

In some cases, however, some unknown parameters are hidden and may be computationally derivable, whereas in others, some parameters may be known with unequal reliability and it may be advisable to use the known parameters directly or indirectly in the adjustment procedure. The concept of self-calibration addresses itself to the former cases, while the utilization of constraints is applicable to the latter cases. Such constraints are meant to enforce the measuring-cum-adjusting process to conform to some functional or geometric relationships or to conform to the degree of reliability as defined by "weighting".

The value of such considerations lies in the ability to utilize the available information to the greatest extent in reducing the number of unknowns or in reducing the magnitude of error propagations. It may be pertinent to express here that for any given problem, more than one least squares solutions are theoretical possible in view of the various 'forms' the mathematical model can assume. It is in the formulation of the mathematical model that one can exercise imaginative skill and improvisation. It has been demonstrated (Chapters 4 and 5, for example) that in developing mathematical models, one can often eliminate or introduce parameters or can simplify by manipulating the observation/condition equation. It is in this philosophical context that the following discussions are presented.

9.1 SELF-CALIBRATION

One of the most interesting applications of collinearity equations was made by Brown (1968) when he developed an analytical calibration technique which admits an infinite number of frames to a solution for a single set of interior oreintation parameters and lens distortion coefficients presumed common to all frames. This, *Simultaneous Multi-frame Analytical Calibration (SMAC),* assumes photography over a precisely surveyed test range, thereby eliminating the need to consider the coordinates of the ground control points as variables. We have noticed, however, significant errors in certain test ranges, at least at individual points.

Furthermore, there are cases (e.g., close-range and micro-range applications) where a test range does not exist, or exterior/interior geometry parameters are not fully known. Such problem cases prompted the development of the Self-calibration technique.

The basis of this approach can be found in Brown *et al.*, (1964), the formulation in which permitted introduction of *a priori* constraints on one or more of the exterior orientation parameters and/or object points by treating the *a priori* knowledge as direct observations of these parameters. Some developments (e.g., Kenefick *et al.*, 1972) specifically provide for the interior orientation parameters also. One may view this as a photogrammetric procedure in which the calibration parameters are recovered analytically, without the necessity for three-dimensional control in the object space. This is accomplished by introducing an error model for the specific parameters in the computation procedure.

Kenefick *et al.*, (1972) reported on the use of this technique for in-flight calibration of a camera used on a space flight around the Moon, for which there was no control in the object space. They had, however, certain orbital information, some camera parameters (from camera calibration) and convergence angles as known values. Maune (1973) and Adiguzel (1985) used this technique in calibrating electron microscopes by using two-dimensional grids (for the test range) and sets of highly convergent micrographs.

Consider the case of 'complete' calibration of a camera. The collinearity equations provide the basis for such an analytical calibration scheme. The equations may be augmented with the parameters of 'interior' orientation as follows:

$$\left.\begin{aligned} &\bar{x}_{ij} + F(K).\bar{x}_{ij} + F(P).\left\{P_1\,(r_{ij}^2 + 2\bar{x}_{ij}^2) + P_2\,(2\bar{x}_{ij}\bar{y}_{ij})\right\} \\ &\quad = f_x \frac{(X_j - X_{oi})A_i + (Y_j - Y_{oi})B_i + (Z_j - Z_{oi})\,C_i}{(X_j - X_{oi})A_i'' + (Y_j - Y_{oi})B_i'' + (Z - Z_{oi})\,C_i''} \\ &\bar{y}_{ij} + F(K).\,\bar{y}_{ij} + F(P).\left\{P_2\,(r_{ij}^2 + 2\bar{y}_{ij}^2) + P_1(2\bar{x}_{ij}\bar{y}_{ij})\right\} \\ &\quad = f_y \frac{(X_j - X_{oi})A_i' + (Y_j - Y_{oi})B_i' + (Z_j - Z_{oi})\,C_i'}{(X_j - X_{oi})A_i'' + (Y_j - Y_{oi})B_i'' + (Z - Z_{oi})\,C_i''} \end{aligned}\right\} \tag{9.1}$$

where subsripts refer to: o for the perspective center,
i for the photograph, and
j for the object (ground) point;

$$\left.\begin{aligned} \bar{x}_{ij} &= x_{ij} - x_c \\ \bar{y}_{ij} &= y_{ij} - y_c \end{aligned}\right\}$$

x_{ij}, y_{ij} being the observed photo-coordinates of the image points, and

x_c, y_c being the observed photo-coordinates of the principal point, assumed constant;

$$r_{ij}^2 = (\bar{x}_{ij}^2 + \bar{y}_{ij}^2)$$

$$F(K) = K_0 + K_1 r_{ij}^2 + K_2 r_{ij}^4 + K_3 r_{ij}^6 + \ldots$$

= function of symmetrical radial distortion (see Eq. 5.5.), assumed constant over all photographs;

$$F(K) = 1 + P_3 r_{ij}^2 + P_4 r_{ij}^4 + \ldots$$

= function of tangential distortion (see Eq. 5.7), also assumed as constant over all photographs;

P_1, P_2 = are correction coefficients for decentering distortion (see Eq. 5.7), also assumed constant over all photographs;

f_x, f_y = are effective focal lengths, in the *x*- and *y*-directions, respectively, separate in view of affine deformation in photo, assumed constant over all photographs;

A, B, C
A′, B′, C′
A″, B″, C″ = are the elements of the orthogonal orientation matrix ***M*** of the photograph, functions of three rotational angles (cf. Eq. 4.8);

and
$$\boldsymbol{M}_i = \begin{bmatrix} A_i & B_i & C_i \\ A_i' & B_i' & C_i' \\ A_i'' & B_i'' & C_i'' \end{bmatrix}$$

Such an expression can be expanded to include other necessary parameters; e.g., Maune (1973) included spiral distortion parameters as contributors to the interior geometry of the SEM system. The equations are linearized by Taylor expansion about the measured quantities x_{ij}, y_{ij} and initial approximate values of the unknown parameters. If all linearized equations are collected, they may be written in matrix notations as below (*cf.* Eq. 8.6):

$$V + \dot{\boldsymbol{B}}\,\dot{\delta} + \ddot{\boldsymbol{B}}\,\ddot{\delta} = \in \tag{9.2}$$

where, considering m number of photographs and n number of object points, and that all points appear on all photographs (note, this is nothing but a simultaneous multi-photo solution),

$\underset{2mn,1}{V}$ = is the vector of residuals of measured photo coordinates;

$\underset{2mn,\,9+6m}{\dot{\mathbf{B}}}\quad \underset{2mn,\,3n}{\ddot{\mathbf{B}}}$ = are the matrices of the partial derivatives of Eq. 9.1, evaluated with measured quantities and the current values of the unknowns;

$\underset{9+6m,1}{\dot{\delta}}\quad \underset{3n,1}{\ddot{\delta}}$ = are the vectors of corrections to the current values of the parameters;

and $\underset{2mn,1}{\in}$ = is the discrepancy vector.

Note: In view of customary practices (see Ghosh, 1975), single dotted matrices here are those associated with parameters of interior and exterior orientations, whereas double dotted ones are associated with the object point coordinates. In some practices (e.g., Halim Munji, 1986) the parameters may be grouped into three or more categories, like interior orientation elements, exterior orientation elements and object point coordinates or other convenient number of categories. Such considerations would naturally lead into additional **B** matrics and associated δ vectors of corrections as well.

Kenefick *et al.*, (1972) suggested to consider supplemental observation equations arising from *a priori* knowledge regarding any of the parameters in Eqs 9.1. Such supplemental equations may be grouped according to the subset of parameters involved, just for convenience,

$$\dot{v} - \dot{\delta} = \dot{\in}$$

$$\ddot{v} - \ddot{\delta} = \ddot{\in} \tag{9.3}$$

where $\underset{9+6m,1}{\dot{\delta}}$ $\underset{3n,1}{\ddot{\delta}}$ = are vectors of observational corrections to the parameters;

and $\underset{9+6m,1}{\dot{\in}}$ $\underset{3n,1}{\ddot{\in}}$ = are discrepancy vectors, between observed values and current (in iterative solutions) values of the parameters.

The entire set of observation equations (Eqs 9.2 and 9.3) can be merged into one expression:

$$\bar{V} + \bar{B}\bar{\delta} = \bar{\in} \tag{9.4}$$

where $\underset{k,1}{\bar{V}} = (v, \dot{v}, \ddot{v})^{T}$

$$\underset{k,\ell}{\bar{B}} = \begin{bmatrix} \dot{B} & \ddot{B} \\ -I & 0 \\ 0 & -I \end{bmatrix} \quad \underset{\ell,1}{\bar{\delta}} = (\dot{\delta}, \ddot{\delta})^{T}$$

and $\underset{k,1}{\bar{\in}} = (\in, \dot{\in}, \ddot{\in})^{T}$

Further, $k = 2mn + 9 + 6m + 3n$ and $\ell = 9 + 6m + 3n$

The covariance matrix associated with the merged observation equation is:

$$\underset{k,k}{\bar{\Sigma}} = \begin{bmatrix} \Sigma & 0 & 0 \\ 0 & \dot{\Sigma} & 0 \\ 0 & 0 & \ddot{\Sigma} \end{bmatrix}$$

where $\underset{2mn,2mn}{\Sigma}$ = is the covariance matrix for the observed photo coordinates, 2×2 block diagonal where coordinates are assumed uncorrelated;

$\underset{9+6m,9+6m}{\dot{\Sigma}}$ = is the covariance matrix for the interior and exterior orientation parameters;

and $\underset{3n,3n}{\ddot{\Sigma}}$ = is the covariance matrix for the object point coordinates, 3×3 block diagonal where coordinates are assumed uncorrelated.

The general form of the 'normal' equations, as formed from the 'condition' equations (Eq. 9.4) is:

$$N\delta = c \tag{9.5}$$

where $N = \bar{B}^{T} P \bar{B}$; $c = \bar{B}^{T} P \in$

and P is the weight (inverse of covariance) matrix.

After appropriate operations, the general form of the normal equations, partitioned (after Brown, 1960), in this case is:

$$\left[\begin{array}{c|c} \dot{\boldsymbol{N}} + \dot{\boldsymbol{P}} & \bar{\boldsymbol{N}} \\ \hline \bar{\boldsymbol{N}}^{\mathrm{T}} & \ddot{\boldsymbol{N}} + \ddot{\boldsymbol{P}} \end{array}\right] \cdot \left[\begin{array}{c} \dot{\delta} \\ \hline \ddot{\delta} \end{array}\right] = \left[\begin{array}{c} \dot{c} - \dot{\boldsymbol{P}}_{\in} \\ \hline \ddot{c} - \ddot{\boldsymbol{P}}_{\in} \end{array}\right] \tag{9.6}$$

where

$$\left.\begin{array}{l} \underset{9+6\mathrm{m},\,9+6\mathrm{m}}{\dot{\boldsymbol{N}}} = \dot{\boldsymbol{B}}^{\mathrm{T}}\boldsymbol{P}\dot{\boldsymbol{B}} \\ \underset{3\mathrm{n},\,3\mathrm{n}}{\ddot{\boldsymbol{N}}} = \ddot{\boldsymbol{B}}^{\mathrm{T}}\boldsymbol{P}\ddot{\boldsymbol{B}} \end{array}\right\} \quad \underset{9+6\mathrm{m},\,3\mathrm{n}}{\bar{\boldsymbol{N}}} = \dot{\boldsymbol{B}}^{\mathrm{T}}\boldsymbol{P}\ddot{\boldsymbol{B}} \quad \left\{\begin{array}{l} \underset{9+6\mathrm{m},\,1}{\dot{c}} = \dot{\boldsymbol{B}}^{\mathrm{T}}\boldsymbol{P}\in \\ \underset{3\mathrm{n},\,1}{\ddot{c}} = \ddot{\boldsymbol{B}}^{\mathrm{T}}\boldsymbol{P}\in \end{array}\right.$$

and

$$\boldsymbol{P} = \Sigma^{-1} \quad \dot{\boldsymbol{P}} = \dot{\Sigma}^{-1} \quad \ddot{\boldsymbol{P}} = \ddot{\Sigma}^{-1}$$

This concept has been applied with great success to Block Triangulation by the 'Simultaneous' method (also known as 'Bundle Adjustment') in order to increase the final overall accuracy (Ebner, 1976). In such applications, however, two problems persist. The first one involves the proper choice of the additional parameters (photo-, strip- or block-dependent). A general concept for the choice of such parameters has yet to be agreed upon in the scientific community for works on specific problems. The second problem arises from highly correlated or insignificant parameters which may cause comparative instability in the adjustment procedure and create somewhat critical geometry.

Somewhat unusual but interesting extension of the self-calibration technique as applicable to Bundle Block Adjustment has been suggested by Ebner (1976) in which additional parameters to consider systematic image (film) deformation (two-dimensional) and model deformation (three-dimensional) are included. Computationally, these could be handled by *stochastic mathematical models* (by treating the additional parameters as free unknowns) or by treating them as *Collocation* problems (Moritz, 1973) in terms of prediction and filtering of noise and signals. Skeptics may scoff at some of these attempts, which indicate the scientists' yielding to the mighty computer without really justifying the natural science. These, however, do point out the unlimited scopes of the modern analytical photogrammetric procedures. The technique of 'In Flight' calibration discussed by Anderson and Lee (1975) also follows the same general concept.

A recent development of the concept by Schlöler (1986) seems to be specially practicable in close-range applications. The basic idea is to derive individual data of interior orientation for a photograph from depth differences between control points around the perimeter of an object. On the other hand, if a suitable pattern of ground control can be established, it would be possible to perform a complete field calibration (along with radical and tangential distortion data) of aerial or terrestrial cameras.

The method of self-calibration has been considerably developed during the last two decades, leading to operational computer programs and practical applications in various conventional and unconventional approaches. The method used in block adjustment of photo-triangulation can easily yield a consistent precision level of the order of $\sigma_0 < 3$ μm for image coordinates provided instrumental errors (for both reading and point transfer) are negligible (Ackermann, 1984).

A computer program for self-calibration developed at the Laval University is appended (Appendix C). This program is flexible enough to be used in conventional (terrestrial, aerial or satellite imaging) as well as unconventional (like X-ray or Electron micrography) systems. Photo coordinates of desired points (along with certain points in adequate number on the original negatives read at a precision comparator are directed to a micro-computer using this program. This makes calculations of the exterior and interior orientation parameters of the cameras. Thereafter, the 3-D coordinates of points are calculated by spatial intersection, through the same program.

To give an example, four different cameras were used in a project (two above and two below a transparent glass plate on which were placed the object to be studied and mapped. The average object distance was ±1m. The cameras were amateur (Minolta SRT-100) with B & W film (ASA 400) being used. All photo coordinates were obtained at a Wild STK-1 stereocomparator. An IBM-PC micro-computer was used. The final precision obtained was better than ±0.5 mm on the object.

9.2 CONSTRAINTS

9.2.1 Weight Constraint

Comparative reliability amongst various parameters can be enforced by utilizing the constraint of weight. This is done by using the standard deviations of various parameters in the condition equations. As an example, consider that the standard deviations of the perspective center coordinates (X_{oi}, Y_{oi}, Z_{oi}) in the working system are known or can be approximated from previous experience or from some auxiliary data sources. The covariance matrix of the camera station coordinates then is:

$$\Sigma_i = \begin{bmatrix} \sigma^2_{X_{oi}} & \sigma_{X_{oi}Y_{oi}} & \sigma_{X_{oi}Z_{oi}} \\ \sigma_{X_{oi}Y_{oi}} & \sigma^2_{Y_{oi}} & \sigma_{Y_{oi}Z_{oi}} \\ \sigma_{X_{oi}Z_{oi}} & \sigma_{Y_{oi}Z_{oi}} & \sigma^2_{Z_{oi}} \end{bmatrix} \tag{9.7}$$

in which each off-diagonal element, for the sake of convenience and simplification, may be considered in practice as zero. This means that they can safely be considered as diagonal matrices, thereby assuming that there is no correlation between coordinates.

Note : Some recent studies (for example, Maarek, 1973) suggest that mathematical correlation between coordinates, in practice, can be neglected at all times without causing any appreciable change in the results.

Furthermore,

$$\boldsymbol{P}_i = \Sigma_i^{-1} \tag{9.7a}$$

Similarly, the weight matrices of the other exterior orientation parameters, object point coordinates or the interior orientation parameters can be determined. In order to utilize such weight matrices in the solution, the partitioned normal equations take the form as expressed in Eq. 9.6. Case (1961) is known to be the first to discuss the subject of constraints in photogrammetry.

Schmid and Schmid (1965) discussed a general procedure for the method of Least Squares, where all elements of the mathematical model are considered as observation data; the burden of classification being on the 'weight matrix'. The relative strengths of $\dot{P}$ and $\ddot{P}$ will have significant influence on the final results of Eq. 9.6. As an extreme case, for example, consider $\ddot{P}$ to be infinity. this is when the object point coordinates are fully known and are unchangeable (one may call it *Absolute Constraint)*. This makes it a case of *Space Resection.* Where $\dot{P}$ is infinity would, accordingly, correspond to *Space Intersection,* the case of the other extreme.

9.2.2 Functional Constraint

The functional relationship between various parameters would provide the functional constraints, which may be applied to the interior or exterior orientation parameters, or even to the object point coordinates. Consider an example case in which the perspective center coordinates (X_{oi}, Y_{oi}, Z_{oi}) are functions of parameters s, t and u:

$$X_{oi} = F_1(s, t, u) \qquad Y_{oi} = F_2(s, t, u) \quad \text{and} \quad Z_{oi} = F_3(s, t, u) \tag{9.8}$$

Note here, as before, i refers to photos and j refers to points. Furthermore, $\dot{\delta}$ can be considered in two parts, viz., $\dot{\delta}'$ for the perspective center parameters and $\dot{\delta}''$ for the rest of interior and exterior orientation parameters.

By considering the differentials, then

$$\dot{\delta}' = \begin{bmatrix} \delta X_{oi} \\ \delta Y_{oi} \\ \delta Z_{oi} \end{bmatrix} = \begin{bmatrix} \frac{\partial X_{oi}}{\partial s} & \frac{\partial X_{oi}}{\partial t} & \frac{\partial X_{oi}}{\partial u} \\ \frac{\partial Y_{oi}}{\partial s} & \frac{\partial Y_{oi}}{\partial t} & \frac{\partial Y_{oi}}{\partial u} \\ \frac{\partial Z_{oi}}{\partial s} & \frac{\partial Z_{oi}}{\partial t} & \frac{\partial Z_{oi}}{\partial u} \end{bmatrix} \begin{bmatrix} \delta s \\ \delta t \\ \delta u \end{bmatrix} = U_i' \dot{\delta}' \tag{9.9}$$

In order to utilize the functional constraints in this case, one merely substitutes the relationships of Eqs. 9.8 and 9.9 in the applicable places of the basic condition equation (Eq. 9.2), which becomes

$$V_{ij} + \dot{B}_{ij}(\dot{\delta}_i'' + U_i' \dot{\delta}') + \ddot{B}_{ij} \ddot{\delta}_{ij} = \epsilon_{ij} \tag{9.10}$$

where $\qquad \dot{\delta}_i'' = [\delta x_c, \delta y_c, \delta f_x, \delta f_y, \delta\omega, \delta\phi, \delta_\kappa]_i^T$

and, naturally, σ_{ij} is a function of s, t and u (indirectly) rather than directly of X_{oi}, Y_{oi} and Z_{oi}. The most likely corrections δs, δt, and δu to the current (initially assumed) values of s, t and u are determined as a result of the solutions of Eq. 9.10. In such a case an alternate solution of obtaining the final values of X_{oi}, Y_{oi} and Z_{oi} can be made by substituting the adjusted values of s, t and u in Eq. 9.8, directly. Such functional constraints may be utilized to reduce the number of unknown parameters in the condition equations. In the case of correlated parameters, if one or more of the original parameters are unknown, use of such constraints becomes of considerable help.

Apart from giving interesting theoretical ideas, Case (1961) has discussed some examples of various types of such constraints. Interesting ideas on the procedures of Least Squares solutions in the presence of various constraints can be obtained from the works of Mikhail (1970, 1976). It is, however, expected that by adding constraints to any system, the residuals (indicated by $V'PV$ matrix) should generally increase.

BIBLIOGRAPHY

Ackermann, F.; "Report on activities of Working Group III-1 during 1980-84'', *ISPRS Archives for 25th Congress,* Rio-de-Janeiro (1984).

Adiguzel, M.; *Problems Related to Three Dimensional Mapping with Electron Micrographs* (Ph.D. Thesis, Laval University, Quebec: 1985).

Anderson, James M. and Clement Lee; "Analytical In-Flight Calibration," *PERS* 41, No. 11 (1975).

Brown, Duane C.' "Results in Geodetic Photogrammetry", *PE* 26, No. 3 (1960).

Brown, Duane C., R.G. Davis and F.C. Johnson; "The Practical and Rigorous Adjustment of Large Photogrammetric Nets'', *Report on US Air Force Contract No. AF-30(602)-3007;* DBA System, Inc., Florida (1964).

Brown, D.C.; "Advanced Methods for the Calibration of Metric Cameras," *Report on US Army Contract No. DA-44-009-AMC-1457(X);* DBA System, Inc., Florida (1968).

Case, James, B.; "The Utilization of Constraints in Analytical Photogrammetry", *PE* 27, No. 5 (1961).

Ebner, H.; "Self-calibrating Block Adjustment", *Bildmessung und Luftbildwesen,* Heft 4 (1976).

Ghosh, Sanjib K.; *Phototriangulation* (Lexington Books, Lexington, Mass.: 1975).

Ghosh, Sanjib K., Monir Rahimi and Zhengdong Shi; "Calibration of an Amateur Camera for Various Object Distances," *Proceedings of ISPRS (Kyoto) Congress* (1988).

Halim Munjy, Raidh A.; "Self-Calibration Using the Finite Element Approach," *PERS* 52, No. 3 (1986).

Kenefick, John F., M.S. Gyer and B.F. Harp; "Analytical Self-Calibration," *PE* 38, No. 11 (1972).

Kupfer, G.; "Improvement of Analytical Aerial Triangulation by Field Calibration," *Proceedings of the Conference of Working Group on Image Geometry,* ISP Commission I; Ottawa, Canada (1975).

Light, Donald L.; "Altimeter Observations as Orbital Constraints," *PE* 38, No. 4 (1972).

Maarek, A.; "New Math Model for Independent-Model Triangulation," *PE* 39, No. 10 (1973).

Maune, David F.; *Photogrammetric Self-Calibration of a Scanning Electron Microscope* (Ph.D. Dissertation, The Ohio State Univ., Columbus, Ohio: 1973).

Mikhail, Edward M.; "Parameter Constraints in Least Squares," *PE* 36, No. 12 (1970).

Mikhail, Edward M.; *Observations and Least Squares* (IEP-A Dun-Donnelly Publishers, New York: 1976).

Moritz, Helmut; "Least-Squares Collocation," *Deutsche Geodatische Kommission, Reihe A,* Heft 75 (1973).

Moritz, Helmut; "Statistical Foundations of Collocation," *US Air Force Geophysics Laboratory Document* No. AFGL-TR-78-0182 (1978).

Schmid, H.H. and E. Schmid; "A Generalized Least Squares Solution for Hybrid Measuring Systems", *The Canadian Surveyor* 9, No. 1 (1965).

Schöler, H.; "Zur Selbstkalibrierung von Aufnahmekammern, insbesondere bei der photogrammetrischen Vermessung im Nahbereich," *Vermessungstechnik 34;* Heft 8 (1986).

APPENDICES

APPENDIX A

PARTIAL DERIVATIVES, COLLINEARITY CONDITION EQUATIONS

The collinearity condition equations as given in Chapter 4 are :

$$x = -f\,\frac{M_1\bar{X}}{M_3\bar{X}} \qquad \text{and} \qquad y = -f\,\frac{M_2\bar{X}}{M_3\bar{X}} \qquad \text{...(4.9)}$$

For reasons of clarity and operational ease, symbolize the first one as function one (F_1) and the second one as function two (F_2). Due to the rather complicated nature of the derivations, determinant notations are utilized here. We obtain :

$$\frac{\partial F_1}{\partial \omega} = \frac{f}{(M_3\bar{X})^2}\begin{vmatrix} M_3\bar{X} & M_1\bar{X} \\ \dfrac{\partial (M_3\bar{X})}{\partial \omega} & \dfrac{\partial (M_1\bar{X})}{\partial \omega}\end{vmatrix} = \frac{f}{(M_3\bar{X})^2}\left(M_3\bar{X}\cdot M_{\omega_1}\bar{X} - M_1\bar{X}\cdot M_{\omega_3}\bar{X}\right)$$

$$= \frac{f}{M_3\bar{X}}\left(M_{\omega_1}\bar{X} - \frac{x}{f}M_{\omega_3}\bar{X}\right) \qquad \text{...(A.1)}$$

Similarly,

$$\frac{\partial F_1}{\partial \phi} = \frac{f}{M_3\bar{X}}\left(M_{\phi_1}\bar{X} - \frac{x}{f}M_{\phi_3}\bar{X}\right) \qquad \text{...(A.2)}$$

$$\frac{\partial F_1}{\partial \kappa} = \frac{f}{M_3\bar{X}}\left(M_{\kappa_1}\bar{X} - \frac{x}{f}M_{\kappa_3}\bar{X}\right) \qquad \text{....(A.3)}$$

$$\frac{\partial F_1}{\partial x} = \frac{f}{M_3\bar{X}}\left(m_{11} - m_{31}\frac{x}{f}\right) \qquad \text{...(A.4)}$$

$$\frac{\partial F_1}{\partial Y} = \frac{f}{M_3\bar{X}}\left(m_{12} - m_{32}\frac{x}{f}\right) \qquad \text{...(A.5)}$$

$$\frac{\partial F_1}{\partial Z} = \frac{f}{M_3\bar{X}}\left(m_{13} - m_{33}\frac{x}{f}\right) \qquad \text{...(A.6)}$$

$$\frac{\partial F_1}{\partial X_O} = -\frac{f}{M_3\bar{X}}\left(m_{11} - m_{31}\frac{x}{f}\right) \quad \text{...(A.7)}$$

$$\frac{\partial F_1}{\partial Y_O} = -\frac{f}{M_3\bar{X}}\left(m_{12} - m_{32}\frac{x}{f}\right) \quad \text{...(A.8)}$$

$$\frac{\partial F_1}{\partial Z_O} = -\frac{f}{M_3\bar{X}}\left(m_{13} - m_{33}\frac{x}{f}\right) \quad \text{...(A.9)}$$

and

$$\frac{\partial F_2}{\partial \omega} = \frac{f}{M_3\bar{X}}\left(m_{\omega_2}\bar{X} - \frac{y}{f}M_{\omega_3}\bar{X}\right) \quad \text{...(A.10)}$$

$$\frac{\partial F_2}{\partial \phi} = \frac{f}{M_3\bar{X}}\left(m_{\phi_2}\bar{X} - \frac{y}{f}M_{\phi_3}\bar{X}\right) \quad \text{...(A.11)}$$

$$\frac{\partial F_2}{\partial \kappa} = \frac{f}{M_3\bar{X}}\left(m_{\kappa_2}\bar{X} - \frac{y}{f}M_{\kappa_3}\bar{X}\right) \quad \text{...(A.12)}$$

$$\frac{\partial F_2}{\partial X} = \frac{f}{M_3\bar{X}}\left(m_{21} - m_{31}\frac{y}{f}\right) \quad \text{...(A.13)}$$

$$\frac{\partial F_2}{\partial Y} = \frac{f}{M_3\bar{X}}\left(m_{22} - m_{32}\frac{y}{f}\right) \quad \text{...(A.14)}$$

$$\frac{\partial F_2}{\partial Z} = \frac{f}{M_3\bar{X}}\left(m_{23} - m_{33}\frac{y}{f}\right) \quad \text{...(A.15)}$$

$$\frac{\partial F_2}{\partial X_O} = -\frac{f}{M_3\bar{X}}\left(m_{21} - m_{31}\frac{y}{f}\right) \quad \text{...(A.16)}$$

$$\frac{\partial F_2}{\partial Y_O} = -\frac{f}{M_3\bar{X}}\left(m_{22} - m_{32}\frac{y}{f}\right) \quad \text{...(A.17)}$$

$$\frac{\partial F_2}{\partial Z_O} = -\frac{f}{M_3\bar{X}}\left(m_{23} - m_{33}\frac{y}{f}\right) \quad \text{...(A.18)}$$

It may be noted that the above derivatives are given in general terms and some expressions in these equations are equal to zero, e.g., $M_{\omega_3} = 0$, which would then modify equations (A.1) and (A.10) into the following forms :

$$\frac{\partial F_1}{\partial \omega} = \frac{f}{M_3\bar{X}}\left(M_{\omega_1}\bar{X}\right), \qquad \frac{\partial F_2}{\partial \omega} = \frac{f}{M_3\bar{X}}\left(M_{\omega_2}\bar{X}\right)$$

Further simplifications may also be possible, e.g., when $M_{\kappa=0}$ or $M_{\kappa=\omega=0}$ matrices are used instead of the *M* matrix.

PARTIAL DERIVATIVES, COPLANARITY CONDITION EQUATIONS

The coplanarity condition equation as given in Chapter 4 is :

$$F_i = \begin{vmatrix} b_X & b_Y & b_Z \\ X_{1i} & Y_{1i} & Z_{1i} \\ X_{2i} & Y_{2i} & Z_{2i} \end{vmatrix} = 0 \qquad ...(4.17)$$

Equation 4.22 defines $[A_i]$:

$$[A_i] = \left[\frac{\partial F_i}{\partial x_{1i}} \ \frac{\partial F_i}{\partial y_{1i}} \ \frac{\partial F_i}{\partial x_{2i}} \ \frac{\partial F_i}{\partial y_{2i}} \right] \qquad ...(4.22)$$

From corresponding equations in Chapter 4,

$$\frac{\partial F_i}{\partial x_{1i}} = \begin{bmatrix} bx & by & bz \\ m_{11}^1 & m_{12}^1 & m_{13}^1 \\ X_{2i} & Y_{2i} & Z_{2i} \end{bmatrix} = \begin{bmatrix} bx & by & bz \\ 1 & 0 & 0 \\ X_{2i} & Y_{2i} & Z_{2i} \end{bmatrix} = (bz \cdot Y_{2i} - by \cdot Z_{2i}) \qquad ...(B.1)$$

$$\frac{\partial F_i}{\partial y_{1i}} = \begin{bmatrix} bx & by & bz \\ m_{21}^1 & m_{22}^1 & m_{23}^1 \\ X_{2i} & Y_{2i} & Z_{2i} \end{bmatrix} = \begin{bmatrix} bx & by & bz \\ 0 & 1 & 0 \\ X_{2i} & Y_{2i} & Z_{2i} \end{bmatrix} = (bx \cdot Z_{2i} - bz \cdot X_{2i}) \qquad ...(B.2)$$

$$\frac{\partial F_i}{\partial x_{2i}} = \begin{bmatrix} bx & by & bz \\ X_{1i} & Y_{1i} & Z_{1i} \\ m_{11}^2 & m_{12}^2 & m_{13}^2 \end{bmatrix} = \begin{bmatrix} bx & by & bz \\ x_{1i} & y_{1i} & -f \\ \cos\phi\cos\kappa & \begin{matrix}\cos\omega\sin\kappa \\ +\sin\omega\sin\phi\cos\kappa\end{matrix} & \begin{matrix}\sin\omega\sin\kappa \\ -\cos\omega\sin\phi\cos\kappa\end{matrix} \end{bmatrix}$$

...(B.3)

$$\frac{\partial F_i}{\partial y_{2i}} = \begin{bmatrix} bx & by & bz \\ X_{1i} & Y_{1i} & Z_{1i} \\ m_{21}^2 & m_{22}^2 & m_{23}^2 \end{bmatrix} = \begin{bmatrix} bx & by & bz \\ x_{1i} & y_{1i} & -f \\ -\cos\phi\cos\kappa & \begin{matrix}\cos\omega\sin\kappa \\ +\sin\omega\sin\phi\sin\kappa\end{matrix} & \begin{matrix}\sin\omega\sin\kappa \\ +\cos\omega\sin\phi\sin\kappa\end{matrix} \end{bmatrix} \quad \text{...(B.4)}$$

Equation 4.23 defines $[B_i]$:

$$[B_i] = \left[\frac{\partial F_i}{\partial bY_2} \; \frac{\partial F_i}{\partial bz_2} \; \frac{\partial F_i}{\partial \omega_2} \; \frac{\partial F_i}{\partial \phi_2} \; \frac{\partial F_i}{\partial \kappa_2} \right] \quad \text{...(4.23)}$$

$$\frac{\partial F_i}{\partial by_2} = -\begin{bmatrix} X_{1i} & Z_{1i} \\ X_{2i} & Z_{2i} \end{bmatrix} \quad \text{...(B.5)}$$

$$\frac{\partial F_i}{\partial bz_2} = \begin{bmatrix} X_{1i} & Y_{1i} \\ X_{2i} & Y_{2i} \end{bmatrix} \quad \text{...(B.6)}$$

$$\frac{\partial F_i}{\partial \omega_2} = \begin{bmatrix} bx & by & bz \\ X_{1i} & Y_{1i} & Z_{1i} \\ \frac{\partial X_{2i}}{\partial \omega_2} & \frac{\partial Y_{2i}}{\partial \omega_2} & \frac{\partial Z_{2i}}{\partial \omega_2} \end{bmatrix} = \begin{bmatrix} bx & by & bz \\ x_{1i} & y_{1i} & -f \\ \frac{\partial X_{2i}}{\partial \omega_2} & \frac{\partial Y_{2i}}{\partial \omega_2} & \frac{\partial Z_{2i}}{\partial \omega_2} \end{bmatrix} \quad \text{....(B.7)}$$

From Eq. 4.19, for the above,

$$\frac{\partial X_{2i}}{\partial \omega_2} = 0$$

$$\left.\begin{aligned} \frac{\partial Y_{2i}}{\partial \omega_{2i}} = \; & x_{2i}\,(\cos\omega\sin\phi\cos\kappa - \sin\omega\sin\kappa) \\ & - y_{2i}\,(\sin\omega\cos\kappa + \cos\omega\sin\phi\sin\kappa) + f\cos\omega\cos\phi \end{aligned}\right\}$$

and

$$\left.\begin{aligned} \frac{\partial Z_{2i}}{\partial \omega_2} = \; & x_{2i}\,(\cos\omega\sin\kappa + \sin\omega\sin\phi\cos\kappa) \\ & + y_{2i}\,(\cos\omega\cos\kappa - \sin\omega\sin\phi\sin\kappa) + \mathrm{f}\sin\omega\cos\phi \end{aligned}\right\}$$

$$\frac{\partial F_i}{\partial \phi_2} = \begin{bmatrix} bx & by & bz \\ X_{1i} & Y_{1i} & Z_{1i} \\ \frac{\partial X_{2i}}{\partial \phi_2} & \frac{\partial Y_{2i}}{\partial \phi_2} & \frac{\partial Z_{2i}}{\partial \phi_2} \end{bmatrix} = \begin{bmatrix} bx & by & bz \\ x_{1i} & y_{1i} & -f \\ \frac{\partial X_{2i}}{\partial \phi_2} & \frac{\partial Y_{2i}}{\partial \phi_2} & \frac{\partial Z_{2i}}{\partial \phi_2} \end{bmatrix} \quad \text{...(B.8)}$$

Here, for the above, from Eq. 4.19,

$$\frac{\partial X_{2i}}{\partial \phi_2} = -x_{2i} \sin\phi \cos\kappa + y_{2i} \sin\phi \sin\kappa - f\cos\phi$$

$$\frac{\partial Y_{2i}}{\partial \phi_2} = x_{2i} \sin\omega \cos\phi \cos\kappa - y_{2i} \sin\omega \cos\phi \sin\kappa - f\sin\omega \sin\phi$$

and $$\frac{\partial Z_{2i}}{\partial \phi_2} = -x_{2i} \cos\omega \cos\phi \cos\kappa + y_{2i} \cos\omega \cos\phi \sin\kappa + f\cos\omega \sin\phi.$$

Finally,

$$\frac{\partial F_i}{\partial \kappa_2} = \begin{bmatrix} bx & by & bz \\ X_{1i} & Y_{1i} & Z_{1i} \\ \frac{\partial X_{2i}}{\partial \kappa_2} & \frac{\partial Y_{2i}}{\partial \kappa_2} & \frac{\partial Z_{2i}}{\partial \kappa_2} \end{bmatrix} = \begin{bmatrix} bx & by & bz \\ x_{1i} & y_{1i} & -f \\ \frac{\partial X_{2i}}{\partial \kappa_2} & \frac{\partial Y_{2i}}{\partial \kappa_2} & \frac{\partial Z_{2i}}{\partial \kappa_2} \end{bmatrix} \quad \text{...(B. 9)}$$

where, from Eq. 4.19,

$$\frac{\partial X_{2i}}{\partial \kappa_2} = -x_{2i} \cos\phi \sin\kappa - y_{2i} \cos\phi \cos\kappa$$

$$\frac{\partial Y_{2i}}{\partial \kappa_2} = x_{2i} (\cos\omega \cos\kappa - \sin\omega \sin\phi \sin\kappa) - y_{2i} (\cos\omega \sin\kappa + \sin\omega \sin\phi \cos\kappa)$$

$$\frac{\partial Z_{2i}}{\partial \kappa_2} = x_{2i} (\sin\omega \cos\kappa + \cos\omega \sin\phi \sin\kappa) - y_{2i} (\sin\omega \sin\kappa - \cos\omega \sin\phi \cos\kappa)$$

Forms and sizes of the matrices :

Let n = Number of observed values of observable quantities
u = Number of unknown quantities (= 5, here, being the elements of relative orientation)
r = Number of condition equations where both observed and unknown quantities are present

Here, $n = 4r$, since there are four coordinate readings for each point. The sizes of the matrices in Eq. 4.21 are, therefore,

$$_r[\mathbf{A}]_n \, _n(\mathbf{V})_1 + \, _r[\mathbf{B}]_u \, _u\Delta_1 + \, _r\mathbf{F}_{o1} = \, _r\mathbf{O}_1 \quad \text{...(4.21)}$$

$$_r\mathbf{A}_n = \begin{bmatrix} A_1 & 0 & 0 \cdots 0 \\ 0 & A_2 & 0 \cdots 0 \\ 0 & 0 & A_3 \cdots 0 \\ \vdots & \vdots & \vdots \\ 0 & 0 & 0 \cdots A_r \end{bmatrix}$$

$$
= \begin{bmatrix} XXXX & & & & & \\ & XXXX & & & & \\ & & XXXX & & & \\ & & & \ddots & & \\ & & & & \ddots & \\ & & & & & XXXXX \end{bmatrix}_{r \times n}
$$

$$
{}_r\mathbf{B}_u = \begin{bmatrix} B_1 \\ B_2 \\ B_3 \\ \vdots \\ B_r \end{bmatrix} = \begin{bmatrix} X & X & X & X & X \\ X & X & X & X & X \\ X & X & X & X & X \\ \vdots & \vdots & \vdots & \vdots & \vdots \\ X & X & X & X & X \end{bmatrix}_{r \times 5} \quad \text{Full matrix}
$$

$$
{}_r\mathbf{F}_{o1} = \begin{bmatrix} F_{o1} \\ F_{o2} \\ F_{o3} \\ \vdots \\ F_{or} \end{bmatrix}_{r \times 1}
$$

$$
{}_u\Delta_1 = \begin{bmatrix} \delta by \\ \delta bz \\ \delta\omega \\ \delta\phi \\ \delta\kappa \end{bmatrix}_{5 \times 1}
$$

$$
{}_n\boldsymbol{V}_1 = \begin{bmatrix} \underset{4\times 1}{V_1} \\ \underset{4\times 1}{V_2} \\ \underset{4\times 1}{V_3} \\ \vdots \\ \underset{4\times 1}{V_r} \end{bmatrix}_{n \times 1}
$$

APPENDIX C

PROGRAM FOR ANALYTICAL SELF-CALIBRATION
[Including an example]

```
C*************************************************************
C
C      PROGRAM FOR ANALYTICAL SELF-CALIBRATION
C
C      @ UNIVERSITE LAVAL
C
C*************************************************************
C
C       MAIN PROGRAM - AUTOCAL1
C
C*************************************************************
C
$NOFLOATCALLS
$STORAGE:2
$LARGE
      IMPLICIT INTEGER*4 (I-N)
      IMPLICIT REAL*8 (A-H,O-Z)
      CHARACTER*40 ITITLE
      DIMENSION WE(6),WS(3),EE(6),POINT(2)
C
C=============================================================
C       IP=TOTAL NB. OF UNIQUE POINTS     MAX=30
C       N =NB. OF PHOTOS                  MAX= 4
C       K1=3*IP
C       J1=6*N+9
C       JA11=J1*(J1+1)/2
C
C       DIMENSION SIZES AS FOLLOWS:
C
C       A11(JA11), A12(J1,K1), A22(K1,3), A22T(K1+3,J1+3)
C       X(K1), Y(K1), Z(K1),
C       WX(K1), WY(K1), WZ(K1),
C       KEY(IP), IST(IP+4)
C
C       DIMENSIONS SHOULD BE GRATER THAN OR EQUAL TO THE
C       MINIMUM REQUIRED FOR PARTICULAR BLOCK
C
C       ONLY THESE DIMENSIONS NEED TO BE CHANGED FOR A
C       PARTICULAR BLOCK. ALSO CHANGE VARIABLES "NPH" AND "IIP"
C
C=============================================================
C
      DIMENSION A11(561),A12(33,090),A22(090,3),A22T(093,36)
      DIMENSION IST(34),X(090),Y(090),Z(090),WX(090),WY(090)
      DIMENSION WZ(090),KEY(30)
      INTEGER   CYCLE
      COMMON IEL
```

```
C
C=================================================================
C       THE FOLLOWINGS ARE CHECK VALUES TO TEST FOR ARRAY OVER-
C       FLOWS.
C      THE ACTUAL DIMENSIONNING IS LEFT UP TO THE USER.
C
C      NPH=CURRENT MAX NO. OF PHOTOS ** OVERFLOW = STOP 88 **
C      IIP=CURRENT MAX NO. OF POINTS ** OVERFLOW = STOP 77 **
C=================================================================
C
    5  WRITE(*,1900)
 1900  FORMAT(5X,'HOW MANY OBJECT POINTS ?')
       READ (*,1910) IIP
 1910  FORMAT (I5)
       IF(IIP.LE.0) THEN
           WRITE(*,1920)
 1920      FORMAT(///,5X,'ERROR... BAD NUMBER OF POINT',
     1               //,5X,'START AGAIN!')
           GOTO 5
       ENDIF
       NPH=4
C
C=================================================================
C       INPUT DATA IN ORDER AND FORMAT AS FOLLOWS:
C       ~~~~~~~~~~~~~~~~~~~~~~~~~~~~~~~~~~~~~~~~~~~~~~~~
C
C      # RECORD DESCRIPTION:
C        ------------------
C
C     1 JOB TITLE AND NO. OF ITERATIONS - ONE RECORD PER JOB
C 2000 FORMAT(10A4,I5)
C
C     2 CAMERA CONSTANT, PHOTO COORD., STD.ERR., SIGMA A PRIORI
C 2010 FORMAT(3F10.3)             --- IN MILIMETERS
C
C     3 CONTROL POINT FORMAT - FM1 - ONE RECORD PER JOB
C 2040 FORMAT(10A8)
C
C     4 PHOTO COORD. FORMAT - FM2 - ONE RECORD PER JOB
C 2040 FORMAT(10A8)
C
C     5 EXT. ORIENT. FORMAT - FM3 - ONE RECORD PER JOB
C 2040 FORMAT(10A8)
C
C     6 INT. ORIENT. FORMAT - FM4 - ONE RECORD PER JOB
C 2040 FORMAT(10A8)
C
C     7 CONTROL POINT NO., X, Y, Z, STD. ERRORS ON X, Y, Z
C      ONE RECORD PER CONTROL POINT ** END CONTROL WITH -99 **
C      FM1 - USER SUPPLIED              <---   IN METERS
C
C     8 PHOTO NO. - ONE RECORD PER PHOTO ** END PHOTO WITH -999 **
C      FM2 - USER SUPPLIED
C
```

```
C     9 EXT. ORIENT PARAMETERS XO, YO, ZO, KAPPA, PHI, OMEGA
C       ONE RECORD PER PHOTO       ----  IN METERS & RADIANS
C       FM3 - USER SUPPLIED
C
C    10 STD. ERRORS ON EXT. ORIENT. PARAMETERS
C       ONE RECORD PER PHOTO       ----  UNITS: SAME AS 9
C       FM3 - USER SUPPLIED
C
C    11 POINT NO., X, Y PHOTO COORD.    ---- IN MILLIMETERS
C       ONE RECORD PER PHOTO OBSERVATION  ** END PHOTO WITH -99 **
C       FM2 - USER SUPPLIED
C
C    12 CURRENT APPROX. OF INT. ORIENT. PARAMETERS
C       ONE RECORD PER JOB                ----- IN MILLIMETERS
C       FM4 - USER SUPPLIED
C
C    13 STD. ERRORS FOR INT. ORIENT. PARAMETERS
C       ONE RECORD PER JOB                ---- IN MILLIMETERS
C       FM4 - USER SUPPLIED
C===================================================================
C
C       FOUR REQUIRED FILES ARE AS FOLLOWS
C
C       IRD = READ FROM INPUT DATA FILE
C       IWT = WRITE TO OUTPUT LISTING FILE
C       IDK = DIREST ACCESS (BINARY) SCRATCH FILE
C                   (DELETED AT END OF JOB)
C       IA2 = SEQUENTIAL (BINARY) SCRATCH FILE
C                   (DELETED AT END OF JOB)
C       IREC = 8*NPH*(IIP+1)
C       IWDS = 124
C       DEFINE FILE IDK (IREC,IWDS,U,IEL)
C===================================================================
C
      OPEN(10,FILE='B:LECTURE1.DAT',STATUS='OLD',ACCESS='SEQUENTIAL
     A      FORM='FORMATTED')
      OPEN(30,FILE='B:ECRIS1.DAT',STATUS='NEW',ACCESS='SEQUENTIAL
     B      ,FORM='FORMATTED')
      OPEN(40,FILE='B:BIDON1.DAT',STATUS='NEW',ACCESS='DIRECT'
     1      RECL=200)
C===================================================================
C       READ TITLE, NO. OF ITERATIONS
C===================================================================
C
      READ (10,2000) ITITLE,CYCLE
 2000 FORMAT(A40,I5)
C===================================================================
C       READ CAMERA CONSTANT, PHOTO COORD. STD. ERROR
C===================================================================
      READ (10,2010) CC,WM,SIG
 2010 FORMAT(3F10.3)
      WM=SIG/WM**2
      WRITE (30,2020) WM
 2020 FORMAT(//,' WT ON PHOTO COORD. = ',E12.5)
      WRITE (30,2030)
```

```
 2030 FORMAT(//,26X,'SURVEY COORD. AND STD ERROR',/,2X,
     A       'PT NO',7X,'X',9X,'Y',9X,'Z',8X,'WX',8X,'WY',8X,
     B        'WZ',/)
C==========================================================================
C      LIST OF INPUT FORMATS
C==========================================================================
 2035 FORMAT(I8,6F8.5)
 2036 FORMAT(5X,I5,2F10.4)
 2037 FORMAT(6F10.5)
C==========================================================================
C      READ PT. NO., X, Y, Z, STD ERRORS ON X, Y, Z.
C==========================================================================
      I=1
   10 READ(10,2035) IST(I),X(I),Y(I),Z(I),WX(I),WY(I),WZ(I)
      IF(IST(I).EQ.-99) GO TO 20
      IF(I.GT.IIP) STOP 77
      WRITE(30,2050) IST(I),X(I),Y(I),Z(I),WX(I),WY(I),WZ(I)
 2050 FORMAT(1X,I4,2X,3F10.4,3E11.4)
      IF(WX(I).NE.0) WX(I)=SIG/WX(I)**2
      IF(WY(I).NE.0) WY(I)=SIG/WY(I)**2
      IF(WZ(I).NE.0) WZ(I)=SIG/WZ(I)**2
      I=I+1
      GO TO 10
   20 IP=I-1
      WRITE(30,2060)
 2060 FORMAT(//,' INPUT DATA FOR CALIB')
      IEL=2
C==========================================================================
C      READ PHOTO NO.
C==========================================================================
      I=1
   30 READ(10,2036) K
      IF(K,EQ.-999) GO TO 90
      WRITE(30,2070) K
 2070 FORMAT(/,5X,'PHOTO',I4)
C==============================
C      READ EXTERIOR ORIENTATION (XO,YO,ZO,KAPPA,PHI,OMEGA)
C==============================
      READ(10,2037) EE
C==============================
      READ(10,2037) WE
      DO 40 J=1,6
      IF(WE(J).NE.0.0) WE(J)=SIG/WE(J)**2
   40 CONTINUE
      WRITE(30,2080) EE
 2080 FORMAT(6F10.4)
      WRITE(30,2090) WE
 2090 FORMAT(1P6E10.2)
C==============================
C      READ PT. NO., PHOTO COORDS., X, Y.
C==============================
      IJK=0
   50 READ(10,2036) ID1,POINT
      IF(ID1.EQ.-99) GO TO 80
      IJK=IJK+1
```

```
      DO 60 ID=1,IP
      IF(ID1.EQ.IST(ID)) GO TO 70
   60 CONTINUE
      WRITE(30,2100)ID1,I
 2100 FORMAT(/,5X,'NO SURVEY COORDINATES FOR PT. ,I4,
     A       'PHOTO NO.',I4)
      STOP 11
   70 WRITE(30,2110) IST(ID),POINT
 2110 FORMAT(I5,2F10.3)
      WRITE(40,REC=IEL) ID,POINT,X(ID),Y(ID),Z(ID),X(ID),Y(ID),
     A                Z(ID),WX(ID),WY(ID),WZ(ID)
      IEL=IEL+1
      GO TO 50
   80 IF(IJK.LT.3) STOP 99
      IL=IEL
      IEL=IEL-IJK-1
      WRITE(40,REC=IEL) IJK,EE,EE,WE
      IEL=IL+1
      I=I+1
      GO TO 30
   90 N=I-1
      IF(N.LE.0) STOP 66
      IF(N.GT.NPH) STOP 88
      K1=3*IP
      J1=6*N+9
      JA11=J1*(J1+1)/2
      IP4=IP+4
      CALL CALIB1 (A11,A12,A22,A22T,X,Y,Z,WX,WY,KEY,
     A            POINT,CC,N,IP,WM,K1,J1,JA11,ITITLE,CYCLE,EE,
     B            WE,WS,IST,SIG,IP4)
      STOP
      END
```

```
$NOFLOATCALLS
$STORAGE:2
$LARGE
      SUBROUTINE CALIB1 (A11,A12,A22,A22T,U1,U2,AW,DE,DS,
     A            KEY,POINT,CF,N,IP,WM,K1,J1,JA11,
     B            ITITLE,CYCLE,EE,WE,WS,IST,SIG,IP4)
C
      IMPLICIT INTEGER*4 (I-N)
      IMPLICIT REAL*8(A-H,O-Z)
C-----------------------------------------------------------------
C
C     ONLY THESE DIMENSIONS NEED TO BE CHANGED FOR A
C     PARTICULAR BLOCK (i.e. for a particular "NPH"
C     and "IIP")
C
```

```
C-----------------------------------------------------------------------
      DIMENSION A11(561),A12(33,90),A22(90,3)
      DIMENSION A22T(93,36),IST(34)
      DIMENSION U1(90),U2(90),AW(90),DE(90),DS(90),KEY(30)
C-----------------------------------------------------------------------
C     UNVARIABLE DIMENSIONS
C-----------------------------------------------------------------------
      DIMENSION ATEMP(9,2),WS(3),WI(9),W(2),POINT(2),BI(2,9)
      DIMENSION XE(6),EE(6),ED(6),B1(2),C(2),XS(3),ES(3),E(2)
      DIMENSION R(6),Q(2),XI(9),EI(9),RDC(2),BE(2,6),BS(2,3)
      DIMENSION WE(6)
      CHARACTER*40 ITITLE
      REAL*8     KI,K2,K3
      INTEGER    CYCLE
      EQUIVALENCE (CC,XI(3)),(KI,XI(4)),(K2,XI(5)),(K3,XI(6)),
     A            (P1,XI(7)),(P2,XI(8)),(P3,XI(9))
      COMMON IEL
      OPEN(50,FILE= B:BIDON2.DAT ,STATUS='NEW')
C-------
      WRITE(*,9999) IP,N
 9999 FORMAT(5X,'IP=',I5,//,5X,'N =',I5)
C
      WU=1,E-25
      F1=1,D6
      F2=F1*F1
      F12=F1*F2
C=====================================================
C     CC=FOCAL LENGTH (TAKEN NEGATIVE)
C=====================================================
      CC=CF
C--------
C     INTERIOR ORIENTATION DATA
C     XI - CURRENT APPROX. OF INTERIOR ORIENT.
C     EI - INITIAL ESTIMATES OF INTERIOR ORIENT.
C.........
C     ORDER OF IO IS ; XC,YC,C,KI,K2,K3,P1,P2,P3
C-------------------------------------------------------------
      DO 133 I=1,9
      READ(10,4000) XI(I)
 4000 FORMAT(9F10.4)
 4400 FORMAT(9F8.4)
  133 EI(I)=XI(I)
      WRITE(30,800)
  800 FORMAT(///,5X,'ESTIMATES OF INTERIOR ORIENTATION'
     A        'ELEMENTS AND THEIR WEIGHTS'/)
      WRITE(30,810) EI
  810 FORMAT(T10,3(5X,1P1E10.3))
C-------------
C     READ WEIGHT MATRIX FOR INTERIOR ORIENT.
C-------------
      READ(10,4400) WI
      DO 132 I=1,9
      IF(WI(I).NE.0.D0) WI(I)=1.D0/WI(I)**2
  132 WI(I)=SIG*WI(I)
      WRITE(30,810) WI
```

```
C---------------
C      INITIALIZE INTERIOR PARAMETERS
C---------------
       IOUT=0
       ICYCLE=0
C---------------
C      PHOTO COORDINATE WEIGHT MATRIX
C---------------
       W(1)=WM
       W(2)=WM
       WRITE(30,512)
  512 FORMAT(7(/),'RESIDUAL AND OBSERVATION EQUATION BEFORE ',
     A       '1ST CYCLE',//,3X,' PHOTO PT RES.IN X RES.IN Y')
C-----------------
C      RETURNS TO HERE OR NEXT CARD FOR ITERATION
C-----------------
    4 ICYCLE=ICYCLE+1
       NDF=0
       VPV=0.D0
C---------------
C      CHANGE 514 TO 516 ON NEXT STATEMENT
C---------------
       IF(ICYCLE.GT.1) GOTO 514
       GOTO 514
  516 II=1
       WI(II)=0.0
       IF(II.EQ.9.OR.II.GT.9) GOTO 514
       II=II+1
       GOTO 516
C----------------------
C      CLEAR NORMALS
C----------------------
  514 DO 5 I=1,IP
    5 KEY(I)=0
       DO 2 I=1,J1
       U1(I)=0.D0
       DO 2 J=1,K1
    2 A12(I,J)=0.D0
       DO 7 I=1,JA11
    7 A11(I)=0.D0
       DO 3 I=1,K1
       U2(I)=0.D0
       DO 3 J=1,3
    3 A22(I,J)=0.D0
C-------------------
C      FORMING A11 AND U1 DUE TO INTERIOR ORIENTATION
C      CONSTRAINTS.
C-------------------
       IA11=0
       DO 8 I=1,9
       IA11=IA11+I
       IF(WI(I).LE.WU) GOTO 8
       NDF=NDF+1
       VPV=VPV+WI(I)*(EI(I)-XI(I))**2
       A11(IA11)=WI(I)
```

```
      U1(I)=WI(I)*(XI(I)-EI(I))
    8 CONTINUE
C---------------
C     CALL PHOTO DATA
C---------------
      IPC=1
      IEL=1
      DO 100 J=1,N
C-------------------
C      XE - CURRENT APPROX. OF EXTERIOR ORIENT.
C      EE - INITIAL ESTIMATES OF EXTERIOR ORIENT.
C      WE - WEIGHT OF EXTERIOR ORIENT. PARAMETERS
C-------------------
      READ(40,REC=IEL) K,XE,EE,WE
      IEL=IEL+1
C-------------------
C     SIN OF KAPPA, PHI, OMEGA AND
C     COS OF KAPPA, PHI, OMEGA
C-------------------
      R(1)=DSIN(XE(4))
      R(2)=DSIN(XE(5))
      R(3)=DSIN(XE(6))
      R(4)=DCOS(XE(4))
      R(5)=DCOS(XE(5))
      R(6)=DCOS(XE(6))
C-------------------
C     ADDING TERMS DUE TO CONSTRANITS ON EXTERIOR
C     ORIENTATION ELEMENTS
C-------------------
      L=6*(J-1)+9
      IA11=L*(L+1)/2
      DO 10 II=1,6
      IA11=IA11+L+II
      IF(WE(II).LE.WU) GO TO 10
      NDF=NDF+1
      VPV=VPV+WE(II)*((EE(II)-XE(II))**2)
      IIL=II+L
C-------------------
C     CARDS PERTAINING TO FORMATION OF MATRICES WILL HAVE
C     5 C'S
C
C     -W(E)*E(E)
C-------------------
      U1(IIL)=U1(IIL)+WE(II)*(XE(II)-EE(II))
C-------------------
C     +W(E)
C-------------------
      A11(IA11)=A11(IA11)+WE(II)
   10 CONTINUE
C--------------------------------------------------------
C     CALL POINT DATA
C--------------------------------------------------------
      DO 100 I=1,K
      READ(40,REC=IEL) NP,POINT,XS,ES,WS
      IEL=IEL+1
```

```
      LL=3*(NP-1)
C-------------------
C     NP     - POIND ID
C     POINT  - X, Y PHOTO COORD.
C     XS     - CURRENT APPROX. OF SURVEY COORDS.
C     ES     - INITIAL ESTIMATES OF SURVEY COORDS.
C     WS     - SURVEY COORD. WEIGHTS
C
C     CALL PARTIALS
C-------------------
      CALL COFEI(XS,R,BE,BS,XE,CC,XC,YC)
C-------------------
C     COMPUTE NORMALS
C     TERMS DUE TO INTERNAL ORIENTATION PARAMETERS
C-------------------
      TEMP1=POINT(1)-XI(1)
      TEMP2=POINT(2)-XI(2)
      R2=TEMP1**2+TEMP2**2
      R4=(R2*R2)/F2
      R6=(R4*R2)/F1
      RPF=1.D0+KI*R2/F1+K2*R4+K3*R6
      CP1=R2+2.D0*TEMP1**2
      CP2=R2+2.D0*TEMP2**2
      CP3=2.D0*TEMP1*TEMP2
      CP4=1.D0+P3*R2/F12
      RDC(1)=P1*CP1/F1+P2*CP3/F2
      RDC(2)=P1*CP3/F1+P2*CP2/F2
      XC=XC/RPF
      YC=YC/RPF
      E(1)=TEMP1-XC+RDC(1)*CP4/RPF
      E(2)=TEMP2-YC+RDC(2)*CP4/RPF
      IF(ICYCLE.LE.1)THEN
          WRITE(30,511) J,IST(NP),E(1),E(2),
  511     FORMAT(I5,I5,F10.3,F10.3)
      ENDIF
      NDF=NDF+2
      VPV=VPV+W(1)*E(1)**2
      VPV=VPV+W(2)*E(2)**2
      BI(1,1)=-1.D0
      BI(1,2)= 0.D0
      BI(1,3)=-XC/CC
      BI(2,1)=0.D0
      BI(2,2)=-1.D0
      BI(2,3)=-YC/CC
      Q(1)=XC/RPF-RDC(1)*CP4/RPF
      Q(2)=YC/RPF-RDC(2)*CP4/RPF
      DO 122 II=1,2
      BI(II,4)=Q(II)*R2/F1
      BI(II,5)=Q(II)*R4
      BI(II,6)=Q(II)*R6
      DO 121 JJ=1,6
  121 BE(II,JJ)=BE(II,JJ)/RPF
      DO 122 JJ=1,3
  122 BS(II,JJ)=BS(II,JJ)/RPF
      BI(1,7)=(CP1*CP4/F1)/RPF
```

```
      BI(1,8)=(CP3*CP4/F2)/RPF
      BI(1,9)=(RDC(1)*R2/F12)/RPF
      BI(2,7)=(CP3*CP4/F1)/RPF
      BI(2,8)=(CP2*CP4/F2)/RPF
      BI(2,9)=(RDC(2)*R2/F12)/RPF
C-------------------
C     FORMING A11 DUE TO INTERIOR ORIENTATION
C-------------------
      DO 123 II=1,9
      DO 123 JJ=1,2
C----------------------
C     B(I)T*W
C----------------------
  123 ATEMP(II,JJ)=BI(JJ,II)*W(JJ)
      KA11=0
      DO 128 II=1,9
      IA11=KA11
      DO 124 JJ=1,II
      IA11=IA11+1
      KA11=IA11
      TEMP=0.D0
      DO 125 KK=1,2
C----------------------
C     B(I)T*W*B(I)
C----------------------
  125 TEMP=TEMP+ATEMP(II,KK)*BI(KK,JJ)
  124 A11(IA11)=A11(IA11)+TEMP
      IA11=L*(L+1)/2+II
      DO 126 JJ=1,6
      TEMP=0.D0
      DO 146 KK=1,2
C----------------------
C     B(I)TW*B(E)
C----------------------
  146 TEMP=TEMP+ATEMP(II,KK)*BE(KK,JJ)
      A11(IA11)=A11(IA11)+TEMP
  126 IA11=IA11+L+JJ
      DO 127 JJ=1,3
      TEMP=0.D0
      LJ=LL+JJ
      DO 147 KK=1,2
C-----------------------
C     B(I)TW*B(S)
C-----------------------
  147 TEMP=TEMP+ATEMP(II,KK)*BS(KK,JJ)
  127 A12(II,LJ)=A12(II,LJ)+TEMP
      DO 128 KK=1,2
C------------------------
C      B(I)TW*E
C------------------------
  128 U1(II)=U1(II)+ATEMP(II,KK)*E(KK)
C-----------------------------------------------------------------
C     TEST FOR FIRST-TIME SURVEY POINT
C-----------------------------------------------------------------
```

```
      ITEST=1
      IF(IPC.GT.IP) GO TO 12
      DO  11 II=1,IPC
      IF(NP.EQ.KEY(II)) GO TO 12
   11 CONTINUE
      KEY(IPC)=NP
      IPC=IPC+1
      ITEST=0
   12 DO 15 II=1,6
      DO 15 JJ=1,2
C-------------------
C      B(E)T*W
C-------------------
   15 ATEMP(II,JJ)=BE(JJ,II)*W(JJ)
C-----------------------------------------------------------------
C     COMPUTE A11
C-----------------------------------------------------------------
      IA11=L*(L+1)/2
      DO 17 II=1,6
      IA11=IA11+L
      IIL=II+L
      DO 16 KK=1,2
C-------------------
C     B(E)TW*E
C-------------------
   16 U1(IIL)=U1(IIL)+ATEMP(II,KK)*E(KK)
      DO 17 JJ=1,II
      IA11=IA11+1
      DO 17 KK=1,2
C-------------------
C     B(E)TW*B(E)+W(E)
C-------------------
   17 A11(IA11)=A11(IA11)+ATEMP(II,KK)*BE(KK,JJ)
C-----------------------------------------------------------------
C     COMPUTE A12
C-----------------------------------------------------------------
      DO 19 II=1,6
      IIL=II+L
      DO 19 JJ=1,3
      LJ=LL+JJ
      DO 19 KK=1,2
C-------------------
C     B(E)TW*B(S)
C-------------------
   19 A12(IIL,LJ)=A12(IIL,LJ)+ATEMP(II,KK)*BS(KK,JJ)
C-----------------------------------------------------------------
C     COMPUTE A22
C-----------------------------------------------------------------
      DO 23 II=1,3
      DO 23 JJ=1,2
C-------------------
C     B(S)T*W
C-------------------
   23 ATEMP(II,JJ)=BS(JJ,II)*W(JJ)
      DO 27 II=1,3
```

```
      M=LL+II
      DO 26 KK=1,2
C--------------------
C     B(S)TW*E
C--------------------
      U2(M)=U2(M)+ATEMP(II,KK)*E(KK)
      DO 26 JJ=1,3
C--------------------
C     B(S)TW*B(S)
C--------------------
   26 A22(M,JJ)=A22(M,JJ)+ATEMP(II,KK)*BS(KK,JJ)
      IF(ITEST.EQ.1) GO TO 27
C--------------------
C     ADDING TERMS DUE TO CONSTRAINT ON SURVEY COORDINATES
C--------------------
      IF(WS(II).LE.WU) GO TO 27
      NDF=NDF+1
      VPV=VPV+WS(II)*((ES(II)-XS(II))**2)
C-----------------------
C     B(S)TWB(S)+W(S)
C-----------------------
      A22(M,II)=A22(M,II)+WS(II)
C-----------------------
C     W(S)*E
C-----------------------
      U2(M)=U2(M)+WS(II)*(XS(II)-ES(II))
   27 CONTINUE
  100 CONTINUE
C-------------------------------------------------------------------
C     INVERT A22 MATRIX
C-------------------------------------------------------------------
      DO 34 II=1,IP
      II3=3*(II-1)
      A22((II3+1),1)=1.D0/A22((II3+1),1)
      DO 34 JJ=1,2
      LI=JJ+1
      L=II3+LI
      DO 48 I=1,2
      B1(I)=0.D0
   48 C(I)=0.D0
      DO 49 J=1,JJ
      DO 49 K=1,JJ
      II3K=II3+K
      B1(J)=B1(J)-A22(II3K,J)*A22(L,K)
   49 C(K)=C(K)-A22(II3K,J)*A22((II3+J),LI)
      D=A22(L,LI)
      DO 30 J=1,JJ
   30 D=D+C(J)*A22(L,J)
      D=1.D0/D
      DO 31 J=1,JJ
      II3K=II3+J
      A22(II3K,LI)=C(J)*D
      A22(L,J)=B1(J)*D
      DO 31 K=1,JJ
   31 A22(II3K,K)=A22(II3K,K)+B1(K)*C(J)*D
   34 A22(L,LI)=D
```

```
C-----------------------------------------------------------------------
C      FORMING A22T
C-----------------------------------------------------------------------
       DO 35 I=1,IP
       M=3*(I-1)
       DO 35 J=1,3
       II=M+J
       DO 35 K=1,J1
       A22T(II,K)=0.D0
       DO 35 L=1,3
   35  A22T(II,K)=A22T(II,K)+A22(II,L)*A12(K,(M+L))
       REWIND 50
       DO 8000 IIK1=1,K1
       DO 8000 IIJ1=1,J1
 8000  WRITE(50,*)A22T(IIK1,IIJ1)
       REWIND 50
       IA11=0
       DO 37 I=1,J1
       DO 37 J=1,I
       IA11=IA11+1
       DO 37 K=1,K1
   37  A11(IA11)=A11(IA11)-A12(I,K)*A22T(K,J)
C-----------------------------------------------------------------------
C      INVERTING A11
C-----------------------------------------------------------------------
       EPS=1.D-12
       CALL DSINV(A11,J1,JA11,EPS,IER)
C-----------------------------------------------------------------------
C      IER = 0 ---- NO ERROR
C      IER =-1 ---- MATRIX IS NOT POSITIVE DEFINITE
C      IER = K ---- LOSS OF SIGNIFICANCE
C-----------------------------------------------------------------------
       IF(IER) 139,138,140
  139  WRITE(30,3013)
 3013  FORMAT('0A11 IS NOT A POSITIVE DEFINE SYMETRIC MATRIX'
     A          -- EXECUTION TERMINATED')
       STOP
  140  WRITE(30,3014)IER
 3014  FORMAT('0A LOSS OF SIGNIFICANCE OCCURED IN A11 ,I4)
  138  IF(IOUT.EQ.1) GO TO 302
       DO 36 I=1,J1
       DO 36 L=1,IP
       M=3*(L-1)
       DO 36 J=1,3
       JJ=M+J
       A22T(JJ,I)=0.D0
       DO 36 K=1,3
       KK=M+K
   36  A22T(JJ,I)=A22T(JJ,I)+A12(I,KK)*A22(KK,J)
       DO 38 I=1,J1
       KA11=I*(I-1)/2
       DO 38 J=1,K1
       A12(I,J)=0.D0
       IA11=KA11
       DO 38 K=1,J1
```

```
      IA11=IA11+1
      IF(K.GT.I) IA11=IA11+K-2
   38 A12(I,J)=A12(I,J)-A11(IA11)*A22T(J,K)
      DO 40 I=1,J1
      DE(I)=0.D0
      IA11=I*(I-1)/2
      DO 39 J=1,J1
      IA11=IA11+1
      IF(J.GT.I) IA11=IA11+J-2
C-----------------------------------------------------------------
C     SOLVING FOR DELTA(I) AND DELTA(E)
C-----------------------------------------------------------------
   39 DE(I)=DE(I)-A11(IA11)*U1(J)
      DO 40 J=1,K1
   40 DE(I)=DE(I)-A12(I,J)*U2(J)
C-------------------------------
C     RESTORE FOR ORIGINAL A22T
C-------------------------------
      DO 8010 IIK1=1,K1
      DO 8010 IIJ1=1,J1
 8010 READ(50,*)A22T(IIK1,IIJ1)
C-----------------------------------------------------------------
C     SOLVING FOR DELTA(S)
C-----------------------------------------------------------------
      DO 42 II=1,IP
      II3=3*(II-1)
      DO 42 JJ=1,3
      I=II3+JJ
      DO 45 J=1,K1
      DS(J)=0.D0
      DO 45 K=1,J1
   45 DS(J)=DS(J)+A22T(I,K)*A12(K,J)
      A22T(I,JJ)=DS(I)
      AW(I)=0.D0
      DO 42 J=1,K1
   42 AW(I)=AW(I)+DS(J)*U2(J)
      DO 43 I=1,IP
      KEY(I)=0
      M=3*(I-1)
      DO 43 J=1,3
      JJ=M+J
      DS(JJ)=0.D0
      DO 43 K=1,3
   43 DS(JJ)=DS(JJ)+A22(JJ,K)*U2(M+K)
      DO 44 I=1,K1
      DS(I)=AW(I)-DS(I)
      DO 44 J=1,J1
   44 DS(I)=DS(I)-A12(J,I)*U1(J)
C-----------------------------------------------------------------
C     APPLY ALTERATIONS TO UNKMOWNS
C-----------------------------------------------------------------
      DO 130 I=1,9
C-----------------------------------------------------
C     UPDATING CURREN APPROX. OF INTERIOR ORIENT.
C-----------------------------------------------------
```

```
 130 XI(I)=XI(I)+DE(I)
 302 NDF=NDF-K1-J1
     VAR=VPV/NDF
     IF(ICYCLE.EQ.CYCLE)WRITE(30,604)ICYCLE,VAR,NDF
 604 FORMAT(//,' ICYCLE=',I5,5X,'VARIANCE=',1PD14.6,5X,'NDF=',I5)
     IF(ICYCLE.EQ.CYCLE) IOUT=1
     DO 306 I=1,J1
     KA11=I*(I-1)/2
     DO 306 K=1,J1
     KA11=KA11+1
     IF(K.GT.I) KA11=KA11+K-2
C-----------------------------------------------------------------------
C    FORMATION OF VARIANCE - COVARIANCE MATRIX
C-----------------------------------------------------------------------
  306 A12(I,K)=A11(KA11)*VAR
      DO 66 I=1,9
   66 ATEMP(I,1)=DSQRT(A12(I,I))
      IF(ICYCLE.EQ.CYCLE)WRITE(30,3000) CHAR(012),ITITLE,N,IP,NDF,
     -ICYCLE,VAR
 3000 FORMAT(A1,11X,'CALIBRATION OF THE ',A40,/,28X,
     A     'NO. OF PHOTOS:',4X,I5,/,24X,'NO. OF CONTROL POINTS:',
     B     I10,/,25X,'DEGREES OF FREEDOM:',2X,I5,/,28X,'NO. OF CYCLES:',
     C     5X,I5,/,18X,'VARIANCE OF UNIT WEIGHT = ',1P1E12.5,
     D     ///,34X,'RESULTS',/,27X,'INTERIOR ORIENTATION',//,
     E     T23,'X',T39,'Y',T53,'F'//)
      IF(ICYCLE.EQ.CYCLE)WRITE(30,3001)(XI(I),I=1,3),(ATEMP(J,1),J=1,3)
     A (WI(JJ),JJ=1,3)
      IF(ICYCLE.EQ.CYCLE) THEN
      WRITE(30,4001)(XI(I),I=4,6),(ATEMP(J,1),J=4,6),
     A (WI(JJ),JJ=4,6)
       WRITE(30,4002)(XI(I),I=7,9),(ATEMP(J,1),J=7,9),
     A (WI(JJ),JJ=7,9)
      ENDIF
 4001  FORMAT(T20,'K1.D-6',T36,'K2.D-12',T50,'K3.D-18',//,
     @T14,F15.8,T30,F15.8,T44,F15.8,/,T5,'STD ERROR',T13,
     F          F15.8,T28,F15.8,T43,F15.8,/,T5,'WEIGHT',T16,1PE15.8,
     G          T29,1PE15.8,T44,1PE15.8,6(/))
 4002  FORMAT(T20,'P1.D-6',T36,'P2.D-12',T50,'P3.D-18',//,
     @T14,F15.8,T30,F15.8,T44,F15.8,/,T5,'STD ERROR',T13,
     F          F15.8,T28,F15.8,T43,F15.8,/,T5,'WEIGHT',T16,1PE15.8,
     G          T29,1PE15.8,T44,1PE15.8,6(/))
 3001 FORMAT(T17,F9.2,T33,F9.2,T48,F9.2,/,T5,'STD ERROR',T16,
     F          F11.2,T31,F11.2,T46,F11.2,/,T5,'WEIGHT',T16,1PE11.2,
     G          T32,1PE11.2,T47,1PE11.2,6(/))
      IEL=1
      DO 115 I=1,N
      READ(40,REC=IEL) K,XE,EE,WE
      IEL=IEL+1
      LL=6*(I-1)+9
      DO 101 IZ=1,6
      KK=LL+IZ
C-------------------------------------------------------
C     EE - EXTERIOR ORIENTATION STD. ERROR
C-------------------------------------------------------
      ED(IZ)=DSQRT(A12(KK,KK))
```

```
C-----------------------------------------------------------------------
C      UPDATING EXTERIOR ORIENT.
C-----------------------------------------------------------------------
  101 XE(IZ)=XE(IZ)+DE(KK)
      IEL=IEL-1
      WRITE(40,REC=IEL) K,XE,EE,WE
      IEL=IEL+1
C--------------------------------
C      SIN OF K,P,O AND COS OF K, P, O
C--------------------------------------
      R(1)=DSIN(XE(4))
      R(2)=DSIN(XE(5))
      R(3)=DSIN(XE(6))
      R(4)=DCOS(XE(4))
      R(5)=DCOS(XE(5))
      R(6)=DCOS(XE(6))
      IF(I.GT.1) GO TO 61
C
C
      IF(ICYCLE.EQ.CYCLE)WRITE(30,3006)
 3006 FORMAT (15X,'COVARIANCE/VARIANCE/CORRELATION COEFFICIENT
     1               'MATRIX')
C
C^^^^^^^^^^^^^^^^^^^^^^^^^^^^^^^^^^^^^^^^^^^^^^^^^^^^^^^^^^^^^^^^^^^^^^^
C
      NVAL=9
      IF(ICYCLE.EQ.CYCLE) NVAL=J1
      DO 60 II=1,NVAL
      TEMP=A12(II,II)
      I2=II
      IF(ICYCLE.EQ.CYCLE) I2=1
      DO 55 KK=I2,J1
C-----------------------------------------------------------------------
C      CALCULATE AND WRITE THE CORRELATION-COEFFICIENT MATRIX
C-----------------------------------------------------------------------
   55 A12(II,KK)=A12(II,KK)/DSQRT(TEMP*A12(KK,KK))
C
C
      IF(ICYCLE.EQ.CYCLE)WRITE(30,3002) II
 3002 FORMAT (//,T2,'ROW',I4)
      IF(ICYCLE.EQ.CYCLE)WRITE (30,3003) (A12(II,J),J=1,J1)
 3003 FORMAT(T12,1P3E15.6)
C
C^^^^^^^^^^^^^^^^^^^^^^^^^^^^^^^^^^^^^^^^^^^^^^^^^^^^^^^^^^^^^^^^^^^^^^^
C
   60 A12(II,II)=TEMP
   61 IF(ICYCLE.EQ.CYCLE)WRITE(30,3007)
 3007 FORMAT(7(/))
      IF(ICYCLE.EQ.CYCLE)WRITE(30,3100)I
 3100 FORMAT(30X,'EXTERIOR ORIENTATION',//,1X,'PHOTO NO.',I4)
      IF(ICYCLE.EQ.CYCLE)WRITE(30,3110)
 3110 FORMAT(//,20X,'VALUE',13X,'STD ERROR',10X,'WEIGHT')
      IF(ICYCLE.EQ.CYCLE)WRITE(30,3120)XE(1),ED(1),WE(1)
 3120 FORMAT(2X,'XO',6X,3(4X,1PE15.6))
```

```
      IF(ICYCLE.EQ.CYCLE)WRITE(30,3130)XE(2),ED(2),WE(2)
 3130 FORMAT(2X,'YO',6X,3(4X,1PE15.6))
      IF(ICYCLE.EQ.CYCLE)WRITE(30,3140)XE(3),ED(3),WE(3)
 3140 FORMAT(2X,'ZO',6X,3(4X,1PE15.6))
      IF(ICYCLE.EQ.CYCLE)WRITE(30,3150)XE(4),ED(4),WE(4)
 3150 FORMAT(//,2X,'KAPPA(RAD)',2X,3(1PE15.6,4X))
      IF(ICYCLE.EQ.CYCLE)WRITE(30,3160)XE(5),ED(5),WE(5)
 3160 FORMAT(2X,'PHI(RAD)',3(4X,1PE15.6))
      IF(ICYCLE.EQ.CYCLE)WRITE(30,3170)XE(6),ED(6),WE(6)
 3170 FORMAT(2X,'OMEGA(RAD)',2X,3(1PE15.6,4X),///)
      IF(ICYCLE.EQ.CYCLE)WRITE(30,3004)
 3004 FORMAT(26X,'RESIDUALS ON CONTROL POINTS',/,31X,
     E        '(MICROMETER UNITS)',///,15X,'POINT NO.',7X,
     F        'RESIDUALS IN X',6X,'RESIDUALS IN Y')
      RMSX=0.D0
      RMSY=0.D0
      DO 116 J=1,K
      READ(40,REC=IEL) NP,POINT,XS,ES,WS
      IEL=IEL+1
      NP3=3*(NP-1)
      DO 114 IZ=1,3
C-----------------------------------------------------------------------
C     UPDATING CURRENT APPROX.OF SURVEY COORDS.
C-----------------------------------------------------------------------
  114 XS(IZ)=XS(IZ)+DS(NP3+IZ)
      IEL=IEL-1
      WRITE(40,REC=IEL) NP,POINT,XS,ES,WS
      IEL=IEL+1
      DX=XS(1)-XE(1)
      DY=XS(2)-XE(2)
      DZ=XS(3)-XE(3)
C-----------------------------------------------------------------------
C     SUBSTITUING IN GENERAL PROJECTIVE EQUATIONS
C-----------------------------------------------------------------------
      XT=DX*R(5)*R(4)+DY*(R(6)*R(1)+R(3)*R(2)*R(4))+DZ*(R(3)*
     &R(1)-R(6)*R(2)*R(4))
      YT=-DX*R(5)*R(1)+DY*(R(6)*R(4)-R(3)*R(2)*R(1))+DZ*(R(3)*
     %R(4)+R(6)*R(2)*R(1))
      ZT=DX*R(2)-DY*R(3)*R(5)+DZ*R(6)*R(5)
      TEMP1=POINT(1)-XI(1)
      TEMP2=POINT(2)-XI(2)
      R2=TEMP1**2+TEMP2**2
      R4=(R2*R2)/F2
      R6=(R4*R2)/F1
      RPF=1.D0+KI*R2/F1+K2*R4+K3*R6
      CP1=R2+2.D0*TEMP1**2
      CP2=R2+2.D0*TEMP2**2
      CP3=2.D0*TEMP1*TEMP2
      CP4=1.D0+P3*R2/F12
      RDC(1)=P1*CP1/F1+P2*CP3/F2
      RDC(2)=P1*CP3/F1+P2*CP2/F2
      XC=(CC*XT/ZT)/RPF
      YC=(CC*YT/ZT)/RPF
```

```
C-----------------------------------------------------------------------
C       COMPUTING RESIDUALS
C-----------------------------------------------------------------------
        E(1)=TEMP1-XC+RDC(1)*CP4/RPF
        E(2)=TEMP2-YC+RDC(2)*CP4/RPF
        IF(ICYCLE.EQ.CYCLE)WRITE(30,3005) IST(NP),E(1),E(2)
 3005   FORMAT(15X,I5,3X,3P2F20.1)
        RMSX=RMSX+E(1)*E(1)
  116   RMSY=RMSY+E(2)*E(2)
        RMSX=DSQRT(RMSX/K)
        RMSY=DSQRT(RMSY/K)
  115   IF(ICYCLE.EQ.CYCLE)WRITE(30,6500) RMSX,RMSY
 6500   FORMAT(//,16X,'RMS = ',1X,3P2F20.1)
        IF(IOUT.EQ.1) GO TO 5000
        IF(ICYCLE.LT.CYCLE) GO TO 4
 5000   IF(ICYCLE.EQ.CYCLE)WRITE(30,5001) CHAR(012)
 5001   FORMAT(A1,5X,'ADJUSTED SURVEY COORDINATES',//,5X,
      A        'POINT',10X,'X',15X,'Y',15X,'Z')
        IEL=1
        DO 5007 I=1,N
        READ(40,REC=IEL) JJ,XE,EE,WE
        IEL=IEL+1
        DO 5007 K=1,JJ
        READ(40,REC=IEL) NP,POINT,XS,ES,WS
        IEL=IEL+1
        DO 5008 L=1,IP
        IF(IST(L).EQ.IST(NP).AND.KEY(L).EQ.0) GO TO 5002
 5008   CONTINUE
        GO TO 5007
 5002   KEY(L)=1
C-----------------------------------------------------------------------
C       ADJUSTED SURVEY COORDINATES
C-----------------------------------------------------------------------
        IF(ICYCLE.EQ.CYCLE)WRITE(30,5003) IST(L),XS
 5003   FORMAT(/,6X,I5,3F15.4)
 5007   CONTINUE
        IF(ICYCLE.EQ.CYCLE)WRITE(30,5004) CHAR(012)
 5004   FORMAT(A1,5X,'STD. DEV. OF SURVEY COORDINATES (MM)',//,
      A        5X,'POINT',10X,'X',15X,'Y',15X,'Z')
        DO 5005 I=1,IP
        I3=I*3
        I2=I3-1
        I1=I3-2
        XSTD=DSQRT((A22(I1,1)-A22T(I1,1))*VAR)
        YSTD=DSQRT((A22(I2,2)-A22T(I2,2))*VAR)
        ZSTD=DSQRT((A22(I3,3)-A22T(I3,3))*VAR)
C-----------------------------------------------------------------------
C       PRINT OUR STANDARD DEVIATIONS FOR
C       ADJUSTED SURVEY COORDINATES
C-----------------------------------------------------------------------
 5005   IF(ICYCLE.EQ.CYCLE)WRITE(30,5009) IST(I),XSTD,YSTD,ZSTD
 5009   FORMAT(/,6X,I3,3P3F15.4)
        CLOSE (50)
        RETURN
        END
```

```
      SUBROUTINE COFEI(D,R,B,BS,XO,CC,XC,YC)
C=======================================================================
C
C     COMPUTES "B" FOR EXTERIOR ORIENTATION ELEMENTS
C     INCLUDING "CC".
C     REQUIRED ORDER  XO(X0,Y0,Z0,K,P,W)
C     CAMERA CONSTANT TAKEN NEGATIVE
C     B = COEFFICIENT MATRIX-EXTERIOR ORIENTATION
C     BS= COEFFICIENT MATRIX-OBJECT COORDINATES
C     D = MATRIX  (X,Y,Z)
C     R = MATRIX  (SK,SP,SW,CK,CP,CW)
C=======================================================================
C
      IMPLICIT REAL*8(A-H,O-Z)
      DIMENSION R(6),D(3),XO(6),B(2,6),BS(2,3)
      SK=R(1)
      SP=R(2)
      SW=R(3)
      CK=R(4)
      CP=R(5)
      CW=R(6)
      DX=D(1)-XO(1)
      DY=D(2)-XO(2)
      DZ=D(3)-XO(3)
      XT= DX*CP*CK+DY*(CW*SK+SW*SP*CK)+DZ*(SW*SK-CW*SP*CK)
      YT=-DX*CP*SK+DY*(CW*CK-SW*SP*SK)+DZ*(SW*CK+CW*SP*SK)
      ZT= DX*SP-DY*SW*CP+DZ*CW*CP
      XC=CC*XT/ZT
      YC=CC*YT/ZT
      COZ=CC/ZT**2
      B(1,1)=-COZ*(ZT*CP*CK-XT*SP)
      B(1,2)=-COZ*(ZT*(CW*SK+SW*SP*CK)+XT*SW*CP)
      B(1,3)=-COZ*(ZT*(SW*SK-CW*SP*CK)-XT*CW*CP)
      B(1,4)= COZ*(-DX*CP*SK+DY*(CW*CK-SW*SP*SK)+
     1        DZ*(SW*CK+CW*SP*SK))*ZT
      B(1,5)= COZ*(ZT*(-DX*SP*CK+DY*SW*CP*CK-DZ*CW*CP*CK)-
     2        XT*(DX*CP+DY*SW*SP-DZ*CW*SP))
      B(1,6)= COZ*(ZT*(DY*(CW*SP*CK-SW*SK)+DZ*(CW*SK+SW*SP*CK))
     3        +XT*(DY*CW*CP+DZ*SW*CP))
      B(2,1)= COZ*(ZT*CP*SK+YT*SP)
      B(2,2)=-COZ*(ZT*(CW*CK-SW*SP*SK)+YT*SW*CP)
      B(2,3)=-COZ*(ZT*(SW*CK+CW*SP*SK)-YT*CW*CP)
      B(2,4)= COZ*(ZT*(-DX*CP*CK-DY*(CW*SK+SW*SP*CK)+
     4        DZ*(CW*SP*CK-SW*SK)))
      B(2,5)= COZ*(ZT*(DX*SP*SK-DY*SW*CP*SK+DZ*CW*CP*SK)-
     5        YT*(DX*CP+DY*SW*SP-DZ*CW*SP))
      B(2,6)= COZ*(ZT*(-DY*(SW*CK+CW*SP*SK)+DZ*(CW*CK-
     6        SW*SP*SK))+YT*(DY*CW*CP+DZ*SW*CP))
      DO 126 I=1,3
      BS(1,I)=B(1,I)
  126 BS(2,I)=B(2,I)
      DO 130 I=1,2
      DO 130 J=1,6
  130 B(I,J)=-B(I,J)
      RETURN
      END
```

```
      SUBROUTINE DSINV(A,N,N2,EPS,IER)
C=============================================================
C  FACTORIZE GIVEN MATRIX BY MEANS OF SUBROUTINE MFSD
C  A = TRANSPOSE(T)*T
C=============================================================
C
      IMPLICIT REAL*8(A-H,O-Z)
      DIMENSION A(N2)
      CALL MFSD(A,N,N2,EPS,IER)
      IF(IER) 9,1,1
C-----------------------------------------
C     INVERT UPPER TRIANGULATION MATRIX T
C      PREPARE INVERTION-LOOP.
C------------------------------------------
    1 IPIV=N2
      IND=IPIV
C------------------------------------------
C     INITIALIZE INVERTION-LOOP
C------------------------------------------
      DO 6 I=1,N
      DIN=1.D0/A(IPIV)
      A(IPIV)=DIN
      MIN=N
      KEND=I-1
      LANF=N-KEND
      IF (KEND) 5,5,2
    2 J=IND
C------------------------------------------
C     INITIALIZE ROW-LOOP.
C------------------------------------------
      DO 4 K=1,KEND
      WORK=0.D0
      MIN=MIN-1
      LHOR=IPIV
      LVER=J
C------------------------------------------
C     START INNER-LOOP.
C------------------------------------------
      DO 3 L=LANF,MIN
      LVER=LVER+1
      LHOR=LHOR+L
    3 WORK=WORK+A(LVER)*A(LHOR)
C------------------------------------------
C     END OF INNER-LOOP.
C------------------------------------------
      A(J)=-WORK*DIN
    4 J=J-MIN
C------------------------------------------
C     END OF ROW-LOOP.
C------------------------------------------
    5 IPIV=IPIV-MIN
    6 IND =IND-1
C------------------------------------------------------------------
C     END OF INVERTION-LOOP.
```

```
C      CALCULATE INVERSE(A) BY MEANS OF INVERSE(T).
C      INVERSE(A)=INVERSE(T)*TRANSPOSE(INVERSE(T))
C      INITIALIZE MULTIPLICATION-LOOP.
C-----------------------------------------------------------------------
       DO 8 I=1,N
       IPIV=IPIV+I
       J=IPIV
C--------------------------------
C      INITIALIZE ROW-LOOP.
C--------------------------------
       DO 8 K=I,N
       WORK=0.D0
       LHOR=J
C--------------------------------
C      START INNER-LOOP.
C--------------------------------
       DO 7 L=K,N
       LVER=LHOR+K-I
       WORK=WORK+A(LHOR)*A(LVER)
     7 LHOR=LHOR+L
C--------------------------------
C      END OF INNER-LOOP.
C--------------------------------
       A(J)=WORK
     8 J=J+K
C-----------------------------------------------------------------------
C      END OF ROW-LOOP AND MULTIPLICATION-LOOP.
C-----------------------------------------------------------------------
     9 RETURN
       END
```

```
       SUBROUTINE MFSD(A,N,N2,EPS,IER)
C
C
       IMPLICIT REAL*8(A-H,O-Z)
       DIMENSION A(N2)
C--------------------------------------
C      TEST ON WRONG INPUT PARAMETER "N"
C--------------------------------------
       IF (N) 12,12,1
     1 IER=0
C----------------------------
C      INITIALIZE DIAGONAL-LOOP.
C----------------------------
       KPIV=0
       DO 11 K=1,N
       KPIV=KPIV+K
       IND =KPIV
       LEND=K-1
```

```
C------------------------------------
C       CALCULATE TOLERANCE "C"
C------------------------------------
        TOL=DABS(EPS*A(KPIV))
C--------------------------------------------------
C       START FATORIZATION-LOOP OVER K-TH ROW
C--------------------------------------------------
        DO 11 I=K,N
        DSUM=0.D0
        IF(LEND) 2,4,2
C------------------------------------
C       START INNER-LOOP.
C------------------------------------
      2 DO 3 L=1,LEND
        LANF=KPIV-L
        LIND=IND-L
      3 DSUM=DSUM+A(LANF)*A(LIND)
C------------------------------------
C       END OF INNER LOOP.
C       TRANSFORM ELEMENT A(IND)
C------------------------------------
      4 DSUM=A(IND)-DSUM
        IF (I-K) 10,5,10
C----------------------------------------------------------------------
C       TEST FOR NEGATIVE ELEMENT AND FOR LOST OF SIGNIFIANCE
C----------------------------------------------------------------------
      5 IF (DSUM-TOL) 6,6,9
      6 IF (DSUM) 13,13,7
      7 IF (IER) 8,8,9
      8 IER=K-1
C------------------------------------
C       COMPUTE PIVOT ELEMENT
C------------------------------------
      9 DPIV=DSQRT(DSUM)
        A(KPIV)=DPIV
        DPIV=1.D0/DPIV
        GO TO 11
C------------------------------------
C       CALCULATE TERMS IN ROW
C------------------------------------
     10 A(IND)=DSUM*DPIV
     11 IND=IND+I
C------------------------------------
C       END OF DIAGONAL-LOOP.
C------------------------------------
        RETURN
C
C
     13 WRITE (*,14) DSUM
     14 FORMAT(10X,'DSUM =',D20.6)
     12 IER=-1
        RETURN
        END
```

WT ON PHOTO COORD. = .15625E+05

SURVEY COORD. AND STD ERROR

PT NO	X	Y	Z	WX	WY	WZ
22	1.0000	2.6000	2.0000	.2500E-03	.2500E-03	.5000E-03
26	1.8000	2.6000	2.0000	.2500E-03	.2500E-03	.5000E-03
29	2.4000	2.6000	2.0000	.2500E-03	.2500E-03	.5000E-03
37	2.0000	2.4000	2.0000	.2500E-03	.2500E-03	.5000E-03
48	2.2000	2.2000	2.0000	.2500E-03	.2500E-03	.5000E-03
46	1.8000	2.2000	2.0000	.2500E-03	.2500E-03	.5000E-03
43	1.2000	2.2000	2.0000	.2500E-03	.2500E-03	.5000E-03
54	1.4000	2.0000	2.0000	.2500E-03	.2500E-03	.5000E-03
57	2.0000	2.0000	2.0000	.2500E-03	.2500E-03	.5000E-03
69	2.4000	1.8000	2.0000	.2500E-03	.2500E-03	.5000E-03
65	1.6000	1.8000	2.0000	.2500E-03	.2500E-03	.5000E-03
62	1.0000	1.8000	2.0000	.2500E-03	.2500E-03	.5000E-03
73	1.2000	1.6000	2.0000	.2500E-03	.2500E-03	.5000E-03
76	1.8000	1.6000	2.0000	.2500E-03	.2500E-03	.5000E-03
88	2.2000	1.4000	2.0000	.2500E-03	.2500E-03	.5000E-03
84	1.4000	1.4000	2.0000	.2500E-03	.2500E-03	.5000E-03
93	1.2000	1.2000	2.0000	.2500E-03	.2500E-03	.5000E-03
102	1.0000	1.0000	2.0000	.2500E-03	.2500E-03	.5000E-03
106	1.8000	1.0000	2.0000	.2500E-03	.2500E-03	.5000E-03
109	2.4000	1.0000	2.0000	.2500E-03	.2500E-03	.5000E-03

INPUT DATA FOR CALIB

```
   PHOTO    1
  1.8890   -5.0500    4.0650    -.0320     .0130    1.2730
2.50E+01  2.50E+01  2.50E+01  2.50E+01  2.50E+01  2.50E+01
 22      -7.935     2.154
 26        .214     2.391
 29       6.342     2.614
 37       2.291     1.917
 48       4.494     1.409
 46        .205     1.257
 43      -6.228     1.071
 54      -4.206      .521
 57       2.394      .724
 65      -2.068      .005
 76        .187     -.630
 84      -4.593    -1.472
 93      -7.191    -2.334
102      -9.953    -3.221
106        .161    -2.896
109       7.759    -2.661

   PHOTO    2
 -5.0350    1.7040    4.0700   -1.5600   -1.2700     .0440
2.50E+01  2.50E+01  2.50E+01  2.50E+01  2.50E+01  2.50E+01
 22      -9.986    -3.237
```

```
 26      -8.8[illegible]6      -.228
 29      -8.163       1.589
 37      -6.432        .478
 48      -4.1[illegible]7       1.136
 46      -4.357       -.117
 43      -4.776      -2.278
 54      -2.235      -1.439
 57      -2.026        .582
 69        .186       1.895
 65        .167       -.618
 62        .136      -2.884
 76       2.430        .078
 88       4.491       1.456
 84       4.940      -1.186
102      10.292      -2.615
106       9.244        .302
109       8.594       2.124

   PHOTO    3
  1.7170     8.6300     4.0702     3.1110     -.0116    -1.2710
2.50E+01  2.50E+01  2.50E+01  2.50E+01  2.50E+01  2.50E+01
 22      10.330      -2.607
 26        .162      -2.905
 29      -7.437      -3.162
 37      -2.291      -2.178
 48      -4.605      -1.513
 46        .173      -1.355
 43       7.372      -1.114
 54       4.839       -.508
 57      -2.139       -.721
 65       2.452        .116
 62       9.264        .321
 73       6.810        .918
 76        .189        .649
 84       4.494       1.411
 93       6.502       2.063
102       8.411       2.666
106        .209       2.384
109      -5.926       2.226

   PHOTO    4
  8.6340     1.8920     4.0540     1.5820     1.2700     -.0450
2.50E+01  2.50E+01  2.50E+01  2.50E+01  2.50E+01  2.50E+01
 22       8.426       2.670
 26       9.272        .298
 29      10.033      -1.808
 37       7.176       -.414
 48       4.965      -1.185
 46       4.730        .156
 43       4.412       1.994
 54       2.363       1.318
 57       2.510       -.583
 65        .193        .683
 62        .218       2.419
 73      -1.878       1.812
```

76	-2.071	-,053
88	-4.612	-1.444
84	-4.093	1.142
93	-6.063	1.645
102	-7.957	2.150
106	-8.869	-.231
109	-9.678	-2.386

ESTIMATES OF INTERIOR ORIENTATIONELEMENTS AND THEIR WEIGHTS

```
                .000E+00          .000E+00      -8.000E+01
   .000E+00          .000E+00          .000E+00
   .000E+00          .000E+00          .000E+00
               1.000E+00         1.000E+00         1.000E+00
  1.000E+00         1.000E+00         1.000E+00
  1.000E+00         1.000E+00         1.000E+00
```

RESIDUAL AND OBSERVATION EQUATION BEFORE 1ST CYCLE

PHOTO	PT	RES.IN X	RES.IN Y
1	22	.077	-.320
1	26	.161	-.344
1	29	.226	-.318
1	37	.172	-.345
1	48	.205	-.356
1	46	.162	-.371
1	43	.087	-.351
1	54	.107	-.369
1	57	.179	-.376
1	65	.135	-.325
1	76	.161	-.368
1	84	.106	-.358
1	93	.077	-.397
1	102	.035	-.413
1	106	.156	-.404
1	109	.238	-.407
2	22	.113	-.532
2	26	.116	-.462
2	29	.122	-.469
2	37	.144	-.464
2	48	.163	-.479
2	46	.167	-.491
2	43	.165	-.522
2	54	.196	-.507
2	57	.195	-.497
2	69	.212	-.425
2	65	.224	-.465

2	62	.223	-.488
2	76	.239	-.507
2	88	.271	-.427
2	84	.272	-.475
2	102	.334	-.529
2	106	.324	-.494
2	109	.318	-.459
3	22	.316	-.435
3	26	.200	-.429
3	29	.121	-.459
3	37	.177	-.421
3	48	.153	-.433
3	46	.200	-.419
3	43	.289	-.395
3	54	.252	-.420
3	57	.183	-.421
3	65	.227	-.392
3	62	.306	-.394
3	73	.268	-.357
3	76	.200	-.424
3	84	.244	-.395
3	93	.276	-.376
3	102	.304	-.376
3	106	.207	-.407
3	109	.138	-.376
4	22	.280	-.610
4	26	.282	-.672
4	29	.282	-.693
4	37	.255	-.655
4	48	.228	-.654
4	46	.232	-.671
4	43	.228	-.618
4	54	.209	-.661
4	57	.201	-.676
4	65	.173	-.630
4	62	.179	-.599
4	73	.162	-.599
4	76	.156	-.666
4	88	.121	-.613
4	84	.131	-.632
4	93	.120	-.633
4	102	.089	-.607
4	106	.068	-.630
4	109	.061	-.656

ICYCLE= 3 VARIANCE= 1.607476D+00 NDF= 142

CALIBRATION OF THE

NO. OF PHOTOS: 4
NO. OF CONTROL POINTS: 20
DEGREES OF FREEDOM: 142
NO. OF CYCLES: 3
VARIANCE OF UNIT WEIGHT = 1.60748E+00

RESULTS
INTERIOR ORIENTATION

	X	Y	F
	.09	-.31	-80.98
STD ERROR	.25	1.17	.40
WEIGHT	1.00E+00	1.00E+00	1.00E+00

	K1.D-6	K2.D-12	K3.D-18
	-.38185225	-.0000355	.00000000
STD ERRO	1.25315797	1.26786268	1.26786268
WEIGHT	1.00000000E+	1.00000000E+00	1.00000000E+00

	P1.D-6	P2.D-12	P3.D-18
	.00301680	.0000000	.00000000
STD ERRO	1.26752306	1.26786268	1.26786268
WEIGHT	1.00000000E+	1.00000000E+00	1.00000000E+00

COVARIANCE/VARIANCE/CORRELATION COEFFICIENT MATRIX

ROW . 1

1.000000E+00	-1.605660E-01	1.339265E-01
-8.778242E-03	-1.209489E-06	-1.279368E-10
-9.388552E-02	-3.178883E-09	-2.649781E-20
-9.038974E-02	1.177604E-01	-1.021395E-01
5.456920E-02	-9.764943E-01	-1.678329E-01

1.355723E-01	5.044374E-02	-1.323676E-01
-9.855257E-01	1.568241E-01	-9.844393E-01
7.989658E-02	-1.571485E-01	-1.620883E-01
7.205575E-02	9.766754E-01	1.656709E-01
-1.328677E-01	-1.330180E-01	-1.252198E-01
-9.839405E-01	-1.565705E-01	9.829421E-01

ROW 2

-1.605660E-01	1.000000E+00	-8.434161E-01
4.767288E-03	8.867383E-07	1.196014E-10
-7.730839E-04	-2.141966E-09	-2.360513E-22
1.127752E-01	-8.421428E-01	7.924834E-01
-3.155793E-01	1.012154E-02	9.993219E-01
-8.434239E-01	-1.141575E-01	7.878324E-01
2.246537E-01	-9.992297E-01	2.244297E-01
-1.258907E-01	8.433443E-01	7.999505E-01
-3.279442E-01	-1.190326E-02	-9.993316E-01
8.375504E-01	1.107045E-01	7.872890E-01
2.344566E-01	9.991864E-01	-2.345528E-01

ROW 3

1.339265E-01	-8.434161E-01	1.000000E+00
1.740460E-02	4.064753E-06	5.766334E-10
4.050120E-04	-1.033260E-08	-3.925412E-23
-1.604308E-01	9.946055E-01	-9.288413E-01
2.614008E-01	-1.093147E-02	-8.437280E-01
9.964164E-01	1.498469E-01	-9.292376E-01
-1.906367E-01	8.430332E-01	-1.903286E-01
8.997011E-02	-9.951722E-01	-9.322303E-01
2.887183E-01	-7.822811E-04	8.441702E-01
-9.963748E-01	-1.333740E-01	-9.214240E-01
-1.971107E-01	-8.443265E-01	1.972629E-01

ROW 4

-8.778242E-03	4.767288E-03	1.740460E-02
1.000000E+00	-2.723858E-06	-2.799677E-10
-4.731254E-05	2.763419E-10	-3.953846E-24
-5.313370E-03	3.232608E-02	-3.451817E-02
-1.365980E-03	7.752593E-03	5.244365E-03
3.557367E-02	4.263487E-03	-3.943968E-02
9.246229E-03	-5.375874E-03	9.246137E-03
1.721011E-02	-3.271963E-02	-3.522443E-02
9.783909E-04	-6.219681E-03	-5.234674E-03
-3.522386E-02	7.210812E-03	-3.626426E-02
1.070187E-02	5.062156E-03	-1.075506E-02

ROW 5

-1.209489E-06	8.867383E-07	4.064753E-06
-2.723858E-06	1.000000E+00	-3.589200E-14
-7.138374E-09	4.344418E-14	-1.321126E-27
1.499942E-07	5.133059E-06	-5.162014E-06

-5.938754E-07	1.189322E-06	9.266228E-07
5.621012E-06	5.947682E-07	-5.859692E-06
1.294161E-06	-9.447717E-07	1.296413E-06
2.750894E-06	-5.190847E-06	-5.221503E-06
3.306761E-07	-7.774041E-07	-9.219561E-07
-5.527475E-06	8.350580E-07	-5.410539E-06
1.476356E-06	9.038695E-07	-1.484702E-06

ROW 6

-1.279368E-10	1.196014E-10	5.766334E-10
-2.799677E-10	-3.589200E-14	1.000000E+00
-8.256952E-13	5.500001E-18	-1.382863E-31
8.640181E-11	6.640020E-10	-6.526708E-10
-1.009467E-10	1.356900E-10	1.229193E-10
7.224355E-10	7.827963E-11	-7.329742E-10
1.387188E-10	-1.250703E-10	1.391081E-10
3.742108E-10	-6.714700E-10	-6.566969E-10
5.818081E-11	-6.832542E-11	-1.220284E-10
-7.064706E-10	6.903131E-11	-6.743946E-10
1.573867E-10	1.201148E-10	-1.583207E-10

ROW 7

-9.388552E-02	-7.730839E-04	4.050120E-04
-4.731254E-05	-7.138374E-09	-8.256952E-13
1.000000E+00	7.893012E-12	-1.672307E-22
-5.701640E-04	3.275976E-04	4.044107E-05
-2.982801E-04	9.321771E-02	-1.852549E-04
4.345646E-04	6.651700E-04	-3.110832E-04
9.141334E-02	1.072408E-03	9.132327E-02
2.201878E-04	-5.190907E-04	-9.775869E-04
-3.314690E-04	-9.357573E-02	9.633508E-05
-4.018762E-04	-3.871675E-04	-3.176570E-04
8.964892E-02	-1.130657E-03	-8.966236E-02

ROW 8

-3.178883E-09	-2.141966E-09	-1.033260E-08
2.763419E-10	4.344418E-14	5.500001E-18
7.893012E-12	1.000000E+00	1.102840E-32
-4.577427E-10	-1.039123E-08	9.157403E-09
.5.412007E-09	3.162272E-09	-2.083637E-09
-1.041937E-08	-1.663662E-09	8.928210E-09
2.957518E-09	2.111744E-09	2.996721E-09
-4.457695E-09	1.039582E-08	9.319513E-09
-7.012097E-09	-3.960493E-09	2.092762E-09
1.040016E-08	1.416582E-09	8.383666E-09
2.893927E-09	-2.058930E-09	-2.894707E-09

ROW 9

-2.649781E-20	-2.360513E-22	-3.925412E-23
-3.953846E-24	-1.321126E-27	-1.382863E-31
-1.672307E-22	1.102840E-32	1.000000E+00

-1.185922E-21	-1.313184E-22	2.676345E-22
4.102581E-22	2.610167E-20	-7.433461E-23
2.178517E-23	2.654062E-21	1.731989E-23
2.538134E-20	3.172373E-22	2.533620E-20
1.786007E-21	-9.094960E-23	-2.669389E-22
1.391054E-22	-2.609436E-20	3.991746E-23
4.507617E-23	-1.056923E-21	8.679382E-23
2.511225E-20	-3.379734E-22	-2.510010E-20

ROW 10

-9.038974E-02	1.127752E-01	-1.604308E-01
-5.313370E-03	1.499942E-07	8.640181E-11
-5.701640E-04	-4.577427E-10	-1.185922E-21
1.000000E+00	-1.739970E-01	1.591165E-01
-3.927174E-01	2.272768E-01	1.134349E-01
-1.564285E-01	-1.362899E-02	1.804442E-01
9.403077E-02	-1.089465E-01	9.329180E-02
-7.087744E-02	1.627526E-01	1.600680E-01
5.427955E-02	-8.030821E-02	-1.125480E-01
1.641114E-01	8.849947E-03	1.098318E-01
9.584078E-02	1.168901E-01	-9.410221E-02

ROW 11

1.177604E-01	-8.421428E-01	9.946055E-01
3.232608E-02	5.133059E-06	6.640020E-10
3.275976E-04	-1.039123E-08	-1.313184E-22
-1.739970E-01	1.000000E+00	-9.343511E-01
2.644251E-01	3.082215E-03	-8.422868E-01
9.914741E-01	1.511458E-01	-9.241952E-01
-1.747779E-01	8.418474E-01	-1.749147E-01
8.986482E-02	-9.902430E-01	-9.315445E-01
2.865785E-01	-1.649446E-02	8.423826E-01
-9.914728E-01	-1.279345E-01	-9.159020E-01
-1.812618E-01	-8.432097E-01	1.810002E-01

ROW 12

-1.021395E-01	7.924834E-01	-9.288413E-01
-3.451817E-02	-5.162014E-06	-6.526708E-10
4.044107E-05	9.157403E-09	2.676345E-22
1.591165E-01	-9.343511E-01	1.000000E+00
-1.903188E-01	-1.267953E-02	7.797425E-01
-9.259028E-01	-1.127504E-01	8.576128E-01
1.563029E-01	-7.928676E-01	1.516381E-01
-9.228151E-02	9.287230E-01	8.405085E-01
-2.861424E-01	2.271966E-02	-7.960426E-01
9.248718E-01	1.457917E-01	8.585846E-01
1.621964E-01	7.930685E-01	-1.665910E-01

ROW 13

5.456920E-02	-3.155793E-01	2.614008E-01
-1.365980E-03	-5.938754E-07	-1.009467E-10

```
           -2.982801E-04    5.412007E-09    4.102581E-22
           -3.927174E-01    2.644251E-01   -1.903188E-01
            1.000000E+00   -6.487402E-02   -3.207186E-01
            2.533409E-01    2.196904E-02   -3.263946E-01
           -6.906643E-02    3.060076E-01   -7.040497E-02
           -5.101772E-02   -2.603363E-01   -2.593136E-01
           -1.362384E-01   -6.603473E-03    3.139109E-01
           -2.687497E-01   -4.800254E-03   -1.527679E-01
           -7.639697E-02   -3.253507E-01    7.487677E-02


ROW   14
           -9.764943E-01    1.012154E-02   -1.093147E-02
            7.752593E-03    1.189322E-06    1.356900E-10
            9.321771E-02    3.162272E-09    2.610167E-20
            2.272768E-01    3.082215E-03   -1.267953E-02
           -6.487402E-02    1.000000E+00    1.756855E-02
           -1.199101E-02   -3.186347E-02    2.249814E-02
            9.520259E-01   -5.919843E-03    9.508766E-01
           -6.948858E-02    3.432007E-02    4.655521E-02
           -7.422340E-03   -9.767614E-01   -1.521965E-02
            1.140824E-02    1.136314E-01    4.263979E-03
            9.491607E-01    6.930968E-03   -9.478787E-01


ROW   15
           -1.678329E-01    9.993219E-01   -8.437280E-01
            5.244365E-03    9.266228E-07    1.229193E-10
           -1.852549E-04   -2.083637E-09   -7.433461E-23
            1.134349E-01   -8.422868E-01    7.797425E-01
           -3.207186E-01    1.756855E-02    1.000000E+00
           -8.437476E-01   -1.173169E-01    7.886901E-01
            2.316654E-01   -9.984664E-01    2.319192E-01
           -1.254924E-01    8.434046E-01    8.034471E-01
           -3.264046E-01   -1.913185E-02   -9.983536E-01
            8.379618E-01    1.088752E-01    7.873245E-01
            2.414584E-01    9.985186E-01   -2.410787E-01


ROW   16
            1.355723E-01   -8.434239E-01    9.964164E-01
            3.557367E-02    5.621012E-06    7.224355E-10
            4.345646E-04   -1.041937E-08    2.178517E-23
           -1.564285E-01    9.914741E-01   -9.259028E-01
            2.533409E-01   -1.199101E-02   -8.437476E-01
            1.000000E+00    1.476276E-01   -9.266447E-01
           -1.919173E-01    8.436567E-01   -1.915380E-01
            9.450130E-02   -9.921906E-01   -9.287325E-01
            2.979617E-01    1.629879E-03    8.442613E-01
           -9.933617E-01   -1.323710E-01   -9.231603E-01
           -1.984193E-01   -8.438676E-01    1.986211E-01
```

ROW 17

5.044374E-02	-1.141575E-01	1.498469E-01
4.263487E-03	5.947682E-07	7.827963E-11
6.651700E-04	-1.663662E-09	2.654062E-21
-1.362899E-02	1.511458E-01	-1.127504E-01
2.196904E-02	-3.186347E-02	-1.173169E-01
1.476276E-01	1.000000E+00	-1.415766E-01
-2.038013E-01	1.119448E-01	-2.170939E-01
-7.753157E-03	-1.464807E-01	-1.657309E-01
1.047006E-02	2.850310E-02	1.115935E-01
-1.490048E-01	-9.072957E-02	-1.338828E-01
-7.323229E-02	-1.144433E-01	6.937146E-02

ROW 18

-1.323676E-01	7.878324E-01	-9.292376E-01
-3.943968E-02	-5.859692E-06	-7.329742E-10
-3.110832E-04	8.928210E-09	1.731989E-23
1.804442E-01	-9.241952E-01	8.576128E-01
-3.263946E-01	2.249814E-02	7.886901E-01
-9.266447E-01	-1.415766E-01	1.000000E+00
1.815346E-01	-7.733823E-01	1.817198E-01
-5.225414E-02	9.244960E-01	8.674589E-01
-1.823617E-01	-1.552017E-03	-7.883866E-01
9.306192E-01	1.207904E-01	8.264320E-01
1.916501E-01	7.921060E-01	-1.913413E-01

ROW 19

-9.855257E-01	2.246537E-01	-1.906367E-01
9.246229E-03	1.294161E-06	1.387188E-10
9.141334E-02	2.957518E-09	2.538134E-20
9.403077E-02	-1.747779E-01	1.563029E-01
-6.906643E-02	9.520259E-01	2.316654E-01
-1.919173E-01	-2.038013E-01	1.815346E-01
1.000000E+00	-2.210603E-01	9.988891E+01
-8.547414E-02	2.131480E-01	2.147014E-01
-9.147488E-02	-9.524547E-01	-2.296015E-01
1.889715E-01	1.522573E-01	1.786831E-01
9.773809E-01	2.206054E-01	-9.764169E-01

ROW 20

1.568241E-01	-9.992297E-01	8.430332E-01
-5.375874E-03	-9.447717E-07	-1.250703E-10
1.072408E-03	2.111744E-09	3.172373E-22
-1.089465E-01	8.418474E-01	-7.928676E-01
3.060076E-01	-5.919843E-03	-9.984664E-01
8.436567E-01	1.119448E-01	-7.733823E-01
-2.210603E-01	1.000000E+00	-2.207505E-01
1.293837E-01	-8.429757E-01	-7.992995E-01
3.376733E-01	8.869851E-03	9.985753E-01
-8.367335E-01	-1.104669E-01	-7.905427E-01
-2.306592E-01	-9.980268E-01	2.308177E-01

```
ROW  21
          -9.844393E-01    2.244297E-01   -1.903286E-01
           9.246137E-03    1.296413E-06    1.391081E-10
           9.132327E-02    2.996721E-09    2.533620E-20
           9.329180E-02   -1.749147E-01    1.516381E-01
          -7.040497E-02    9.508766E-01    2.319192E-01
          -1.915380E-01   -2.170939E-01    1.817198E-01
           9.988891E-01   -2.207505E-01    1.000000E+00
          -8.360822E-02    2.123695E-01    2.187013E-01
          -8.980186E-02   -9.511266E-01   -2.288896E-01
           1.887197E-01    1.484989E-01    1.778615E-01
           9.763196E-01    2.204490E-01   -9.747290E-01

ROW  22
           7.989658E-02   -1.258907E-01    8.997011E-02
           1.721011E-02    2.750894E-06    3.742108E-10
           2.201878E-04   -4.457695E-09    1.786007E-21
          -7.087744E-02    8.986482E-02   -9.228151E-02
          -5.101772E-02   -6.948858E-02   -1.254924E-01
           9.450130E-02   -7.753157E-03   -5.225414E-02
          -8.547414E-02    1.293837E-01   -8.360822E-02
           1.000000E+00   -1.093016E-01   -1.013667E-01
           3.827298E-01    2.155084E-01    1.267913E-01
          -8.615801E-02   -4.387013E-03   -1.218500E-01
          -8.471571E-02   -1.214844E-01    8.414393E-02

ROW  23
          -1.571485E-01    8.433443E-01   -9.951722E-01
          -3.271963E-02   -5.190847E-06   -6.714700E-10
          -5.190907E-04    1.039582E-08   -9.094960E-23
           1.627526E-01   -9.902430E-01    9.287230E-01
          -2.603363E-01    3.432007E-02    8.434046E-01
          -9.921906E-01   -1.464807E-01    9.244960E-01
           2.131480E-01   -8.429757E-01    2.123695E-01
          -1.093016E-01    1.000000E+00    9.356185E-01
          -2.945909E-01   -2.553608E-02   -8.443785E-01
           9.919639E-01    1.376311E-01    9.171371E-01
           2.196161E-01    8.441722E-01   -2.201487E-01

ROW  24
          -1.620883E-01    7.999505E-01   -9.322303E-01
          -3.522443E-02   -5.221503E-06   -6.566969E-10
          -9.775869E-04    9.319513E-09   -2.669389E-22
           1.600680E-01   -9.315445E-01    8.405085E-01
          -2.593136E-01    4.655521E-02    8.034471E-01
          -9.287325E-01   -1.657309E-01    8.674589E-01
           2.147014E-01   -7.992995E-01    2.187013E-01
          -1.013667E-01    9.356185E-01    1.000000E+00
          -2.265889E-01   -3.719431E-02   -7.882667E-01
           9.290293E-01    1.044707E-01    8.542125E-01
           2.211517E-01    8.011887E-01   -2.170102E-01
```

ROW 25

7.205575E-02	-3.279442E-01	2.887183E-01
9.783909E-04	3.306761E-07	5.818081E-11
-3.314690E-04	-7.012097E-09	1.391054E-22
5.427955E-02	2.865785E-01	-2.861424E-01
-1.362384E-01	-7.422340E-03	-3.264046E-01
2.979617E-01	1.047006E-02	-1.823617E-01
-9.147488E-02	3.376733E-01	-8.980186E-02
3.827298E-01	2.945909E-01	-2.265889E-01
1.000000E+00	7.655372E-02	3.341548E-01
-2.775570E-01	-2.482103E-02	-3.680160E-01
-8.939721E-02	-3.169110E-01	9.088711E-02

ROW 26

9.766754E-01	-1.190326E-02	-7.822811E-04
-6.219681E-03	-7.774041E-07	-6.832542E-11
-9.357573E-02	-3.960493E-09	-2.609436E-20
-8.030821E-02	-1.649446E-02	2.271966E-02
-6.603473E-03	-9.767614E-01	-1.913185E-02
1.629879E-03	2.850310E-02	-1.552017E-03
-9.524547E-01	8.869851E-03	-9.511266E-01
2.155084E-01	-2.553608E-02	-3.719431E-02
7.655372E-02	1.000000E+00	1.716840E-02
1.484203E-03	-1.131525E-01	-5.711509E-03
-9.491723E-01	-7.348548E-03	9.480776E-01

ROW 27

1.656709E-01	-9.993316E-01	8.441702E-01
-5.234674E-03	-9.219561E-07	-1.220284E-10
9.633508E-05	2.092762E-09	3.991746E-23
-1.125480E-01	8.423826E-01	-7.960426E-01
3.139109E-01	-1.521965E-02	-9.983536E-01
8.442613E-01	1.115935E-01	-7.883866E-01
-2.296015E-01	9.985753E-01	-2.288896E-01
1.267913E-01	-8.443785E-01	-7.882667E-01
3.341548E-01	1.716840E-02	1.000000E+00
-8.383158E-01	-1.140460E-01	-7.885728E-01
-2.393392E-01	-9.984384E-01	2.399003E-01

ROW 28

-1.328677E-01	8.375504E-01	-9.963748E-01
-3.522386E-02	-5.527475E-06	-7.064706E-10
-4.018762E-04	1.040016E-08	4.507617E-23
1.641114E-01	-9.914728E-01	9.248718E-01
-2.687497E-01	1.140824E-02	8.379618E-01
-9.933617E-01	-1.490048E-01	9.306192E-01
1.889715E-01	-8.367335E-01	1.887197E-01
-8.615801E-02	9.919639E-01	9.290293E-01
-2.775570E-01	1.484203E-03	-8.383158E-01
1.000000E+00	1.226067E-01	9.171489E-01
1.941571E-01	8.392360E-01	-1.941083E-01

```
ROW  29
          -1.330180E-01   1.107045E-01  -1.333740E-01
           7.210812E-03   8.350580E-07   6.903131E-11
          -3.871675E-04   1.416582E-09  -1.056923E-21
           8.849947E-03  -1.279345E-01   1.457917E-01
          -4.800254E-03   1.136314E-01   1.088752E-01
          -1.323710E-01  -9.072957E-02   1.207904E-01
           1.522573E-01  -1.104669E-01   1.484989E-01
          -4.387013E-03   1.376311E-01   1.044707E-01
          -2.482103E-02  -1.131525E-01  -1.140460E-01
           1.226067E-01   1.000000E+00   1.168898E-01
           2.899432E-01   1.083492E-01  -3.014325E-01


ROW  30
          -1.252198E-01   7.872890E-01  -9.214240E-01
          -3.626426E-02  -5.410539E-06  -6.743946E-10
          -3.176570E-04   8.383666E-09   8.679382E-23
           1.098318E-01  -9.159020E-01   8.585846E-01
          -1.527679E-01   4.263979E-03   7.873245E-01
          -9.231603E-01  -1.338828E-01   8.264320E-01
           1.786831E-01  -7.905427E-01   1.778615E-01
          -1.218500E-01   9.171371E-01   8.542125E-01
          -3.680160E-01  -5.711509E-03  -7.885728E-01
           9.171489E-01   1.168898E-01   1.000000E+00
           1.778540E-01   7.728912E-01  -1.798799E-01


ROW  31
          -9.839405E-01   2.344566E-01  -1.971107E-01
           1.070187E-02   1.476356E-06   1.573867E-10
           8.964892E-02   2.893927E-09   2.511225E-20
           9.584078E-02  -1.812618E-01   1.621964E-01
          -7.639697E-02   9.491607E-01   2.414584E-01
          -1.984193E-01  -7.323229E-02   1.916501E-01
           9.773809E-01  -2.306592E-01   9.763196E-01
          -8.471571E-02   2.196161E-01   2.211517E-01
          -8.939721E-02  -9.491723E-01  -2.393392E-01
           1.941571E-01   2.899432E-01   1.778540E-01
           1.000000E+00   2.307449E-01  -9.989901E-01


ROW  32
          -1.565705E-01   9.991864E-01  -8.443265E-01
           5.062156E-03   9.038695E-07   1.201148E-10
          -1.130657E-03  -2.058930E-09  -3.379734E-22
           1.168901E-01  -8.432097E-01   7.930685E-01
          -3.253507E-01   6.930968E-03   9.985186E-01
          -8.438676E-01  -1.144433E-01   7.921060E-01
           2.206054E-01  -9.980268E-01   2.204490E-01
          -1.214844E-01   8.441722E-01   8.011887E-01
          -3.169110E-01  -7.348548E-03  -9.984384E-01
           8.392360E-01   1.083492E-01   7.728912E-01
           2.307449E-01   1.000000E+00  -2.306232E-01
```

ROW 33

9.829421E-01	-2.345528E-01	1.972629E-01
-1.075506E-02	-1.484702E-06	-1.583207E-10
-8.966236E-02	-2.894707E-09	-2.510010E-20
-9.410221E-02	1.810002E-01	-1.665910E-01
7.487677E-02	-9.478787E-01	-2.410787E-01
1.986211E-01	6.937146E-02	-1.913413E-01
-9.764169E-01	2.308177E-01	-9.747290E-01
8.414393E-02	-2.201487E-01	-2.170102E-01
9.088711E-02	9.480776E-01	2.399003E-01
-1.941083E-01	-3.014325E-01	-1.798799E-01
-9.989901E-01	-2.306232E-01	1.000000E+00

EXTERIOR ORIENTATION

PHOTO NO. 1

	VALUE	STD ERROR	WEIGHT
XO	1.890285E+00	3.504329E-03	2.500000E+01
YO	-5.057287E+00	3.378101E-02	2.500000E+01
ZO	4.069987E+00	1.101265E-02	2.500000K+01
KAPPA(RAD)	-3.142700E-02	6.385527E-04	2.500000E+01
PHI(RAD)	1.398531E-02	3.061434E-03	2.500000E+01
OMEGA(RAD)	1.273402E+00	1.446456E-02	2.500000E+01

RESIDUALS ON CONTROL POINTS
(MICROMETER UNITS)

POINT NO.	RESIDUALS IN X	RESIDUALS IN Y
22	7.4	11.2
26	.1	-11.8
29	-2.3	18.4
37	-8.7	-8.3
48	.4	-6.2
46	2.6	-16.1
43	1.0	-6.6
54	-3.6	-5.9
57	-2.1	-9.7
65	2.2	24.4
76	4.0	14.8

84	1.1	14.8
93	1.7	-5.2
102	-7.5	-10.6
106	2.6	2.6
109	1.1	-5.7
RMS =	4.0	12.1

EXTERIOR ORIENTATION

PHOTO NO. 2

	VALUE	STD ERROR	WEIGHT
XO	-5.039631E+00	3.364324E-02	2.500000E+01
YO	1.706529E+00	3.637329E-03	2.500000E+01
ZO	4.076303E+00	1.109865E-02	2.500000E+01
KAPPA(RAD)	-1.556032E+00	1.010099E-02	2.500000E+01
PHI(RAD)	-1.271541E+00	1.444876E-02	2.500000E+01
OMEGA(RAD)	4.825042E-02	1.058337E-02	2.500000E+01

RESIDUALS ON CONTROL POINTS
(MICROMETER UNITS)

POINT NO.	RESIDUALS IN X	RESIDUALS IN Y
22	4.1	-10.5
26	-2.1	18.9
29	-.1	-8.5
37	-.2	5.2
48	-4.7	-12.9
46	-1.6	-2.5
43	-1.7	-14.4
54	2.3	2.0
57	.9	-14.6
69	-4.1	20.5
65	5.1	9.6
62	.7	19.4
76	-3.4	-17.9
88	4.9	16.0

84	-1.1	15.3
102	-5.0	-6.6
106	1.3	-11.3
109	4.5	-7.9
RMS =	3.2	13.1

EXTERIOR ORIENTATION

PHOTO NO. 3

	VALUE	STD ERROR	WEIGHT
XO	1.714057E+00	3.394284E-03	2.500000E+01
YO	8.638126E+00	3.363637E-02	2.500000E+01
ZO	4.070931E+00	1.091827E-02	2.500000E+01
KAPPA(RAD)	3.110026E+00	5.911072E-04	2.500000E+01
PHI(RAD)	-1.339149E-02	3.051694E-03	2.500000E+01
OMEGA(RAD)	-1.272568E+00	1.446354E-02	2.500000E+01

RESIDUALS ON CONTROL POINTS
(MICROMETER UNITS)

POINT NO.	RESIDUALS IN X	RESIDUALS IN Y
22	.6	-12.3
26	-.4	5.8
29	.4	-10.3
37	.2	5.4
48	1.1	-4.3
46	-2.3	9.4
43	5.0	14.5
54	-2.0	-2.4
57	4.0	6.3
65	-.1	-1.6
62	1.3	-9.5
73	-8.6	20.5
76	-3.3	-12.1
84	-5.7	-11.9
93	2.0	7.7
102	5.4	.0
106	1.6	-18.9
109	.8	13.6
RMS =	3.4	10.8

EXTERIOR ORIENTATION

PHOTO NO. 4

	VALUE	STD ERROR	WEIGHT
XO	8.639454E+00	3.382968E-02	2.500000E+01
YO	1.894222E+00	3.913530E-03	2.500000E+01
ZO	4.057086E+00	1.101385E-02	2.500000E+01
KAPPA (RAD)	1.588644E+00	1.040007E-02	2.500000E+01
PHI (RAD)	1.274053E+00	1.444472E-02	2.500000E+01
OMEGA (RAD)	-4.989863E-02	1.087105E-02	2.500000E+01

RESIDUALS ON CONTROL POINTS (MICROMETER UNITS)

POINT NO.	RESIDUALS IN X	RESIDUALS IN Y
22	1.5	18.4
26	1.0	-13.6
29	-3.6	-4.0
37	.3	4.8
48	.0	16.3
46	3.5	-10.8
43	-1.8	9.8
54	3.3	-17.5
57	-.3	-8.2
65	-5.1	-5.5
62	-4.7	9.3
73	4.3	8.8
76	2.4	-12.4
88	2.8	21.7
84	-1.5	-12.1
93	7.4	-14.8
102	-3.6	2.8
106	-8.1	7.8
109	2.4	-.8
RMS =	3.7	11.9

ADJUSTED SURVEY COORDINATES

POINT	X	Y	Z
22	1.0000	2.6001	2.0000
26	1.8001	2.6000	2.0000
29	2.4000	2.6000	1.9997
37	1.9999	2.4000	2.0004
48	2.1999	2.2001	1.9998
46	1.8001	2.2000	1.9992
43	1.1999	2.1999	2.0001
54	1.4000	2.0000	1.9990
57	1.9999	1.9999	1.9989
65	1.6001	1.8000	2.0011
76	1.8001	1.6002	1.9989
84	1.4002	1.4001	2.0004
93	1.2000	1.2000	1.9995
102	.9998	1.0000	1.9993
106	1.8000	1.0000	1.9993
109	2.4000	.9999	1.9999
69	2.4001	1.8000	2.0008
62	1.0000	1.8000	2.0009
88	2.2000	1.4000	2.0016
73	1.2001	1.6000	2.0012

STD. DEV. OF SURVEY COORDINATES (MM)

POINT	X	Y	Z
22	.2928	.2919	.4691
26	.2867	.2870	.4279
29	.2912	.2908	.4594
37	.2857	.2858	.4184
48	.2866	.2860	.4210
46	.2840	.2841	.4030
43	.2865	.2860	.4221
54	.2842	.2839	.4029
57	.2845	.2841	.4041
69	.3162	.3037	.5528
65	.2834	.2832	.3954
62	.2994	.2884	.4540
73	.3008	.3021	.4889
76	.2840	.2837	.4001
88	.3141	.2891	.4894
84	.2850	.2850	.4100
93	.2890	.3013	.4600
102	.2918	.2922	.4614
106	.2886	.2882	.4374
109	.2961	.2934	.4822

INDEX